Essential Papers on Jewish-Christian
Relations in the United States

ESSENTIAL PAPERS ON JEWISH STUDIES
General Editor: Robert M. Seltzer

Essential Papers on Judaism and Christianity in Conflict:
From Late Antiquity to the Reformation
Edited by Jeremy Cohen

Essential Papers on Hasidism: Origins to Present
Edited by Gershon David Hundert

Essential Papers on Jewish-Christian Relations in the United States:
Imagery and Reality
Edited by Naomi W. Cohen

Essential Papers on Israel and the Ancient Near East
Edited by Frederick E. Greenspahn

ESSENTIAL PAPERS ON JEWISH-CHRISTIAN RELATIONS IN THE UNITED STATES

Imagery and Reality

Edited by
Naomi W. Cohen

NEW YORK UNIVERSITY PRESS
New York and London

Library of Congress Cataloging-in-Publication Data
Essential papers on Jewish-Christian relations in the United States :
imagery and reality / edited by Naomi W. Cohen.
p.   cm. — (Essential papers on Jewish studies)
Includes index.
ISBN 0-8147-1445-5—ISBN 0-8147-1446-3 (pbk.)
1. Jews—United States   2. Jews—United States—Public opinion.
3. Public opinion—United States.   4. Christianity and antisemitism.
5. Judaism—Relations—Christianity.   6. Christianity and other
religions—Judaism.   7. United States—Ethnic relations.   I. Cohen,
Naomi Wiener   II. Series.
E184.J5E78   1990
305.892'4073—dc20   90-42878
                               CIP

New York University Press books are printed on acid-free paper,
and their binding materials are chosen for strength and durability.

Book design by Ken Venezio

To the Three A's,
who didn't make it the last time

Contents

Preface

The papers in this reader address different facets of the relations between American Jews and Christians. The book is not, however, a collection of landmark essays in theology or the philosophy of religion. Nor, at the other extreme, is it intended to prescribe how Jews and Christians should interact. Rather, it aims at introducing the state of the field, both with respect to the substance of the theme and to the scholarship that the theme and its subthemes have generated. With a few exceptions, the focus is slanted to historical and sociological interpretations. Although the published material on contemporary interfaith matters overwhelmingly reflects the different viewpoints of the participants themselves, most essays reproduced here are by social scientists who have critically explored and assessed certain issues in their past or present American context. All of the selections were published in the 1970s or 1980s. Since the original footnotes of the articles are reproduced, and since the introductions to the various sections cite additional books or articles, the interested student can proceed to more intensive study.

Admittedly, a limited number of essays do scant justice to the complexities of the subject. As all students of American religion know, it is impossible to designate any one position as *the* view of Protestantism or Judaism. Multiple responses within each camp have always abounded on major social issues; frequent divisions between the leadership and the rank and file cause further fragmentation. Moreover, the reader should remember that ethnicity as well as religion have separated American groups, and ethnic lines can either temper or reinforce religious distinctions. For example, many German Jewish immigrants of the nineteenth century participated in cultural activities with non-Jewish Germans, thus dulling the importance of religious differences. On the other hand, ethnic rivalry fed religious animosity in the notorious attack by Irish Catholics on New York Jews in 1902 at the funeral of Rabbi Jacob Joseph.

Some of the categories overlap. Most papers can be filed under the heading of Antisemitism or, for that matter, under Dialogue. The essay by Franklin H. Littell fits as easily under Holocaust and under Zionism as it does under Antisemitism. The short introduction preceding each section attempts to explain the significance of each piece under a particular rubric. Only on the issue of the Holocaust were articles by Christians rather than Jews purposely chosen.

Friends and colleagues generously assisted in the preparation of this reader. I am especially grateful to Judith Herschlag Muffs and Judith H. Banki, experts in the field of Jewish-Christian relations, for directing me to important materials. Robert M. Seltzer, who invited me to participate in the series under his editorship, offered wise counsel and constructive suggestions. He read portions of the manuscript, as did Jeremy Cohen. I am also grateful to Kitty Moore, editor at New York University Press, for her sustained encouragement. She and her associates handled the numerous technical tasks involved in preparing the reader for publication. The responsibility for the choice of materials and overall interpretation is mine alone.

Essential Papers on Jewish-Christian Relations in the United States

Introduction

The subject of Jewish-Christian relationships in the United States encompasses a wide range of topics. It deals with theology, sociology, and politics; it includes patterns of thought and behavior that run the gamut from hostility and outright violence to amity and cooperative ventures. Its multifaceted dimensions cut through time, incorporating precedents of the past, the changing realities of the present, and goals for the future.

Jewish-Christian relations as a field of critical study is comparatively recent. To be sure, popular writers and trained theologians of every era have examined credal distinctions between the two faiths and recounted episodes of enmity and persecution. Nevertheless, serious and dispassionate exploration of interreligious relations in America began in earnest after the Holocaust and the creation of the state of Israel. Vatican Council II some fifteen years later significantly advanced that interest. Organized efforts at interfaith cooperation are not much older; a pioneer agency, the National Conference of Jews and Christians (its name was changed in the 1930s) was founded in 1927. Today, Jewish and Christian organizations maintain interfaith departments, sponsor conferences, and encourage research to deal with different areas of interreligious concern. Independent scholars also recognize the subject as one that merits serious analysis, and work in the history and sociology of intergroup relations is slowly increasing.

Throughout history Jews faced non-Jewish majorities, and America was no different. Since Jews have always been a very small minority of the population, most interreligious encounters, and the materials relating to them, find the Christian as the initiator and the Jew the reactor or adapter. What Jew-hatred has meant and how it has been acted upon, or what Christian textbooks have said about Jews, are far more significant historically, and far more important to interfaith relations, than Christian-hatred on the part of Jews or what Jewish texts might say about Christians. Or, on another level, the behavior of the majority carries greater influence with the minority, particularly an accommodationist one, than the reverse. Jews adapted numerous Christian ideas and institutions to their own needs—the mode of synagogue services, the Sunday school, circuit preaching, the social gospel (in the Jewish case the social justice) movement. Perhaps most telling, the American Jewish minority, like their ancestors, constantly worried about "mah yomru hagoyim," what will the gentiles say. The Christian majority had no comparable concern.

The relationship of Jews and Christians in the United States is predicated on Old World foundations, specifically the theological framework of each group that transcended national boundaries. To be sure, in the religious milieu of the ancient world the resemblances between the two faiths overshadowed the differences. Not only were both monotheistic, but Christianity retained the Jewish Scripture, prophets, and the basic mode of worship. Only when Christianity triumphed over paganism, did the distinctions between the mother and daughter religions stand out more sharply. The rise of Protestantism altered neither the essential legacy on which Christianity built nor the fundamental views that earlier Christians had formulated about Judaism and Jews.

In age-old Christian thought, Jews were the perfidious people, those who had spurned and crucified the true messiah. They in turn were rejected by God and superseded by the Christians, the new children of Israel, armed with a new covenant and a new mission. In the religious design Christians could not extirpate Judaism or completely annihilate its followers. Judaism was the stock from which the younger faith sprang, and Jews, the original chosen people, were to bear witness to the truth of Scripture and to the second coming of Jesus. Yet, the scepter had departed from Judah. Until the end of days Jews were consigned to inferior status and eternal wandering. Individually they could escape their destiny only by conversion to the true faith. For its part the church was ready to show Jews the error of their ways and accept them into the fold.

The masses of Christians may not have understood the theological fine points, but they grasped full well the negative images that were projected—the Jew as Christ-killer, the Jew as eternal alien, the Jews as the stiff-necked people that resisted salvation. During the Middle Ages, as the Jew was virtually diabolized, other popular images—e.g., the Jew as ritual murderer—took root. Since pre-modern Jews and Christians generally moved in separate orbits that offered only limited contact, daily living failed to dislodge myth. Over the course of centuries that imagery became fixed. Historical experience showed that the negative images proved more potent than the positive ones of "the people of the Book" or God's first chosen. In the name of Christianity, Jews as a group were often fair game for persecution, forcible conversion, and expulsion.

Images of the Jews permeated Christian literature and folklore. One study of England during the period of Jewish exile from that land has shown that anti-Jewish sentiment could thrive even without the presence of Jews (Bernard Glassman, *Anti-Semitic Stereotypes without Jews*). The same images were transported to America in the cultural baggage of European immigrants. Many Christians had perceptions of Jews even if they knew no Jews. Professor Jacob Rader Marcus tells the story of Joseph Jonas, the first known Jew to arrive in Ohio in the early nineteenth century. Jonas was approached by an old Quaker woman who asked: "Art thou a Jew? . . . Wilt thou let me examine thee?" She turned him around and announced (doubtless disappointedly, says Marcus): "Well, thou art no different to other people" (Marcus, *Memoirs of American Jews*, I:203). The mythic Jew rather than the real Jew was the object of concern when Americans in the era of constitution-drafting debated the issue of individual political rights. Even Roger Williams, a pioneer champion of universal religious liberty, thought about Jews under the familiar Anglican rubric of "Jews, Turks, and Infidels."

Early American colonists hewed to the dichotomy in Christian thought between the admired patriarchs of the Old Testament and their ignoble descendants of post-Jesus times. The Puritans of Massachusetts Bay, the architects of a new Jerusalem or the city on the hill, studied the Hebrew language, gave Biblical names to their settlements and children, and looked to Mosaic law to regulate their daily lives. But they did not welcome the descendants of the ancient Israelites in seventeenth-century Boston. The Old Testament figures were God's chosen, the contemporary Jews the displaced. Religious imagery frequently ignited impassioned popular accusations against the Jews well into the nineteenth century. The charge of deicide reverberated in respectable as well as extremist circles. During the Civil War, when Judaeophobia was rampant both North and South, one periodical asked whether the treacherous Jews aimed to crucify Lincoln as they had Jesus. The image of the eternal alien also surfaced, usually as the base on which to question Jewish loyalty to the country. Particularly in wartime moods of hypernationalism, the figure of the Jew symbolized the quintessential outsider. Ezra Stiles, a Congregationalist minister and usually sympathetic friend of colonial Jews in Newport, Rhode Island, suspected the existence of a central Jewish intelligence agency in London that used its coreligionists in America to inform on supporters of the Revolutionary cause. Nor had the ritual murder or blood libel image been laid to rest in the New World. As recently as 1928 the disappearance of a small child in Massena, New York, two days before Yom Kippur, prompted local officials to query Jews on their alleged custom of using Christian blood for Jewish ritual purposes. The officials may have confused the holidays— the myth usually dealt with Passover—, but they remembered the essence of the image.

Negative religious imagery in the United States did not remain static. In some Christian circles the Jew as anti-Christ fused with images of Jewish lust for money and economic power (the Shylock myth) and developed into fears of a Jewish monied conspiracy to destroy Christian civilization. A popular theme of the twentieth century, the Jew as Bolshevik, may logically have been the antithesis of the "international banker," but it too built on the anti-Christ motif. Here, Jews spearheading international communism menaced the Christian order. These images, like the older ones, stigmatized the Jewish group as a whole and branded individual Jews regardless of different origins or behavior. When in the nineteenth century police blotters entered arrests of a "Jew criminal," or when John Quincy Adams in Congress referred to a Jewish colleague as the "Jew delegate," the particular Jew was masked by preconceptions of a larger group.

Some analysts have argued against overemphasis of Christian imagery. They suggest that negative images were tempered by America's democratic foundations, or by a concurrent strand of philosemitism, or by the affinity of the open American economic structure with Jewish values. Furthermore, if images were not acted upon, their significance was academic at best. Even if such suggestions are valid, the historical experience of Jews in a given particular time frame proves that they felt menaced by the imagery alone. For example, Reform Jewish leadership at the turn of the century railed against Zionism almost hysterically, in part because it conjured up the image of Jew as alien. Similarly, Jews during the early cold war years feared that a strict separationist stand on church-state matters would raise the charge of atheistic Jewish Communist. Jewish leaders expended immeasurable energy in seeking ways to counter Christian myths; they themselves often resorted to the same images when counseling modes of proper communal behavior. Obsession with image could and did on occasion result in demoralization, passive resignation, or communal paralysis. All told, images may rarely have triggered dramatic forms of hostility, but they left distinct impressions on American Jewish behavior.

Predicated on Judaism but affirming its supersession of the mother faith, Christianity was inseverably bound to its progenitor. Judaism, on the other hand, had an independent integrity and was under no constraints to iterate its superiority over the rival religion. At least on a theological level it was free to ignore Christianity. But Jews lived in a Christian world, and they brought their images of the regnant faith to America. Their pre-modern religious authorities had not uniformly tagged Christianity as idolatry, and some even saw its legitimacy in the divine plan, but Jews consistently maintained that Jesus of Nazareth was a false messiah, one of several spawned by the turbulence of first-century Judea. Just as they looked to the coming of their own redeemer, so did they continue to believe that they were God's elect. Reform Judaism in nineteenth-century America may have fashioned a style of synagogue worship along Protestant lines, but it distanced itself totally from Christianity with a renewed emphasis on the mission of Israel and Israel's role as the priest people. Without distinction between Catholic and Protestant or among the various Protestant churches, the Jewish image of *the* Christian was essentially that of persecutor, a composite of the Crusaders, Torquemada, and the pogrom-happy Russian peasant. Philosemites among the Christians were often suspect as would-be missionizers. Even if they failed, their very object, resting on the premise of the inferiority of Judaism, was an insult and humiliation. As late as 1890 some Jews feared that William Blackstone's widely circulated petition for opening up Palestine to the Jews was a conversionary scheme. The same fear erupted with the onset of the "goodwill" or incipient interfaith move-ment in the 1920s. Such images made early American Jews reluctant to form alliances with Christian groups until well into the twentieth cen-tury. Christian crusades for whatever cause—abolition and prohibition and not only conversion and Sunday laws—frightened Jews, for they augured ill for all nonconformists. In the era of Know-Nothingism, an hysterical outburst of anti-Catholicism before the Civil War, some prom-inent Jewish leaders advised their community to steer clear of both Protestant persecutors and Catholic victims. Defended on grounds of communal security as well as the need to preserve religious law (e.g., dietary laws, marriage within the fold), isolation from Christians evoked in turn the criticism of Jewish clannishness and separatism.

Both Jews and Christians held discrete images of themselves and each other that flowed from their respective theologies and history, but Jewish imagery was in no position to rival the Christian. The sheer numbers of each group created an imbalance from the outset. Although the status of Judaism rose in America, it never equaled Protestantism or Catholicism with regard to resources, political influence, or international clout. Until very recently Jews were hardly able to contest Christian religious teach-ings about Jews in the marketplace of ideas. Some nineteenth-century Jewish tracts against missionaries coupled a defense of Judaism with attacks against Christian doctrine, but fortunately for the Jews, they were never compelled to engage in public theological disputations. Nor could American Judaism hope to compete, even if it had so desired, with the major Christian denominations in this-worldly matters of potential converts, public support, or government favors. Whereas fear of a legally recognized Christian America haunted American Jews into the first de-cade of the twentieth century, Christians other than the lunatic fringe had little reason to fear Jewish political or economic strength. Thus, minority status in addition to fixed Christian imagery imposed two handicaps on the struggle to achieve full equality for Jews and for Judaism.

Interreligious encounters in the United States are distorted if examined only through a theological or European prism. They have been shaped at least as much by environmental influences—social, economic, politi-cal—which, operating on Jews and Christians indiscriminately, are sin-gularly American. Individually, each of those factors significantly altered the ways in which different religious groups met and interacted. Together, they accounted for the rise and acceptance of religious pluralism. Acceptance of pluralism in turn explains how Jews, ever a tiny fraction of the population, could ultimately be ranked with Protestants and Catholics in the oft-used tripartite formula of religious America.

From the beginning, the New World setting promised a society markedly distinct from its European antecedents. For example, the absence of a feudal legacy or a caste system, as Crèvecoeur explained some two hundred years ago, was critical in defining the new breed of Americans. It also redefined the traditional Jewish-Christian relationship. America never thought of separate corporate existence for Jews or of legally prescribed ghettos. The drama of Jewish emancipation, which in Europe divided critics and defenders of the old order, did not play in America. Jews settled in most colonies and eventually spread out to all states and territories of the United States. Barriers based on pre-modern religious usages did not impede their entry into all economic pursuits and professions. Even the military, traditionally the conservative bailiwick of European nations, accepted Jews. (A Jew, one Simon Levy, graduated in the first class of West Point in 1802.)

The absence of a feudal heritage proved salutary for all religions in America. Here, as opposed to Europe, religion and the church had no historic association with aristocratic or anti-democratic forces; church affiliation always cut through social classes and political parties. It followed, as has been pointed out, that within the *American* democratic setting religion generally could take root and flourish, contributing to and entwined in the liberal ethos of the nation. Distinctions along traditional European lines were also untenable in a land that cried out for manpower during most of its history. Colonial America needed settlers to clear the wilderness, create a viable economy, and defend the territory. Rapid advances in technology required hordes of others to build the factories and railroads, man the machines, and distribute and consume the industrial output. Immigrants of many ethnic and religious backgrounds responded to those economic pulls, and in the resultant diversified population hard-and-fast barriers separating churches or ethnic groups gradually eroded. Where various types of Jews, Protestants, Catholics, and non-believers lived and worked side by side, religious pluralism was a reality long before it received lip service from the major churches.

For most immigrant groups that arrived in the United States, the house of worship constituted the hub of their transplanted existence. Retaining Old World customs and language, it anchored them in an unfamiliar society. The ethnic trappings were usually sloughed off as acculturation and assimilation took their toll. Besides, the United States frowned upon permanent, discrete national subgroups; it was prepared, however, to accept religious variations. In response to those stimuli, third-generation immigrants identified themselves sooner by religion than by country of origin. Thus, secured by the realities of the American scene, both church and synagogue endured. Religious spokesmen and organizations of all major denominations have consistently commanded greater respect from other Americans than their ethnic or lay counterparts. The house of worship and its leaders played different roles in different eras, but similarities in experience and function narrowed the divide between church and synagogue.

Many immigrants prospered in a burgeoning economy and fluid social structure, and Jews as a group were a notable example. Their experience in commerce and crafts enabled them to develop areas in merchandizing, light industry, and services that benefited them and the nation at large. In all periods their conduct as a group displayed the so-called Puritan or middle-class virtues—prudence, thrift, sobriety, diligence. Jewish economic success did not go unnoticed. Although some observers lauded "Jewish skills" as exemplary American traits, others continued to lash out at the ruthless, acquisitive Shylock. The rapid mobility of the Jews after the Civil War contributed in a major way to heightened anti-Jewish animosity and social discrimination. At times both Jews and non-Jews also criticized the so-called abnormalities of Jewish economic distribution, i.e., heavy concentration in manufacturing and trade, underrepresentation in agriculture and manual labor. Whether or not the charge of abnormal Jewish economic behavior is justified, the "abnormalities" shrank, as sociologist Nathan Glazer points out, with the upward movement of Americans as a whole to business, service industries, and the professions. From the beginning, then, Jews figured actively if not importantly in the national economy, part of the American reality that operated to integrate them into an overwhelmingly Christian society.

Religious leveling under law, or the concept that no one church in the United States enjoyed a superior legal status, stemmed from the existence of a democratic government separated from religion by fundamental law. Article 6 of the Constitution, banning religious tests for federal officeholders, and the prohibitions of the First Amendment—no establishment of religion or congressional restraints on the free exercise of religion—set the tone. In advance of the practices of the colonies or the original states, where freedom of conscience but not necessarily state impartiality was accepted, the Constitution announced that the new government closed its eyes to differences among the churches if not to religion generally. The federal example contributed to the liberalization of the religion clauses in the state constitutions, and by 1860 most guaranteed equal political rights as well as religious freedom to all inhabitants. The states were further limited in 1940, when the Supreme Court ruled that they, like Congress, were bound by the religion clauses of the First Amendment.

To be sure, not all Americans agreed with the idea of government neutrality or with rigorous separation. Before the First World War, state lawmakers and courts frequently acted on the assumption that Christianity, even Protestantism exclusively, was *the* American religion. The Supreme Court held twice, once in 1892 and again in 1931, that the United States was in fact a "Christian nation." Public opinion also lagged on the issue of separationism. Many Protestants saw no inconsistencies between their support of Sunday laws or readings from the King James Bible in the public schools and the theory of church-state separation. Echoes of an extremist demand for a religious amendment to the Constitution that would have the government recognize Christianity resonated into the 1950s. But constitutions that held majorities in check by limiting sheer numerical advantage succeeded over the long haul in preserving the legal equality of minorities.

Within a democratic context, the search for a common denominator among religions could only result in greater latitude for all. America's heterogeneous population thus contributed to an easing of legal distinctions among different faiths. The rights of dissenters and minorities demanded recognition in colonial America if only for the preservation of civil peace. Religious minorities were rarely enamored of each other, but advantages that accrued to one group were usually applied to others. Similarly, the rights won in later years by Christian Sabbatarians and Jews, Catholics, Jehovah's Witnesses, or the Amish aided other groups in their quest for legal protection. In this way minorities forged precedents for extending the boundaries of religious freedom.

Since the government never officially identified with any one religion, the churches were forced on their own. Their successes depended on voluntaryism, or how well they scored in the open, competitive religious market, and on their inner vitality. In one way government impartiality drew the different faiths together. If the very nature of the state encouraged the inroads of secularization, all religions stood to lose. Any church, regardless of the number of adherents, felt more comfortable in a society that accepted the axiom of man's need for religion. A secularist creed, even if less militant than the kind that arose in revolutionary France, was abhorrent to the faithful of whatever creed. American ministers, priests, and rabbis alike railed against irreligion and its evil social consequences. In the nineteenth century, atheists and "nothingarians" generally ranked lowest on all religious totem poles. When in the struggle against "godless" totalitarianism during the Second World War, spokesmen of all the major faiths affirmed the religious roots of American democracy. Whether they acknowledged it or not, Jews and Christians desired the same climate of opinion. Since government cooperation was at best uncertain, the menace of increasing secularization—an aspect of the American reality—automatically created a base for mutual understanding and common activity among the faiths.

At the same time that opposition to secularism as a creed forged a bond among the churches, secularization blunted the force of religious animosities. People less sensitive to religious stimuli would be far less likely to respond to negative religious images. One example will suffice. In 1896 William Jennings Bryan turned imagery into political advantage when he appealed to the antisemitic strand in Populist thought. His oft-quoted words, "you shall not crucify mankind upon a cross of gold," effectively harnessed contemporary grievances against "international Jewish bankers" with the latent but still potentially volatile myth of Jew as Christ-killer. Almost forty years later Franklin Roosevelt attempted in his first inaugural address to give hope to a nation in the grip of a major depression. However, it was a changed America, one where the old-time commitment to religion had paled after the First World War and where, according to church historian Robert Handy, the "second disestablishment," or the toppling of Protestant hegemony, was well under way. Thus, when Roosevelt invoked a New Testament metaphor—"The money changers have fled from their high seats. . . . We may now restore the temple to the ancient truths"—the image was neither calculated to incite anti-Jewish feeling nor did it cause any popular ripple whatsoever.

The factors here discussed constructed a social reality that went a long way toward mitigating the tensions of pre-modern imagery and traditions. In essence they rectified much of the imbalance between majority and minority; they also created a pool of common experience in which the major American religions shared. Obviously, they failed to erase all suspicions or distinctions. Individuals switched affiliation from one church to another, but, despite observations on a common core that characterized the major faiths, no notion of merging Protestantism with Catholicism or Judaism with Christianity into new American churches could hope to succeed. As the smallest group, Jews might have been most tempted. In the nineteenth century some did leave the fold to follow Felix Adler into the Ethical Culture movement, and a few, dissatisfied with the blandness of Reform Judaism, did suggest that Jews as a group join the Unitarians. But never was mass defection likely. Jews identified themselves as a people as well as a religion, and the ethnic component—which traditional Christian thought also recognized—continued to distance them from Christians regardless of whether they were Orthodox, Reform, or secularist.

Although boundaries separating the major faiths remained fixed, the American experience indelibly marked each one—in customs and traditions, theological bent, and views of other religious groups. According to Will Herberg, author of the classic socioreligious study, *Protestant-Catholic-Jew,* the result has been a common allegiance to the American way of life on the part of the three major faiths. That shared allegiance has made the American component of American Protestantism, Judaism, or Catholicism as significant as the noun that the adjective "American" modifies.

The American experience permitted the different religions to flourish equally and autonomously. Indeed, no other land created opportunities so ripe for interfaith dialogue and cooperation. Predicated on the interplay between imagery and social reality, the relations between Jews and Christians in America have assumed a quality never before seen in the Western world.

I

ENCOUNTERS IN THE PUBLIC SQUARE

In the open society of the United States, the church and synagogue meet in different arenas—political, economic, social. They address each other through words and through actions. They can look upon each other with friendship, hostility, or indifference; at times they cooperate and at times they compete. All those variables produce innumerable combinations and permutations that defy simple categorization or hard-and-fast patterns of behavior. What obtains on one issue at a specific time does not necessarily insure the same configuration for a different issue or a different time. A particular matter can join the three major faiths together, pit one against one, or one against two. No standing alliances mobilize the Jewish and Catholic minorities against the Protestant majority, or Jews and Protestants against Catholics, or Christians against Jews.

Complicating matters still further is the impossibility of defining *one* Jewish, Protestant, or Catholic point of view. None of the American religious triumvirate is a monolith. At least in the Protestant and Jewish experience, the accepted congregationalist pattern has effectively militated against the imposition of a single, hierarchical stand within the denominations themselves. To be sure, certain questions elicit more consistent responses than other—e.g., Jews will usually lobby for American aid to Israel, Catholics will generally support public aid to parochial schools—but even on such matters there are differing opinions within each camp. Moreover, like Orthodox Jews who agree with Catholics on the issue of parochial schools, members of one religion can resemble their counterparts of an opposite faith sooner than their own coreligionists.

The selections that follow illustrate only four of the countless stages on which Jews and Christians have met. The institutional or group focus does scant justice to the myriad encounters, many deviating from the expected norm, between individual, ordinary Jews and Christians. (Under what general rubric, for example, does the experience of Lazarus Straus fit? Straus, a small merchant of Talbotton, Georgia, conducted serious discussions of biblical passages with local clergymen before the Civil War.) Nevertheless, a sampling of various intergroup experiences from the nineteenth and twentieth centuries elucidates some of the issues that have borne and still bear on overall Jewish-Christian relationships. Parenthetically, the prominence of lay figures and secular organizations on the Jewish side of the interreligious encounter should be noted.

Judaism like Christianity affirms a mission that is central to its theology. However, tradition and history (particularly pre-modern Christian bans on proselytization by Jews) kept American Jews from competing in the religious market. Individual converts came into the fold, but not until the 1980s, when Reform Jews in the United States inaugurated an "outreach" program, did Jews seriously consider missionizing. Besides, had earlier American Jews been uninhibited about proselytizing, their prospects would have been chimerical. If only for the wherewithal to deliver this-worldly benefits, Christianity clearly had the edge in the competition for souls.

On the other hand, nineteenth-century Jews were targeted by Christian missions in Europe and the United States with renewed interest. Different from missions to other non-Christians, an element of obligation or reparation colored the approach to the Jews. One World Missionary Conference said: "The Jewish people have a peculiar claim upon the missionary activities of the Christian Church. Christianity is preeminently theirs by inheritance. The Church is under special obligation to present Christ to the Jew. It is a debt to be repaid, a reparation to be fully and worthily made." (Quoted in John S. Conway, "Protestant Missions to the Jews 1810–1980: Ecclesiastical Imperialism or Theological Aberration?" *Holocaust and Genocide Studies* 1 [1986]:132.) American Jews, like their European brethren, were an object of conversionary societies ever since the early Republic. Crude measures like forcible entry into homes and synagogues, or bribing children to attend missionary classes, may be relics of the past, but the idea of the ultimate conversion of the Jews to the one true faith has lived on.

In antebellum America, Christian missionary activity ranked high on Jewish defense priorities. Even if few Jews succumbed to the religious propagandists, missionaries who denigrated the Jewish religion and its adherents and who spread their jaundiced views throughout the territories posed a stumbling block to the quest for full equality—equality for both Jews and for Judaism. The theory behind Christian missions to the Jews, i.e., the fulfillment of Judaism through Christianity, still hinders open dialogue between the church and synagogue.

The essay by Jonathan D. Sarna is one of several insightful pieces that he has written on American Jews and the missionaries. (Other Jewish treatment of the subject appears in articles and a recent book, *Defending the Faith: Nineteenth-Century American Jewish Writings on Christianity and Jesus,* by George L. Berlin and a book by David Max Eichhorn, *Evangelizing the American Jew.*) Sarna's analysis of nineteenth-century anti-missionary strategies and arguments invites two side observations: first, the security that Jews felt obviously permitted them, a young and largely immigrant community, to indulge in seemingly audacious counterattacks; second, the response, even in its polemical dimension, involved Jews largely untrained in religious dialectics.

Writing in American journals over one hundred years ago, two Jewish women faulted religious catechism and other Sunday school materials for inculcating anti-Jewish sentiment (Nina Morais in *North American Review* 133[1881]; Alice Hyneman Rhine in *Forum* 3[1887]). To be sure, the charge could well have been leveled against the public schools as well, for, as historian Ruth Miller Elson has shown in *Guardians of Tradition, American Schoolbooks of the Nineteenth Century,* a similar bias against Jews and Judaism was aired in nineteenth-century textbooks. While public textbooks were emended as the schools lost their Protestant coloration, the imagery in religious teachings remained constant. It followed that protestations of mutual understanding by religious leaders and institutions lacked substance so long as church members were simultaneously taught that other faiths were less legitimate or respectable than their own.

The American Jewish Committee, the oldest Jewish defense agency on the contemporary scene, has long been interested in the problem of images purveyed by Christian textbooks. Under the Committee's encouragement, a major self-study of Protestant materials was undertaken in the 1950s by Bernhard Olson of the Yale Divinity School. Olson's findings, published in *Faith and Prejudice: Intergroup Problems in Protestant Curricula*, exposed the negative imagery employed about Jews, and it reaffirmed the centrality of Christian education to bigoted beliefs.

Judith H. Banki of the Committee recounts the principal developments in the field after Olson's pioneer work. Summarizing the material of a later study by Gerald S. Strober, she shows how few of Olson's lessons have been incorporated by Protestant textbooks. Catholic materials remain similarly flawed, although progress has been made since Vatican II. Banki underscores those themes which are most likely to produce negative images of Jews, and she elucidates an underlying problem: How far can Christian texts and teachers go in rectifying that imagery without contradicting the intrinsic meaning of the New Testament?

In recent years the attention of Jewish defense organizations to Christian teaching materials is matched by similar interest on the part of Christian groups. (The entire issue of the *Journal of Ecumenical Studies* in which Banki's article appeared was devoted to the theme of Jews and Judaism in Christian education.) Although an interest in the obverse side of the coin, the treatment of Christianity in Jewish textbooks, has also been manifested by Jewish institutions since World War II, that subject understandably never received similar emphasis. Important and detailed research by Judith Herschlag Muffs of the Anti-Defamation League has recently appeared in her article, "Jewish Textbooks on Jesus and Christianity," in *Fifteen Years of Christian-Jewish Dialogue (Teologia e Filosofia*, XI[1988]).

The voice of religious groups on social policy issues has been heard since the beginning of the Republic. Today, like the powerful secular agencies, the churches speak out on all sorts of issues, from abortion to civil rights to foreign policy. Confronting a specific matter, each group factors in its immediate interests as well as its ideology and historical experience. The dynamics of the interplay between the churches and the state is treated by Richard E. Morgan in *The Politics of Religious Conflict. How* religion should undergird social action by the churches is drawing increased attention in *intra* and *inter*faith deliberations. See, for example, Eugene J. Fisher and Daniel F. Polish, eds., *The Formation of Social Policy in the Catholic and Jewish Traditions*.

On the one hand, a shared American experience can create common viewpoints and transcend religious dogma. Catholic use of contraception is a case in point. On the other hand, theological principles applied to social issues frequently divide the major faiths. Writing in 1956 ("Issues That Divide," *Journal of Social Issues*), Leo Pfeffer, a foremost authority on matters of church and state, outlined major areas of friction: religion and education, public morals and censorship (prohibition, lotteries, Sunday laws, sexual behavior), family relationships (divorce, adoption, birth control), and political affairs (ambassador to the Vatican, McCarthyism, communism). Pfeffer elaborated on those themes three years later in a full-length book, *Creeds in Competition: A Creative Force in American Culture.* Overall, the broad area known as "church and state" has generated most interreligious tension. Clashes over public and institutional policy, notably in the matter of religion in the public schools, often resulted in litigation involving the religion clauses of the First Amendment.

The source of the tension may be described as follows: what Catholics and Jews historically regarded as improper religious intrusion into the public domain—e.g., Sunday laws, Protestant trappings in the schools, prohibition—Protestants considered part of the American way of life. All three faiths had to adjust to American realities, Judaism and Catholicism to the position of dissident minority, Protestantism to the unfolding reality of religious pluralism. (For the history of the Protestant design see Robert T. Handy, *A Christian America: Protestant Hopes and Historical Realities;* on the clash between majority and minorities over church-state matters and minority "adjustments" see Anson Phelps Stokes' classic three-volume *Church and State in the United States* and Leo Pfeffer's *Church, State, and Freedom.*) Over the course of two centuries, internal differences have plagued each camp, and even majority opinion within a group (as in the case of Catholic support of Sunday laws or prayer in the schools) could and did at times reverse itself. Of the three major religious bodies American Jews consistently score highest on graphs of church-state separation. The strict separationist stand has been somewhat chipped away over the past thirty years, but it continues to reflect majority opinion within the community.

The article by David G. Singer compares the views of the American Jewish Congress, the most outspokenly separationist of Jewish defense agencies, with those of the Catholic church on political and judicial issues, 1945–1977. Nineteenth-century patterns of Catholics and Jews on the defensive against militant Protestants had long since changed. After World War II both groups emerged more confident and assertive, and how they interacted on church-state matters in a period of heightened Supreme Court involvement sheds light on the new strengths and weaknesses of both non-Protestant minorities.

None can disagree with the popular observation that intermarriage is a natural consequence of life in an open society. Charles Silberman has succinctly summarized the ways in which Jews and Christians meet: "in school, on the job, at cocktail parties, jogging, sitting on the front stoop of the house in which both live, and in a host of other casual and serendipitous settings." (Silberman examines the issue in a detailed chapter of his recent book, *A Certain People: American Jews and Their Lives Today*.) But intermarriage did not become an issue of intense focus, or concern, until the 1960s. (An early but important sociological study that appeared in 1964 was *Intermarriage: Interfaith, Interracial, Interethnic* by Rabbi Albert I. Gordon.) Today, as sociologists study interreligious unions and their ramifications—i.e., conversion of one spouse, religious identification after marriage, children of the intermarried—and popular books advise on how to build a successful intermarriage, Jewish and Christian religious leaders and institutions counsel concerned couples, run workshops, and write discussion guides.

The intermarriage rate has risen dramatically, from well below 10 percent for Jews until 1960 to over 30 percent by 1972. (Some analysts dispute that figure. Silberman, for example, arrives at an estimate of 24 percent, and conversely others put the rate way above 30 percent.) Similarly, the attitudes both of Jews and gentiles to the incidence of intermarriage have changed markedly. As a small minority, Jews are still more fearful than Christians. Some worry that intermarriage, compounded by the relatively low birth rate among Jews, will steadily erode the community. The traditional American Jewish viewpoint, lasting well into the twentieth century, considered intermarriage an outrage, a betrayal of the Jewish people, virtually an act of apostasy. Nevertheless, sociological samplings indicate that Jewish parents are now far more accepting of the intermarriage of their children, and rabbis (except perhaps for the Orthodox) are concentrating primarily on winning the intermarried couple and their children for Judaism.

Sociologist Egon Mayer has studied intermarriage for many years. The selection include here, co-authored with Carl Sheingold, is from his earlier research, but the research is still ongoing. (See Mayer's more recent study with Amy Avgar, *Conversion among the Intermarried: Choosing to Become Jewish,* and his *Children of Intermarriage: A Study in Patterns of Identification and Family Life.*)

1

The American Jewish Response to Nineteenth-Century Christian Missions

Jonathan D. Sarna

Kenneth Scott Latourette properly characterized the nineteenth century as the "Great Century" of Christian expansion: the age when missionary activities spread to cover all corners of the world. Numerous facets of this development have been investigated.[1] We know a great deal about the origins, growth, and impact of the missionary movement. But the immediate response of the missionized, their counteractive programs and battle for cultural survival, has received surprisingly scant attention. Most scholars continue to view the "unenlightened" only as objects of history, shaped by others.[2] . . .

Organized Protestant efforts to convert American Jews began only in the nineteenth century. *Annus mirabilis* was 1816, a year that saw the establishment both of the Female Society of Boston and the Vicinity for Promoting Christianity among the Jews and of the American Society for Evangelizing the Jews. Post-Edwardsian theology, the Second Great Awakening, the growth of the London Society for Promoting Christianity amongst the Jews, and the Peace of Ghent form the background for these developments. In addition, a man sailed into New York harbor in 1816 who had become famous for the leading role he had played in founding the London conversionist society: Joseph Samuel Christian Frederick Frey.[3]

Frey (1771–1850), a native of Franconia, converted in 1798 and

Reprinted in part by permission from the *Journal of American History* 68, no. 1 (June 1981): 35–51.

immigrated to London in 1801. Though originally slated to work for the London Missionary Society in Africa, he soon commenced labors among his "brethren and kinsmen according to the flesh." In 1809, he helped organize the London Society for Promoting Christianity amongst the Jews. Seven years later, following the publication of his best-selling autobiography and in the wake of an ugly scandal (according to one source Frey seduced a convert named Mrs. Josephson), Frey came to the United States.[4]

Frey's arrival, and the initial attention lavished upon him in New York, brought about the first American response to missionary activities directed at Jews. European polemics and counter-polemics, including the works of David Levi in London, had appeared in New York bookstores earlier—thanks in part to Jewish printers. George Bethune English's idiosyncratic, eccentric, and highly Judeophilic *The Grounds of Christianity Examined, by Comparing the New Testament with the Old* (1813), had also stirred up a predictable storm of controversy.[5] But *Tobit's Letters to Levi; or A Reply to the Narrative of Joseph Samuel C. F. Frey* (1816) was different. Personalities rather than theologies dominated its pages. It sought to puncture the halo around Frey—whose original name was Levy—and tried to prove from "common sense" that money should not be "squandered in America, in . . . the conversion of the Jews." "Tobit" claimed both membership in a Christian church and adherence to "the doctrine of Jesus Christ as contained in the New Testament."[6] Be this as it may, his work—especially in its attacks on Christian divisions and prejudices—reads like one that was Jewish-inspired. European Jews often subsidized philo-Semitic tracts. The same may well have been true in America.[7]

Four years after Tobit's publication, the American Society for Evangelizing the Jews received a state charter. The organization's list of officers reads like a Who Was Who of New York: Elias Boudinot, former president of the Continental Congress, stood at the helm. Below him sat many, obviously honorific, vice presidents, including John Quincy Adams, Jeremiah Day, Ashbel Green, Philip Milledoler (presidents respectively of Yale, Princeton, and Rutgers), William Phillips, and Stephen Van Rensselaer. Rounding out the list of officers was the treasurer, Peter Jay, son of diplomat John Jay. Even this formidable assembly, however, failed to convince the legislature to grant the desired charter. Disturbed by the implications of state-sanctioned evangelization, and embarrassed by the presence in Albany of Mordecai Noah, the Jewish editor of the *National Advocate,* New York City's Tammany newspaper, the legislature insisted on a new name for the evangelization society. From 1820 onward, the organization was known as the American Society for Meliorating the Condition of the Jews.[8]

Open and direct American Jewish responses to Christian missions properly date to this 1820 incorporation. Only then did the melioration society become an active force, funded by hundreds of auxiliary organizations that poured money into its coffers and promised full support for its activities.[9] Though the society initially claimed to be interested only in "melioration," and only in those already converted abroad, American Jews understandably took fright. They feared for their survival. Being small in number (about 3,000), they could ill afford to lose adherents to the majority faith.[10] But fear was not the whole of it. Historically, Christianity posed a menacing challenge to the Jewish people. By undertaking active missions, Christians forced Jews back into an age-old battle. Not only live souls were at stake; centuries of martyred souls were too. In Jewish eyes, the war against missionaries became a war of affirmation, a war to prove that eighteen hundred years of Jewish civilization had not been in vain.[11]

The symbolic importance of the missionary battle explains the magnitude of the Jewish response. Beginning in 1820 with a work entitled *Israel Vindicated* (allegedly authored by "An Israelite" but probably written by the non-Jewish George Houston with the help and financial assistance of Jews)[12] and continuing down through the nineteenth century, the small Jewish community devoted a substantial portion of its resources to various forms of polemics. Solomon Jackson devoted his entire *The Jew* (1823–1825), the first Jewish periodical in America, to "a defence of Judaism against all adversaries."[13] Later Jewish works, if less single-minded, never strayed far from "the challenge." As far as Jews were concerned, nothing was more important.

The most traditional form of Jewish polemic dealt with theology— specifically, the wearisome arguments over the meaning of the Hebrew Bible and the validity of the Christian one. The points of contention scarcely changed over time.[14] As a result, Jews freely borrowed from past masters. A work composed in eighteenth-century England but first printed in nineteenth-century America, *A Series of Letters on the Evidences of Christianity* by Benjamin Dias Fernandes, proved spectacularly popular. Its arguments drew heavily from the classic polemical works of Isaac Troki (1533–1594) and Isaac Orobio de Castro (1620–1687).[15] A later American volume, Selig Newman's *The Challenge Accepted,* was completely derivative:

The following work does not profess to be original as the subjects on which it treats, have been already fully and ably discussed by former writers, defenders of Judaism. Therefore, the learned reader will here find nothing that is new. . . . It is for the use of the less informed of our co-religionists who are almost strangers to all but the English language, that the discussions and writings of the ancient and modern defenders of our Faith have herein been collected and exhibited in an English dress, to enable them to stand in self-defence, when challenged respecting certain predictions of our Prophets, and perverted constructions of Scripture are sought to be forced upon them.

Like others of its genre, *The Challenge Accepted* explained crucial biblical passages, mostly in Genesis and Isaiah, and then moved on to question the authenticity of the gospel literature based on alleged inner contradictions.[16]

Works like these demonstrated their modern character through their emphasis on reason. No standard of truth stood higher. Following Moses Mendelssohn, the great eighteenth-century Jewish philosopher, most insisted that nothing in Judaism was "contrary to, or above, reason." Noah called Judaism "the religion of nature—the religion of reason and philosophy." Isaac Mayer Wise, the pioneer of American Reform Judaism, entitled his first theological polemic "Reason and Faith," and he later stated as a principle that "nothing which reason rejects is to be accepted." By invoking reason Jews proclaimed themselves blissfully modern. They relegated Christianity to a lower level, one reserved for religions repugnant to reason: "The credo which establishes this doctrine is so full of contradictions and inconsistencies, that I challenge any person to compose, within the same compass of words, anything equal to it, or more repugnant to reason and common sense." They implied that Judaism would win out in the end.[17]

A variant form of theological polemic, while dependent on reason, departed from Jewish arguments and relied instead on enlightenment, deistic, and freethought ones: works by John Toland, Anthony Collins, and Paul Henry Thiry, Baron d'Holbach. *Israel Vindicated* falls into this category—not surprisingly, since its presumed author, Houston, had translated Holbach's *Ecce Homme.* English's *The Grounds of Christian-*

ity Examined drew from similar sources. Both employed the same arguments: "Christians . . . adopt, without examination, the most contradictory facts, the most incredible actions, the most amazing prodigies, the most unconnected system, the most unintelligible doctrine, and the most revolting mysteries." Judaism, by contrast, was thoroughly reasonable. Jews promoted and printed these volumes, just as later they publicized the "heretical" findings of David Strauss and Ernest Renan. They aimed to show, as Wise admitted, that Christians and infidels had already "shorn the Christian story of the last prestige." The polemical corollary was obvious: if Christians could not even convince their own adherents, why should Jews pay them heed? [18]

By employing for polemical purposes non-Jewish, anti-Christian works, Jews courted great danger. The impious and nonbeliever held low esteem in America; irreligion and immorality were assumed to go hand in hand.[19] Furthermore, many of the authors whom Jews happily quoted in attacks on the Gospels had on other occasions attacked Judaism with equal vehemence. Why would Jews want to associate with such people? The needs of the hour, however, took precedence over due caution. As had been true in the Middle Ages in eighteenth-century Germany, Jews risked temporary alliances with outcast dissenting Christians for the sake of their more urgent battle against onslaughts from mainstream missionaries. In times of religious war, polemics made strange bedfellows.[20]

Jews stood on safer terrain when they employed a third kind of theological polemic, one that might be called Mendelssohnian or even antipolemical. These works invoked the spirit of Mendelssohn's *Jerusalem* and his letter to Lavater, both of which were known in America, and they professed a "disinclination to enter into religious controversy" of any sort. Isaac Leeser, a leading Jewish minister, editor, and publicist in the antebellum period, employed this type of argument in his *The Jews and the Mosaic Law* (1834) and *The Claims of the Jews to an Equality of Rights* (1841). In both volumes he condemned Christian missionaries without specifically attacking Christianity itself. Though his later synagogue discourses were at times full of theological polemics, Leeser in these early works acknowledged and praised the kind treatment he had received at non-Jewish hands. If only Jews could disabuse their neighbors of "any unfounded suspicions they might be induced to adopt concerning us," he mused, conversionist efforts might lose public support.[21] Leeser did his best to educate Christians, but as a strategy his proved thoroughly unsuccessful—which perhaps led him to abandon it in later years. By not challenging Christian arguments, he had unwittingly opened himself to the charge of being unable to challenge them. Missionaries claimed victory by default.[22]

The failure of the Mendelssohnian approach points up a more general dilemma that American Jews met in their missionary encounters. If they ignored missionaries, they faced charges of cowardice or tacit acquiescence. If, on the other hand, they debated missionaries, they risked angering and offending all Christians, even those with whom they had established social relations. Civil society frowned on religious disputations. It viewed Jews who undertook them as medieval, insular, and intolerant. It made no provisions, however, for how Jews should respond when attacked. Jews did not know either.[23]

By the end of the nineteenth century, some Jews had found a way out of this dilemma. They employed special antimissionary crusaders, like Adolph Benjamin, who defended Judaism with all necessary weapons. These crusaders scorned civility and accepted on their own heads the "medieval taint." Meanwhile, the wealthy, socially active Jews who secretly supported them—men like the banker Jacob Schiff—could proclaim themselves progressively modern and thoroughly tolerant.[24] The compromise may look hypocritical. In fact, it was an effort by some Jews to assimilate socially while simultaneously holding fast to their Jewish identities. The result was ambivalence: manners went one way, money the other.

Historical polemics, those that dealt with the medieval and modern worlds rather than with the biblical one, proved less risky than theological disputes. Furthermore, Jews's relative success in America made these polemics particularly effective. To view the Jewish experience, as many Christians had, as a "tedious succession of oppressions and persecutions" or as "a standing monument of the truth of the christian religion"[25] did not square with obvious facts of American Jewish history. "In this country," as Tobit pointed out, "a Jew is equally as proud a man as a Christian . . . [nor] is it incompetent for a Jew to be the first magistrate, the President of these United States."[26] It followed that past persecutions were not divinely inspired at all, but rather the products of human intolerance. While Christians blamed Jewish intransigence and God's wrath for medieval persecutions, Jews blamed the church "whose principles, condensed into a small compass, appear to be, all who are one way are legitimized; all not are cut off."[27] Jews and Christians agreed on the basic facts of medieval Jewish history; only their interpretations differed.

For a while, Jews had more trouble when Christians pointed to the Jewish diaspora as proof of divine wrath, an argument easily buttressed by Jewish sources. In the late nineteenth century, however, Jews, particularly Reform Jews, provided an answer for this claim as well: "We do not look upon this dispersion as a curse; on the contrary, we regard it as a blessing—a blessing for you and all mankind." This account viewed the diaspora as God's means of spreading his message to the world. Far from being a cursed figure, the wandering Jew had been transformed into a hero: an authentic Jewish missionary.[28]

Jewish historical polemics depended on Jewish current events. The more Jews succeeded, the easier it was to claim that God still loved his people Israel and had never rejected them. In boasting of their success, however, Jews sometimes overstated their case—disastrously. Such claims as "there are upwards of seven millions of Jews, known to be in existence, throughout the world; a number greater than at any period of our history; and possessing more wealth, activity, influence and talents than any body of people of their number on earth" provided grist for the anti-Semite's mill. The same claims to power which negated an old stereotype—"the ever-persecuted Jew"—confirmed a new one—"the all-powerful Jew." Polemics had Jews caught in a double-bind.[29]

As a result, some Jews reworded this argument and substituted a new phrase: "the accepted Jew." Prestige replaced power as a mark of success. The new answer to the myth of the accursed, wandering Jew was a proud, well-mannered and well-groomed Jew who "enjoy[ed] excellent social positions."[30]

Historical polemics based on Christian history posed considerably less danger and shifted the argument to the enemy's turf. Consequently, Jews employed them as often as possible. A hardy perennial, deeply rooted in medieval disputations, was the proof from world events. Writers on this theme borrowed liberally from Troki's list of twenty "prophecies which are unfulfilled, and are yet to come to pass in the days of the expected Messiah." These include everything from "the ingathering of the Ten Tribes" and "the rise of Gog and Magog" to "peace and harmony" and the rebuilding of the temple. Dias Fernandes reprinted these unfulfilled prophecies in their entirety, with full attribution. Others reduced them to their barest essence: "great events are contingent on the appearance of the Messiah which have not yet been realized."[31] In either case, Jews forced missionaries to respond. Without explicitly saying so, they warned that missions could ultimately backfire, as Christians exposed to Jewish arguments began to question their own faith.

Similarly well rooted in the past was the argument from Christian divisions. A variety of denominations missionized simultaneously among American Jews, each claiming truth for its own views. Noah and other Jew posed the obvious question: "how are we to choose?" The question was rhetorical. Since Christians "contradict each other on vital principles and condemn each other most recklessly," Jews like Wise argued that they were better off keeping to their own firmly held convictions. Wise suggested, as others had before him, the Christianity put its own house in order before daring to venture into Jewish-held territory.[32]

In this defensive strategy Jews did not merely refer to Christian divisions. Being thoroughly familiar with the Christian scene, they knew, in Leeser's words, of "multitudes in America who never enter a church, who never have been in Sunday School, who never had a preacher's voice reaching their ears."[33] Jews urged missionaries to attend to these unfortunates and to leave them alone. In some cases, though not that of Wise, they even supported Christian foreign missions and Bible societies. They did not care where the Christian army marched, so long as it kept out of Jewish domains.[34]

Jews trumpeted two other Christian problems. In these cases, however, they aimed not to deflect Christianity, but rather to demonstrate its waning influence in order to deter potential newcomers from signing up. First, they pointed to the "rapid progress of Unitarianism." To Abraham Collins this indicated the indubitable quality of Unitarian arguments and the abiding power of its reason—as contrasted with that of the missionaries. To the typically more exuberant Noah, the same evidence showed broader influences at work, ones that might ultimately lead to the reunification of Christianity with Judaism—largely on Jewish terms. Both men thought that Uniterianism was on the rise and evangelical Protestantism on the decline. Neither hesitated to exploit this "fact" for its polemical possibilities. After the Civil War this argument largely died. Unitarianism became a threat to Judaism, luring away those on the fringes of the Reform movement.[35] But there remained another sign of weakness for Jews to exploit: Christian conversions to Judaism.

The fact that Christian conversions to Judaism took place at all in early America is remarkable. In England, through most of the nineteenth century, synagogues refused to accept proselytes because of fear of popular, clerical, and government reaction. Where converts found acceptance, as in Holland, nobody boasted about them. Jews rather took pride in their lack of evangelical zeal. They made a positive virtue of historical necessity and stressed the ethnic aspects of the faith.[36] Logically, however, no Jewish argument had better polemical potential than proselytism. Converts demonstrated that Judaism was a vibrant religion, one worth leaving Christianity to join. Why then, Jews asked, should anyone want to leave Judaism? By no coincidence, Christians often trumpted Jewish conversions for the opposite reason: to stimulate backsliding Christians.

The centuries-old taboo on discussing proselytization did not break easily. Strategic considerations, however, finally won out. Jackson admitted in *The Jew* to having on file "a score or more" names of converts to Judaism. He revealed no particulars. Leeser also overcame early hesitations. By 1844 he justified reports of proselytization as an "offset to the occasional apostasy of Jews to Christianity." Wise hardly hesitated at all. He enjoyed taunting missionaries with tales of proselytization and went so far as to inform his readers that if non-Jews mastered his *Essence of Judaism,* he would consider their "confessions." Unfortunately, we have no record of how many confessions he heard. At least one missionary, however, sadly admitted that conversions of Gentiles to Judaism were "not uncommon."[37]

The argument from proselytization stands as one of American Jewry's most original and important contributions to counter-missionary polemics. Its significance lies primarily in its daring. By trumpeting conversions, American Jews insisted on their right to battle Christianity on equal terms—no holds barred. If Christians could convert Jews, Jews could convert Christians. Religious liberty, according to this view, meant nothing less than religious anarchy. All sects had the right to fight among themselves for new members. The same "voluntary system" that permitted Protestant denominations to compete with one another, and permitted Catholics to make converts, must allow Jews to proselytize as well.[38]

Earlier, some Jews had propounded a different view. *Israel Vindicated* considered missions to American Jews "contrary to the true spirit and meaning of the *constitution.*" Leeser used a similar phrase, arguing that it was "contrary to the spirit of the constitution of the country for the many to combine to do the smallest minority the injury of depriving them of their conscientious conviction by systematic efforts."[39] According to this understanding of the First Amendment, all sects, Christian and non-Christian, had the right to exist unmolested and unmissionized. The "spirit of the constitution," however, never became enshrined into law. By the mid-1840s at the latest, most American Jews realized this. They understood that they had to fight missionaries, and they proceeded to do so with all means at their disposal.

Polemics formed only one means of countering missionaries. They covered a broad range of subjects—often borrowing arguments from both theology and history—and they aimed at a wide variety of audiences. Still, something was missing. Missions aroused the deepest of passions in American Jews: intellectual arguments, no matter how forceful, did not give them vent. Jews needed a vituperative outlet, a place where they could rage, roar, and respond with feeling. They employed for this purpose their Jewish newspapers.

Angry rebuttals consumed many pages of the Jewish press. *The Jew* specialized in point-by-point refutations of the melioration society's missionary sheet, *Israel's Advocate*. Leeser, who promised in the first issue of the *Occident* to keep "a watchful eye" on missionaries, picked his targets more selectively. He once devoted six passionate pages to a minute examination of the thirty-sixth annual report of the London Society for Promoting Christianity in order to prove that the magnitude of the society's expenses stood in stark contrast to the insignificance of its achievements. On other occasions, he found friends and relatives eager to watch missionaries for him. They furiously denied the alleged deathbed conversions of such people as Charleston's "Dr. D" (De La Motta) and Savannah's "Miss H."[40] Perhaps Leeser's greatest coup came in 1853 when Rabbi E. Marcussohn personally took to the *Occident*'s columns to refute missionary claims of his conversion. The private record suggests that Marcussohn, a heavy drinker, may not have been nearly so innocent as he maintained. In the antimissionary battle, however, propaganda needs took precedence over fine points of fact. Leeser and his readers enjoyed their victory.[41]

No editor vented more rage at missionaries than Wise. He considered it a "sacred duty" to expose missionaries' "rascality" and wasted no opportunity to catch them at their "lying." Wise's passionate diatribes, however, by no means confined themselves to defensive rebuttals. By his own admission, he assumed the role of "malicious, biting, pugnacious, challenging, and mocking monster of the pen." His "peeps into the missionary efforts" conveniently summarize the major accustations made against missionaries by large numbers of Jews throughout the nineteenth century.[42]

Bribery and fraud held pride of place in Wise's standard litany of charges. Hyprocrisy, deception, impertinence, imposition, laziness, immorality, and false piety rounded out the sordid picture. When Wise opened his columns to a non-Jew, Theodore Norman, the message did not change. Norman dutifully revealed that missionaries "deceive, cheat and impose on mankind in general."[43] A single aim underlay all of these charges: the desire to prove missionaries depraved. If Christians considered them miscreants—evil, immoral, and corrupt—then they might refuse them support. They might even succumb to fallacious logic by deciding that the quality of missionary arguments was no better than the quality of the missionaries themselves. By the same token, if Jews considered them miscreants, then they would have more reason than ever to battle against them. They could rest secure that in opposing missionaries they were patriotically working to bring about moral reform.

Mighty as American Jewish pens were in the battle against missionaries, they still could not substitute for concrete actions. Christians, after all, had foot soldiers, tracts, institutions, and funding on their side. Jews needed to respond with more than printed words alone. And they did. At the most passive level, they attempted to talk with missionaries—especially the converts among them—hoping to show them the errors of their way. Occasionally this succeeded, and converts returned.[44] Most often, however, the tactic backfired. Reports of the conversations would appear in the missionary press as evidence that Jews had begun to "see the light." When he realized this, Leeser urged his readers to desist from conversations: "refrain from holding intercourse in any measure with these renegadoes." Many Jews apparently heeded his call. Missionaries increasingly reported finding Jews uncoopertive and unwilling to open their doors.[45]

Snubbing may have functioned as a form of Jewish passive resistance to missionaries. Still, Jews yearned for more active strategies—ones that promised to have far greater impact. Back in the 1820s, Noah intimidated the melioration society by appearing at their annual meetings. His presence, eloquent in its silence, served as indubitable public testimony of missionary failure. In 1843, Joseph Simpson attempted to invoke the president's aid against the melioration society. He asked John Tyler to censure Gen. Winfield Scott for presiding at a missionary conference while on the public payroll. Tyler, who considered the matter a private one, refused.[46] A few Jews may have found other creative or political means of frustrating the hated missionary, but the average Jew could not always control his feelings. He viewed missionaries, especially if they were converts, as traitors and provocateurs, yet found no one in government interested in protecting him. So he lashed out on his own. In most cases, situations did not develop beyond the stage of malicious language and angry threats. At that point missionaries generally left the scene. As early as 1864, however, a stone-throwing incident took place at the New York City Mission School. More serious and widespread violence and rioting came later, in the 1890s, after the immigrant population grew and missionaries opened up conversionist centers in ghetto storefronts.[47]

Jewish leaders never encouraged antimissionary violence. They feared for the Jewish image and for Jews' acceptance into civil society. They also understood, however vaguely, that in the long run defensive actions —those aimed at strengthening the Jewish community internally—held far more promise of solving the missionary problem once and for all. Leading Jews preferred analysis to violence. They studied missionary successes to learn where their own society had failed. They saw how missionaries met needs that the Jewish community had ignored. Then, they imitated missionaries in order to defeat them. They created Jewish functional alternatives to missionary activities—alternatives that would keep Jews firmly within the fold.[48]

The most obvious weaknesses pointed up by pre-Civil War missionaries were Jewish ignorance and communal disunity. Before the rise of the melioration society, the Jewish community had no newspaper, no certified rabbi, few textbooks, and no central leader. All of this changed once missionaries began their work. Within months of the appearance of their Israel's Advocate, The Jew rose up to answer it. Though neither lasted more than a few years, a pattern was set. In 1843, it repeated itself: the missionaries issued the Jewish Chronicle; Leeser responded with his Occident. Leeser may have been planning his newspaper for some time and for different reasons. The missionary challenge, however, transformed his ideas into action. From the very beginning the two periodicals functioned, in Leeser's words, as "two such little planets revolving around their peculiar axis, the former to malign Jews and to report all their faults and apostacies, the latter to be in a measure their *advocate* and to reprove without hesitation and reserve when errors and wrongs are discovered."[49]

The *Occident* benefited the Jewish community in two ways: it drew disparate settlements together, and it armed Jews with the kinds of information they needed to rebut missionary claims. The periodical could not substitute, however, for the textbooks, tracts, and English-language Bibles that missionaries provided Jews for free. Jews needed educational volumes of their own, and, thanks largely to the work of Leeser, these volumes came into being. Leeser personally translated into English catechisms, readers, even the Bible, and what he did not do himself, he urged others to do. The resulting books always mirrored Christian ones in form and style. But though outwardly the same, they differed in content. In a sense, this is symbolic of all Jewish counter-missionary activities: outwardly Jews conformed, inwardly they maintained their identity.[50]

The American Jewish Publication Society (1845–1851) expanded on Leeser's work, but kept only adult needs in mind. Rather than textbooks, the society printed popular literature—exclusively the kind, however, that challenged "the secret attacks and open assaults by specious arguments of those whose darling object is to break down the landmarks of Judaism." The society's first book, *Caleb Asher,* typifies the rest: it was an antimissionary satire.[51]

Other developments in the antebellum Jewish community—the publication of new books and periodicals, the creation of Jewish schools, hospitals, and synagogues, the appointment of foreign rabbis to be American religious leaders, and the drafting of plans for Jewish colonies in America and Palestine—also relate to the missionary challenge.[52] In each case, other motivating factors were at work, particularly the growth of Jewish immigration. "The activity and missionary zeal of all the [Protestant] sects," however, always played a part in Jewish planning.[53] Indeed, the conversionist threat frequently proved the decisive argument —the one that convinced thrifty Jews to contribute their hard-earned money.

The only weapon that Jews refused to employ in their anticonversionist war was the missionary weapon itself. Leeser, imitating "the activity and the missionary zeal of all the sects which surround us," once called for "Israelites of every degree to become missionaries," but only to carry the good tidings to "the bosom of their own families, to their neighbors, to their friends"—not apparently, to Christians. A decade later, he suggested the creation of a Jewish missionary organization for the same purpose.[54] Leeser also advocated a Hebrew Foreign Mission Society aimed at sending Jews to China and "other quarters of the globe" that required "the presence of enlightened Israelites" to ward off "Christian soldiers." The philanthropost Judah Touro willed this society $5,000 in capital, and Julius Eckman, followed by the traveler I. J. Benjamin, agreed to undertake the arduous journey. In the end, however, no missionaries ever set out. Apathy, internal squabbling, charges that the society acted "contrary to Judaism," and the outbreak of Civil War brought the whole Jewish foreign missionary enterprise to a premature conclusion.[55]

After the Civil War, Jewish missions never received serious consideration. "Missionizing" became something that Christians did and Jews did not do.[56] Otherwise, the antebellum dynamic remained the same. Missionaries probed the underside of the Jewish community and uncovered areas of Jewish need. Alarmed Jews, in turn, probed the missionaries. Having learned about Jewish needs secondhand, they then proceeded to fill them. In so doing, they subverted the missionaries by imitation. The New York example is typical. Missionaries created schools, dispensaries, and ghetto charities designed to meet immigrant needs. This led to a Jewish survey of ghetto conditions. Ultimately, Jews created free schools, dispensaries, and philanthropies of their own.[57] And then the cycle began all over again.

By the end of the nineteenth century, missionaries actually posed only a petty threat to American Jewry. They continued to ply their trade, and American Jewry continued to battle them. But outsiders knew that widespread conversions would never take place. Eight decades of struggle had sensitized Jews to their own identities and past history. They had learned the value of education, organization, and leadership. They had even discovered how to use the missionary threat as a specter—an evil portent menacing enough to frighten the community into undertaking defensive actions, self-analyses, and constructive new projects. Occasionally, missionaries did succeed in luring a few troubled souls away. In the final analysis, however, their impact was precisely the opposite of what they intended.[58] Instead of converting the American Jewish community, they helped transform it into a more cohesive and more secure body than it had ever been before.

NOTES

1. Kenneth Scott Latourette, *The Great Century: A.D. 1800–A.D. 1914, Europe and the United States of America* (New York, 1941); this is volume IV of his *A History of the Expansion of Christianity* (7 vols., New York, 1937–1945). See also Stuart Piggin, "Assessing Nineteenth-Century Missionary Motivation: Some Considerations of Theory and Method," in *Religious Motivation: Biographical and Sociological Problems for the Church Historian*, ed. Derek Baker (Oxford, Eng., 1978), 327–37; John K. Fairbank, ed., *The Missionary Enterprise in China and America* (Cambridge, 1974); James P. Ronda and James Axtell, *Indian Missions: A Critical Bibliography* (Bloomington, Ind., 1978); John McCracken, *Politics and Christianity in Malawi, 1875–1940: The Impact of the Livingstonia Mission in the Northern Province* (Cambridge, Eng., 1977).

2. An important exception is Louise H. Hunter, *Buddhism in Hawaii* (Honolulu, 1971). See also James P. Ronda, " 'We Are Well as We Are': An Indian Critique of Seventeenth-Century Christian Missions," *William and Mary Quarterly*, 34 (Jan. 1977), 66–82.

3. *Religious Intelligencer*, 1 (Jan. 25, 1817), 555–58. On early American Jewish missions generally, see David Max Eichhorn, *Evangelizing the American Jew* (New York, 1978); Max Eisen, "Christian Missions to the Jews in North America and Great Britain," *Jewish Social Studies*, 10 (Jan. 1948), 31–66; Marshall Sklare, "The Conversion of the Jews," *Commentary*, 56 (Sept. 1973), 44–53; Lee M. Friedman, "The American Society for Meliorating the Condition of the Jews and Joseph S.C.F. Frey," in Lee M. Friedman, *Early American Jews* (Cambridge, 1934), 96–112; Lorman Ratner, "Conversion of the Jews and Pre-Civil War Reform," *American Quarterly*, 13 (Spring 1961), 43–54; and Louis Meyer, "Hebrew-Christian Brotherhood Unions and Alliances of the Past and Presentm," *Minutes of the First Hebrew-Christian Conference of the United States. Held at Mountain Lake, Md., July 28–30, 1903* (Pittsburgh, 1903), 16–31. On British missions to the Jews, see Todd M. Endelman, *The Jews of Georgian England, 1714–1830: Tradition and Change in a Liberal Society* (Philadelphia, 1979), 71–76, 285–86; Harvey W. Meirovich, "Ashkenazic Reactions to the Conversionists, 1800–1850," *Transactions of the Jewish Historical Society of England*, 26 (1979), 8–25; and Bill Williams, *The Making of Manchester Jewry, 1740–1875* (Manchester, Eng., 1976), 45–48, 148–50. On German missions, see David C. Smith, "The Berlin Mission to the Jews its Ecclesiastical

and Political Context, 1822–1848," *Neue Zeitschrift für Missionswissenschaft*, 30 (1974), 182–90. The only general survey of the field remains A. E. Thompson, *A Century of Jewish Missions* (Chicago, 1902).

4. On Joseph Samuel Christian Frederick Frey see, in addition to works already cited, George Harvey Genzmer, "Joseph Samuel Christian Frederick Frey," *Dictionary of American Biography* (20 vols., New York, 1928–36), VII, 28–29; George J. Miller, "David A. Borrenstein: A Printer and Publisher at Princeton, N.J., 1824–28," *Papers of the Bibliographical Society of America*, 30 (1936), 1–6; and Harry Simonhoff, *Jewish Notables in America, 1776–1864: Links of an Endless Chain* (New York, 1956), 176–80.

5. *Christian Disciple*, 4 (Aug. 1816), 249–52; (New York) *Jewish Chronicle*, 10 (March 1854), 248; David Levi, *Letters to Dr. Priestly, in Answer to Those He Addressed to the Jews; Inviting them to an Amicable Discussion of the Evidences of Christianity* (New York, 1794); David Levi, *A Defence of the Old Testament, in a Series of Letters Addressed to Thomas Paine* (New York, 1797); George Bethune English, *The Grounds of Christianity Examined, by Comparing the New Testament with the Old* (Boston, 1813); and Edward Everett, *A Defense of Christianity, against the Work of George B. English* (Boston, 1814).

6. *Tobit's Letters to Levi; or A Reply to the Narrative of Joseph Samuel C. F. Frey* (New York, 1916), 1,36. See also the American reprint of a Liverpool polemic, Jacob Nikelsburger, *Koul Jacob in Defence of the Jewish Religion: Containing the Arguments of the Rev. C. F. Frey* (New York, 1816).

7. Alexander Altmann, *Moses Mendelssohn: A Biographical Study* (University, Ala., 1973), 449–61, 512; and more generally Hans Joachim Schoeps, *Philosemitismus im Barock: Religions-und geistgeschichtliche Untersuchungen* (Tübingen, Ger. 1952).

8. American Society for Meliorating the Condition of the Jews, *Constitution of the American Society for Ameliorating the Condition of the Jews; with an Address from the Hon. Elias Boudinot . . . And the Act of Incorporation Granted by the Legislature of the State of New York* (New York, 1820); Joseph Samuel C. F. Frey, *Judah and Israel: Or, the Restoration and Conversion of the Jews and the Ten Tribes* (New York, 1840), 81–93; Joseph L. Blau and Salo W. Baron, eds., *The Jews of the United States, 1790–1840: A Documentary History* (3 vols., New York, 1963), III, 714–73; Jonathan D. Sarna, *Jacksonian Jew: The Two Worlds of Mordecai Noah* (New York, 1981), 56–57.

9. The early support for the American Society for Meliorating the Condition of the Jews is chronicled in its annual reports (especially 1820–1825) and in its *Israel's Advocate* (1823–1827). For details of the Philadelphia auxiliary, see Marion L. Bell, *Crusade in the City: Revivalism in Nineteenth-Century Philadelphia* (Lewisburg, Pa., 1977), 137–59.

10. Ira Rosenswaike, "The Jewish Population of the United States as Estimated from the Census of 1820," *American Jewish Historical Quarterly*, 53 (Dec.

1963), 148; Bertram W. Korn, "Factors Bearing upon the Survival of Judaism in the Ante-Bellum Period," *ibid.*, 53 (June 1964), 341–51; and more generally, Malcolm H. Stern, "The 1820s: American Jewry Comes of Age," in *A Bicentennial Festschrift for Jacob Rader Marcus*, ed. Bertram Wallace Korn (New York, 1976).

11. On the background of the Jewish-Christian encounter in the United States, see Hans Joachim Schoeps, *The Jewish-Christian Argument: A History of Theologies in Conflict*, trans. David E. Green (New York, 1963); Oliver Shaw Rankin, *Jewish Religious Polemic of Early and Later Centuries, a Study of Documents Here Rendered in English* (Edinburgh, 1956); Kenneth R. Stow, "The Church and the Jews: From St. Paul to Paul IV," in Lawrence V. Berman, et al., *Bibliographical Essays in Medieval Jewish Studies* (New York, 1976), 109–65; and Frank Ephraim Talmage, *Disputation and Dialogue: Readings in the Jewish-Christian Encounter* (New York, 1975), especially the bibliographic essay, 361–83.

12. Jonathan D. Sarna, "The Freethinker, the Jews and the Missionaries: George Houston and the Mystery of *Israel Vindicated*," *AJS Review*, 5 (1980), 101–14.

13. *The Jew*, 1 (March 1823), 1.

14. See, in addition to works cited in note 14, Daniel J. Lasker, *Jewish Philosophical Polemics against Christianity in the Middle Ages* (New York, 1977).

15. Benjamin Dias Fernandes, *A Series of Letters on the Evidences of Christianity* (Philadelphia, [1853]), 2,250–58. Isaac Leeser briefly traces the history of these letters in his introduction to the 1853 edition. See also *The Jew*, 1 (July 1823), 85. Reprints of this polemic appeared in 1858 and in 1869, and a "revised and enlarged" edition was printed serially in *Israelite*, 14–15 (1868–1869). See Isaac Mayer Wise's praise of the book as "one of the best polemical works on this topic ever published by a Hebrew in the English language." *Israelite*, 12 (1864), 149.

16. Selig Newman, *The Challenge Accepted: A Dialogue between a Jew and a Christian: The Former Answering a Challenge Thrown Out by the Latter, Respecting the Accomplishment of the Prophecies Predictive of the Advent of Jesus* (New York, 1850), iii. On Selig Newman, see Endelman, *Jews of Georgian England*, 244, 285. For another example of a theological polemic from this period, see the unpublished manuscript of Jacob Mordecai, Mordecai Family Papers (American Jewish Archives, Cincinnati, Ohio).

17. Moses Mendelssohn to Elkan Herz, July 22, 1771, quoted in Altmann, *Moses Mendelssohn*, 249; Mordecai M. Noah, *Discourse Delivered at the Consecration of the Synagogue K. K. Shearith Israel in the City of New York* (New York, 1818), 24; James G. Heller, *Isaac M. Wise: His Life, Work, and Thought* (New York, 1965), 140–41, 535; Dias Fernandes, *Series of Letters*, 149; see generally, Schoeps, *Jewish-Christian Argument*,

103–5; and Arthur Hertzberg, *The French Enlightenment and the Jews* (New York, 1968), 256–58.

18. An Israelite [George Houston], *Israel Vindicated; Being a Refutation of the Calumnies Propagated Respecting the Jewish Nation* (New York, 1820), 30; Sarna, "The Freethinker, the Jews and the Missionary," 105–6. Abraham De Sola republished George Bethune English's work in 1852, and readers were urged to buy it in *Occident*, 11 (Sept. 1853), 324. For Wise, see Heller, *Isaac M. Wise*, 641; and *Israelite*, 12 (1866), 396.

19. Robert T. Handy, *A Christian America: Protestant Hopes and Historical Realities* (New York, 1971), 30–42; see also John Webb Pratt, *Religion, Politics, and Diversity: The Church-State Theme in New York History* (Ithaca, N.Y. 1967), 121–57.

20. Hertzberg, *French Enlightenment and the Jews*, 268–313; Jacob Katz, *From Prejudice to Destruction: Anti-Semitism, 1700–1933* (Cambridge, 1980), 23–33; S. Ettinger, "Jews and Judaism as Seen by English Deists of the Eighteenth Century" [in Hebrew], *Zion*, 29 (no. 3–4, 1964), 182–207; Moshe Pelli, "The Impact of Deism on the Hebrew Literature of the Enlightenment in Germany," *Journal of Jewish Studies*, 24 (Autumn 1973), 127–46; David Berger, "Christian Heresy and Jewish Polemic in the Twelfth and Thirteenth Centuries," *Harvard Theological Review*, 68 (July–Oct. 1975), 287–303; Lasker, *Jewish Philosophical Polemics*, 164–65.

21. Moses Mendelssohn, "Letter to Johann Casper Lavater," in *Disputation and Dialogue*, ed. Talmage, 266; Isaac Leeser, *The Claims of the Jews to an Equality of Rights* (Philadelphia, [1841]), 4, 8–13, 92–97; Isaac Leeser, *The Jews and the Mosaic Law* (Philadelphia, [1834]), 228; *Occident*, 9 (1852) supplement, iii–xx, 1–115; *Israelite*, 1 (1854), 132–33; and, for a later example, *Sabbath Visitor*, 22 (1893), 324. More generally, see Bertram Wallace Korn, "German-Jewish Intellectual Influences on American Jewish Life, 1824–1972," in *Tradition and Change in Jewish Experience*, ed. A. Leland Jamison (Syracuse, N.Y., 1978), 106–40; and Maxine S. Seller, "Isaac Leeser: A Jewish-Christian Dialogue in Antebellum Philadelphia," *Pennsylvania History*, 35 (July 1968), 231–42.

22. See the bound compendium of issues from *The Jew*, S. H. Jackson, ed., *The Jew; Being a Defence of Judaism against All Adversaries, and Particularly against the Insidious Attacks of "Israel's Advocate"* (New York, 1824), vii. "In the present enlightened age, not to defend Judaism, would be considered a tacit acknowledgement that it was indefensible, or at least that we thought so."

23. For this theme in a different context, see John Murray Cuddihy, *The Ordeal of Civility: Freud, Marx, Lévi-Strauss, and the Jewish Struggle with Modernity* (New York, 1974), 13–14.

24. Eichhorn, *Evangelizing the American Jew*, 178–80.

25. Hannah Adams, *The History of the Jews from the Destruction of Jerusalem to the Nineteenth Century* (2 vols., Boston, 1812), I, iii, iv. See *Christian*

Disciple, 4 (Aug. 1816), 250; Blau and Baron, eds., *Jews of the United States*, I, 88–89; Anita Libman Lebeson, "Hannah Adams and the Jews," *Historia Judaica*, 8 (Oct. 1946), 113–34; and C. Conrad Wright, "Hannah Adams," *Notable American Women: 1607–1950: A Biographical Dictionary*, ed. Edward T. James, Janet Wilson James, and Paul S. Boyer (3 vols., Cambridge, 1971), I, 9–11. Hannah Adams's view of Jewish history can be traced back to Jacques Basnage. See Hertzberg, *French Enlightenment and the Jews*, 47.

26. *Tobit's Letters to Levi*, 55. Christians themselves realized that "America was different," but this had little bearing on their arguments. See *Israel's Advocate*, 1 (Feb. 1823), 29; American Society for Meliorating the Condition of the Jews, *Interesting Documents* (New York, 1822), 11; and Aaron Bancroft, *A Discourse Delivered before the Worcester Auxiliary Society for Meliorating the Condition of the Jews, April 28, 1824* (Worcester, Mass., 1824), 11.

27. "Honestus," *A Critical Review of the Claims Presented by Christianity for Inducing Apostacy in Israel* (New York, 1852), 30.

28. Bernhard Felsenthal, *The Wandering Jew: A Statement to a Christian Audience, of the Jewish View of Judaism* (Chicago, 1872), 5. Cf. Haim Hillel Ben-Sasson, "Galut," *Encyclopedia Judaica* (16 vols., Jerusalem, 1971), VII, 275–94. See also Max Wiener, "The Conception of Mission in Traditional and Modern Judaism," *Yivo Annual of Jewish Social Sciences*, 2–3 (1947–1948), 9–24.

29. Abraham Collins, *The Voice of Israel, Being a Review of Two Sermons Preached in the City of New York* (New York, 1823), 20. See also "Honestus," *Critical Review*, 21; and Sarna, *Jacksonian Jew*, 122.

30. Felsenthal, *Wandering Jew*, 4.

31. [Isaac Troki], *Faith Stengthened*, trans. Moses Mocatta (New York, 1970), 32–36; Dias Fernandes, *Series of Letters*, 250–58; *New York Sunday Times and Noah's Weekly Messenger*, April 14, 1850, p. 2. See also Collins, *Voice of Israel*, 80.

32. M. M. Noah, *Discourse on the Restoration of the Jews: Delivered at the Tabernacle, Oct. 28 and Dec. 2, 1844* (New York, 1845), 27.; F. C. Gilbert, *From Judaism to Christianity and Gospel Work among the Hebrews* (Concord, Mass., 1911), 85; *Israelite*, 1 (1854), 36; *ibid.*, 4 (1857), 4. See also M. M. Noah in *New York Evening Star*, June 14, 1836, p. 2; Isidor Kalisch, *A Guide for Rational Inquiries into the Biblical Writings* (Cincinnati, 1857), ix; [Houston], *Israel Vindicated*, 9; Leeser, *Claims of the Jews*, 14.

33. *Occident*, 3 (May 1845), 99. See also *ibid.*, 6 (May 1848), 101; *Israelite*, 3 (1856), 172.

34. Abraham Collins, "Introduction," to John Oxlee, *Three Letters Humbly Submitted . . . on the Inexpediency and Futility of Any Attempt to Convert the Jews to the Christian Faith* (Philadelphia, 1843), ii; Mordecai M. Noah, *Travels in England, France, Spain, and the Barbary States, in the Years*

1813–14 and 15 (New York, 1819), 56; Noah, *Discourse Delivered at the Consecration of the Synagogue*, 43; S. M. Isaacs in *London Voice of Jacob*, Aug. 4, 1853, p. 214B.

35. Collins, *Voice of Israel*, iv; Sarna, *Jacksonian Jew*, 131; Benny Kraut, "Judaism Triumphant: Isaac Mayer Wise on Unitarianism and Liberal Christianity," unpublished typescript, 1980 (American Jewish Archives), 49.

36. "Proselytes," *Encyclopaedia Judaica*, XIII, 1182–93; Joseph R. Rosenbloom, *Conversion to Judaism: From the Biblical Period to the Present* (Cincinnati, 1978), 67–89.

37. *The Jew*, 1 (Dec. 1823), 222; *ibid.*, 2 (April 1824), 294; *Occident*, 2 (July 1844), 216; *Israelite*, 12 (1868), 76; *Israelite Indeed*, 7 (March 1864), 213. For other examples, see *Occident*, 3 (May 1845), 42; *ibid.*, 6 (Dec. 1848), 456–67; *ibid.*, 8 (May 1850), 59; *Israelite*, 3 (1856), 52, 412; *ibid.*, 6 (1860), 210, 249; *ibid.*, 9 (1863), 220. For comparable Catholic arguments, see Aaron I. Abell, ed., *American Catholic Thought on Social Questions* (Indianapolis, 1968), xvi–xvii, 13, 14.

38. The *London Voice of Jacob*, Sept. 29, 1843, p. 7B, viewed American Jews' daring with trepidation, and hoped "that forbearance will continue to characterize the English Jews." Anglo-Jewish passivity was attacked in *Israelite*, 3 (1856), 147.

39. [Houston], *Israel Vindicated*, ibid.; *Occident*, 3 (May 1845), 42. See also *New York Evening Post*, March 15, 1829, p. 2.

40. *The Jew*, 1 (Nov. 1823), 191; *Occident*, 7 (July 1849), 223; *ibid.*, 2 (Aug. 1844), 255–56; *ibid.*, 4 (Oct. 1846), 355–57. Cf. (New York) *Jewish Chronicle*, 3 (Nov. 1846), 142, (May 1847), 346.

41. *Occident*, 10 (Oct. 1852), 352–60; E. R. McGregor to Isaac Leeser, Oct. 5, 1852, Dec. 6, 1852, microfilm 200, Isaac Leeser Papers (American Jewish Archives); C. D. Oliver to Leeser, Oct. 20, 1853, *ibid.*; S. Cellner to Leeser, Aug. 23, 1852, *ibid.*; E. Marcussohn to Leeser, Jan. 1, 1853, *ibid.*; Stephen A. Speisman, *The Jews of Toronto: A History to 1937* (Toronto, 1979), 26–27.

42. *Israelite*, 4 (1858), 237; Isaac M. Wise, *Reminiscences*, trans. David Philipson (New York, 1973), 273; Isaac Mayer Wise "The World of My Books," trans. Albert H. Friedlander, in *Critical Studies in American Jewish History: Selected Articles from* American Jewish Archives, ed. Jacob R. Marcus, (3 vols., Cincinnati, 1971), I, 173–75; Heller, *Isaac M. Wise*, 652–57. See also Samuel Sandmel, "Isaac Mayer Wise's 'Jesus Himself,' " in *Essays in American Jewish History: To Commemorate the Tenth Anniversary of the Founding of the American Jewish Archives under the Direction of Jacob Rader Marcus* (New York, 1975), 325–58.

43. *Israelite*, 1 (1854), 36; *ibid.*, 3 (1856), 12, 268; *ibid.*, 5 (1859), 302. For the Theodore Norman exposés, see *ibid.*, 1 (1854), 39, 52, 68. Leeser employed proselyte Warder Cresson for a similar purpose. See *Occident*, 6 (Dec. 1858), 456–60.

44. (New York) *Jewish Chronicle*, 3 (June 1847), 370; *Israelite Indeed*, 1 (July 1857), 7–8; *Israelite*, 10 (1864), 347.

45. *Occident*, 7 (July 1849), 223 Cf. *ibid.*, 1 (April 1843), 43–47; (New York) *Jewish Chronicle*, 1 (Dec. 1844), 142; *Israelite Indeed*, 2 (Dec. 1858), 125.

46. Sarna, *Jacksonian Jew*, 56–57; N. Taylor Phillips, "Items Relating to the History of the Jews of New York," *Publications of the American Jewish Historical Society*, 11 (1903), 158–59.

47. Notices of violence include, (New York) *Jewish Chronicle* 1 (Aug. 1844), 43, (Jan. 1845), 177, (April 1845), 270, 274–75, (May 1845), 306; *ibid.*, 4 (May 1848), 336; *ibid.*, 8 (Aug. 1851), 45; *Israelite*, 2 May 24, 1868, p. 4; *Israelite Indeed*, 8 (July 1864), 10–11; Church Society for Promoting Christianity amongst the Jews, *Annual Report*, 1 (1879), 24; *New York Evening Post*, June 17, 1899, in *Portal to America: The Lower East Side, 1870–1925*, ed. Allon Schoener (New York, 1967), 63–65. See also Speisman, *Jews of Toronto*, 131–44; R. Gruneir, "The Hebrew-Christian Mission in Toronto," *Canadian Ethnic Studies*, 9 (no. 1, 1977), 18–28.

48. The contrast to the situation in Germany is striking; see Eleonore Sterling, "Jewish Reaction to Jew-Hatred in the First Half of the Nineteenth Century," *Leo Baeck Institute Year Book*, 3 (1958), 103–21.

49. *Occident*, 6 (Oct. 1848), 362. Cf. *ibid.*, 1 (April 1843), 43–44; and (New York) *Jewish Chronicle*, 1 (July 1844), 1. The *Jewish Chronicle* appeared in a newsletter format before 1844. Leeser issued a prospectus for the *Occident* in 1842. See Nathan M. Kaganoff, "Supplement III: Judaica Americana Printed before 1851," in *Studies in Jewish Bibliography, History and Literature in Honor of I. Edward Kiev*, ed. Charles Berlin (New York, 1971), 193.

50. Moshe Davis, *The Emergence of Conservative Judaism: The Historical School in Nineteenth Century America* (Philadelphia, 1963), 34–64; Hyman B. Grinstein, "In the Course of the Nineteenth Century," in *A History of Jewish Education in America*, ed. Judah Pilch (New York, 1969), 25–50; Lloyd P. Gartner, ed. *Jewish Education in the United States: A Documentary History* (New York, 1969), 50–79. For a related problem, see Lloyd P. Gartner," Temples of Liberty Unpolluted: American Jews and Public Schools, 1840–1875," in *Bicentennial Festschrift for Jacob Rader Marcus*, ed. Korn, 157–89.

51. *Occident*, 2 (Jan. 1845), 511–14; *Caleb Asher* (Philadelphia, 1845). See also Davis, *Emergence of Conservative Judaism*, 51–53, 367–69; and Solomon Grayzel, "The First American Jewish Publication Society," *Jewish Book Annual*, 3 (1944–45), 42–44.

52. *Occident*, 1 (December 1843), 411; Hyman B. Grinstein, *The Rise of the Jewish Community of New York, 1654–1860* (Philadelphia, 1945), 156, 234, 386; S. Joshua Kohn, "Mordecai Manuel Noah's Ararat Project and the Missionaries," *American Jewish Historical Quarterly*, 55 (Dec. 1965), 162–96; S. Joshua Kohn, "New Light on Mordecai Manuel Noah's Ararat

Project," *ibid.*, 59 (Dec. 1969), 210–14; Allan Tarshish, "Jew and Christian in a New Society: Some Aspects of Jewish-Christian Relationships in the United States, 1848–1881," in *Bicentennial Festschrift for Jacob Rader Marcus*, ed. Korn, 565–87; Allan Tarshish, "The Rise of American Judaism (A History of American Jewish Life from 1848 to 1881)" (Ph.D. diss., Hebrew Union College, 1938), 321–83.

53. *Occident*, 2 (May 1844), 63.
54. *Occident*, 2 (May 1844), 63; *ibid.*. 11 (Aug. 1853), 245. Cf. *Israelite*, Aug. 23, 1867, p. 4.
55. *Occident*, 10 (March 1853), 583; *ibid.*, 11 (May 1853), 83–84, (June 1853), 180–84, (Aug. 1853) 275–76, (Nov. 1853), 409–13, (Jan. 1854), 510–15, (March 1854), 597; *ibid.*, 18 (June 7, 1860), 66, (June 14, 1860), 71, (June 26, 1860), 108; *Asmonean*, 7 (Jan. 14, 1853), 149, (March 11, 1853), 245, (March 18, 1853), 257; *Israelite*, 7 (1860), 14; Leon Huhner, *The Life of Judah Touro (1775–1854)* (Philadelphia, 1946), 172; H. G. Reissner, "The German-American Jews (1800–1850)," *Leo Baeck Institute Year Book*, 10 (1965), 105; Davis, *Emergence of Conservative Judaism*, 78–79; I. J. Benjamin, *Three Years in America: 1859–1862*, trans. Charles Reznikoff (2 vols., Philadelphia, 1956), I, 318–33; Gershon Greenberg, "A German-Jewish Immigrant's Perception of America, 1853–54," *American Jewish Historical Quarterly*, 67 (June 1978), 338; and Michael Pollak, *Mandarins, Jews, and Missionaries: The Jewish Experience in the Chinese Empire* (Philadelphia, 1980), 176–86.
56. *Israelite Indeed*, 12 (July 1868), 10–16; Jacob J. Weinstein, *Solomon Goldman: A Rabbi's Rabbi* (New York, 1973), 267; Ida Cohen Selavan, "The Founding of Columbian Council," *American Jewish Archives*, 30 (April 1978), 32–33; Joseph R. Rosenbloom, "Intermarriage and Conversion in the United States," in *Bicentennial Festschrift for Jacob Rader Marcus*, ed. Korn, 496.
57. Alexander M. Dushkin, *Jewish Education in New York City* (New York, 1918), 54, 468–69; *Year Book of the Central Conference of American Rabbis, 1890–91* (Cincinnati, 1891), 122; Moses Rischin, *The Promised City: New York's Jews, 1870–1914* (Cambridge, 1962), 101, 107, 199; Lloyd P. Gartner, "The Jews of New York's East Side, 1890–1893," *American Jewish Historical Quarterly*, 53 (March 1964), 264–81.
58. For what may have been the first understanding of this impact, see Isaac M. Wise, "Had a Contrary Effect," *Israelite*, 7 (1861), 300.

2

The Image of Jews in Christian Teaching

Judith H. Banki

Jews have long been concerned that certain Christian teachings and preaching about Jews and Judaism represented one of the deep-seated and enduring sources of Antisemitism. However, the question of how to bring systematic scholarship to bear on such problems is both complex and sensitive. The American Jewish Committee's approach to these questions was to stimulate a series of textbook self-studies, which began as early as the 1930s but became more systematic and concentrated in the late 1950s and 1960s, when the consequences of unbridled Antisemitism were laid bare, and the need to trace and confront its roots became inescapable.

PROTESTANT STUDIES

The Protestant self-study was undertaken over a seven-year period at Yale University Divinity School by Bernhard Olson, and published in book form as the classic *Faith and Prejudice*.[1] Olson asked the following questions: Do Protestant church school lesson materials tend to foster prejudice? What images of outside groups do they present? What are the factors that make for negative or positive portrayals? How can negative images, if there are such, be corrected within the faith perspective of the in-group? The last question is particularly cogent, because Olson understood that it would do no good to give uniform advice to all Protestants;

Reprinted in part by permission from the *Journal of Ecumenical Studies* 21 (Summer 1984): 1–15.

rather, each group should be addressed from within its own theological perspective. The study consisted of an analysis to determine how a variety of racial, ethnic, national, and non-Protestant religious groups were portrayed in Protestant teaching materials.

While some thirty Protestant denominations were initially surveyed, Olson chose four distinct curricula for intensive analysis, each representing a basic variation of Protestant thought, tradition, and theology. The four faith perspectives selected were: fundamentalism (represented by the materials of the Scripture Press); classical conservatism (represented by the Lutheran Church-Missouri Synod curriculum); liberalism (represented by the Unitarian-Universalist Beacon Press series); and neo-orthodoxy, specifically, a neo-Reformation viewpoint (represented by the curriculum of what was then the Presbyterian Church in the USA). All the Christian educational materials of these four groups were subjected to painstaking content analysis.

Finding terms such as "prejudice" and "tolerance" difficult to measure, Olson chose the concept of ethnocentrism, defined as "a pervasive and rigid ingroup-outgroup distinction; it involves stereotyped positive imagery and submissive attitudes regarding ingroups, and a hierarchical, authoritarian view of group interaction in which ingroups are rightly dominant, outgroups subordinate."[2] Olson found that anti-ethnocentrism was also a distinct and measurable quality. Anti-ethnocentrics support the rights and freedoms of other groups and are able to criticize their own. His findings challenged two popular preconceptions of the time: the assumption by Christian educators that intergroup attitudes— while a commendable subject for research—had little to do with Christian education; and the assumption that prejudice was a unified phenomenon rooted in a particular personality type, i.e., if one hated one group, one hated them all.

Olson discovered that "Protestant religious textbooks incorporate an astonishingly high percentage of lessons in which other groups are spoken of, incidentally or in detail."[3] Reference to outside groups ranged from sixty-seven percent in one curriculum to eighty-eight percent in another. Moreover, Protestants were considerably more preoccupied with outside religious groups (mentioned in ten to sixty-six percent of all lessons) than with black-white relations (three to nine percent) or other ethnic groups (three to seven percent), and they had more difficulty in depicting religious groups positively. In terms of prejudice, the real problems of Protestant education were found in the area of interreligious relations.

Protestant lessons referred more frequently to Jews and Judaism than to any other group mentioned in the literature. Jewish references ranged from forty-four percent of all lessons in one curriculum to sixty-six percent in another. The conspicuousness of Jews in Protestant education is neither unexpected nor invidious, since biblically rooted Protestantism cannot be set forth without reference to Judaism. Nevertheless, it does create hazards. "As a minority which inescapably figures in the foreground of Christian thought—and remains an accessible minority in a society which contains deep strains of anti-Semitism—the Jewish community easily becomes a vulnerable target," Olson commented, continuing:

There are instances cited in this study where the Jew is used as a convenient whipping boy for human ills and failings simply because he is "there" in the biblical material and therefore was suggested to the writer as the most relevant object of criticism. That the writers may have in mind only biblical Jewry does not make the problem less serious, since this distinction is seldom made. For the Jew to be under the continual scrutiny of the pupil and teacher with their open textbook is to expose him to potential hazards; in the Christian era, the Jew has infrequently escaped these dangers unharmed.[4]

Among the themes which posed the knottiest problems of intergroup writing for Protestant educators were the Crucifixion, the conflict between Jesus and the Pharisees, the early conflict between church and synagogue, the question of Gentile inclusion, the themes of rejection and unbelief, and Jewish resistance to Christian missionary efforts.

Jews have frequently wondered, publicly and privately, whether Antisemitism is, in fact, rooted in Christian Scripture and thus an inevitable component of Christian teaching. Olson pointed out that, while Scripture can and does affect references to Jews, it does not alone determine the overall Jewish portrait in Protestant lessons. Cultural, social, and political viewpoints, unrelated to Scripture, find expression in the lessons. Moreover, he noted that a point of view is brought to Scripture as well as derived from it: "The biblical text determines the theme; but the mind-sets of the different writers to Jews leads them to quite different inferences."[5] Olson showed, for example, how a single biblical passage was interpreted negatively for Jews by one denomination and positively by another. There are significant differences in the ways Scripture is invoked by Protestants to support their interreligious teachings. One group quotes Scripture at a ratio of nine to one against various forms of interreligious action (cooperation, interfaith activities, etc.); another finds authority in Scripture for exactly the opposite viewpoint by a ratio of six to one.

Whatever one's faith, it is possible to view other groups positively, Olson concluded, but paradoxically it was precisely in the attempts to set forth the faith that negative scores and ambiguous images of other groups appeared in his study. Lessons produced specifically in the area of intergroup relations were invariably positive. It was in the lessons intending to expound Scripture or doctrine—wherein other groups were mentioned marginally, incidentally, or unintentionally—that prejudice emerged. What were the reasons for this? In some respects a negative intergroup portrait was simply a matter of "bad theology"—not by Olson's standards, but by the standards of the group itself, that is, a fragmentary statement of faith which did not draw upon doctrines and convictions existing within the theology of the particular group. Sometimes lesson writers were simply not aware that statements they made about other groups in a historic or doctrinal context might affect attitudes toward contemporary people. Because of these problems, Olson recommended that the churches set up a process for reviewing Christian education materials in light of their impact on intergroup attitudes, particularly those toward Jews.

A follow-up study by Gerald Strober,[6] undertaken nine years after *Faith and Prejudice* was published, showed unfortunately how little had been done. The Strober study, sponsored and published by the American Jewish Committee and the National Conference of Christians and Jews, covered teaching materials issued by ten denominations and two publishing houses. Six of the denominations and the two publishing houses represented conservative Protestant viewpoints; the other four denominations were mainstream Protestant. All together, some 3,000 lessons used by junior high, senior high, and adult students and teachers were subjected to content analysis.

The chief insights gained by the inquiry may be summarized as follows:

(1) The Yale study did not have the long-term effect which its initial reception seemed to promise. For the most part, the defects uncovered by Olson persisted in then-current teaching materials. Certain key themes were still presented in ways likely to foster hostiliy against Jews and

their religion and experience. Chief among such themes were the following: the nature of Judaism, Jesus' relation to his Jewish contemporaries, the Pharisees, the Jews' rejection of Jesus as the Messiah, and the Crucifixion. In conservative publications, the handling of these topics remained predominantly negative, even though in each case there were some lessons with a positive tendency. The Missouri Synod Lutheran Church was the only important exception; several of its publications were comprehensively revised in response to the Olson study. In the materials issued by mainstream Protestant denominations, the negative tendency was somewhat less pronounced but still clearly present.

(2) Recent and current developments in Christian-Jewish relations were rarely reflected in teaching materials, and then only superficially. Subjects such as the official rejection of Antisemitism by the Roman Catholic church and by several Protestant bodies, the spread of Christian-Jewish dialogue, and the meaning and problems of Israel got short shrift in materials of both conservative and mainstream denominations.

(3) The teaching materials addressed to black Protestant audiences— as represented by the publications of the two black Baptist bodies—did not show any special kind of animosity in the way they dealt with Jews and Judaism. Their approach resembled that of the other Protestant materials so closely that it was not necessary to treat them separately in reporting the findings.

(4) Not many Protestant bodies have been prompted to develop explicit intergroup relations policies or to set up procedures for reviewing practices and publications from this angle. The lessons did exhibit an increased interest in discussing and confronting prejudice, and they often took a strong, unconditional stand against racial bias. However, where religious bias was concerned, the concern appeared to be much less intense. Moreover, in the conservative literature, combating prejudice figured less as an ethical imperative demanded by the Christian faith than as a preliminary requirement for winning converts.

Addressing himself to specific items, Strober wrote that "Christianity has traditionally taken a jaundiced view of the Jewish religion in Jesus' time and thereafter. The role of Judaism in Jesus' own life has been minimized. The teachings of Jesus have been placed in spurious opposition to Jewish beliefs and practices. Christianity has been deemed to have made Judaism obsolete, and as a result the survival of Judaism as a living religion has often been lost sight of."[7]

All these misperceptions were represented in the lesson material. The image of Judaism in Jesus' day as a worn-out, formalistic creed still turned up in many Protestant texts—usually in connection with the miracle at Cana, where Jesus changed water into wine (John 2:1–12). More often than not, the lesson materials tended to isolate Jesus and his closest followers from their Jewish contemporaries: "They are made to look like a new kind of group thrust into the midst of first-century Jewish life, without roots in, or sympathy for, Jewish history, tradition, or religious values."[8] Only a minority of lesson writers placed Jesus within a Jewish context.

The Pharisees, Strober noted, continued to be vilified in curriculum materials, although more often by conservative than by mainstream denominations. A body of Christian scholarship underscoring the Pharisees' role as creative religious reformers, many of whose teachings and values were shared by Jesus, seemed not to have made a dent in the traditional formula of depicting them as self-righteous hypocrites. One example of what Strober calls "a typically devastating group portrait"[9] will suffice:

The Pharisees . . . were full of sin—the sin of pretense, of sham, of hypocrisy— Oh, the irony of Jesus!—implying that the Pharisees were "whole" when they, of all people, were most sick and fragmented and diseased and in greatest need of a physician, and implying that they were "righteous" when they were full of spite and resentment and hatred and prejudice and greed and lust and were in desperate need of repentance and forgiveness![10]

Also widely prevalent, particularly in the conservative literature, were passages asserting that God has passed judgment on, or rejected, the Jews as a group for their alleged collective failure to recognize and accept Jesus as the Messiah. Some lessons suggested that this judgment manifested itself with the end of the Jewish nation in Palestine and the diaspora.

On a more positive note, Strober found that lesson materials dealing with the Crucifixion proved to be "considerably less unanimous in representing Jewry as villanous than lessons on other themes involving the reaction of Jews to Jesus."[11] He attributes this increase in "fairness and balance" in both conservative and mainstream instructional materials to the formal rejection by numerous Christian bodies of the deicide charge against the Jewish people (following the catastrophe of European Jewry in World War II), to the "burgeoning ecumenical spirit among Christians and Jews in the United States and, in this limited area, to the work done by Bernhard Olson." [12]

Strober found a paucity of materials on the subject of the Holocaust and, within these materials, the tendency to abstract the event as an example of "evil," to ignore its unique and specific consequences for Jews (except in lessons emphasizing how some Christians helped and protected Jews), and to avoid the issue of Antisemitism, particularly its religious roots. Interestingly, I found parallel tendencies in a study of Christian press reactions to the trial of Adolf Eichmann: an intense preoccupation with the legalities and forthcoming verdict of the trial, an emphasis on Christians who saved and helped Jews (surely, such noble souls, including many who were martyred for their efforts, deserve acknowledgment—and they have been honored by the Jewish community—but their courageous acts should not be represented as the major pattern of Christian behavior during the Holocaust), a leaning toward moral abstractions, and an apparent unwillingness to confront the Christian sources of Antisemitism.

Fewer than half of one percent of the lessons analyzed by Strober mentioned the State of Israel, and more than half of these viewed it through dispensationalist theological lenses—as a signal that the end of time is drawing near.

ROMAN CATHOLIC STUDIES

The Roman Catholic textbook self-study project, carried out at St. Louis University under the supervision of Trafford Maher, and summarized in book form by John Pawlikowski in *Catechetics and Prejudice*,[13] pointed to similar problems. While the literature and social studies materials revealed very few instances of prejudice against Jews, they also contained very few specific references of Jews. As might be surmised, the problems were found in the religion and church history materials. These texts included many positive statements about humanity in general, such as the admonition that God loves all persons. There were also a number of references to Jews which were scored as positive by the researcher on grounds we would consider questionable today; for example:

News of the birth of Jesus Christ, the Son of God, had been brought to the Jews by angels. The Jews, however, formed only a small part of the whole human race living on earth at that time. Gentiles, or non-Jews, were to be saved by Jesus as well as Jews.[14]

Pawlikowski cogently observed:

While the above was scored as positive for Jews, it is clearly implied that the Judaism which is praised culminated in Christianity; the Jews who are esteemed are praised for their implied acceptance of Christianity. While the textbooks acknowledge the spiritual wealth of Judaism, they infer that these riches were totally absorbed by Christianity. Judaism's value as a religion appears to be exhausted in its contribution to the Christian heritage.[15]

The overwhelming majority of negative references concerning Jews were concentrated around the themes of the Jewish rejection of Christianity and the consequent divine curse inflicted on this people, the Jewish role in the Crucifixion, and comments regarding the Pharisees. In light of the progress toward Christian understanding of Jews and Judaism in recent years, it is somewhat shocking to look back on some of the excerpts found in Catholic textbooks most commonly used at the time of the St. Louis University research. Accusations of collective guilt and assertions that Jews are a people accursed and rejected by God found frequent expression in these texts, as did the charge that the Jews willfully and culpably blinded themselves to Jesus' significance. Pawlikowski noted—as did Olson before him—that statements stressing the universal theological significance of the Crucifixion were not infrequent in the materials. For example:

Why Christ suffered. That *all* men might be united in love and peace with one another, and that all men might be united in love with God . . .[16]

The difficulty was that this universal viewpoint got lost when the lessons dealt with the events leading up to the Crucifixion. Thus, the Catholic student might be informed in other lessons that the "sins of all men" were responsible, but "in the representative excerpts from the religion materials, it is *Jewish* cupability for the suffering and death of Christ that is stressed, rather than the sins of all mankind."[17] A single example will suffice:

However, when the mob saw this, the chief priests took up a cry that put a curse on themselves and on the Jews for all time: "His blood be upon us and our children."[18]

As for references to the Pharisees—described by Pawlikowski as among the most negative encountered in the textbooks—some were so distorted "that the student would find it virtually impossible to sense any human identification with them or to believe that they acted out of human motivation." [19]

Two additional Roman Catholic self-studies, carried out at different institutions in Europe in the 1960s, supplemented the growing research in the field. One was conducted at the International University of Social Studies, Pro Deo, in Rome, an institution under papal patronage; the other, at the Catholic University of Louvain, Belgium, with the personal endorsement of the Archbishop of Malines and Brussels, Leo Jozef Cardinal Suenens. Both were sponsored by the Sperry Center for Intergroup Cooperation, established by American Jewish Committee leaders.

The Pro Deo study dealt with textbooks for Catholic religious teaching that were published for use in Italian and Spanish schools, from the elementary to the senior or college level, between 1940 and 1964. A brief supplementary study covered texts issued after Vatican II. The survey focused mainly on Jews and Judaism but also dealt with references to other religious, ethnic, political, and cultural groups outside the Roman Catholic church. A report on the Pro Deo research, by Otto Klineberg et al., was published in Italy as a paperback entitled *Religione e pregiudizio: Analisi di contenuto dei libri cattolici di insegnamento religioso in Italia e in Spagna.*[20]

The Louvain research consisted of two distinct phases. The first was an analysis of religious textbooks from French-speaking countries— France, Belgium, Switzerland, and Canada—published between 1949 and 1964, and used in both public and Catholic secondary schools. The second was an opinion survey exploring what ideas about Jews and Judaism were held by persons who had been exposed to Catholic teaching. The Louvain studies were fully reported in two volumes by François Houtart et al., under the general title, *Les Juifs dans la catéchèse.*[21] The volume on textbook analysis is subtitled *Etude des manuels de la catéchèse le langue francaise* (1969); that containing the opinion survey is subtitled *Etude sur la transmission des codes religieux* (1971). The Pro Deo and Louvain studies were summarized in English by Claire Huchet Bishop in *How Catholics Look at Jews.*[22] . . .

The Pro Deo researchers, assessing their survey findings as a whole, were struck by the amount of hostility they uncovered toward Jews and other groups in both the Italian and the Spanish materials. However, Bishop notes, the time patterning of the findings gave grounds for optimism. The Louvain report noted that unfavorable statements reached a peak in books dating from 1963 and 1964, then ebbed sharply in 1965 and 1966. Similarly, the 1965–67 survey by Pro Deo found twenty-one negative statements in books dating from 1965, four in those published in 1966, and none in the two titles issued in 1967. Bishop observed: "It seems reasonable to assume that these figures reflect the Church's adoption of a new, positive policy toward Jews and Judaism at the Second Vatican Council."[23]

The assumption that Roman Catholic teaching materials produced after Vatican II would be more sympathetic to Jews and Judaism is borne out by Eugene Fisher's updated study of Catholic textbooks used in the United States. It covered sixteen major religion series currently in use on the grade and high school levels. The 161 student texts and 113 teachers' manuals were published between 1967 and 1975. The findings of that study—along with general observations and recommendations, guidelines for the evaluation of the treatment of Jews and Judaism in catechetical materials, and authoritative church documents—were published in 1977 under the title *Faith without Prejudice.*[24]

Focusing on specific themes which are critical to Christian-Jewish relations today, Fisher found great improvement in the treatment of many of them. For example, he found clear references to the Jewishness of Jesus. (In contrast, some of the earlier materials appeared to go to great lengths to avoid identifying the Jews as Jesus' people.) He found the notion of Jewish suffering as an expression of divine retribution completely eliminated from the textbooks. (The only references to this notion clearly condemned it.) He found that references to the Holocaust were handled with great sensitivity. While not negative or hostile, he found that references to violence against Jews occasioned by the Crusades and the Inquisition and references to the modern State of Israel were "inadequate." Despite overwhelmingly positive references to Judaism in *general* terms, however, textbook treatments of the events of Jesus' passion trigger some of the old negative generalizations, and, throughout all the textbooks, the Pharisees "are painted in dark, evil colors."[25]

These problems reveal themselves, statistically, in interesting ways. After noting that the visibility (technically, the percentage of preoccupation) of Jews and Judaism in Catholic elementary (Grades 1–8) texts leaped from twenty-three percent in 1961 to nearly forty-two percent at the time of his study, but it was much lower (seventeen percent) in high-school-level textbooks, Fisher observed: "Because of the impact of Vatican II's declaration and more recent episcopal statements, it was expected that textbooks today would be more positive toward Judaism than those written before the Council. This proved to be true for the high school texts. . . . But the elementary texts . . . actually went down, . . . reflecting a higher percentage of negative statements than in 1961. What can account for this?"[26] His answer points to the depth of the remaining problems:

[T]he critical area for Jewish-Christian relations as revealed in the study lies in our treatment of New Testament themes and events. . . . Since the elementary-level textbooks use the New Testament much more now than before the Council, these key problem areas come up more frequently. Almost all of the negative references to Jews and Judaism occur in statements dealing with New Testament themes. . . . Vestiges of the old polemics still remain, and, in view of the author, the teachers' manuals fail to give an adequate background for the correct interpretation of difficult New Testament passages, such as those in Matthew and John.[27]

Fisher also found some instances of lingering triumphalism—including the tactic of taking basic Jewish tenets from the Hebrew Scriptures, subsuming them into Christianity, and then using them to "prove" that Christianity is superior to the Judaism which gave birth to these ideas. Nevertheless, he concluded that the positive changes since Vatican II "are almost overwhelming in their honesty and integrity of vision."[28]

GERMAN STUDIES

Chronologically, the last, but certainly not least, of the self-study projects are those undertaken in West Germany by research groups at the University of Duisburg (Protestant), under the direction of Professors Heinz Kremers and Michael Brocke, and the University of Freiburg (Roman Catholic), under the direction of Professors Günter Biemer and Peter Fiedler. The projects, undertaken with the cooperation of the American Jewish Committee, include the preparation of textbooks, teachers' manuals, and supplementary information for distribution in German schools, some of which are still in preparation. The findings of the analytic research, however, corroborate the findings of the other studies discussed here, and the problematic themes are the same.

At a symposium convened by the Evangelical Academy in Arnold-
shain in December, 1981, the following deficiencies were noted in Protestant religious books in the primary and secondary grades: Jesus is
depicted as apart from, and in conflict with, the Judaism of his time; his
Jewishness seems accidental; Old Testament lessons are limited to the
Exodus and the Patriarchs, but the latter are de-Judaized (that is, they
are portrayed as "pre-Christians," or as timeless symbols, rather than as
individuals rooted in the culture of their time), and the relation between
the Exodus tradition and Christianity remains unclear; in New Testament lessons, Jews appear almost exclusively as opponents of Jesus and
in confrontation with him; Jewish law is depicted as harsh and oppres-
sive, and Jesus as totally opposed to it; New Testament references (twelve
percent of the New Testament represents sixty-five percent of all New
Testament references in the texts) concentrate on and repeat those passages which interpret Jews most negatively; the works on Jesus are
mostly constructed on the principle of confrontation (Jesus against the
Jews, new waves against the Old World, liberation against attachment
to tradition, merciful God against unmerciful God, love against legality,
etc.); and the portrayal of the Pharisees as self-righteous, hypocritical,
power-hungry legalists is another "beloved cliche."

While this report dealt with the studies of Protestant books conducted
at Duisburg, it was noted that the parallel research on Catholic school
books at Freiburg arrived at the same fundamental conclusions.

CONCLUSIONS

Since the time of the earlier studies—and perhaps in large part due to
them—major church groups and religious leaders have issued exemplary
statements on Christian-Jewish relations, repudiating the myth of collective guilt, condemning Antisemitism, and affirming the eternal validity
of God's covenant with the Jewish people. The question remains to what
extent these very significant statements and guidelines have been translated into the teaching process. With regard to this question, there is
good news and bad news. The good news is that significant progress *has*
been made. Much of the hostile invective has been eliminated from
current materials, along with the deicide charge and the obscene notion
of Jewish suffering as the result of divine retribution. There is an abundance of good-will and increased sensitivity among growing numbers of

Christian clergy and educators as to the impact of their teachings on attitudes toward Jews. The bad news is that certain religious and historical themes, particularly those deriving from conflicts described in New Testament writings (e.g., the struggle between the early church and the synagogue, the Pharisees, the Jewish rejection of Jesus as Messiah) can still call forth negative stereotypes and inaccurate generalizations about "the Jews." If the earlier textbook research showed how wide the problems were, more recent research indicates how deep the remaining problems go.

These problems have no easy or simplistic solutions. How *does* a church school teacher with the best of intentions but little or no advanced theological training explain Matt. 27:25 to a class? Or John's polemical use of the term "the Jews" to designate the enemies of Jesus? Surely, Jews cannot ask Christians to censor or delete from their Sacred Scriptures. Nevertheless, there is much that can be done, both in textbook preparation and in teacher training, if the will is there. As previously noted, Olson found that the images of Jews projected in the materials he analyzed were drawn as much from extrabiblical as from biblical sources:

[T]he difficulty . . . in setting forth a positive and constructive view of Jews and Judaism is the result of perspectives that go beyond, and perhaps may be more basic than, scripture as such. These influences are usually compounded by exegetical views, theological commitments, and other teachings about Jews that derive from tradition and from attitudes formed by social and cultural forces.[29]

Olson also noted a phenomenon he called "downgrading" and "upgrading" from the biblical text:

Downgrading takes various forms. Sometimes disparaging statements about Jews foreign to the text are injected into the commentary. Or derogatory passages are singled out and enlarged upon, while contradictory passages are ignored. Or a hostile reaction occasioned by a given passage may be fortified by bringing in other unfavorable, though often loosely related, passages from scripture. Other practices are to attribute contemptible hidden motives to Jewish figures or to misstate the facts of their behavior. Often the Jewish personages whose actions are being condemned are labeled "Jews," while the exemplary personages are not. Finally, the lesson writer may resort to stereotypes, verbal tags, and other rhetorical devices of invective. . . . By "upgrading" is meant that the writer does more than simply ignore, reject, or explain negative elements in the text. He assigns valued and distinctively human motives to the Jewish figures; he corrects typical and unfavorable distortions; he warns against prejudice and misunderstanding; he expresses himself in honorific language, such as "devout" or "pious," where the hostile writer uses negatively charged expressions. In controversial areas such as when discussing the Pharisees, he provides explanatory background material that illuminates the actions of Jesus' critics and those who opposed the message and work of the early Church. Beyond this, he is careful to comment on biblical-historical context.[30]

In these passages, in the other textbook research, and in the subsequent writings of these and other scholars, there are sufficient clues for textbook publishers and writers seriously interested in coming to grips with remaining elements of the anti-Jewish polemic embedded in Christian tradition. In addition to a sensitive handling of conflict themes, the inclusion of some positive information about Judaism as a continuing and developing religion would be helpful. For perfectly understandable reasons, Jews and Judaism tend to drop out of Christian religious education and church history materials after the emergence of Christianity —except as antagonists—and, while some of the newer textbooks do take note of contemporary Jewish celebrations and religious festivals, I would guess that the most widespread misconception about Judaism among Christians today is that it is the "religion of the Old Testament." In addition, the "law versus love" dichotomy embodied in this perception is still common.

In terms of process, Strober, noting that Protestant denominations have allocated funds and staff to work systematically toward the resolution of racial problems, called for the same degree of commitment in the area of Christian-Jewish relations:

For the National Council of Churches and for those denominations which have formally gone on record against anti-Semitism, the next step logically is to form task forces of Old and New Testament scholars, church historians, religious educators and program specialists who will reexamine the tradition of teaching concerning Jews and Judaism. The same task forces also ought to explore how a truthfully balanced portrait of Jews and Judaism may be introduced into curriculums—indeed, into the very life of the Church and the individual Christian.[31]

Unfortunately, this suggestion has not been implemented. A few Protestant and Catholic publishers of religious education textbooks have set up procedures for reviewing publications from the perspective of their impact on Jewish-Christian understanding; others have not. Perhaps because the Roman Catholic church has established a Secretariat on Catholic-Jewish Relations, with a full-time professional devoted to this area who has produced helpful catechetical guidelines and suggestions for enriching curriculum materials, current Roman Catholic textbooks appear to be more responsive to contemporary biblical and historical scholarship.

Since texts are only as good as the teachers who use them, the question of teacher training is also critical to the process. In this area, the Office of Jewish-Christian Relations of the National Council of Churches of Christ in the U.S.A. has initiated two pilot programs which it hopes will serve as models nationally. The problem, I believe, is not malice, but lack of priority.

Although this article has been confined to an exploration of the image of the Jews in Christian religious education materials, the dimensions of the challenge extend into many other areas. The public worship of the church surely merits consideration, because problematical passages from Scripture, presented in a liturgical setting without the opportunity for interpretation and explanation, have a powerful emotional impact, and becaues the juxtaposition of readings from the Hebrew Scriptures and the New Testament according to the "promise-fulfillment" model in some major denominations offers little space for a Judaism with its own validity. Moreover, the implications of recent Christian affirmations that the Jewish covenant is binding and eternal have hardly been explored in the teaching of the Hebrew Scriptures, the New Testament, church history, homiletics, and systematic theology. And religio-cultural expressions such as passion plays still seem centered on the model of confrontation and malice in order to satify the needs of dramatic convention. In some, Jews are represented as blood-thirsty villains; in almost all, the political realities and religious complexities of Roman-occupied, first-century Palestine are ignored.

We have come a long way, indeed, but we have much work to do together.

NOTES

1. Bernhard E. Olson, *Faith and Prejudice: Intergroup Problems in Protestant Curricula* (New Haven and London: Yale University Press, 1963).
2. Daniel J. Levinson in T. Adorno et al., *The Authoritarian Personality* (New York: Harper, 1950), p. 150 (cited in Olson, *Faith and Prejudice*, p. 3).
3. Olson, *Faith and Prejudice*, p. 22.

4. Ibid., p. 24.
5. Ibid., p. 40.
6. Gerald S. Strober, *Portrait of the Elder Brother: Jews and Judaism in Protestant Teaching Materials* (New York: The American Jewish Committee and the National Conference of Christians and Jews, second printing, October, 1982).
7. Ibid., p. 15.
8. Ibid., p. 17.
9. Ibid., p. 21.
10. *Come Ye Apart* (Church of the Nazarene), January–March, 1968, p. 31 (cited in Strober, *Portrait*, p. 21).
11. Strober, *Portrait*, p. 32.
12. Ibid., p. 35.
13. John T. Pawlikowski, *Catechetics and Prejudice: How Catholic Teaching Materials View Jews, Preotestants, and Racial Minorities* (New York, Paramus, Toronto: Paulist Press, 1973).
14. Ibid., p. 81.
15. Ibid.
16. Ibid., p. 83.
17. Ibid.
18. Ibid.
19. Ibid., p. 84.
20. (Rome: Capelli, 1968). The Introduction was written by Augustino Cardinal Bea.
21. (Louvain: Centre de Recherches Socio-Religieuses, 1969 and 1971).
22. (New York, Paramus, Toronto: Paulist Press, 1974).
23. Ibid., p. 27.
24. *Faith without Prejudice: Rebuilding Christian Attitudes toward Judaism* (New York, Ramsey, Toronto: Paulist Press, 1977).
25. Ibid., p. 136.
26. Ibid., pp. 128–129.
27. Ibid., p. 129.
28. Ibid., p. 139.
29. Olson, *Faith and Prejudice*, pp. 36–37.
30. Ibid., pp. 40–41.
31. Strober, *Portrait*, pp. 55–56.

3

One Nation Completely under God? The American Jewish Congress and the Catholic Church in the United States, 1945–1977

David G. Singer

The separation of church and state is a fundamental principle of the American Constitution, and adherence to this principle abetted the rise of American Jewry—the largest and most affluent Jewish community in the world. In the post-World War II era, the Roman Catholic bishops of the United States sought to break down the constitutional wall that separated the nondenominational, public sphere from the private, religious one. The bishops and Catholic educators were particularly interested in gaining public financial aid for the nation's parochial schools, as well as introducing some form of religious instruction into the public schools. By 1977, it was clear that the American Catholic Church had failed to achieve these goals. In that year, Jimmy Carter, a "born again" Christian from the predominantly Baptist South, assumed the office of president of the United States, and a wave of evangelical Protestantism was on the ascendancy.

In 1945, however, the Catholic Church was the most militant Christian church in Western Europe and the United States. Christian democratic parties were organized in France, West Germany, Italy, and other countries, and, in the United States, the Church gained in its political and religious influence. A number of well-known individuals, such as Claire Booth Luce, converted to Catholicism, and President Harry S

Reprinted in part by permission from the *Journal of Church and State* 26 (Autumn 1984): 473–90.

Truman attempted to appoint Myron Taylor to serve as the first American ambassador to the Vatican.

In the post–World War II era, the Catholic bishops sought to Christianize the United States or at least to strengthen religious and moral values in many areas of American life. This involved the suppression of antireligious and prurient materials (as they were defined by the Church), a legal ban on abortion and artificial birth control devices, the prohibition of commercial activity on Sunday that might draw congregants away from attendance at Sunday mass, and, above all, the introduction of religious instruction in the public schools and the use of public funds to assist financially the nation's parochial school system.

A majority of American Jews opposed the Catholic bishops in these matters, and the American Jewish Congress (AJC) was among the leading advocates of the continued separation of church and state in American society during the years 1945–77. It should be noted, however, that neither the Catholic nor the Jewish communities in the United States are monolithic ones. Thus, some Orthodox Jews sided with conservative Catholics on the issue of "parochiaid" while *Commonweal*, a liberal Catholic journal, sided with the American Jewish Congress in the debate over the use of Christian symbols on public property. The AJC and other separationist organizations fought for the preservation of the First Amendment to the Constitution, and often won favorable decisions in the law courts partly because of the AJC's outstanding legal staff, which included such noted lawyers as Leo Pfeffer and Will Maslow.[1]

The American Jewish Congress, under the leadership of men like Pfeffer and Israel Goldstein, sought to preserve or even expand the public area of American life wherein the individual's religious affiliation or nonaffiliation would be a neutral factor in such spheres as education, employment, and politics. In pursuit of this aim, Pfeffer opposed governmental financial subsidies to parochial schools. The key question here was not the intervention of the government in the private sphere per se, but what was the purpose of such intervention? If its intent was to achieve greater equality for all Americans in the public sector, then the leaders of the AJC supported such government action. Therefore, Will Maslow advocated federal legislation that would outlaw discrimination against any religious, ethnic, or racial group in the United States.[2]

The Catholic Church also advocated legislation that would help correct what it regarded as one of the most serious problems in post–World

War II American society: the decline of public and private morality that threatened to undermine the family, which is the basic unit of society. Catholic thinkers connected this decay with the decline of traditional religious beliefs and ethics, and therefore sought to raise social and moral values and strengthen family ties in America. Catholic thinkers urged the Jews to join them in this struggle, and, at the beginning of 1946, *The Catholic World* stressed that both Christians and Jews were threatened by naturalistic, godless philosophies.[3]

Many American Jews agreed with this analysis of the malaise in American society and, like the Catholic bishops, sought to raise standards of public and private morality in the United States. This is evidenced by a statewide campaign of the Jewish War Veterans of New York to ban the public display of pornographic literature and a conference on moral standards in American society that was sponsored by the Jewish Theological Seminary in 1953.[4]

The Catholic bishops were encouraged by these developments and urged American Jewry to support them in their effort to heighten the importance of religion and religious values in American life—even if this might possibly involve the curtailment of some civil liberties. The American Jewish Congress, like other Jewish organizations, had always sought to uphold high moral standards in American society, but the AJC, traditionally and now, balked at any infringement of the first ten amendments to the Constitution, generally known as the Bill of Rights.

This became evident in the early 1950s when a New York City censorship board banned the movie *The Miracle* from public showing on the basis that it was sacrilegious. The film was a serious presentation of a young country virgin seduced and impregnated by a bearded stranger, who she believed to be St. Joseph, spouse of the Virgin Mary. A local motion picture distributor challenged the New York statute that established a film censorship board on the ground that such censorship "was a denial of freedom of expression."[5] Subsequently, the American Jewish Congress entered the case with the additional argument that the film censorship statute established "a use of state power to enforce a religious dogma in violation of the first amendment."[6] In 1952, the Supreme Court of the United States declared that the controversial statute was unconstitutional.

The American Jewish Congress was concerned only with the censorship of films as a threat to the freedom of expression and not with the content of *The Miracle*. For their part, Catholic leaders regarded this film as an insult to both Christian theology and sexual standards of morality (the Catholic Church opposes abortion under any conditions and all artificial methods of birth control). Now, in the post–World War II era, the Church supported legislation that would outlaw abortion and ban the public sale and distribution of contraceptives. The American Jewish Congress and other separationist organizations felt that such legislation would not only represent a violation of the First Amendment that separated church and state but would violate the right of every individual to make his own private choice in the area of sex.

This clash was between the accommodationists, who felt that local and state governmental agencies had the right, even the moral duty, to enforce sexual standards and behavior, and the separationists (i.e., those individuals and groups who upheld a strict separation of church and state), who felt that these matters were strictly private concerns and did not follow rigid denominational lines. To a large extent, Orthodox Jews hold the same views on birth control and abortion as do pious Catholics. Orthodox Jews, however, feel that abortion is justified if the mother's life is placed in jeopardy during parturition. Since it was non-Orthodox Jews who sanctioned artificial means of birth control, Catholic writers addressed themselves to these Jews when they criticized the American Jewish community at large for its refusal to support anticontraceptive legislation.

At the end of 1971, a writer of *The New Catholic World* urged non-Orthodox Jews to reassess their attitudes toward birth control and abortion, and noted that "Orthodox Jews always held that abortion is incompatible with Jewish law, that contraception is an offense against God's command to be fruitful and multiply."[7] Florence Julian felt that because the Jews were faithful to this commandment, they replenished those who had been killed during their long, tortured history. At the same time that Julian made these comments, the Catholic hierarchy itself was facing a revolt within the laity and especially among Catholic women against the Church's stand that prohibited all artificial means of birth control—including the then recently developed contraceptive pill. In 1967, Pope Paul VI reaffirmed the Church's traditional ban against all forms of birth control with the exception of the rhythm method. The encyclical, *Humanae Vitae*, disappointed many American Catholics, and, fearful that it might lead to large-scale defections from the Church, the

American bishops emphasized the encyclical's advisory rather than its dogmatic nature.

In actuality, there were few differences in sexual attitudes between Catholics and Protestants in the United States in the mid-1970s.[8] Even with regard to abortion, Catholics generally took a less rigid stand on this matter at this time than they had in previous years.[9] Hence, a wide gap existed between the moral teachings of the Church and the sexual practices of the laity. Indeed, Andrew Greeley blamed most of the Church's problems in the United States during the 1960s and 1970s on *Humanae Vitae*. The encyclical, Greeley wrote, sparked a conflict between the bishops and the parish priests, brought on a shortage of priests, and even caused many to leave the Church altogether.[10] While one may question Greeley's assertion that *Humanae Vitae* led to a decline of American Catholicism, it certainly is true that a substantial number of Catholic women in the United States use contraceptive methods that are morally unacceptable to their Church. Thus, the differences between Catholic and Jewish sexual attitudes in the United States are not as great in practice as they are in theory.

The reasons for this convergence of sexual practices lie in the assimilation of many Jews and Catholics into Anglo-American society and their social advancement in that society. The Catholic and Jewish communities in the United States stem largely from rural and semi-rural areas such as Ireland, southern Italy, Russia, and Poland that had high birth rates. Catholic and Jewish immigrants settled largely in American urban centers, however, where they served as reservoirs of cheap labor. In their urban ghettos, Catholic and Jewish ethnic groups clung to their Old World customs and traditions and these included large, closely knit families.

Gradually, these ethnic ghettos broke up as many Catholics and Jews rose into the middle class. (The pace of non-Protestant social mobility was accelerated by the social and political reforms of the New Deal and the post–World War II prosperity.) An ever-increasing number of Catholics as well as Jewish youth attended institutions of higher learning. As is the case with all highly educated, socially mobile groups, middle-class Catholic families practiced family planning—even if this might involve contraceptive methods that were not sanctioned by their Church.

As has already been seen, the Catholic Church and Orthodox Judaism share similar but not identical sexual values, and this similarity in sexual values elicited the praise of Catholic writers. Unlike Catholics and indeed almost all Christians, however, Jews and particularly Orthodox Jews observe Saturday and not Sunday as a day of rest and prayer, and this presented a dilemma for the Catholic Church. On the one hand, the Catholic bishops sought to raise the general level of religious faith and observance in the United States. From this point of view, the Catholic Church thought more favorably of highly observant Orthodox Jews than they did of non-Orthodox Jews. On the other hand, the Church sought to raise the spiritual meaning and religious observance of Sunday in American life and therefore favored those laws that prohibited commercial activity on Sunday. Some Orthodox Jews owned stores or other commercial enterprises, and they opposed the Sunday closing laws on the grounds that they discriminated against Sabbatarians who closed their businesses on Saturday for religious reasons and on Sunday because the law forced them to do so. Thereby, Jews who strictly observed Saturday as the Lord's day suffered a serious financial loss in those areas where the Sunday closing or blue laws were strictly enforced.

That this situation raised a contradiction among Catholic thinkers can be seen in the initial comments of Robert F. Drinan, a scholar and social activist who advocated a rapprochement between Jews and Catholics. In 1959, Drinan wrote that Catholics oppose and will probably continue to oppose any modifications of the Sunday closing laws. Drinan explained that Catholics regard the movement to abolish these laws as "another application of the secularistic concept that the government may not encourage religion or promote public morality."[11] Drinan further emphasized that many non-Catholics as well as Catholics fear that "frightful competitive practices and Sunday 'bargain days' may tend further to dispel that sense of quiet reverence which law and society have always attached to Sunday as a day of rest and religious observance."[12]

At the same time, Drinan felt that the Catholic community in the United States sympathized with Orthodox Jews, who, like Catholics, are a religious minority in this country, and who, like Catholics, were sometimes inconvenienced or even penalized for their particular religious beliefs and practices.[13] In particular, Drinan felt that Catholics were penalized when they were forced to pay taxes to support the public schools that their children did not attend, but sent their children to non-tax-supported parochial schools.[14]

The legal battle over the Sunday closing laws was ultimately carried to the Supreme Court of the United States. In December 1960, the Court heard arguments for and against the Sunday closing laws of Massachusetts, Pennsylvania, and Maryland, and at the beginning of 1961, Drinan commented that those "aggressive" merchants who sought to abolish the Sunday closing laws were not motivated by religious principles but by the selfish desire to maximize their profits.[15] On 29 May 1961, the Supreme Court ruled that the local laws that prohibited Sunday business activity did not discriminate against Orthodox Jews and other Sabbatarians (e.g., Seventh-Day Adventists), but only made it somewhat more difficult and expensive for them to fulfill their religious obligations on their Sabbath. Drinan concurred with this decision, and again questioned the motivation and sincerity of those Orthodox Jews who wished to keep their businesses open on Sunday.[16]

To a large extent, however, certain social changes and forces proved to be more effective in determining how Americans were to spend their Sundays than the Supreme Court decision of May 1961. Drinan took note of these forces in 1963 when he wrote: "The claims of Sabbatarians . . . were not the only issue in the several states when the enforcement of Sunday laws had become a problem. Equally complex was the challenge to Sunday legislation by suburban discount houses whose very survival depends on high volume and massive weekend sales."[17] Indeed, the Sabbatarians found a new and powerful ally in the suburban commercial interests whose business considerations compelled them to keep their stores open on Sunday. Altogether, in the postwar middle-class suburban milieu, Sunday came to be regarded as a day for shopping, recreation, and leisure rather than a day that was largely devoted to religious observances. This change in the meaning of Sunday was not confined to the new, suburban areas. In the post–World War II area, a vast network of highways was built that linked rural and urban areas and the central cities with the outlying suburbs. This highway system enabled urban dwellers easily to reach recreation areas, and thereby accelerated the tendency to transform Sunday into a secular rather than a religious holiday.

In these postwar years of economic growth and social change, all levels of the American educational system experienced a period of unprecedented expansion. The expansion of American education at this time was necessitated by the postwar rise in the birth rate, and the large number of war veterans who enrolled in American colleges and universities. Through a program of direct and indirect financial grants, the federal government aided and stimulated the expansion of American higher education in the post–World War II era. The Catholic educational system, from the primary grades to graduate schools, shared in this general expansion of American education. Unavoidably, the question of the relationship between religion and education arose at this time.

The Catholic bishops and Catholic educators sought to introduce religious values into the public schools and to obtain public financial support for the nation's parochial school systems. This effort to break down the legal barrier between religion and education precipitated the most serious clash between the Catholic bishops and the American Jewish Congress and its allies in the struggle over the separation of church and state.

Beginning in 1947, the Supreme Court sought to redefine the relationship between church and state in America, and, in particular, the place and role of religion in the public schools. These questions became particularly pressing in 1962 when many of the babies born in the immediate postwar period began to attend school. The Supreme Court generally permitted, even encouraged, studies about religion, but refused to permit the introduction of denominational religious instruction or religious education as such into the public schools or to allow direct federal financial support to church-related primary and secondary schools.

Three important decisions of the post–World War II period clearly revealed the Court's attitudes toward the relationship between religion and public education. In 1947, in *Everson v. The Board of Education,* the Supreme Court allowed the state of New Jersey to continue transporting parochial school students on state-owned buses. In 1948, in *McCollum v. The Board of Education,* the Supreme Court ruled that clergymen could not enter the public schools and conduct religious classes there, i.e., the public school could not provide religious education classes as a part of the public school program. In 1952, in *Zorach v. Clauson,* the Court ruled that the New York City public school system may release students from their regular school schedule so that they might receive religious instruction off public school grounds.

During the 1960s, the Supreme Court heard cases concerning the place of religion in the public schools including such matters as Bible readings and prayers in the classroom. For historical reasons, American Catholics were not so ardent in their support of public school prayers and Bible readings as were fundamentalist Protestants. The Catholic school system was established, in part, as a reaction to the use of the King James version of the Bible and the recitation of Protestant prayers in nineteenth-century American public schools. Many Catholics, however, certainly an overwhelming majority of those who sent their children to parochial schools, fully supported their bishops' campaign to obtain direct (parochiaid) or indirect (tuition reimbursement and tax credits) federal aid for their financially hard-pressed schools.

The Catholic episcopate and Catholic educators appealed to the American people—to non-Catholics as well as Catholics—to win public financial aid for the nation's parochial school system and to introduce religion and religious values into the public schools. As has been already noted, one plan would have permitted clergymen to teach religion and religious ethics in public school classrooms, while another would have allowed public school students to attend classes in religion at private facilities (released time).

In support of these plans, the editors of *America* stressed that a public opinion poll in 1953 revealed that the majority of American women favored the inclusion of some sort of religious instruction in the public school curriculum.[18] True to American tradition, religious readings in the public schools were chosen from the King James version of the Bible —even in states with large Catholic populations. These states included New Jersey where, in 1954, the American Jewish Congress and the local Catholic priest cooperated in instituting what proved to be a successful legal suit that blocked the distribution of the King James version of the Bible in that state's public schools.[19] Because of this and other experiences, the American bishops preferred to strengthen their own parochial school system rather than to introduce religious instruction into the public schools. Faced with limited funds for their educational needs, the bishops appealed to the federal government for financial aid.[20]

Opposed to the bishops' appeal for public financial help was a broad coalition of groups and organizations that represented Protestants, as well as Jews, plus the religiously unaffiliated. This coalition, which ranged from fundamentalist Baptists to liberal Jews, felt that the Catholic Church was asking for special privileges for its own educational system, and that if Catholics wanted to maintain their own separate schools, then they must pay for them and not ask the general, non-Catholic public to provide public funds for their upkeep.[21] Certainly there were Jewish and Protestant school systems, notably a Lutheran one, but the Catholic parochial school system is easily the largest one in the United States. Consequently, any public plan to aid church-affiliated educational institutions in the United States would benefit the nation's Catholic schools much more than those of other denominations.

Catholic writers and educators now appealed to the American people's sense of fairness and justice. These writers and educators argued that Catholic parents had to bear a double educational burden: they had to pay taxes to support their public schools that their children did not attend and then pay again to send their children to parochial schools. As the children who were born in the immediate postwar period reached high school age, the need to expand Catholic secondary and advanced educational facilities became more urgent than at any time since 1945.

In May 1961, Frederick Hochwalt of the National Catholic Welfare Council urged Congress to enact some sort of parochiaid on the basis of the oft-stated argument that denial of such aid constituted, in effect, an injustice to American Catholics. Hochwalt argued that the United States is a unified social entity, and, at the same time, it is a mosaic of many religious and ethnic groups.[22] Federal financial aid to the nation's parochial schools would further enhance the rich diversity of American society and, at the same time, promote the unity of the United States because these schools emphasize patriotism, individual morality, and stress the importance of the family in their curricula. Currently, Hochwalt pointed out, other Western democracies, including the United Kingdom, the Netherlands, and Canada, have successfully worked out arrangements whereby their governments grant financial assistance to church-affiliated schools. The United States, he concluded, would do well to emulate the example that was set by these other democratic nations.

Virgil Blum, a founder and an executive director of Citizens for Educational Freedom, disagreed. Americans do not have to look to foreign paradigms of public aid to private, religious education; rather, the government of the United States has long been offering financial help to church-related schools.[23] The precedent for such financial help was established early in the history of the American republic: "The state of New York . . . made direct [monetary] grants to Baptist, Episcopalian, Unitarian, Lutheran, Presbyterian, Catholic, Jewish and Christian Re-

formed elementary schools from 1795 to 1825."[24] Of greater significance, "In 1832 the federal government gave land grants to Columbia
(Baptist) College, now George Washington University, and in the following year, it gave a similar grant to Georgetown (Catholic) College."[25]
Currently, Blum wrote, the federal government gives massive amounts
of financial aid to church-affiliated schools, both in the form of direct
grants (e.g., research grants) and indirectly in the form of financial
assistance and other kinds of aid to students who attend these schools.

As a religious minority in the United States, Catholics realized that
they would have to win over many non-Catholics to their point of view
concerning parochiaid. For this reason, Blum stressed the gains that
would be made by all religious bodies in the United States through a
program of direct federal aid to the nation's parochial schools. For the
same reason, Catholic educators and writers greeted the establishment
of new and the expansion of already existent non-Catholic parochial
school systems in the United States—including those of Conservative
and even Reformed Jews. It was largely among Orthodox Jewish educators and rabbis, however, that the Catholic bishops found allies in their
push for federal aid to religious schools.

Like the Catholic Church, Orthodox Judaism maintained its own
religious day schools, and, like the Catholic school system, was similarly
hard-pressed for funds in the post–World War II era.[26] Like American
Catholics, Orthodox Jews sought to disseminate their point of view
towards parochiaid in the larger American society as well as among their
coreligionists; the National Jewish Commission on Law and Public Affairs (COLPA), an organization of lawyers and social scientists, and
Agudath Israel represented those Orthodox Jews who advocated public
aid to private, religious schools. Catholic educators and writers now
praised those Orthodox Jews who advocated parochiaid, partly in the
hope that their point of view concerning this matter might become more
popular than it was in the entire American Jewish community.[27]

The Orthodox stand on parochiaid naturally led to disagreements
with separationist Jewish organizations and individuals, including the
American Jewish Congress and Leo Pfeffer who served as the chief legal
counsel of the Congress.[28] COLPA and Agudath Israel represented only
a minority of American Jewry, however, the majority of whom continued to uphold the strict separation of church and state in the area of
education.[29]

The Jesuits of *America* felt that the American Jewish community was hypocritical in its opposition to parochiaid; at the same time that it opposed public financial aid to private, religious schools, it accepted government aid for its own hospitals and other welfare agencies. Jewish leaders and intellectuals justified their separationist stand on the basis that the tortuous history of their people had taught them that the absolute separation of church and state is the best guarantee of religious freedom. If this is the case, however, the Jesuits queried, why has this principle not been applied in the State of Israel?[30]

Catholic accommodationists emphasized that the line that separated church and state was not a clear and absolute one, but rather was often times hazy and indefinite, with much overlapping between the public, secular area and the private, religious one. Because the boundary that demarcates the spheres of religion and government was frequently vague, Catholic accommodationists concluded that it was useless to try to keep these two spheres of society apart—particularly in the area of education. In contrast to the historical experiences of the Jews, the Jesuits of *America* wrote that Christians have learned from the recent past that only antireligious governments, and especially that of the Soviet Union, advocate the complete separation of church and state.[31]

The United States Catholic Conference, the leading Catholic accommodationist organization, often found that the American Jewish Congress was its chief opponent in the movement to break down the wall that separated religion and public education in the United States. This situation led the Jesuits of *America* to criticize the AJC on the grounds that it has refused to support "the Christian and traditionally American position that if religion is indispensable to American society, then our public schools must somehow give instruction in it."[32] Not only the survival of Catholic schools but Jewish ones as well were threatened by the strict separationist stand of the American Jewish Congress, warned Virgil Blum.[33]

Robert Drinan concurred with his fellow Jesuits concerning the need for the inclusion of religious values and attitudes into American public education; therefore, those Jewish leaders who called for a rigorous separation of church and state—although their arguments for this were based on the Constitution itself—are not acting in the best interests of American society. Drinan asserted that "Jewish spokesmen have an obligation to address themselves to the contention that public morality and the moral health of the nation may be endangered by . . . [the] divorce of religion from society."[34] Since religion is the source of moral values, the separation of the religious sphere from society at large could only undermine the nation's basic morality and weaken its social unity, Drinan argued.[35] Drinan, who later became a congressman, the head of the liberal Americans for Democratic Action, and an advocate of Christian support for Israel, then warned American Jewish leaders that inter-religious harmony in the United States would be harmed if they persisted in their support of a strict separationist policy.

These appeals and admonitions failed to convince the American Jewish Congress and all other separationist organizations that they ought to modify their stand concerning church-state relations. This resistance to the aims of Catholic accommodationists evoked, at times, a bitter response from them and particularly from the Jesuits of *America.* In November 1958, they warned American Jewry that their continued support for the separation of church and state would lead to their isolation in American society as an increasing number of Christians came to oppose them on those basic public issues that involved religion.[36] An even stronger warning came from *America* in September 1962. In response to a Supreme Court ruling of June 1962 that banned the recitation of a nonsectarian prayer in the New York public schools, this journal bitterly criticized the American Jewish Congress for its role in this case and then went on to warn all of American Jewry that they well might have to face a resurgence of anti-Semitism in the United States if they continued to adhere to a separationist position.[37]

Certainly, many American Catholics, particularly among the intelligentsia, would not have condoned these harsh words. More importantly, just as the American Jewish community was not monolithic in its attitude towards parochiaid, neither was the Catholic laity in the United States. A small but very articulate group of Catholic thinkers opposed public financial aid to church-affiliated school systems and the introduction of religious instruction in the public schools.

Increasingly, the editors and writers of *Commonweal* adopted a separatist position. As early as December 1956, this journal questioned the wisdom of placing religious symbols on public property. At that time, the school board of Ossining, New York, decided to place a nativity crèche on the lawn of the local high school. This decision sharply divided the residents of this small community. The editors of *Commonweal* commented: "What has been the actual results of the dispute at Ossining? The victory, it seems to us, went not so much to Christianity as to a dangerous kind of formalism—a formalism which sees America as somehow more Christian if only the familiar symbols are displayed as publicly and as 'officially' as possible. The Nativity scene, which is a hallowed symbol of the birth of Christ, has become in Ossining a symbol of community dissension and wrangling . . . and all in the name of the Prince of Peace."[38] When the Jesuits of *America* warned American Jewry that they must back down from their strict separationism, *Commonweal* sharply reprimanded the editors of the former journal.[39]

A decade after this sharp exchange of views, Leonard Swidler stated even more emphatically than had *Commonweal,* that religion—including the teaching of religion and school-sponsored prayers—has absolutely no place in the public schools.[40] The introduction of religion into the public schools, he argued, would constitute a grave injustice against those whose religious views differ from the majority. Indeed, this unjust situation had prevailed in most American schools from the very inception of the public school system until it was corrected only rather recently by the Supreme Court, Swidler wrote.

In an effort to win over non-Jews as well as more Jews to its point of view, the American Jewish Congress also advanced several cogent arguments for the continued exclusion of religion from the public schools and the denial of public funds to parochial school systems. Leo Pfeffer advanced the thesis that the American experiment in the separation of church and state "was not the result of any hostility to religion. On the contrary, it was predicated on a firm belief that religion prospers best when it is divorced from the political state and is inevitably corrupted when it becomes entangled with state."[41] Pfeffer also felt that religious beliefs and practices cannot be taught and conducted in a non-partisan objective manner; therefore, they should be left in the hands of the parochial schools and excluded from the public school curriculum.[42]

Pfeffer's ideas were echoed by Will Maslow, another well-known legal counsel of the American Jewish Congress. In a speech before the American Political Science Association, Maslow declared that any form of public financial aid to any religious group or institution "embroils the state in religious controversies, encourages religious and civil divisiveness, penalizes non-believers, and compels the taxpayers of one faith to support the religious institutions of another in violation of conscience and religious liberty."[43] Moreover, a strict separation of church and state is actually in the best interests of true religious faith because when religious institutions become dependent on governmental support, they fail to develop fully their own inner, spiritual resources.[44]

The Supreme Court apparently agreed with Maslow, Pfeffer, and others who represented separationist organizations, and subsequently banned the introduction of religious symbols and practices into the public schools as well as the direct use of public funds to subsidize public schools. In addition to the arguments that separationists presented before the courts, what other factors contributed to their victory that preserved the traditional separation of the public sector and religious education? . . .

In the prosperous post–World War II years, the secular trends in American life grew stronger and particularly in the new affluent suburbs. Beyond these general trends, part of the answer to this question can be found in the nature of the separationist and accommodationist organizations themselves, and the composition of the loose alliance that supported a continued separation of religion and the state.

Many Protestants, fundamentalist as well as liberal, and religiously unaffiliated Americans supported a separationist stand and opposed the accommodationists in the courts. The organizations that joined in this broad coalition included the Baptist Joint Committee on Public Affairs, the United Presbyterians, the National Council of Churches, the Religious Liberty Association of the Seventh-Day Adventists, and Protestants and Other Americans United for the Separation of Church and State. The separationist coalition also included the American Civil Liberties Union, Americans for Democratic Action, the National Education Association, the American Veterans' Committee, the American Humanist Association, and, at times, the AFL-CIO.[45] In 1967, for example, the ACLU and the United Federation of Teachers joined with the American Jewish Congress in opposition to a provision of the Elementary and Secondary Education Act that would have granted federal financial aid to parochial schools. In the early 1970s, the United States Supreme Court ruled unconstitutional a number of state statutes according such aid.

In contrast to the separationists, the Catholic accommodationists were uncoordinated and fragmented; each diocese and bishop, Citizens for Educational Freedom, the Knights of Columbus, religious orders,

Catholic colleges, and other Catholic groups and organizations all acted independently of each other.[46] The United States Catholic Conference was cognizant of this situation, and, between 1951 and 1971, tried to persuade local Catholic authorities that they were in need of a sophisticated defense and then sought to find legal counsel for them. The Conference did little more than this, however, and refrained from launching its own legal initiatives.

Thus, the struggle over the place of religion in the public sector, and particularly in the primary and secondary schools, ended in victory for the separationists. It was not only a victory for those who upheld a basic principle of American democracy—the strict separation of church and state—but it was also a gain for religion in America. The men who wrote the Constitution sought to avoid the devastating religious conflicts that beset Europe and advanced the principle that all religions were equal before the law. After World War II, the Catholic bishops sought to upset that equality by obtaining special concessions for the Catholic Church. In light of the resurgence of Protestantism in the 1970s and 1980s, American Catholics would have found it difficult to defend the Church's privileged position in a predominantly Protestant country.

NOTES

1. Frank J. Sorauf, *The Wall of Separation: The Constitutional Politics of Church and State* (Princeton, N.J.: Princeton University Press, 1976), 159.
2. Will Maslow, "The Use of the Law in the Struggle for Equality," *Social Research* 22 (1955):298.
3. Herbert N. Hart, "Naturalism and Dogma," *Catholic World* 162 (January 1946):349.
4. Eds., "Current Comment: Jewish War Veterans Fight Smut," *America* 96 (6 July 1957):376; Eds. "Editorials: Conference on Moral Standards," *America* 89 (26 September 1953):618.
5. Will Maslow, "The Legal Defense of Religious Liberty—The Strategy and Tactics of the American Jewish Congress" (Paper prepared for delivery at the annual meeting of the American Political Science Association, St. Louis, Missouri, 6–9 September 1961), 15.
6. Ibid.
7. Florence Julian, "Books: *The Case Against Having Children*," *New Catholic World* 214 (December 1971):137.
8. Andrew Greeley, *The American Catholic: A Social Portrait* (New York: Basic Books, 1977), 247.

9. Ibid., 129, 245.
10. Ibid., 37, 136–37, 143, 157–58, 161; Andrew Greeley, William C. Mc-Cready, and Kathleen McCourt, *Catholic Schools in a Declining Church* (Kansas City: Sheed and Ward, 1976), 260, 263, 280.
11. Robert Drinan, "Sunday Laws in Jeopardy," *America* 101 (6 June 1959):411.
12. Ibid.
13. Ibid.
14. Ibid.
15. Drinan, "The Court Judges Sunday Laws." *America* 104 (21 January 1961): 505. Like Drinan, the Jesuits who published *America* were ambivalent towards those Sabbatarians who wished to conduct business on Sunday.
16. Drinan, "Sunday Laws and the First Amendment," *America* 105 (19 August 1960):629–30.
17. Drinan, *Religion, the Courts, and Public Policy* (New York: McGraw-Hill 1963), 210.
18. Eds., "Current Comment: *Companion Poll on Religious Instruction*," *America* 89 (22 August 1953):49.
19. Maslow, "The Legal Defense of Religious Liberty," 7.
20. Robert G. Glouse, Robert D. Linder, Richard V. Pierard, eds., *Protest and Politics: Christianity and Contemporary Affairs* (Greenwood, S.C.: Attic Press, 1968), 168.
21. Richard E. Morgan, *The Politics of Religious Conflict: Church and State in America* (New York: Pegasus Books, 1968), 50, 52.
22. Frederick G. Hochwalt, "Should Federal Aid Proposals Include Parochial Schools?" *Congressional Digest* 40 (January 1961):220, 222.
23. The membership of Citizens for Educational Freedom, an accommodationist organization, is overwhelmingly Catholic, but nevertheless, it is a lay organization.
24. Virgil C. Blum, *Freedom in Education: Federal Aid for All Children* (Garden City, N.Y.: Doubleday, 1965), 141.
25. Ibid.
26. Gilbert S. Rosenthal, *Four Paths to One God: Today's Jew and His Religion* (New York: Bloch Publishing, 1973), 79.
27. Blum, *Freedom in Education*, 74, 129, 202, 203; Eds., "Minority View," *America* 104 (26 November 1960):286–87.
28. Sorauf, *The Wall of Separation*, 189.
29. Morgan, *The Politics of Religious Conflict*, 189.
30. Eds., "Current Comment: Jewish Congress on Church-State," *America* 80 (10 January 1953):386.
31. Ibid. It should be noted that occasionally the Jesuits of *America* were less intractable in their attitude towards Jewish separationists. In 1954, for example, an editorial that appeared in *America* took a more conciliatory attitude towards the American Jewish separationists. At that time, the Jesuits who published this journal conceded that Jewish fears of a breakdown

in the separation of church and state were understandable in light of the Jews' historical experiences. Eds., "Jewish Tercentennial," 611.

32. Eds., "Current Comment: Jewish Congress on Church-State," 386.
33. Virgil C. Blum, "This Heartless Business," *America* 115 (10 September 1966):247–49.
34. Drinan, *Religion, the Courts, and Public Policy,* 230.
35. Ibid.
36. Eds., "Current Comment: The Jew in the New Germany," *America* 84 (4 November 1958):128. The same editorial warned American Jewry not to oppose the rearmament of Germany.
37. Eds., "To Our Jewish Friends," *America* 107 (1 September 1962):665–66.
38. Eds., "Week by Week: Christ in Christmas," *Commonweal* 65 (21 December 1956):300.
39. Eds., "Religion and Pluralism," *Commonweal* 77 (28 September 1962):5–6.
40. Leonard Swidler, "Editorials: Religion in the Public Schools," *Journal of Ecumenical Studies* 3 (Winter 1966): 148. Swidler is a professor of history at Duquesne University and the editor of the *Journal of Ecumenical Studies.*
41. Earl Raab, ed., *Religious Conflict in America: Studies of the Problems beyond Bigotry* (Garden City, N.Y.: Doubleday, 1964), 162.
42. Leo Pfeffer, *Church, State, and Freedom* (Boston: Beacon Press, 1953), 12.
43. Maslow, *The Legal Defense of Religious Liberty,* 2.
44. Ibid., 12.
45. Morgan, *The Politics of Religious Conflict,* 46–60.
46. Ibid., 64; Sorauf, *The Wall of Separation,* 200.

4

Intermarriage and the Jewish Future
Egon Mayer and Carl Sheingold

THE STUDY

For the purposes of this investigation, intermarriage was deliberately defined in its broadest possible terms to include a marriage between any individual who was born Jewish and one who was not. Thus, the sample included some persons who, from a *halachic* and/or communal point of view, were Jewish, since they had converted to Judaism. This decision was made in hope of shedding some light on the consequences of conversion as well as on the consequences of intermarriage itself. The term "intermarriage" is therefore used in this report as an inclusive term covering all respondents; the term "mixed marriage" refers to marriages in which neither partner had converted; and the term "conversionary marriages" describes marriages in which the born-Gentile spouse had converted to Judaism.[1]

The Respondents

Respondents in this study included 446 intermarried couples, in Cleveland, Dallas, Long Island, Los Angeles, New York City, Philadelphia, San Francisco and Westchester. Both husband and wife filled out identical self-administered questionnaires and participated in identical in-depth interviews.

Two-thirds of the couples consisted of a Jewish man and non-Jewish

Reprinted in part by permission of the American Jewish Committee, New York. Originally published in 1983.

woman, a sex ratio which has, in the past, been typical of the intermarried. There was, however, a greater proportion of Jewish women in the younger age groups of the sample, and it is possible that as the educational and occupational patterns of women become more like those of men, the earlier ratio will be altered.

The family lives of the born-Jewish men were generally more Jewishly oriented than those of born-Jewish women. For instance, 41.4 percent of the born-Jewish men often or always attend High Holy Day services, compared to 30.0 percent of the born-Jewish women. Over 30 percent of the men are affiliated with a synagogue, compared to 23.8 percent of women. And with few exceptions, ritual observances at home, the celebration of religious rites of passage for children, involvement in Jewish organizations, were marked by the same sex differences. Born-Gentile wives married to Jewish men were also more likely to convert to Judaism than were the born-Gentile husbands.

Ninety percent of the marriages studied were intact, and for over 80 percent of the spouses it was their first marriage.

The sample included a full range of age groupings, though the percentage of respondents aged 50 and over was larger than it should have been, given the low rate of intermarriage before the 1950s.

Eighty-five percent of the couples studied were parents, and approximately 30 percent have more than two children.

Educational attainment, occupational status and income were all higher for the respondents than for both the national average and the national Jewish average. Born-Jewish women were more likely than born-Jewish men to have the same level of education as their spouses, and to have met their spouses at college.

The family background of the born-Jewish spouses in this sample closely approximated the religious affiliation patterns of American Jews, including a substantial representation of the Orthodox (see Table 4–1).

Table 4–1
Denominational Backgrounds of Born-Jewish Respondents

	Percent
Orthodox	11.1
Conservative	29.3
Reform	26.7
Not affiliated	32.9

The born-Gentile spouses also represented a variety of religious backgrounds (see Table 4–2).

Just over 21 percent of the non-Jewish respondents and 3.3 percent of the Jewish respondents had converted to their spouses' religion—again figures consistent with data from other studies. The rate of conversion was highest in the 20–39 age groups.

The Sample

The goal of the study was to obtain a large representative sample from the national population of intermarried couples. Because this goal proved difficult to achieve, it is important to indicate some of the limitations of this particular sample.

Since there is no central listing of Jews, much less of marriages and religious backgrounds, it was necessary to rely on a variety of strategies for locating intermarried couples. Most of the couples in this study were identified as intermarried by members of the local Jewish community. Thus, although efforts were made to randomize as much as possible, the respondents do not, in strict sense, constitute a random sample. A number of resulting biases can be identified:

(1) All the Jewish spouses included in the sample had to be known, at least to some members of the Jewish community, as Jewish. Thus, the most assimilated intermarried couples in the community were probably underrepresented.

(2) Ninety percent of the marriages studied were intact. Since this is a higher percentage than for marriages as a whole, intermarried couples with severe marital problems were probably underrepresented.

Table 4–2
Religious Backgrounds of Born-Gentile Respondents

	Percent	
	Converts	Non-Converts
Protestant	53.7	45.1
Catholic	17.7	30.8
Other	13.5	6.3
None	11.4	17.7

Note: Totals across do not equal 100% because some respondents did not answer this question.

(3) As with any study on a sensitive personal topic, the refusal rate (the percentage of people contacted who declined to be interviewed) was high. One obvious result was a smaller sample than had been hoped for. But it is also possible that couples most sensitive about their intermarriage, for whatever reason, were underrepresented.

(4) All the communities studied were large metropolitan areas with sizeable Jewish populations—the kind of communities in which most American Jews live. Couples living in small towns, where both intermarriage and assimilation may be harder to avoid, are not represented in the sample. It is possible that their experiences differ significantly from those of couples who were included.

These biases are important enough to make this investigation less than a definitive study. But there are a number of reasons to view its findings as significant and reliable. In the first place, the study yielded a richer lode of relevant data than most earlier researches in this area. And on those questions where it was possible to compare the results with the more representative National Jewish Population Study, the findings were, for the most part, consistent.

Even more important is the fact that virtually all the biases tended in a similar direction—an overrepresentation of couples with more positive feelings about, and ties to, the Jewish community. Thus, while it is possible that, from a Jewish communal perspective, the effects of intermarriage are more damaging than these data suggest, it is highly unlikely that they are less so. Also from a Jewish communal perspective, the sample contains an overrepresentation of the kind of families most likely to retain some contact with the Jewish community. *They are the group the community has to work with.* If the goal is to develop a viable communal response to intermarriage, then this sample has considerable insight to impart.

THE FINDINGS[2]

One important area probed by both the written questionnaires and the personal interviews was the family background in which the partners to the intermarriage, particularly the born-Jewish spouses, grew up. The findings not only corroborate earlier studies and conventional wisdom to the effect that those who intermarry come from less religious and less intensively Jewish homes than those who don't; they also provide clues as to the religious and cultural background and experiences that those who intermarry bring to their marriage.

Family Background of Born-Jewish Spouses

Almost 70 percent of the parents of the born-Jewish spouses belonged to a synagogue, and over 65 percent were perceived by the respondents to have been "somewhat religious" (as compared to "very religious" or "not at all religious"). It is not clear, however, just how much of a religious involvement these perceptions indicate.

More revealing, perhaps, are the data concerning the religious and ritual objects that were available and/or used in the homes in which the born-Jewish spouses grew up (see Table 4–3).

In interpreting these data it is necessary to take into account the ritual

Table 4–3

Religious and Cultural Objects in the Parental Homes of Born-Jewish Respondents

	Percent		
	Own, Use or Display	*Own But Do Not Use*	*Do Not Own*
Mezuzah	54.7	9.1	36.1
Sabbath Candle	45.2	23.3	31.3
Kiddush Cup	32.8	22.3	44.9
Menorah	66.9	14.7	18.4
Havdalah Set	12.1	6.5	81.4
Talith	27.8	24.4	47.7
T'fillin	14.0	21.8	64.2
Seder Plate	47.2	13.5	39.3
Jewish Bible	35.5	43.7	20.7
Jewish Prayer Book	46.1	31.0	22.9
Jewish Books	47.5	35.0	17.4
Separate Dishes for Meat and Dairy Foods	7.1	22.3	70.6
Kipah	38.5	26.1	27.8
Jewish Musical Records	25.5	22.5	52.0
Jewish Art Objects	44.9	18.6	37.6
Poster, etc.	24.9	14.9	60.3

and religious significance of the various objects checked off by the respondents. Keeping separate dishes for meat and dairy foods, and using a *havdalah* set and *t'fillin,* obviously connote a far deeper religious involvement than owning Jewish books or a menorah, particularly if these are the sole marks of Jewishness in the home. The data suggest that only 10 to 20 percent of the respondents were raised by parents who kept a kosher home or laid *t'fillin,* and a similar percentage were raised by parents who did not even own Jewish books or a menorah. The vast majority grew up in homes with some objects that are generally associated, in at least a minimal way, with Jewish identity; but a considerably smaller number experienced religious observance or practice.

In the fact-to-face interviews, slightly over 10 percent of the respondents described their parents as anti-religious. Approximately 20 percent said their parents had insisted on some ritual observances; most of the rest reported an explicit or implicit desire on the part of their parents for Jewish identity—"a sense of being Jewish"—without much actual religious practice or cultural involvement.

A small minority of the born-Jewish partners had an intensive Jewish education; the largest group had some Jewish education but not a great deal; and a significant group appears to have had no Jewish education at all (see Tables 4–4A and 4–4B).

Though very few of the born-Jewish respondents grew up in an exclusively Jewish environment, the vast majority grew up in neighborhoods where at least half their peers were Jewish, and between 15 and 20 percent were raised in a predominantly non-Jewish environment. The degree of contact with non-Jews increased when dating began, but only a minority said that they dated "mostly non-Jews." Thus, while the typical respondent had extensive social contacts with non-Jews, he or

Table 4–4A
Amount of Jewish Education Reported By Born-Jewish Respondents (By sex)

	Percent	
	Male	Female
1–5 years*	39.0	38.0
6+ years	19.0	8.0
No answer/None	42.0	54.0

* Most respondents in this group had less than four years of Jewish education.

Table 4—4B
Type of Jewish Education Reported By Born-Jewish Respondents (By sex)

	Percent	
	Male	Female
Day School or Yeshiva	11.7	3.0
Sunday or Afternoon School	64.9	62.6
Yiddish School or other		
(e.g. tutoring)	6.5	8.4
Can't recall	16.7	26.0

she also had extensive Jewish contacts. In such a setting, intermarriage must be viewed as a possible, but not as an inevitable outcome.

The born-Jewish partners reported that their parents grew more and more uneasy as their sons' and daughters' contacts with non-Jews moved from friendship to dating to marriage (see Table 4—5). Though a majority of the parents were clearly opposed to their children's intermarriage, most were not strongly opposed; and approximately one-third were perceived by their children as neutral.

In sum, the typical born-Jewish spouses in the sample studied came from homes which, though neither non-Jewish nor anti-Jewish, were not intensively Jewish, particularly in religious terms. While most reported that their parents were opposed to the intermarriage, it did not, in light of their upbringing, represent either an unnatural development or an act of rebellion. Nor was the parents' opposition great enough to rupture their ties to their children when the latter proceeded with the marriage.

Table 4—5
Parents' Attitudes toward Friendship, Dating, and Marriage between Jews and Gentiles

	Father (Percent)			Mother (Percent)		
	Friendship	Dating	Marriage	Friendship	Dating	Marriage
Strongly opposed	0.6	11.5	19.7	0.9	12.7	21.3
Opposed	6.7	33.4	39.5	11.0	38.9	39.7
No opinion	58.0	48.5	35.0	53.9	41.1	33.7
Approved	29.2	6.6	5.8	27.6	6.3	5.1
Strongly approved	5.1	****	****	6.3	0.9	0.3

Family Background of Non-Jewish Spouses

As might be expected, the non-Jewish respondents grew up in a more exclusively non-Jewish environment than did their spouses. Most said they had few, if any, Jewish friends while they were growing up, and the majority reported dating mostly non-Jews. And not surprisingly, the typical non-Jewish respondent was much more ignorant about Jews and Judaism at the time of the marriage than his or her spouse was about Christianity.

The findings also indicate that the parents of the non-Jewish respondents were somewhat more religious than their Jewish counterparts. Approximately three-quarters of these parents belonged to a church; fewer of the fathers were perceived by their children to have been "anti-religious," and more of the mothers were perceived as "very religious." And though many of these parents, too, were opposed to their children's intermarrying, a majority of the respondents said their parents were either neutral or favorably disposed toward their marriage (see Table 4–6).

Married Life

Marital Harmony. Many of the questions in the study were designed to elicit information as to agreement or disagreement between the spouses about lifestyle, religious involvement, child-rearing, and related matters. The vast majority of couples reported family harmony (or at least the absence of intense conflict) on most matters, including ethnic and religious issues. Though self-report data are not altogether reliable, and the high percentage of intact marriages in the sample may have skewed the responses to some degree, they do seem to negate the widely held as-

Table 4–6
Parental Attitudes towards Children's Intermarriage (Non-Jewish Parents)

	Percent	
	Convert	Non-Convert
Favorable	19.5	22.6
Neutral	31.7	29.4
Unfavorable	48.8	48.8

sumption that intermarriage results in friction between the spouses and does not work. In this sample, at least, it seems to have worked well enough.

Extended Family Ties. Another widely held belief about intermarriage is that it tends to damage family ties. If this were true it would, of course, be a tragedy in its own right. It would also eliminate possible sources of Jewish content in the lives of intermarried families. All of the data make it clear, however, that the ties between the couples surveyed and their parents and other relatives were intact. Not only did most of the respondents say they got along well with their families, many even reported that their relationships with their parents were better than before the marriage. They saw their families as regularly as time and distance permitted, and in the vast majority of cases their spouses were accepted into the extended family. None of the respondents reported a total break with their families as a result of their marriage.

Though most respondents, Jewish and non-Jewish, report getting along well with their inlaws, the data suggest that the couples are in closer touch with their Jewish than their non-Jewish parents, perhaps simply because many of the couples live closer to the Jewish parents.

The data also reveal specific ways in which the couples' social ties with their extended families are cemented. . . . A significant minority of the couples celebrate Jewish religious holidays with their Jewish parents (but, except for Passover, a majority do not). The holiday most consistently celebrated with Jewish parents is Thanksgiving; and a sizeable minority of the couples also celebrate Christmas with their Jewish families. . . .

These data sugggest that for many intermarried couples the close ties with Jewish parents and extended Jewish family represent an opportunity to enrich the Jewish content of their family lives. In reality, however, shared holiday observances have more of a social than a religious or ritualistic meaning for most of the families.

Religious and Ethnic Life

If intermarriage is a threat to Jewish continuity, it is so particularly because such families provide so little Jewish upbringing for their children. Thus a major concern of this study was the religious and ethnic life of intermarried families and the level of their Jewish identification.

Because there was a dramatic difference, in virtually every area studied, in the responses of couples whose non-Jewish spouse did not convert (mixed marriages) and the responses of couples whose born-Gentile spouse had converted to Judaism (conversionary marriages), the data for the two groups were considered separately.

Mixed Marriages

Religious Identification. Close to two-thirds of the Jewish respondents among the mixed-marriage couples declared that they thought of themselves as Jews and that being Jewish was important to them. A significant minority, however, indicated indifference to any expression of Jewishness, however minimal.

As might be expected, the vast majority of the non-Jewish spouses who did not convert do not identify as Jews. But surprisingly, close to 12 percent of these spouses do consider themselves Jewish, and another 7.3 percent consider themselves partly Jewish. Only about one-third currently identify with the religion of their birth—roughly half the number that did so prior to their marriage (see Table 4–7). More than three-quarters of the non-Jewish spouses report experiencing religious feelings—however they choose to define that—fairly often.

Organizational Involvement. Twenty-two percent of the mixed-marriage couples report some involvement with Jewish communal organizations and 37 percent contribute to the United Jewish Appeal (UJA). Though this level of involvement is lower than that of endogamous Jewish cou-

Table 4–7
Religious Self-Identification of Born-Gentile Respondents (Non-converts)

	Percent	
	Prior to Marriage	*Currently*
Protestant	45.0	26.0
Catholic	30.0	10.0
Other	6.0	7.0
None/no answer	18.0	57.0

ples, it is not dramatically different. According to the National Jewish Population Study, approximately 40 percent of the Jewish population participates in the activities of Jewish organizations, most of them on a sporadic basis.

Synagogue Involvement. The Jewish involvement that probably exerts the greatest influence on the religious and ethnic identity of young children (and their parents) is participation in synagogue life. The data make clear that while 15 to 20 percent of the mixed-marriage couples surveyed do belong to a synagogue, and attend services with some regularity, the vast majority do not. . . . It should be noted, however, that intermarried couples often find scant welcome in both religious and secular Jewish organizations. Lack of involvement does not always reflect a lack of desire on the part of the intermarried couples to belong.

Home Observances. Not surprisingly, only a handful of the mixed-marriage couples surveyed keep a kosher home, own and use a *havdalah* set or other ritual objects, light Sabbath candles, or otherwise observe the Sabbath with any regularity. . . .

Fewer than half own and use a menorah, and less than one-half often light candles on Hanukkah. Indeed, while roughly one-third of the respondents reported owning and/or using a number of Jewish objects (see Table 4–8), not a single object on the list was owned *and* used by a majority. . . .

Raising Children. At the heart of Jewish concern about intermarriage is whether the children of such marriages will be part of, or lost to, the Jewish fold. The data summarized above bear significantly on this question; but the study provides data even more relevant to the subject.

Approximately one-third of the mixed-marriage couples surveyed said they thought of their children as Jewish, and would be upset if their children did not think of themselves as Jews. Forty-three percent of the respondents reported that their sons had been, or would be, ritually circumcised—a figure greater than might be expected.[3]

But fewer than a third of the couples said that their children had had, or would have, a Bar or Bat Mitzvah—a rite of passage with strong direct impact on the child—and some of the couples reported they were planning to have their children baptized and confirmed. In most cases,

Table 4–8
Ritual and Cultural Jewish Objects in the Homes of Mixed-Marriage Couples

	Percent		
	Own, Use or Display	Own But Do Not Use	Do Not Own
Mezuzah	22.9	6.6	70.5
Sabbath Candle	16.3	16.9	66.8
Kiddush Cup	12.9	12.7	74.4
Menorah	43.5	12.2	44.4
Havdalah Set	2.4	3.8	93.8
Talith	8.8	12.3	78.9
T'fillin	4.9	9.8	85.3
Seder Plate	18.9	5.9	75.2
Jewish Bible	23.5	35.1	41.4
Jewish Prayer Book	23.8	23.0	53.2
Jewish Books	30.6	32.6	36.8
Separate Dishes	5.2	2.4	92.5
Kipah	20.1	26.1	53.8
Jewish Musical Records	18.4	13.2	68.4
Jewish Art Objects	29.6	15.3	55.1
Posters, etc.	15.1	9.3	75.6

however, there were no plans to replace Jewish rites with Christian rites. . . .

Perhaps the most sobering statistic, given the low level of Jewish content in the family life of most mixed-marriage couples, is the small number of such families that provide formal Jewish instruction for their children. Only about one-quarter, at most, of the children whose parents were involved in this study receive a formal Jewish education, and even fewer receive intensive Jewish schooling (see Table 4–9).

What then do the data indicate about mixed-marriage couples and

Table 4–9
Type of Religious Education Currently Given to Children

	Percent
Day School	6
Afternoon/Sunday School	19
Home Instruction	13
Other/None (including non-Jewish)	62

about the Jewish component of their lives? It seems fair to conclude that while most of the Jewish spouses have an abstract sense of Jewish identity, only a minority of them act on it; and even among the latter, very few act on it with any intensity. The majority of these couples express neither desire nor intention to have their children identify as Jews, and only a small proportion of the families studied will provide formal Jewish education or other experiences explicitly designed to raise their children Jewishly. Despite the fact that the sample selected for this study may be expected to skew the responses in the direction of optimism, the Jewish content of family life in mixed marriages is, by every index, less than it is among endogamous marriages.

Conversionary Marriages

Just over 21 percent of the born-Gentile respondents in the sample had converted to Judaism by the time of the study.[4] Of this group, 40 percent converted prior to, and in connection with, the marriage, and another 15 percent before they met their current spouse (often in connection with an earlier marriage). This still leaves a large group (approximately one-third of all the converts) who converted after the marriage (see Table 4–10).

The data indicate that most of these later conversions were not entered into primarily for the sake of the children, but were the culmination of long and thoughtful consideration. The most common reason cited for conversion was the influence of the Jewish spouse and family (see Table 4–11).

Conversion into Judaism was more common among women than men. Twenty-seven percent of the born-Gentile women, compared to 14

Table 4–10
When Did Conversion Occur?

	Percent
Prior to meeting spouse	15.0
Prior to marriage	40.0
Prior to first child, but after marriage	22.0
After first child	6.0
No answer	15.0

Table 4–11
Reasons for Conversion Reported by Converts

	Percent
Personal conviction	32.2
Influence of spouse and in-laws	38.0
For the sake of the children	8.9
Combination of above, and other reasons	20.9

percent of the born-Gentile men, had converted to Judaism by the time of the study.[5]

A larger proportion of converts were between 20 and 39 years of age than was the case with non-converts (see Table 4–12). The data on those under 20 years of age, however, point the other way; but those marrying this young are, in any case, not typical.

As might be expected, conversion was more common where the parents of the Jewish spouse were more religiously involved. In addition, it would appear that religious feelings combined with a lack of identification with the religion of one's birth on the part of the born-Gentile spouse play a part in the impetus for conversion.

The data reveal few significant differences between mixed and conversionary marriages on such matters as education, income, family harmony and ties to extended family. But they point to dramatic and important differences in religious and ethnic identification. Close to 83 percent of the converts consider themselves Jewish and another 6.4 percent consider themselves partly Jewish. The vast majority said that being Jewish was important to them.

Table 4–12
Age Distribution of Converts and Non-Converts

	Percent	
	Converts	Non-Converts
Under 20 years old	1.0	15.2
20–29	18.9	10.3
30–39	41.0	32.9
40–49	22.2	20.3
50–59	13.7	14.6
60 and over	3.1	6.6

Organizational Involvement. The families of converts are more involved in Jewish organizational life than the families of non-converts, but the differences are not dramatic. Thirty-eight percent of the converts said they contribute to the UJA, 9.4 percent said they were frequently involved in the activities of Jewish organizations, and 32.3 percent reported less frequent involvement.

Synagogue Involvement. The vast majority of converts are actively involved in their synagogues, and approximately two-thirds attend services with some regularity (the comparable figure for non-converts is less than one-third). According to the National Jewish Population Study, fewer than half of all endogamous Jewish families are involved in synagogue life, making the affiliation rate of the converts doubly dramatic (see Table 4–13). . . .

Ritual Activities and Objects in the Home. Approximately half of the converts in this study light Sabbath candles, at least some of the time, and more than three-quarters regularly light Hanukkah candles. . . .

As Table 4–8 indicates, the majority of mixed-marriage respondents did not own or use the religious and cultural objects listed in the study. Most of the respondents in the conversionary marriages, however, reported owning virtually all of these items, including items of considerable ritual or religious significance, and a majority said they used these objects. As the data on separate dishes indicate, few of the conversionary-marriage families are strictly observant; but in the homes of most of them, artifacts of Jewish life are visible and used (see Table 4–14).

Table 4–13
Affiliation of Conversionary-Marriage Couples Belonging to Synagogues (68% of total)

Type of Congregation	Percent*
Reform	47
Conservative	18
Orthodox	11
Unidentified	23

*These are percentages *only* of the 68% of the conversionary-marriage couples who belong to synagogues.

Table 4–14
Religious and Cultural Objects in the Homes of Conversionary Marriages

	Percent		
	Own, Use or Display	Own But Do Not Use	Do Not Own
Mezuzah	57	6	32
Sabbath Candle	52	24	19
Kiddush Cup	43	16	36
Menorah	87	3	7
Havdalah Set	8	9	80
Talith	24	17	57
T'fillin	10	14	72
Seder Plate	47	6	43
Jewish Bible	40	38	18
Jewish Prayer Book	52	27	18
Jewish Books	62	20	15
Separate Dishes	9	4	82
Kipah	43	26	26
Jewish Musical Records	30	23	43
Jewish Art Objects	56	6	34
Posters, etc.	35	9	51

Note: Totals across do not equal 100% because some respondents did not answer this question.

Raising Children. Eighty percent of the Jewish spouses in conversionary marriages said they considered their children Jewish and would be upset if their children did not regard themselves as Jewish, compared to about one-third of the Jewish spouses in mixed marriages.

Close to three-quarters of the conversionary-marriage couples provided, or plan to provide, for ritual circumcision of their sons as well as a Bar or Bat Mitzvah for their children (in mixed marriages, close to half of the couples opted for ritual circumcision and less than a third for a Bar or Bat Mitzvah). Fifty-six percent of the conversionary-marriage couples said they were providing a formal Jewish education for their children, and 16 percent were sending their children to Jewish day schools (less than one-quarter of the children of mixed marriages receive a formal Jewish education).

Denominational Background. Based upon the denominational background of the Jewish parents, the rates of conversion were 28 percent for Reform, 19 percent for Conservative, and 31 percent for Orthodox. While the vast majority who converted under Reform or Conservative auspices later affiliated with the same denomination, the vast majority of those who converted under Orthodox auspices are currently affiliated with Reform synagogues. Reform, Conservative and Orthodox converts all scored higher on measures of Jewishness than non-converts, but those who converted under Conservative and Orthodox auspices tended to score higher than the Reform group, and in some cases significantly so. . . .

The Effect of Jewish Background

While there are not enough data to permit a systematic identification of the religious and cultural factors which influence the Jewish component in intermarriage, there is enough information about the background and commitment of the born-Jewish spouse to warrant a brief examination of some relevant data.

Given the relatively low commitment of the born-Gentile spouses to the religion of their birth and their lack of opposition to Jewishness in their family lives, it is reasonable to assume that the level of pre-marital commitment to Judaism by the born-Jewish spouse played an important part in determining the Jewish religious and ethnic content of the couple's family life. This assumption seems to be corroborated by the findings on the Jewish spouses' Jewish education and personal commitment and their parents' synagogue affiliation.

When the data on Jewish education and synagogue affiliation are examined together with the responses of both spouses about how important their religious background had been to them just prior to their marriage, there is little doubt that religious background was subjectively of greater importance to the born-Jewish spouses than to the born-Gentile spouses (see Table 4–15).

The data also highlight the relationship between these background variables and several measures of the Jewishness in the couples' married life.

Jewish Books in the Home. Thirty percent of the born-Jewish spouses who had had no Jewish education reported that they own and read Jewish books, compared with 36 percent for those with one to three

Table 4–15
"Thinking Back to the Time Just Prior to Your Getting Married, How Important Would You Say Your Own Religious Background Was to You?"

	Percent			
	Born-Jewish Spouse		Born-Gentile Spouse	
	Male	Female	Male	Female
Very Important	27.5	32.8	13.9	19.5
Somewhat Important	39.3	27.2	19.1	31.4
Unimportant	27.0	35.1	56.4	41.3
Tried to Avoid It	3.6	3.3	5.4	.9
Rejected It	2.6	1.6	5.8	6.8

years of Jewish education and 48 percent for those with four or more years of Jewish education. Also, 28 percent of those whose parents had not belonged to a synagogue reported that they own and read Jewish books, compared to 43 percent for those whose parents had belonged to a synagogue. Only 18 percent of the born-Jewish spouses who said their religious background had been unimportant to them before marriage said they owned and read Jewish books after marriage, compared with 42 percent for those who said that it had been "somewhat" important and 60 percent for those who considered it "very" important. . . .

Bar or Bat Mitzvah. The percentage of born-Jewish spouses who had celebrated or planned to celebrate a Bar or Bat Mitzvah for their children ranged from 40 percent for those with less than four years of Jewish education to 57 percent for those who had had four years or more. The comparable figures are 38 percent for those whose parents had not belonged to a synagogue, and 49 percent for those whose parents did belong. About one-third of those whose religious background had been unimportant to them before marriage had, or planned to have, a Bar or Bat Mitzvah, compared to over half of those to whom religious background was "somewhat" or "very" important.

Attendance at High Holy Day Services. Thirty-two percent of the born-Jewish spouses with no Jewish education said they regularly attend High Holy Day services, compared to about half of those with four years or more. Half as many (21 percent) of those whose parents had not belonged to a synagogue regularly attended such services as did those (42 percent) whose parents did belong. And the comparable figures were 13 percent for those whose religious background had been unimportant to them before marriage, 42 percent for those to whom it had been somewhat important, and 62 percent for those to whom it had been very important.

All of these data, though admittedly limited in scope, tend to confirm the relationship between the Jewish background of the born-Jewish spouse and the Jewish content of the intermarriage. The strongest influence, it would appear, lies in the importance the individual ascribed to his or her religious background prior to the marriage. An impressive percentage of those who brought into the intermarriage a strong religious involvement in Judaism managed to carry some of that involvement into their family life.

SUMMARY AND CONCLUSIONS

Given the deep feelings about intermarriage in the Jewish community, the findings in this study will inevitably be cited to support a number of contradictory assumptions. In the preceding pages a determined effort has been made to let the data speak for themselves. The final pages will summarize the findings and draw such implications as seem warranted to the researchers and sponsors of the study.

Major Findings

The study indicates that:

—In most mixed marriages, the born-Jewish spouse affirms a Jewish identity, but does little to act on this affirmation. Only a minority, when they become parents, provide formal Jewish education for their children, and in general, the transmission of Jewish knowledge, skills and experience is minimal.

—On every index of Jewish attitudes and practice, couples whose born-Gentile spouses have converted to Judaism scored higher than other intermarried couples. Indeed, based on what is known about the religious and ethnic life in endogamous marriages, the family life of conversionary marriages is more consciously Jewish, both in religious practice and in formal and informal Jewish acculturation of children.

—The factor most responsible for the Jewishness of intermarried families—including the conversion of the born-Gentile spouse—would seem to be the extent of Jewish background, knowledge and commitment of the born-Jewish spouse.

—Lack of Jewish identity and practice in intermarried families is not the result of pressure by the non-Jewish spouse. Most born-Gentile spouses do not identify strongly with the religion of their birth; in fact, even among those who did not convert, a minority reported some identification with Judaism. Very few of the families expressed a desire to raise their children in a religion other than Judaism, and the percentage of children celebrating Christian rites of passage was significantly lower than those experiencing Jewish rites. Most children of intermarriage are being raised without any ethnic or religious identification.

—Differences of religious background do not seem to contribute to estrangement from parents or to conflicts in family decision-making, including decisions about child-rearing. Relationships between both born-Jewish and born-Gentile respondents and their parents were consistently reported to be close and harmonious.

—The responses of mixed-marriage couples married by a rabbi suggested more Jewish practice than of those who were not (though still considerably less than in families where the born-Gentile spouse had converted), though there is no basis in the data for assuming that rabbinic participation was the cause, rather than the result of such greater commitment. In any event, the number of such couples in the sample was so small that any interpretation must be considered highly speculative.

General Implications

The findings summarized above tend to reinforce the fear that intermarriage represents a threat to Jewish continuity. Most non-Jewish spouses do not convert to Judaism; the level of Jewish content and practice in mixed marriages is low; only about one-third of the Jewish partners in such marriages view their children as Jewish; and most such children are exposed to little by way of Jewish culture or religion. Thus, despite the suggestions of some Jews that intermarriage may actually add to the Jewish population by bringing non-Jewish spouses and the children of such unions into the Jewish fold, this study—conducted with a sample that made optimistic conclusions more likely—does not support this hope. It does, however, suggest steps the Jewish community might take to ameliorate the assimilationist threat inherent in intermarriage.

One set of data—the findings on conversionary marriages—merits particular attention and discussion. Conversionary marriages compare favorably not only with mixed marriages, but with endogamous marriages as well. In the conversionary marriage, Jewish identity is not merely asserted; it is acted upon, particularly with respect to religious affiliation and observances. Thus, in some ways, there is more reason for optimism about Jewish continuity in families where the born-Gentile spouse has converted to Judaism than there is in the typical endogamous family.

Identity formation is too complex a process for anyone to conclude from these data how many, and to what degree, the children of conversionary marriages will remain Jewish. It seems clear, however, that where conversion takes place, the fact that one of the spouses was not born Jewish is no obstacle to a Jewish family life. . . .

NOTES

1. Although the study does include a few couples in which the born-Jewish spouse converted from Judaism to another faith, the number was too small to permit analysis.
2. Some tables do not total 100% because of minor deviations due to rounding.
3. The study did not probe why more respondents said they had had, or planned to have, ritual circumcisions for their sons than said that they considered their children Jewish. It is likely that at least some of the respondents ignored the difference between religious and medical circumcision and reported the latter as "ritual circumcision," or that some of the respondents, convinced that circumcision was desirable for medical or hygienic reasons, agreed to ritual circumcision to please the Jewish grandparents.
4. It should be noted that 3.3 percent of the born-Jewish respondents had converted out of Judaism; but this is too small a group to analyze, and no effort was made to do so.
5. This pattern was reversed among the small group of respondents who converted out of Judaism; 11 of the 15 were men.

II

THE CHRISTIAN COMPONENT OF AMERICAN ANTISEMITISM

Precisely because of the centrality of Judaism and Jews in Christian theology, Professor A. Roy Eckardt explains, antisemitism has been nurtured by Christendom throughout history. Unlike Judaism whose essence is independent of Christianity, the church cannot simply ignore Jews. "The anti-Judaism and the anti-Jewishness of Christians and the Christian church find no comparable place in anti-Christianness among Jews" (*Jews and Christians*, p. 8). Yet, although foremost Christian thinkers like Eckardt recognize the importance of religious imagery in antisemitism, many scholars in secular disciplines, usually positing the exceptionalism of America, question the significance of religion as they seek the roots of American discrimination elsewhere.

Serious analysis of the subject by historians began in the 1950s. A pioneer essay by Oscar Handlin, "American Views of the Jews at the Opening of the Twentieth Century" (*Publications of the American Jewish Historical Society,* 1951) was followed a few years later by John Higham's seminal pieces, "Anti-Semitism in the Gilded Age" and "Social Discrimination against Jews" (both reprinted in Higham, *Send These to Me*). The two historians addressed several issues—when American antisemitism began, its causes, and the importance of imagery to its eruption. Neither ranked Christian religious images, negative or positive, high in the antisemitic equation. Indeed, imagery generally did not appear all that important. Both accepted the existence of a parallel, indigenous strand of philosemitism that threaded its way through American thought and countered negative images of different sorts. Handlin, who blamed social antisemitism on a Populist movement gone sour, also played down the significance of antisemitic images by arguing that stereotyping was common to all American minorities. Higham found the primary cause of antisemitism in competition over status between the rapidly mobile Jews and native Americans. Distinguishing between overt and ideological antisemitism, he minimized the importance of myth. His approach has been adapted by social scientists who examine antisemitism under the rubric of "conflict of interests" situations.

Louise A. Mayo examines imagery in greater detail. In the first essay of this section, she traces Christian images of the Jews in religious and secular publications of the nineteenth century. The title of the book from which the piece is drawn, *The Ambivalent Image*, sums up her thesis. She contends that "the religious image of the Jew was filled with ambiguities" and that negative myths were countered by positive views at least as potent. Developing the duality of image originally posited by Handlin, she emphasizes the philosemitic strand. The findings can lead logically to one of two conclusions: either Christianity's responsibility for American antisemitism, or American antisemitism itself, was not all that signficant.

Scholars divide on the proposition that American philosemitism effectively curbed anti-Jewish sentiment. One earlier detailed study, Louis Harap's *The Image of the Jew in American Literature*, places greater emphasis on negative, including religious, images of the Jews. On the other hand, an article by historian Lloyd Gartner published the same year as Mayo's book, "The Two Continuities of Antisemitism in the United States" (in *Antisemitism through the Ages*, edited by Shmuel Almog) agrees with Mayo's assessment. Denying that American Christianity can be treated as a monolith, Gartner writes: "Our point is that, just as Christianity is multifaceted, so are the conceptions of the Jews which it harbors. Undoubtedly, they are mainly negative. However, as a result of the particular character of American Christianity, they are not only part of antisemitic continuity. . . . They are also indicative of the second continuity, that which prevented the spread of antisemitism or limited its scope" (p. 314).

Most American Jewish spokesmen of the nineteenth century would not have agreed with accounts of a strong and pervasive Christian philosemitism. Naomi W. Cohen shows in a historical essay that Jews of the

Gilded Age explained antisemitic eruptions primarily as a recurrent and inescapable function of Christian animosity. Accordingly, they did not admit that the 1870s, the usual date given for the onset of significant anti-Jewish sentiment, were radically different from previous decades. Nor would they have been convinced by later socioeconomic interpretations of discrimination against Jews. They neglected, however, to explain —if Christian antisemitism is a constant—how to account for fluctuations in antisemitic eruptions. The Jewish proclivity to associate discrimination with Christianity was reinforced by the active participation of Christian clergymen of the nineteenth and twentieth centuries in antisemitic movements. (See, for example, *Apostles of Discord: A Study of Organized Bigotry and Disruption on the Fringes of Protestantism* by Ralph Lord Roy and *The Old Christian Right: The Protestant Far Right from the Great Depression to the Cold War* by Leo P. Ribuffo. Several biographies of Father Charles Coughlin, as well as Seymour Martin Lipset and Earl Raab in *The Politics of Unreason,* analyze the antisemitism of that Catholic demagogue.) Cohen's article suggests the importance of analyzing the response of the "victims," or those under fire, to outbreaks of bigotry. A recent study by sociologist Gary A. Tobin, with Sharon L. Sassler, *Jewish Perceptions of Antisemitism,* develops a related theme. Tobin examines the impact of the antisemitic legacy upon contemporary American Jewish thought and how it has affected the Jewish sense of rootedness in a Christian society.

Psychologists and sociologists followed Handlin and Higham into the scholarly debate. Switching the focus from the Jew to the antisemite, they introduced variables of personality, age, income, education, and urbanization by which to measure the bigots. In their studies, too, Christian imagery was at best but one of a series of multiple causes. The implicit aim of the social scientists and their poll data was to isolate, and then prescribe for the elimination of, those conditions that gave rise to bigotry. Their work, like that of the historians, has generated considerable and ongoing analysis. (Two important contributions of this genre are T. W. Adorno et al., *The Authoritarian Personality* and Charles Herbert Stember and others, *Jews in the Mind of America.*)

In the wake of the cemetery desecrations in Germany in 1959, the Anti-Defamation League embarked on a half million dollar project in cooperation with the Survey Research Center of the University of California at Berkeley. Between 1963 and 1975 nine studies of American antisemitism for the series called Patterns of Prejudice were undertaken, one historical and eight contemporary. The latter, based on population sampling, included three projects relating to religion and discrimination. They in turn found their way into two books, *Christian Beliefs and Anti-Semitism* by Charles Y. Glock and Rodney Stark, and *Wayward Shepherds: Prejudice and the Protestant Clergy* by Stark and others.

The selection by Harold E. Quinley and Charles Y. Glock which is reprinted here is from the final "wrap-up" volume of the series, *Anti-Semitism in America*. It summarizes the results of those religious studies. Critics have attacked the findings on methodological grounds—i.e., the nature of the questions posed by the sample—and for its conclusion that hostility toward Jews is more prevalent in the "conservative" as opposed to "liberal" churches. Indeed, for different reasons—e.g., stand on Israel, affirmative action—Jews too over the past twenty years have been rethinking the assumed alliance between "liberal" Christianity and Judaism.

The last selection in this section is by Franklin H. Littell, Methodist minister and professor of religion, who has long fought against antisemitism. In a talk for the International Center for the Study of Antisemitism in Jerusalem (1985), Littell reaffirmed the centrality of religious imagery in antisemitism. He also underscored the importance of the Holocaust in evaluating the religious dimension of Jew-hatred. The Holocaust and the death camps moved the interpretation of antisemitism to a new level, Littell contends, for they laid bare "the endemic antisemitism which has been a malaise of Christendom for centuries." Rejecting the behavioralist approach of the Patterns of Prejudice series, and implicitly dismissing the countervailing strength of American philosemitic images, he focuses on theological and cultural levels of antisemitism which, he argues, cut through the "liberal" and "conservative" American Protestant churches.

Littell also emphasizes the challenge of the state of Israel to traditional Christian teachings. Israel symbolized the right of the Jews to "self-definition," or the right to carve out their own destiny, and it created an independent Jew foreign to the religious images of despised and denigrated people. Thus, Littell challenges American Protestantism to confront its traditional hostility in light of both the burden of the Holocaust and independent Jewish statehood.

Littell's piece is but one illustration of how the Holocaust dramatically revised thinking about antisemitism in both Christian and Jewish circles. As historian Shmuel Ettinger has also explained, the Holocaust reinvigorated the study of the subject, and, more importantly, it shifted concentration from isolated episodes to continuities ("Jew-Hatred in Its Historical Context," in *Antisemitism through the Ages,* edited by Shmuel Almog).

Running through the various approaches to antisemitism is a common concern: can Jew-hatred itself be wiped out? Those who place greatest emphasis on the Christian component are least sanguine. Historian Ben Halpern suggests in a recent essay that antisemitism may be a normal element of Jewish-Christian relations. If the religious roots of antisemitism are not eradicable, and Halpern doesn't see how they can be, then the realistic approach is to preserve a "normal balance" between antagonism and acceptance of the Jew. "Antisemitism, if kept at tolerable levels, is a normal element of Jewish-Christian relations" (*Policy-Oriented Research on Antisemitism: An Inquiry,* p. 12).

5

The Ambivalent Image: Nineteenth-Century America's Perception of the Jew

Louise A. Mayo

THE RELIGIOUS IMAGE

Historically, the religious reaction to the Jew had been the most deeply engrained on the Christian mind. In the United States there was a profound ambivalence toward "God's chosen people who one and the same time, gave us the messiah and rejected him."[1] This basic Christian attitude goes back to the early Christian writers who taught that the dispersion of the Jews was divine retribution for the crucifixion. Judaism in Christ's time, it was assumed, had become a religion without soul, desiccated by its legalism, formalism, and ritual.

Most important, the Jews had rejected and caused the death of their one true leader, like the father who destroys his own child. In this case, the unrepentant father who had killed his child, Jesus, had also rejected his other child, Christianity. Yet Christianity did owe a debt of gratitude to Jews who had preserved the worship of one God. They were the divinely elected upholders of the law, the people from whom Christ came. Many Americans, Protestants and students of the Old Testament, were acutely aware of their Hebrew roots.

A father may be loved as well as feared. The Jew was considered responsible for the crime, but it was a crime from which the Christian reaped moral and psychological benefit—redemption from sin. The Jew

Reprinted in part by permission of Associated University Presses from Louise A. Mayo, *The Ambivalent Image: Nineteenth-Century America's Perception of the Jew* (Rutherford, N.J.: Fairleigh Dickinson University Press, 1988), 20–39, 187–89.

also represented a marvelous and incomprehensible phenomenon. Despite extreme persecution, this strange people had survived for thousands of years. Perhaps this was part of a vast divine plan in which the Jew would be restored to greatness by acknowledging Christian truth.

These religious preconceptions played a significant role in the way in which Americans perceived Jews, particularly earlier in the century. An ambivalence that had been brought over by the Calvinists, was widespread: "The Jews were forever guilty of deicide . . . but as foreordained witnesses to the divine plan of salvation in Christianity, must be tolerated and protected. . . ."[2] The view that the Jew was the Christ-killer, rejected by God and justly punished for his transgressions, was widely accepted.[3] A related popular idea was that the Jewish religion was merely a precursor of Christianity and, therefore, no longer relevant in the modern world. Proselytizers were active, although believing as they did in the central role of the Jew in bringing God's kingdom to earth, not always unsympathetic.

Although many Christian writers supported these attitudes, others, often in secular journals, placed greater emphasis on gratitude to the Jews for bringing religion to the world. They also expressed admiration for the miraculous survival of the Jewish people in spite of oppression, interest in Jewish religious customs and disdain for the futile efforts of the conversionists. They dismissed the crucifixion as either not the fault of the Jews or not related to their modern descendants. The seemingly contradictory attitudes of religious hostility and sympathy existed side by side in America, often on the pages of the same publication. At any rate, the multiplicity of conflicting attitudes was far more characteristic of the American religious reaction to the Jews than elsewhere in the Christian world.

In a discussion of the reasons for anti-Jewish prejudice, *Harper's Magazine* of July 1858 recognized the centrality of religious motivation: "Is it surprising that a civilization called from the name of Christ should hold under perpetual ban of dislike . . . the whole race which is descended from those who rejected the leader of Christendom . . . and who refuse him to this day?" The magazine felt this was a very natural and obvious prejudice and admonished Jews not to expect its rapid disappearance.[4]

Early histories of the Jewish people and Sunday-school texts for children, adults, and teachers illustrated widely held preconceptions, often balanced by expressions of sympathy. In one of the first published histories of the Jewish people (1812), Hannah Adams declared that the persecutions, antiquity, and rites of the Jews were "a standing monument to the truth of the Christian religion." Jews had been selected to preserve the knowledge of God, but after the prophetic age, Jews had corrupted and perverted their religion. When Christ was "ignominiously rejected and put to death by the Jewish nation," the result was terrible calamities and dispersion. Yet it is interesting that, despite this righteous condemnation, she expressed great sympathy for the "cruel oppression and pillages this devoted race have suffered." She admired their survival despite all their misery and hoped for the future conversion of the "descendants of those illustrious patriarchs."[5]

Sunday-school books designed for the young were often particularly severe in their judgments of the Jews. *Sabbath Lessons* by Elizabeth Peabody, for instance, spoke of the "conspiracy of the Jewish rulers against Jesus Christ" and reproofed the Jews for "indulging themselves in reviling, covetousness. . . ." Despite endorsing this view of God's rejection, an 1832 volume, *Annals of the Jewish Nation,* pointedly typified the ambiguities of the attitudes of religious fundamentalists toward the Jews. In spite of all their misdeeds, "an extraordinary providence" attended the Jewish people in fulfillment of the prophecies and in their preservation as a distinct people. They continued to be a "monument of God's displeasure" against the crucifixion. "Still they are preserved in mercy. . . . For it is clear . . . they will be restored to the privileges of the Church" from which they had been temporarily cut off by unbelief.[6]

An 1853 volume, *Stories from the History of the Jews,* presented sympathetic tales for children about the scattering of the Jewish people throughout the world where they remained strangers and were persecuted and massacred; "still we shall find them in quiet industry, making their way." The child was reminded that the Jews had "rejected and murdered the Savior" and that "the punishment, though heavy, was just." The author did, however, firmly believe that it was time for all oppression to end: "If Christians will think and act in the mild spirit of their teacher, the Jew will, in time . . . throw off their coating of pride. . . ."[7] Sunday-school texts have long been identified as sources of anti-Semitism.[8] Works such as these might reinforce the view of the Jew as abandoned by God, yet they strongly opposed modern persecution.

Religious press and books designed for adults and Sunday-school teachers were similar, even in tone and level of sophistication, to those written for children. Occasionally, their tone was far more vitriolic. In 1855 *The Churchman*, an official Episcopal organ, reported an "outrage" to the Christian religion. A rabbi responded to a toast offered to the clergy of the state at a state legislature dinner. In a Christian city, "a disbeliever—a reviler of Christianity" dared to appropriate the finer sentiments to his own "defiant infidel system" and responded from his "evil heart of unbelief" to a Christian assembly! It was "blasphemy" and hypocritical—whoever heard of the Jews regarding gentiles as their "brethren?" [9]

Adult religious books often combined the basic image of the Jew as despised Christ-killer with real, if incongruous, sympathy. In his *A Pictorial Descriptive View and History of All Religions*, Reverend Charles A. Goodrich noted that in the dispersal of the Jews the readers of the Bible would "learn the evil and danger of despising divine admonitions." Still, Goodrich repeated the belief that God must have had a reason to preserve this people "in so extraordinary a manner," with the "same trust in the promise of their God, the same conscientious attachment to the institutions of their fathers," which he described in careful detail. In a similar vein, Hannah W. Richardson, in her 1861 book, *Judea in Her Desolations*, accepted the generally held belief that "the great mass of the Jews ... conspired the death of this just One assuring an awful responsibility." Yet, although the national existence of the Jews was annihilated as a result, "still this sturdy stock resisted the rude blast of centuries ..." surviving to the present as witnesses to the truth that "the savior of the world was a Jew." Therefore, she admonished her readers, Christians must never "despise these now down-trodden ones." [10]

Supposedly more sophisticated works delineated hostile images that found greater favor in the twentieth century. John Mears believed that the Jews could not accept Christ as the Messiah because they had expected a monarch-warrior since "their views and hopes were almost entirely worldly." W. D. Morrison's condemnation in *The Jews under Roman Rule* (1891) could still be heard in the modern world. The Jews were detested in the Roman world because of their practice of refusing to associate with gentiles. This was "utterly opposed to the humane sentiments of national brotherhood which were taking root in the ancient world." The Jews brought contempt upon themselves by their "separatist customs." The inference was clear that this continued to be the case.[11] This accusation has found an echo in modern complaints about "clannishness."

Religious books and publications, whether designed for children or adults, popular or scholarly, tended to reinforce the view of Jews as murderers of God's son, and the Jewish religion as a fossil destined to give way entirely to the "New Israel," Christianity. In his poem "The Star of Calvary," Nathaniel Hawthorne expressed this most basic of all Christian attitudes:

> Behold O Israel! behold,
> It is no Human One
> That ye have dared to crucify
> What evil hath he done?
> It is your King, O Israel!
> The God-begotten Son![12]

Yet God had continued to preserve the Jewish people. There must be some profound divine purpose for this miracle. Religious writers, therefore, frequently cautioned their readers that they must renounce persecution.

Perhaps the reason for the miraculous survival of the Jews was their ultimate conversion. Indeed, this became a basic tenet of fundamentalist ideology. In early America conversion was often the aim of even the most sympathetic Protestant leaders. For example, Ezra Stiles, president of Yale and close friend of the great merchant Aaron Lopez, often expressed the wish that his friend would see the light of truth some day. In his 1798 Life of President Stiles, Reverend Abiel Holmes (the father of Oliver Wendell Holmes) recommended his subject's benevolent approach in seeking the conversion of Jews. Stiles's civility was certainly worthy of imitation in dealing with "this devoted people." Instead of treating them with appropriate "humanity and tenderness," Christians often persecuted and condemned them, tending to "prejudice them against our holy religion, and to establish them in infidelity."[13] . . .

The ardent evangelical admonition to "weep over the unbelieving Jews and pity them and strive to reclaim them" was terribly condescending and naturally resented by Jews. However, the actions of those who zealously accepted such ideas could hardly have been anti-Semitic. Once, one author wrote, Jews feared to lift their heads, but now they do and "rank among the chief men of the earth" whom the Lord will take to rebuild his Holy Land. Another declared that Jews possessed "more native talent, keenness of perception and energy, joined with activity of mind," than any other group. As fellow men they were entitled to both sympathy and equal rights.[14] Unlike Europe, in the United States even the most ardent conversionist tended to favor equal rights.

The secular press showed a continuing fascination with proselytizing, reporting even the meagerest success in converting Jews. Both *Harper's Weekly* and the *New Englander and Yale Review* were enthralled by the "Kishinev" movement of the late 1880s. Its leader, the convert Joseph Rabinowitz, declared that the "lamentable condition" of Eastern European Jews was caused by their rejection of Christ. He hoped to form an independent group of Jewish-Christians (Jews for Jesus?). Since Jews scorned those who reject their own religion, his followers would remain Jews to a certain degree, retaining circumcision and the seventh-day Sabbath. These would not be permanent, but were harmless concessions to the "weaknesses of those who cannot . . . throw off at once all Jewish feelings and prejudices."[15] The intensity of interest in this small and obviously insignificant splinter group was a vivid illustration of the continuing attraction exerted by the prospect of converting the Jews.

More frequently, however, the ardent efforts of the conversionists were ridiculed by the secular press. In the early years of the century *Niles Weekly Register*, a most influential publication that was not particularly kind to the Jews, expressed its cynicism about missionary efforts among the Jews. An 1816 article, for example, commented that in the previous five years $500,000 had been spent for "the conversion, real or supposed, of *five Jews.*" The rate of $100,000 per Jew was a considerable sum to pay even to purchase the "scattered nation. . . . Whether Jews convert Christians or Christians convince Jews, what is it to us in this land of civil and religious liberty?"[16]

Most newspapers showed little patience with missionary efforts, which increased as the number of Jews in America grew. An 1871 editorial in the *Philadelphia Sunday Dispatch* commented on a report issued by the Society for the Promotion of Christianity among the Jews. The association could claim the conversion of only a few Jews over a period of several years, a "miserable return," which the paper estimated as "a sixth of a Jew per annum." Despite funds contributed by "over-zealous Christians," the missionary L. C. Newman was forced to admit that he had not been able to convert even one of New York's one hundred thousand Jews in 1870. The lack of interest in supporting his efforts was, undoubtedly, evidence of the good sense of New York Christians. "New Yorkers know that there can be no hope in attempting to convert the Jews to Christianity as long as they feel Christianity is an untrue doctrine." Jews believed in the Messiah, the paper informed its reader, but held that He was yet to come. The missionary's salary was being increased, so "it may be expected that he will wander drearily about the country, seeking for impossible Jews whom he never expects to convert."[17] . . .

There was more criticism of the feeble efforts of the conversionist movement in the secular press than there was approval of its goals. The ceremonies of the Jews might be mistaken, but America granted freedom to even the most peculiar ideas.

The ever-present current of emotional religiosity in the nineteenth century found its way into popular poems, songs, and novels.[18] These tended to reflect the same mixture of contradictory attitudes toward the Jewish religion, the crucifixion, and the possibilities of conversion as those found in religious nonfiction. Many were impelled by similar motives as the "lo, the poor Indian" genre that was widespread at the same time.

Many early songs and poems were preoccupied with what James Russell Lowell called "thou blind unconverted Jew." These often showed great sympathy for the sufferings of the Jews and concluded that persecution would cease with conversion to the true faith. Songs, such as Mrs. Moran's 1830 "Fallen Is Thy Throne," depicted the plight of poor Jews who had been driven out of their fatherland and taken captive because they rejected the Messiah.[19] "The Jewish Maiden" lamented her lost homeland, "I n'er shall repose on thy bosom again." Reverend Eastburn's "The Hebrew Mourner" acknowledged that Jehovah had forsaken "this city of God," but held forth the prospect "He preserves for his people a city more fair. . . ." Other songs, like "The Maid of Judah," and "The Hebrew Captive," had similar themes. Though conversionist in ideology, they certainly could not be classified as malicious. Rather, their tone tended to be sympathetic.

Religious novels enjoyed great popularity throughout the nineteenth century, particularly in mid-century at the height of religious revivalism.

Some were designed for the edification of children to reinforce the lessons of formal study.[20] The American Sunday School Union was particularly active in their publication. Historical novels for adults with proselytizing themes became very popular starting in the 1830s. The first really successful author in this genre was William Ware, a Unitarian minister. His best seller was *Zenobia,* written in 1837.[21] One character was a religious Jew, Isaac, who was, paradoxically, presented as admirable while Judaism itself was condemned for its aridity and lack of love. Isaac eloquently defends his fellow Jews against charges of avarice and usury. This mixture was typical of the basic ambiguity characteristic of these novels.

A similar ambivalence was apparent in the works of the most popular of the authors of biblical novels, the Episcopal priest Joseph Holt Ingraham. He enjoyed immense success with three novels romanticizing the "grandeur of Hebrew History." His books were so popular that publishers outbid each other to pay him the previously unheard-of sum of $10,000 plus royalties for the second book of his series. *The Prince of the House of David* (1855) went through twenty-three editions and is said to have sold between four and five million copies. *The Pillar of Fire* (1857), the story of Moses and Joseph, was issued nine times. *The Throne of David* (1871) had twelve editions of its tale of David and Solomon.[22] The popularity of these books helped to stir up sentimental sympathy for Jews, overlaying antagonisms. Reverend Ingraham, himself, was careful to dedicate each of the books to American Jews, descendants of the biblical figures, in the expressed hope that they would finally see the light and convert. The inscription to *The Prince of the House of David,* for example, is an interesting illustration of the complex attitudes involved: "To the daughters of Israel, the country-women of Mary . . . this book is inscribed . . . they, as well as the unbelieving gentile, may be persuaded as they read that this is the very Christ."[23] The book is the story of Christ and the heroine is a Jewish convert, but the Jewish origin of Christ and his disciples is made clear. The other two books, dealing with chronologically earlier periods, are more unambiguously complimentary to the biblical Jews, also expressing the hope that modern Jews might one day "see the light."

The climax of the biblical novel was the ever-popular *Ben Hur* by Lew Wallace, which came out in 1880. This most phenomenally successful of all religious novels was typically equivocal in its attitudes toward Jews. The Jewish characters, as a whole, are presented as fine, intelligent, and noble people, the best the world had to offer up to that time. Although the crucifixion was presented in the traditional way, Wallace was careful to note that there were people of many different nationalities present, voicing hatred.[24]

The success of *Ben Hur* led to a flood of novels on biblical themes in the 1880s and 1890s. Most followed a similar pattern.[25] Florence Kingsley, who wrote four popular religious books, was most significant in promoting theological anti-Semitism.[26] The New Sabbath library published the books at five cents a copy and sold over one million, largely to young people. They presented vindictive, bigoted, and evil Jews who contrasted with virtuous Christians who turned the other cheek in the face of Jewish malice. Because of their deicide, the Jews were "a people displeasing to God and enemies to all mankind."

Although many of the biblical romances reflected similar viewpoints, there were some striking exceptions. In *The Archko Volume* (1887), William D. Mahan, a clergyman, attempted to bring humanity to his Jewish characters. He declared, "The Jews were honest in all their dealings with Christ. . . . Hence much of the prejudice among Protestants against the Jews is groundless. There never was a people more honest and more devoted to their country and their God than the Jews."[27] Mrs. T. F. Black, in one of the innumerable variants of the story of Esther, presented the tale as a moral caution against modern anti-Semitism. After two thousand years in the age of Christianity, "in what condition does it find the oppressed race so kindly delivered from persecution by a *heathen* monarch! The cause of this oppressed race is now undergoing the most infamous persecution since the days of the destruction of Jerusalem."[28]

Another popular genre was conversionist fiction in which individuals, or even entire families, were brought into Christianity in vivid contrast to the paltry real results of the proselytizing efforts.[29] Some, such as *The Jewish Twins* by "Aunt Friendly" (Sarah Schoonmaker Baker), were aimed at children. The twins, Muppin and Huppin, convert but remain Jews since, after all, "the Virgin Mary and the twelve disciples were of that people to which the Blessed Savior had chosen to belong. . . ." Mrs. C. A. Ogden's *Into the Light,* written in 1867, was a popular volume in the American Girl Series. All the Jews in the book, with the exception of the villain, convert. The Christian minister-hero tells his Jewish-convert wife, "Let us remember his chosen people and plead for their speedy restoration to the land of their heritage. . . ." "Aunt Hattie" (Henriette N. W. Baker) produced two versions of this theme. In *Lost but Found* (1866) the Seixas family converts and the aloof, cold Mr. Seixas becomes "kind and affable to all." Mrs. Baker expressed the hope that *Rebecca the Jewess* would bring the light of the true religion to "some beloved child of Israel who is groping in the dark." Although Annie Fellows Johnston's *In League with Israel* (1896) indicated that only by accepting Christ could a Jew fulfill his heritage, it was kindly in its portrait of Jews. It condemned Christians for mistreating Jews. The author hoped that her book would "turn all bitterness and prejudice into the broad spirit of brotherhood."

Much of the religious literature reinforced the picture of Jews as Christ-killers and of the Jewish religion as antiquated ritual that must inevitably give way to the higher truths of Christianity. However, there were many benevolent exceptions. The rampant sentimentality of the time was easily extended to a "poor oppressed people."

The secular press tended to oppose negative religious stereotypes for the most part. A reviewer in *Scribner's Monthly* in 1876, discussing George Eliot's influential *Daniel Deronda,* commented on objections to the Jewish element in the novel. Many Christians, the critic noted, remember that Jews killed Christ. They forget "that the race also gave birth to Christ. That Christ should be killed by any people among whom he might appear was inevitable. . . . The exceptional and marvelous thing was his production. . . ." He concluded with the retort of a Jew upon whom a Christian had spat, "that half Christendom worship a Jew and the other half a Jewess." *Harper's Magazine,* in a similar vein, complained in 1879 that "men of no Christian principle whatever flout better men today because other men murdered the founder of Christianity."[30]

An article in the April 1887 issue of *Ironclad Age* presented an interesting theological counterview to the hatred of Jews as deicides. Christians, it argued, could not condemn the Jews for crucifying Christ without condemning the salvation that flowed from that act. It was all part of God's "scheme." Therefore, the magazine concluded, "let us love the Jew for killing Christ."[31]

Even folk humor reflected the view that eighteen hundred or more years was a very long time to hold a grudge against a person or group.[32] Two similar stories from different sections of the country illustrate this. In both tales a Jew (storekeeper in one case, peddler in the other) is knocked down by a cowboy or Tennessee mountaineer who has just attended a camp meeting. When the Jew demands an explanation for this unprovoked violence, the ignorant Christian replies, "You crucified our Lord." The Jew responds that the event in question had occurred more than eighteen hundred years earlier and that he had nothing to do with it. The back country bumpkin apologizes profusely, explaining that he had just heard about the event and, thus, thought that it had happened recently. The joke and its popularity point to the skepticism of the average religious American about any continuing responsibility of the Jewish people for the death of Jesus.

Many writers felt that the Christian world owed the Jews gratitude as the people of the Bible, the originators of Christian belief, and the people who gave the world Christ and his disciples. A July 1826 article in the *North American Review* on interpretations of the New Testament pointed out the necessity of studying the Old Testament, which contains the origin of all Jewish institutions. The author reminded his readers, "Christ came not to destroy the law and the prophets, but to fulfill them." An 1867 review in the *Nation* discussed the Talmud. It acknowledged the ignorance of most Christians about that favorite bugaboo of the anti-Semite. "The morality of the New Testament is not original," the critic noted, it can be found in the Talmud. In that sense, "Christianity popularized Talmudic morality."[33]

The reminder that Christ himself was a Jew was frequently reiterated by those seeking to counter negative stereotypes. *Niles Weekly Register*, in an 1846 report of an "Israelitish Convention" to reform the Jewish religion in Germany, commented that Jews have been called a blot upon mankind, "yet the Redeemer was one of them." His descendants were worthy of respect. Whenever they had the power, "they exert it to elevate their race." They employ wealth to "spread among themselves education—a higher philosophy, a purer charity and a truer religion."[34] The same idea was expressed in 1882 in *Frank Leslie's Illustrated News-*

paper, a publication usually described as unfriendly to Jews. It reprinted a well-known poem by Joaquin Miller that enumerated the debt the world owed to the Jews and concluded:

> Who gave the patient Christ? I say,
> Who gave you Christian creed? Yea, yea,
> Who gave your very God to you?
> The Jew! The Jew! the hated Jew![35]

A few of the respondents in the *American Hebrew* discussion of the causes of anti-Semitism addressed themselves to this issue.[36] Reverend Washington Gladden conceded that prejudice had been fostered "unwittingly" by Sunday School teachings. As a solution, he urged, "We ought to keep it before our children that Jesus himself was a Jew." Oliver Wendell Holmes gave one of the most revealing responses. He noted that his own background had tended to stress the curse upon the Jews for rejecting Jesus. "The Jews are with us as a perpetual lesson to teach us modesty. . . . The religion we profess is not self-evident. It did not convince the people to whom it was sent." In his concluding poem, "At the Pantomime," Holmes described his visit to a theater filled with stereotypical "black-bearded Hebrew" men and "orient-eyed" women. They rushed in, poking him and bringing out his prejudices against the "cursed unbelieving Jew," the "spawn of the race that slew its Lord." Then he looked more closely at the Jew closest to him:

> Soft gentle loving eyes that gleam . . .
>
> So looked that other child of Shem,
> The Maiden's boy of Bethlehem!
> —And thou couldst scorn the peerless blood
> That flows unmingled from the Flood. . . .
>
> Thy prophets caught the Spirit's flame,
> From thee the Son of Mary came'
> With thee the Father deigned to dwell,—
> Peace be upon thee Israel!

In 1891 the *New York Tribune* summarized the attitudes of men of good will in an article on Judaism and Christianity. Benevolence, it declared, was finally eliminating "insensate emnity and antipathy born of ignorance." When our "Jewish brethren" erected a magnificent Temple on Fifth Avenue, the feeling was not that of hatred or envy, but of "generous sympathy." A Christian "cannot help respect a faith out of which his was born." The Jews maintained their ideals through centuries of oppression. Americans must admire "a faith that makes so much for a noble manhood and an exalted ideal of citizenship."[37]

A related favorable image concerned the "marvelous" and mysterious survival of the Jewish people despite centuries of persecution. This aroused a combination of guilt feelings for Christian misdeeds and pride among many Americans who saw their nation as a haven for the oppressed. In 1829 *The Constitutional Whig* ran a series of articles about Judaism by Isaac Leeser, one of the pioneeers of American Judaism. The editor reproved Christians who despised Jews. If, as some believed, the Jews were being punished by God, this "ought to entitle them to the . . . compassion of the more favored Gentile." If, as most people would do, one rejected the idea that "perfect justice can punish the thousandth innocent generation . . . then we ought to admire . . . that high and unbending spirit of the Jews which have preserved their nation. . . ." Christians should feel "awe, admiration, sympathy and reverence" for the Jew who remained the same as the one who worshiped at the Second Temple two thousand years earlier. "We think it a glorious distinction to our country that here the Jews have found a substantial fulfillment of the promise of being restored to the Chosen Land. . . ."[38]

The *North American Review* expressed a similar viewpoint, as did the *Boston Journal*.[39] In an 1831 discussion of Milman's popular history of the Jews, the critic in the *Review* remarked that Jewish history since the destruction of Jerusalem was "truly wonderful." Though scattered, they were able to adapt themselves to each area with "a wonderful flexibility." The character of the modern Jew, particularly his fortitude, was the same as in ancient days. Americans should respect Jews and abandon foolish attempts to convert them. How could anyone expect them to embrace the faith of their persecutors? An 1845 review of four books about Jews in the same magazine also characterized Jewish history as a history "of wonders." They had exerted "a mighty influence over the faith and practice of mankind." Their sufferings, surpassing human endurance, and their survival was "the standing miracle of modern times." An 1837 *Journal* article, "The Jews," noted that, despite inducements to abandon the religion of their forefathers, they had remained Jews. "They have never for a moment forgotten or denied their religion, their customs or NAME. . . ."

Many well-known Americans expressed the same point of view in letters and speeches.[40] Zebulon Vance, in his widely delivered lecture, noted the contradiction of people who despised the Jew "but accept and adore the pure conception of a God which he taught us and whose real existence the history of the Jew more than all else establishes." Every Christian church was an offshoot of its Jewish roots. If one were to eliminate all of Judaism from Christianity, "nothing but an unmeaning superstition" would remain. Jews "may safely defy the rest of mankind to show such undying adherence to accepted faith, such wholesale sacrifice for conscience sake."

Authors and speakers in the last two decades of the century, when foreign persecutions were most intense, were particularly struck by Jewish survival.[41] Sidney Lanier, the poet, in an 1881 lecture at Johns Hopkins, rhapsodized that when he saw even the poorest old clothes dealer, "I seem to feel a little wind fresh off the sea of Tiberius." Although the Jews lacked a homeland, they "made a literature which is at home in every nation." He believed that to gather the Jewish people together and restore them in their "thousand-fold consecrated home" was the noblest mission possible. Crawford Howell Toy, in an 1890 work, *Judaism and Christianity,* praised the religious instinct that had produced prophets and poets inspired by God. "It is a proof of the intense vitality of the Jewish people that they did not . . . succumb to the oppression of foreign religious domination. Their energy came from their . . . consciousness of possession of highest truth. . . ." In the same year, Charles Loring Brace, in *The Unknown God,* concluded, "we do not sufficiently render justice to the Jews' great services in human history . . . they deserve the lasting respect of mankind."

Harper's New Monthly Magazine of January 1894 included an interesting article titled "The Mission of the Jews." The author neatly reversed the common view of the dispersion of the Jews as a sign of God's punishment. Instead, he accepted the Reform Jewish notion that it was an indication of God's mission to serve as priests and prophets. "It was by a wondrous design of Providence that the people of Israel was dispersed over the world, in order that it might penetrate with its spirit the whole humanity." The Jews had achieved through their dispersion a remarkable steadfastness of belief. As a result, Jews had become the "chief bearers of spirituality."[42]

The most passionate defense of the Jews, summarizing many of the themes discussed above, can be found in a mid-century work. *The*

Progress of Religious Ideas through Successive Ages, by Lydia Maria Child.[43] She was a well-known abolitionist and reformer, with the New England interest in the People of the Old Testament. She was most concerned about "the relentless, universal and prolonged" persecution of the Jews. "Their constancy and fortitude equaled their unparalleled wrongs." The "darkest blot" in the history of Christians was their treatment of the Jews even though "we reverence their scriptures . . . Christ and his Mother and Apostles were Jews." Only a very few of the people were responsible for the crucifixion. Even those "acted with the blind bigotry so generally manifested by established churches toward non-conformists." Although so few were actually implicated, the church fathers irrationally condemned all Jews as Christ-killers, "as if each one of them had put him to death." Christians should acknowledge Jewish resisters as heroic martyrs who "at the cost of incredible sacrifice . . . still set their face steadfastly toward Jerusalem." She concluded, "We owe the Jews an immense debt of gratitude."

While Lydia Child's extreme judeophile views were, perhaps, unusual, there was extensive coverage of the Jewish religion in the press. There was a fascination with Jewish customs, practices, and rites, particularly the "exotic." Interest in movements within Judaism and celebrations of the building of synagogues was widespread. The treatment of Judaism showed the same ambivalence as the discussions of the religious history of the Jews. While many of the comments were openly admiring, some others were sternly censorious of "outdated" rituals.

The *North American Review* was particularly concerned with the movement for reform within Judaism as shown by Isaac Harby's pamphlets for the "reformed Society of Israelites."[44] The writer had assumed that "the minds of Israelites were so wedded to their religious peculiarities as to be impenetrable to the spirit of innovation." Jews had been considered to be the most reactionary religious group. Christians, who had observed the "singular rites" in synagogues, had not suspected that there were Jews who had surmounted such peculiarities as an "air of indifference," indistinct and rapid chants, and constant comings and goings. Harby merited praise. Although inwardly a firm Jew, he was willing to accommodate the forms "to the conciliatory, compensating and sacrificing spirit of the age." His opponents' ideas were treated with respect due to their "solemn associations of antiquity," although the author clearly preferred the "new school." In the end, the author felt certain that the spirit of the age would convert the synagogue "with its obsolete ceremonials, its unintelligible language . . . into a more rational sanctuary." This was the viewpoint of an enlightened member of the upper class, probably a Unitarian. The condescension was obvious. It is also revealing, however, that there was not the slightest hint that the Jew should ultimately convert to Christianity. The main hope he expressed was that the new "reformed" temples would attract thousands "to be strengthened and enlightened, and their hearts to be warmed, consoled and purified."

The consecrations of synagogues were reported early and in great detail. Evidently this was a subject of some interest to readers. *Niles Weekly Register* in 1823, for example, described the "impressive ceremony" in the Great Synagogue in London with rolls of law in "peculiar cases, most splendidly ornamental. . . ."[45]

The description of the consecration of "Roudoufe Sholum" of Philadelphia in 1843 by the *United States Gazette* was typical of mid-century press coverage. The ceremony was described in painstaking detail. The scrolls "attracted general and undivided attention." (Christians were often curious about the central importance of the Torah scrolls.) The singing was "beautifully performed" by the (as usual) lovely ladies of the choir. Most of the state justices, a large representation of the Christian clergy, the bar, and the press were present. The building was described in detail as well. . . .[46]

At the other extreme, the Sunday School Union book, *The Jew at Home and Abroad,* condemned many Jewish practices. Even though the Jews were "indestructible" and deserving of gratitude for the Old Testament, their rejection of Jesus had led them into delusion. They had turned to the Talmud, which contained many offensive sections, "ridiculous laws," and directions for "absurd and superstitious practices which are so numerous" in Jewish rites. The author stressed the resemblance between Judaism and "Popery." Both were beset by tradition with little judgment allowed to individuals. Still, the writer cautioned, Christians must continue to show "compassion."[47]

Most of the newspapers regularly reported Jewish festivals and events by the 1870s. The *New York Times,* not yet Jewish-owned, was a good example.[48] Like many other periodicals and newspapers, the *Times* was interested in the rising Reform movement. On 3 April 1870 it reported that "Reformed Judaism" had "excited a good deal of attention in the

Christian world." This movement illustrated the "strange vitality of a downtrodden and persecuted but strong-willed race." The power of amalgamation that was creating a great people out of may diverse elements in America, "has also touched the chosen race and is bringing them more into harmony with the modes of thinking that prevail around them." There followed a continuous stream of editorials commending the "reformed school" as superior to a medieval Orthodoxy, which was oblivious to the needs of a new era. A story, "Jews in America," described the congregations of the city. The finest and costliest was Emanuel, which was the first to declare the "domination of reason over blind and bigoted faith." It stood for the triumph of the "Judaism which proclaims the spirit of religion as being of more importance than the letter." . . .

Cities with small Jewish populations were at least as scrupulous in reporting Jewish holidays and special events. Salt Lake City papers were typical in that respect.[49] The *Salt Lake City Tribune* was particularly conscientious. An issue of 2 October 1872 described "Rosh Hasheno," followed by "the holiest of all Sabbaths, a day observed by Israelites from time immemorial. . . ." The paper noted sadly that the Western world had been contaminated by apostasy and wondered whether any of "our Jewish friends" had caught the disease. It was relieved, on the following day, to witness a large attendance at the service, "indeed we were not previously aware that so many inhabitants of this city were of Jewish extraction." On Yom Kippur the paper was again pleased to report scrupulous observance. The *Tribune* informed its readers during Passover week of 1876 that Jews celebrated the occasion by "abstaining from all food except unleavened bread as commanded by the great lawgiver." Somewhat later, when the cornerstone for a new synagogue was laid, the paper commented enthusiastically, "The building will be an ornament to the city." The dedication services were "impressive and interesting . . . a more attractive place of worship does not exist in the West."

Some observers even responded positively to mysterious Orthodox services, as demonstrated by an 1875 visit to an Orthodox synagogue by a writer for *Liberal Christian*. Although the commentator, like all visitors, noted the "business-like air" and the "walking about and talking," he did not regard these as basic. The service itself was entirely in Hebrew and was "musical, plaintive, devout, triumphant." The reporter queried,

"What Christian church can boast a service of such antiquity? Where is there a ritual so free from idolatry and error? Where is there a service more democratic?" . . .[50]

The arrival of large numbers of Eastern Jews to New York increased the interest in Jewish ceremonial. New York newspapers described "exotic" Jewish holidays in considerable detail for the benefit of their Christian readers.[51] The *New York Tribune* was particularly careful in its descriptions. The New Year was a season of "impressive ceremonies" with "weird, tearful, wailing melodies," which the listener could never forget. Even the Feast of the Tabernacles, with its strange booths, was fully covered. Most of the services took place in "the humble synagogues of the poor." The strongest impulse in the ghetto was the maintenance of religion in these tiny synagogues where one found not a single trace of New York, "not a word of English." The *Evening Post* reported that each little town of the Pale of Jewish settlement was represented by a synagogue in New York. Chanukah was a "merry season of domestic fun making." The *Post* advised people who thought of Jews as "a sullen folk in dismal homes" to witness this celebration. They would find "many prospering lords of large families dispensing 'mehr fun als a circus.' " The *Times* contrasted the Reform and Orthodox services of the rich and poor. On the East Side, the "weeping and wailing of the supplicants could be heard for blocks." In the fashionable temples attended by richly attired men and women, while the services "were also fraught with deep emotion," the worshipers displayed no such open feelings. The rituals of the Eastern Jews were "oriental" and strange. The services of the Reform Jews were certainly more comprehensible and "American" to newspaper observers and, therefore, far more thoroughly reported. . . .

In America the religious image of the Jew was filled with ambiguities. There is no question about the continuing power of the old view of the Jews as crucifiers of the Son of God, a people who had been punished for eternity for that heinous crime. Indeed, that idea of the religious place of the Jew has continued to be potent in the minds of some Americans to the present day. A related view with widespread circulation was that the Jewish religion had existed only as a precursor to Christianity, and had long since outlived its viability in the modern world. Not only did religious and Sunday-school texts propagate this perception of the Jew, but religious novels, some of which were among the most phenomenally successful books of the century, also often reinforced such ideas.

It is also true, on the other hand, that some of the very religious writers were also the most aware of the Jews as the people of the Bible and the originators of Christianity. Even the most ardent conversionists were not always unkind in their estimates of Jews. Believing, as they did, that the Second Coming was dependent upon the restoration of the "chosen people" and their acceptance of the true Messiah, many expressed a benevolent interest in the Jews. Although patronizing or even scornful about Jewish religious rites, most preached that respect and tolerance was the best approach.

In addition, there was a strong countercurrent in America, especially apparent in the secular press. This was the image of the Jews as the ancient people of the Bible who had preserved the worship of one God, who had courageously overcome the most terrible persecution the world had known, and to whom Christians should be grateful for their basic ideas and for Christ himself. It was a great source of pride that these ancient people could worship with complete freedom only in America. This confirmed America's superiority to the bigoted Old World and should not be tampered with. For that reason, the secular press was largely opposed to missionary activities. There was a genuine interest in the religious customs of the Jews, and while this interest was sometimes condescending, it was rarely unkind. The building of synagogues was universally welcomed, and the consecrations were characteristically attended by the leading citizens of the community. While most Christian observers seemed to prefer Reform Judaism as more "American," this was a reflection of the desire to assimilate Jews into the American mainstream, rather than an unfriendly wish to eliminate the Jewish religion. At any rate, by the latter years of the century, hostile religious images of the Jews diminished considerably, a reflection of a more secularized society. By that time, other, nonreligious images—both positive and negative—had become more significant.

NOTES

1. Nicholas Berdyaev, *Christianity and Anti-Semitism* (New York, 1954), 6.
2. Fred Gladstone Bratton, *The Crime of Christendom* (New York, 1969), 168.
3. The continued potency of this religious image of the Jew in the twentieth century can be seen in a study by Charles Y. Glock and Rodney Stark, *Christian Beliefs and Anti-Semitism* (New York, 1969), 62–65.
4. *Harper's Magazine* 17 (July 1858):267.
5. Hannah Adams, *The History of the Jews* (Boston, 1817), 1:7, 43, 53, 287, 290, 543. See also Rev. Michael Russell, *Palestine of the Holy Land* (New York, 1833), 19, 301.
6. Elizabeth Peabody, *Sabbath Lessons* (Salem, Mass., 1813), 32, 49–50, 60; A. A. *Annals of the Jewish Nation* (New York, 1832), iii–iv, 311, 354. See also H. P. Peet, *Scripture Lessons for the Young* (New York, 1846).
7. M. Johnstone, *Stories from the History of the Jews* (New York, 1853), 194, 199–200, 206, 215, 231, 238–39. For similar views see E. C. Forbes, *Easy Lessons on Scripture History* (New York, 1859), 98–99.
8. It should be noted that only in the second half of the twentieth century did Protestant religious groups begin to reexamine Sunday-school texts in the light of studies revealing the extent of anti-Semitism found in these books. A good description of the kind of material in modern Sunday-school books can be found in: James Brown, "Christian Teaching and Anti-Semitism: Scrutinizing Religious Texts," *Commentary*, December 1957, 494–501.
9. *The Churchman*, 24 March 1855, quoted in *American Israelite*, 29 April 1855. Similar views were expressed by the *Christian Intelligencer* and the *Catholic Telegraph*, quoted in *American Israelite*, 7 August 1858 and 29 January 1869.
10. Rev. Charles A. Goodrich, *A Pictorial Descriptive View and History of All Religions* (New York, 1860), 42–44, 52. Hannah W. Richardson, *Judea in Her Desolations* (Philadelphia, 1861), iii, 269–70.
11. W. D. Morrison, *The Jews under Roman Rule* (New York, 1891), 360–61. John W. Mears, *From Exile to Overthrow* (Philadelphia, 1881), 238–45. See also F. W. Farmer, *The Herods* (New York, 1898).
12. Nathaniel Hawthorne, "The Star of Calvary," in *An American Anthology, 1781–1900* ed. Edmund Stedman (New York, 1900), 191.
13. Quoted in Adams, *History*, 2:214–15.
14. Moses Stuart, *Sermon at the Ordination of the Reverend G. Schouffler as Missionary to the Jews* (Andover, Mass., 1831), 5–8, 19, 20. Also, Alexander Keith, *The Land of Israel* (New York, 1844), 381. This reflected views similar to those popularized by the English author, Rev. H. H. Milman, *The History of the Jews* (New York, 1832). Milman was widely read in the United States. For a typically ambiguous mixture of admiration, condemna-

tion, and conversionist fervor, see also, American Sunday School Union, *The Jew at Home and Abroad* (Philadelphia, 1845).

15. *Harper's Weekly* 32 (3 March 1888): 155–56; and *New Englander and Tale Review* 16 (March 1890): 245–50. Support for conversion attempts exists in modern America. In the Glock and Stark study 48% of all Protestants supported efforts to convert the Jews (p. 66).

16. *Niles Weekly Register* 11 (14 December 1816) :260. Also, 26 (17 July 1824):326; 30 (3 June 1826): 234.

17. *Philadelphia Sunday Dispatch*, 28 May 1871.

18. Religious literature is covered more extensively in Louis Harap, *The Image of the Jew in American Literature* (Philadelphia, 1974), 135–88.

19. All the songs quoted in this chapter come from the collection of the Newberry Library, Chicago.

20. Some good examples are: Rev. Jarvis Gregg, *Selumiel* (Philadelphia, 1833); *Hadassah, the Jewish Orphan* (Philadelphia, 1834); Sarah Pogson Smith, *Zerah, the Believing Jew* (Philadelphia, 1837).

21. William Ware, *Zenobia* (New York, 1843).

22. Lee M. Friedman, "Jews in Early American Literature," *More Books: The Bulletin of the Boston Public Library* 17, no. 10, 463; Don B. Seitz, "A Prince of Best Sellers," *Publishers Weekly*, 21 February 1931, 940.

23. Joseph Holt Ingraham, *Prince of the House of David* (Philadelphia, 1855), vii, 400. Also J. H. Ingraham, *Pillar of Fire* (Boston, 1888), i.

24. Lew Wallace, *Ben Hur, A Tale of Christ* (New York, 1880), 545.

25. Some examples are F. Marion Crawford, *Zoroaster;* Elizabeth Stuart Phelps, *The Master of Magicians* and *The Story of Jesus Christ;* Rose Porter, *A Daughter of Israel;* Eldbridge Brooks, *Son of Issacher;* E. F. Burr, *Aleph, the Chaldean;* J. Breckinridge Ellis, *Shem;* Mary Elizabeth Jennings, *Asa of Bethlehem;* Caroline Atwater Mason, *The Quiet King;* William A. Hammond, *The Son of Perdition;* all published from 1885 to 1900.

26. Florence M. Kingsley, *Titus* (New York, 1894), *Stephen* (New York, 1896), *Paul* (New York, 1897), and *The Cross Triumphant* (New York, 1898). The quote is from *Paul*, 348, vi.

27. William D. Mahan, *The Archko Volume* (Philadelphia, 1887), 16–17.

28. Mrs. T. F. Black, *Hadassah* (Chicago, 1895), 196.

29. Sarah Schoonmaker Baker, *The Jewish Twins* (New York, 1860), 134; Mrs. C. A. Ogden, *Into the Light* (Boston, 1899), 322; Henriette N. W. Baker, *Lost But Found* (Boston, 1871), 322, and *Rebecca the Jewess* (Boston, 1879), i; H. H. Boyeson, *A Daughter of the Philistines* (Boston, 1883), 176; Annie F. Johnston, *In League with Israel* (New York, 1896), 303.

30. *Scribner's Monthly* 13 (November 1876): 130; *Harper's Magazine*, October 1879.

31. *Ironclad Age*, 26 April 1887, quoted in *Israelite*, 6 May 1887.

32. Cited in Rudolf Glanz, *The Jew in Old American Folklore* (New York, 1961), 13.

33. *North American Review* 33 (July 1826): 102–4; *Nation* 5 (14 November 1867): 388. For a similar point of view, see also Thomas Jefferson's letter to Joseph Marx, cited in Abraham Karp, ed., *The Jewish Experience in America* (New York, 1969), 26.

34. *Niles Weekly Register* 69 (3 January 1846): 283–48.

35. *Frank Leslie's Illustrated Newspaper*, 4 November 1882.

36. Philip Cowen, ed., *Prejudice against the Jews* (New York, 1928), 62, 18–19. This was a republication of a symposium in the *American Hebrew*, 4 April 1890.

37. *New York Tribune*, 27 September 1891.

38. *Constitutional Whig*, 9 January 1829.

39. *North American Review* 32 (January 1831): 254, 263; 60 (April 1845): 330; *Boston Journal*, quoted in Philip S. Foner, *Jews in American History* (New York, 1945), 50.

40. Zebulon Vance, "The Scattered Nation," in Clement Dowd, *The Life of Zebulon Vance* (Charlotte, N.C., 1897), 371–74, 385. Similar ideas were expressed by Daniel Webster, quoted in Bertram Korn, *Eventful Years and Experiences* (Cincinnati, 1954), 49; and by Theodore Parker, in John Weiss, ed., *The Life and Correspondence of Theodore Parker* (New York, 1969), 2: 497.

41. Sidney Lanier, quoted in Joseph L. Baron, ed., *Stars and Sand* (Philadelphia, 1943), 431–32; Crawford Howell Toy, *Judaism and Christianity* (Boston, 1890), 237; Charles Loring Brace, *The Unknown God* (New York, 1890), 72.

42. *Harper's New Monthly Magazine* 88 (January 1894): 262–64.

43. Lydia Maria Child, *The Progress of Religious Ideas through Successive Ages* (New York, 1855), 2:152–53; 3: 439–42.

44. *North American Review*, July 1824, 113.

45. *Niles Weekly Register* 25 (1 November 1823); 26 (13 March 1824).

46. *United States Gazette*, 14, 15, 16 April 1843.

47. *Jew at Home*, 111, 114, 120, 123.

48. *New York Times*, 3 April, 1870; 5 September 1870; 16 October 1870; 8 January 1871; 18 December 1870; 10 March 1872; 22 April 1872; 12 May 1878.

49. Quoted in Leon L. Watters, *The Pioneer Jews of Utah* (New York, 1952), 73–75, 85–86.

50. Quoted in *American Israelite*, 13 August 1875.

51. *New York Tribune*, 10 October 1894; 6 September 1896; 24 September 1899; 6 April 1898; 16 February 1896; *Evening Post*, 25 September 1897; 12 December 1895; *New York Times*, 7 October 1897.

6

Antisemitism in the Gilded Age: The Jewish View

Naomi W. Cohen

Over the past twenty-five years, several significant studies have appeared on the genesis of American antisemitism. Although no consensus has been reached on whether hostility toward Jews was an example of ethnic prejudice which was also felt by the Irish, Italians, and Germans, or whether it more closely resembled religious bigotry experienced by Catholics, most scholars agree that it was not significant until the last quarter or even last decade of the nineteenth century. Some accounts have noted the ambivalent feelings of Americans toward Jews, along with a countervailing current of philosemitism, and a case has been made for distinguishing between ideological antisemitism, or the images of the Jew as Christ-killer and Shylock, and the actual eruption of discrimination. For the catalyst which triggered late nineteenth-century hostility, status rivalry and narrow nationalism have been singled out as have the Populists and agrarian radicalism.[1]

In all these studies, scant attention has been paid to the testimony of "the victims"—their interpretations of what threatened them, how seriously they took isolated attacks, and how they proposed to respond. Victims or participants are hardly the most objective analysts, but in this case the explanations by Jews who experienced or reported on nineteenth-century antisemitism suggest parameters of the problem that historians have generally overlooked.

Reprinted in part by permission from *Jewish Social Studies* 41 (Summer–Fall 1979): 187–210.

The term antisemitism was coined in western Europe in the 1870s[2] and only slowly came into use in the United States. American Jews did not refer to themselves as Semites; some even thought that it was more polite to say Israelite or Hebrew rather than Jew.[3] There was less agreement on how to define a Jew. All said that he was first a member of a religious body, but they did not satisfactorily resolve how to designate a heritage which included components other than matters of faith. Since the term ethnic was unknown, they used loose labels—a people, a nationality, a race—with utter lack of consistency or precision. When they analyzed discrimination in the Gilded Age they generally saw themselves as victims of religious bigotry. Since prejudice affected the secularist and infidel as much as the observant Jew, however, they had to admit that, whatever its genesis, hostility against the Jews was directed against an entire people.

American Jewish spokesmen would not have agreed that the Seligman-Hilton affair of 1877, often highlighted as the start of social discrimination, marked a novel departure in Christian behavior. The well-known story of the exclusion of the famous banker from Saratoga's Grand Union Hotel excited Christian America just because it involved Joseph Seligman, the head of the prominent banking firm and personal friend of President Grant.[4] The Jews had noted social ostracism even before. In 1864, an article in the *Jewish Messenger* of New York stated that Jews were barred from the "favored circles of society."[5] Two years later, it editorialized on the same theme: "We are unable to deny . . . that even among the so-called educated classes there is a distaste for, and apprehension of, *fraternity* for the Jew, which often inclines them to wish that their ancestors had not so readily granted *liberty* and *equality* to the non-Christian."[6] Oscar Straus, who later became minister to Turkey and a member of Theodore Roosevelt's cabinet, recorded his own taste of discrimination at that time. He entered Columbia College in 1867, where, he said, "I was under many disadvantages, comparatively poor, not as well dressed as most of my class-mates, with no social standing and a Jew. For the latter offense I was even excluded from the literary society of the undergraduates."[7] That Christians shunned the presence of Jews was verified in a book about New York, written by reporter Matthew Hale Smith. Calling Jews a "nuisance to any Christian neighborhood," Smith described the reverse pattern of exclusiveness, i.e., how Christians deserted residential and resort areas when they became "infested" by Jews.[8] . . .

True, the Seligman affair followed by the Corbin episode in 1879, which involved the plan to bar Jews from Manhattan Beach, heralded an increase in social exclusionary patterns as well as an awareness of their pervasiveness.[9] However, to the Anglo-Jewish press which had exposed hostility to the Jew since the 1840s, nothing qualitatively new had transpired. The Jewish population in the United States did not reach 250,000 until 1880, but to nineteenth-century Jews that was no reason to minimize the significance of earlier hostility. Since they did not distinguish between ideological Jew-hatred and actual discrimination—between a Good Friday sermon which charged them with deicide and a school which excluded Jewish students—the existence of antisemitism depended neither on numbers nor the visibility of Jews. "Rishuth" as they called it (literally Hebrew for wickedness) cropped up at different times and in various forms.

Jews living one hundred years ago would also have questioned the reasoning which fixed upon the 1870s on economic grounds. To say that by then the German Jews who had arrived in the 1840s and 1850s had attained positions of affluence, which in turn aroused jealousy and resentment,[10] implies that their rapid mobility had gone unnoticed before. Not so, said Isaac Leeser, prominent Philadelphia rabbi and editor of the *Occident,* who was one of the most knowledgeable about the contemporary Jewish scene. He claimed as early as 1863 that the increase in numbers and prosperity of the Jews was attracting attention and causing a "sentiment inimical to Judaism."[11] Two years later he added:

With the great increase of Hebrew residents in America, their general prosperity has also augmented in the same ratio, and in most large cities Jewish people occupy some of the finest residences. Now, if nothing else would cause prejudice, this circumstance will do so to a certainty. . . . While we are poor and unsightly, we may be tolerated; but let us only look up, and become the social equals of our neighbors, and their ire will be at once roused.[12]

The *American Israelite,* the influential organ of reform Judaism under the editorship of Rabbi Isaac Mayer Wise of Cincinnati, explained that the seeds of social prejudice had been sown during the Civil War. At that time, according to the paper, the mischief was started in Washington, D.C., by public figures and newspaper correspondents who delighted in vilifying the Jew. This alarming upsurge of prejudice testified to the social upheaval brought about by the war: "A revolution of the government had just been accomplished, and the highest had become the lowest, and the lowest had become the highest. . . . [A] lower stratum had been brought to the surface, and with it all the virtues and vices of upstarts in this world; hence also prejudices against the Jew." Washington society was infected, and the poison spread throughout the country, leaving long-lasting damage to Jewish/Christian relations.

That same editorial mentioned a second, and indeed, more substantial cause of the new Jew-hatred. It blamed the religious revival begun during the war and carried over into the political arena for wielding a "nugatory influence" on the behavior of Christians toward Jews.[13] Wise's line of reasoning, which merits consideration in light of some aspects of religious ferment in the postwar period, not only points to the earlier terminus ad quo for nineteenth-century antisemitism but indicates as well the need to look beyond social competition or agrarian radicalism for an understanding of anti-Jewish sentiment in the Gilded Age. . . .

Well into the nineteenth century, the Jews had ample reason to fear the influence of Christian teachings on their political rights and status in society. Orthodox Protestants invoked the deicide charge in order to justify the retention of the ban against officeholding by Jews in Maryland. Governor J. H. Hammond of South Carolina saw no cause to formulate his Thanksgiving Day proclamation in nonsectarian terms; Jews whose ancestors had crucified Jesus had to understand that the United States was a Christian country. Another South Carolinian, Judge John O'Neal, wrote into a Sunday law decision that Christianity was the source and standard of true morality.[14] Many such disabilities and slurs were cleared up when Jews or their defenders raised the issue. If, however, traditional intolerance were invigorated by new religious agitation, the prospects for total amelioration could grow dimmer. Thus, when the Jews as a group denounced the spirit of Know-Nothingism, it was not because of a love for Catholics but from fear that any minority group could become a target for renewed persecution if one denomination could dominate others.[15] Some were uneasy too about the antebellum reform movements such as temperance and abolition, which in large measure were spurred by the social activism of the churches. If they became religious causes, those crusades, no different from the Sunday law agitation, harbored the possibility of an adverse fallout on a non-Christian minority.[16] Furthermore, as long as public officials acted out the precepts of fundamentalist Christianity, and as long as Christian leaders fused those precepts with political activity, it was meaningless to distinguish between ideological Jew-hatred and overt hostility.

Before the Civil War, the Jews reacted to separate instances of disabilities or prejudice in a pragmatic fashion. It would have been futile to champion the absolute separation of church and state, for the social climate of the age underscored the importance of organized religion. Also, since it was unlikely that Christians would modify their teachings radically or quickly, Jews believed that they could do little more than ask for public recognition, at least under law, of Judaism's equality with Christianity. This was their approach whether fighting for the right to hold office or to gain exemption from Sunday laws for those who kept Saturday as a holy day, or when renouncing the Christian wording of Thanksgiving Day proclamations or sectarian teaching in the public schools. They pleaded that their faith inculcated principles of virtue and good citizenship and that its followers were entitled to the same civic privileges enjoyed by others. When New York's oldest synagogue petitioned the state legislature for aid to its religious school, it asked only for "the same countenance and encouragement which has been exhibited to others."[17] Often Jews invoked the American principle of freedom of religion to silence their detractors. In reality, however, they were fusing two concepts under that rubic, freedom of conscience and equality of religion.

New heights in Jew-hatred were reached during the Civil War. In the fall of 1862 General Grant expelled the Jews as a class from military territories in the border states on the grounds that they were engaged in illegal trading ventures beyond the Union lines. Understandably, American Jewry was stunned. This act was qualitatively different from the more typical slights they suffered when Lincoln ordered strict observance of Sunday in the armed forces (and did not consider privileges for Sabbath observers) and when Congress decided against providing for Jewish chaplains.[18] Again, Isaac Leeser found the underlying source for the order and America's willingness to accept it in Christian prejudice. The church, he said, "is the seat of danger to liberty of conscience and perhaps the permanence of free institutions of all kinds." Leeser bitterly attacked the secular press for keeping silent: "[T]he matter did not concern them of course, the parties threatened with such ill-usage were not Christians, not even negroes, nothing but Jews! . . . and those, every one knows, are enemies of Christ and his apostles."[19]

Leeser reported heightened religious sentiment during the Civil War which he, like Wise, interpreted to mean increased hostility toward the Jew. The war had inflamed religious passion; Jews, despite their military service in both the Union and Confederacy, were singled out for all sorts of "crimes." In the North where the churches had thrown themselves into the antislavery movement, abolition was considered a victory for Christianity, and Jews were criticized for not having been sufficiently outspoken against slavery. Their general prosperity nurtured the mounting antipathy, for how could unbelievers enjoy earthly rewards which rightly belonged to members of the saving church?[20]

More threatening was the possibility that the new religious fervor would spill over into the political area and cause dissenters from the majority position to forfeit civil rights. Despite America's tradition of religious freedom, that possibility did not appear too far-fetched after a war which signaled a major constitutional and social upheaval, particularly to a people whose history was punctuated by suffering at the hands of churches or church-dominated states. No wonder then that Jews took seriously the growing momentum of the movement to engraft Christianity upon the Constitution. Just before the war, a small group of Presbyterians had met in Allegheny, Pennsylvania, and petitioned the Senate for a constitutional amendment acknowledging the authority of God, Jesus, and Scriptural law. After 1861 the group drew support from the belief that the destruction and suffering of the war were marks of God's vengeance against a nation which was not sufficiently Christian. By 1863 the movement was considerably more significant, having attracted other denominations and even some prominent public officials, and it continued to expand from year to year. Jews derived hope for its defeat in the divisions which precluded a unified stand among the multiple Protestant denominations, but Leeser, for one, sketched the dire results should rights to vote or hold office be predicated upon a religious base.[21]

Leeser's apprehensions, which were shared by the young Jewish defense agency, the Board of Delegates of American Israelites, resulted in a remonstrance to the Senate against the amendment by the Board. Still

more interesting was the *Occident*'s tacit admission that America was
not different. Just as Jews throughout their history had lived with persecution spawned by religious bigotry so would they face similar cycles of
both tribulation and respite in the United States.[22]

The promoters of the constitutional amendment organized themselves
into a national association and dispatched a delegation to present their
aims to President Lincoln. After the war, clergymen and religious periodicals took up the cause and spread the message that it was both "an
error and an evil" for the Constitution not to acknowledge God or Jesus.
The association, standing for a Christian nation resting on Christian
beliefs, pitted itself against those "baneful" views which were being
heard in politics: "That civil government is only a social compact; That
it exists only for secular and material, not for moral ends; That Sabbath
Laws are unconstitutional, and that the Bible must be excluded from our
Public Schools." If the stated purpose alone did not prove that the
association included Jews among its opponents, the speeches at the national conventions were more explicit. One clergyman uttered a blanket
condemnation: "The enemies of our movement naturally draw into their
ranks all infidels, Jews, Jesuits, and all opposers of Him who is Lord
over all, our Lord Jesus Christ." Another cited the "confederacy of the
Jesuit and Jew, infidel and atheist" for attacking the Bible in the schools.
Those elements had no common aim, "but they have stricken hands
like Herod and Pontius Pilate in the common work of crucifying Christ."[23]

The Jews could not ignore the movement, especially since it was
headed in the early 1870s by Supreme Court Justice William Strong and
included several governors, state judicial officers, and academicians among
its vice presidents. The *Jewish Messenger* argued several points at once:
the greatness of the Constitution and the Founding Fathers just because
they eschewed an established religion; the evils of a church/state combination; and the fact that Jewish teachings were the base of so-called
Christian virtue. When in 1874 the House Judiciary Committee turned
down the association's petition for an amendment, the paper happily
suggested that the members offer their services to Bismarck (who was
having trouble with the Church) or to the "valorous women who expect
to conquer the rum sellers by prayer."[24]

The clamor for an amendment abated for a while but other manifes-
tations of religious intolerance persisted. New Hampshire did not permit

non-Protestants to hold office until 1877. In Massachusetts and Pennsylvania, Jews were far more numerous, but those states still required all to refrain from work on the Christian Sabbath despite their possible observance of Saturday as the day of rest. The Centennial Exhibition held in Philadelphia in 1876 was closed on Sundays in deference to Christian pressure, and Jews felt slighted still further when Bishop Matthew Simpson, who offered the opening prayer, referred to America's Christian civilization. It was strange, the *American Israelite* observed, that in the year celebrating a century of progress and enlightenment, such anachronisms, inconsistencies, and hypocrisies could still exist. Yet Americans had been governed by "rings, cliques and vestrys [sic]" since 1861; when priests and deacons decided otherwise, the Constitution and the statutes on religious liberty were not insurmountable. Jews wanted no special legislation, the paper insisted, but merely freedom based upon justice and equality.[25]

The winter of 1875–76 also marked a high point in the revivalist crusade of Reverend Dwight L. Moody. The popular preacher, who reached tens of thousands through meetings conducted in major cities, did not ignore the Jews. Not only did he repeat the deicide accusation— recounting the story of the crucifixion in gripping, dramatic detail[26]— but he also once claimed that at a meeting of one thousand Jews in Paris in 1873 they had boasted of killing the Christians' God. Rabbi Sabato Morais of Philadelphia, the city in which the incident took place, said: "None of us would have believed, before he undertook an ostensibly holy mission, that the attempt to inflame the passions of multitudes against law-abiding Hebrews would have been tried . . . two days before the Centennial year was ushered in." Moody was denounced in the secular and Jewish press and the story of the Paris meeting exposed as a falsehood. Isaac Mayer Wise challenged Moody repeatedly to debate the deicide charge, but the latter took no notice. He later claimed that he had been misquoted, that he never passed a Jew without wanting to take off his hat to the people who were destined to convert the world to Christianity.[27] That Moody was interested in converting Jews was true. That he honored them is highly questionable, for years later he had no qualms about inviting Adolf Stoecker, ex-court chaplain and notorious Jew-baiter of Bismarck's Germany, to share a pulpit with him.[28]

Moody spelled danger to Jewish spokesmen because he appealed to emotions instead of reason and because he invoked inflammatory images. Furthermore, like all evangelical Protestants, he stood for a religious or Protestant base for American society.[29] To write him off as an illiterate demagogue, however, the way the *American Israelite* tried to do, was inaccurate. Moody was not the stereotyped backwoods revivalist. He was the preacher who brought traditional religion to native Americans on the urban frontier, and his messages bridged their former way of life with the new industrial reality. His audiences were middle class in aspirations and values—he even had the financial support of some postwar millionaires—uncomfortable as yet with the Darwinist and secularist challenges to religion.[30] Moody shared their attitudes; he identified with businessmen and applied business principles to his own revival campaign.

Indeed, nineteenth-century Jews overlooked the real significance that Moody's crusade may have held for them. It is conceivable that those he addressed, not of the patrician class but pushing to be in society, were of the same cloth as those most eager to exclude Jews from summer resorts. Also, Moody's religious message may well have intensified the feeling of those Christian businessmen competing with the Jews for social status.

A constitutional amendment, Dwight Moody, Sunday laws and the Centennial—all in the decade when social discrimination began claiming increased attention. Therefore, to connect religious ferment with the discrimination, the way Rabbi Wise did, was not unreasonable. If Christian hostility were a constant, the degree of political and social activism on the part of religious groups or individuals could account at least in part for changes in attitude or ups and downs in eruptions of prejudice. It was an *aggressive* Christianity, the *American Israelite* explained, one which saw itself superior to other religions, which was out of harmony with modern ideas of liberty and justice.[31]

Jewish spokesmen remained alert in the last quarter of the nineteenth century to the causes undertaken by militant Protestants. The latter were then seeking popular support and protective legislation in a desperate attempt to stem the sweeping currents of secularization. Their particular concern was the city, where new industrial patterns were undermining fixed social traditions and where hordes of Catholic and Jewish immigrants from southern and eastern Europe were neutralizing the Protestant flavor of established customs. To retain the religious component of Americanism as they knew it, they breathed new life into old ventures, such as missionary drives, Bible reading and sectarian teachings in the public schools, the religious amendment movement (which sputtered again in the 1890s), prohibition, and stricter Sunday laws. The last was spurred significantly in the 1880s by the work of the National Reform Association and the Women's Christian Temperance Union (WCTU), and reached a climax in Senator Henry Blair's bills of 1888 and 1890 proposing a national day of rest.[32]

On most of those issues the Jewish press had long since recorded its opposition, and its favorite targets remained the missionaries, Sunday laws, and sectarianism in the schools.[33] Since Jews recognized that the different causes and their sponsors were connected in the underlying purpose of safeguarding Christian morality through law, they also denounced any incident, no matter how insignificant, which could be construed as an entering wedge. Thus, they noted and criticized gubernatorial proclamations addressed to Christian citizens,[34] the demand to close the 1893 Chicago Fair on Sunday,[35] the attempt in New York to make Good Friday a legal holiday,[36] and even a proposal by the congressional representative from the territory of Wyoming for paintings on the Capitol walls depicting the life of Jesus. That last episode, incidentally, was upsetting, since members of Congress upbraided its sponsor not for his idea but merely for his insertion of a lengthy, undelivered, speech into the *Congressional Record*.[37]

What the Jews resented as much as the inconveniences which Sunday laws worked on Sabbath observers or the psychological alienation which sectarian teachings in the public schools meant for their children[38] was the stigma of second-class citizenship inherent in the concept of a legally recognized Christian country.[39] Their fear that religious activism produced a higher popular level of anti-Jewish hostility seemed to have been borne out, too. The *American Israelite*, for example, noted bitterly that a minister injected the deicide charge in an argument with a rabbi about Sunday laws in Arkansas, while a Methodist newspaper singled out the Jews for blame when voters rejected prohibition in North Carolina.[40] At the end of the century Jews strongly deplored the anti-Catholic activity of the American Protective Association, for they were combating the very same forces of religious bigotry. Some even feared that the prejudice against Catholics might be turned upon them.[41] It is not surprising, therefore, that as they watched the injection of religious issues into politics, American Jews gravitated increasingly into a position favoring a secularist state.[42]

Jews were also uneasy about ministers and priests who attacked the Jews and could thereby fan the flames of popular hostility. While the mainstream of the American clergy would never have condoned downright Jew-baiting, individual hatemongers arose from the evangelical or missionary elements. Preaching antisemitism was not necessarily their purpose, but they invoked stock motifs of antisemitic propaganda in delivering messages usually related to the fulfillment of biblical prophecies. For example, in 1879 Reverend L. C. Newman (probably a missionary for the Society for the Promotion of Christianity among the Jews) lectured in New York on "Jerusalem and Its Future." He lauded the achievements of the Jews in the face of incessant persecution and he predicted their restoration to Palestine and the emergence of Jerusalem as the "metropolis of the world." In the course of his remarks, which were devoid of any malice, he said: "They [the Jews] control the finances of Europe . . . and they are now more prosperous than at any time since the destruction of Jerusalem. The Jewish community throughout the world is united by a bureau of correspondence and they hold conventions, to which delegates come from the outermost parts of the earth."[43] Around the same time a preacher in Washington repeated the theme that Jews like the Jesuits were organized into societies throughout the world and that their organization had ordered their return to Palestine.[44] Some twenty years later, Reverend Doctor Isaac Haldeman of New York's First Baptist Church discoursed on the degree of Jewish economic power. Already the financial masters of the world, they would soon control all the professions: all this since God promised them the wealth of the gentiles before restoring them to their own land. The next stage prior to their ultimate conversion called for an anti-Christ arising from among the Jews who would "devastate the nations of Europe and build up a kingdom in Palestine."[45] Haldeman, similar to others, was concerned with restoration to Palestine as a harbinger of Jewish conversion, but in the meantime, he joined in spreading charges of an international Jewish secret organization and of Jewish economic domination over the gentiles.

The antisemitic themes were more carefully worked out in a full-length book (printed in two editions) by Samuel H. Kellogg, a Presbyterian missionary who in 1878 became Professor of Theology at Western Theological Seminary. Kellogg postulated that everything that had happened or would happen to the Jews was foretold in Old and New Testament prophecies. According to divine plan, Jews were accumulating the wealth of the world from the gentiles who had oppressed them, while simultaneously gaining control of the press and prominence in world politics. Kellogg documented those new charges primarily from European sources; he drew much from Stoecker and, in his second edition, from Edouard Drumont, the notorious Jew-baiter in France. More interesting was how Kellogg pinpointed the fulfillment of the prophecy that Israel would be God's instrument for the overthrow of the gentiles. Not only were Jews currently engaged in abusing and denigrating Christianity, Kellogg said, but they also were responsible for the birth of pantheistic rationalism (Spinoza) and of socialism and communism (Marx, Lasalle, et al.). The same people who had crucified the Messiah had engineered these deadly assaults upon Christian civilization.[46]

Kellogg's work was used and embellished by a Reverend L. B. Woolfolk of Cincinnati whose book *Great Red Dragon* also appeared in two editions. The Dragon, drawn from an image in Revelations, symbolized the evolution of the "Money Power" or the Jewish economic masters of the world. The Money Power worked secretly and underhandedly as it dispossessed honest labor and asserted control over all aspects of commerce and manufacturing. Through organization, political manipulation, and the use of carefully placed agents, it worked solely for its own gain while threatening the survival of republican institutions and Christian churches. A union of the money evil with the devil, the Dragon was the anti-Christ and the head of the Money Power the destined Jewish messiah.[47]

Just how many people were influenced by such clergymen is impossible to estimate, but those who were could not help but fear and hate the Jews. Even if they accepted the view that the Jew's behavior conformed to biblical prophecies and would ultimately bring about the millennium, it was not a cheerful prospect to be one of the generation to fall to the Jew on his way to salvation. More likely there were those who would remember the power and danger of the Jew much sooner than the biblical message.

For the historian looking back, the preachers and their theories attest to the interplay of European and American thinking about the Jews. They also represent a stage in the evolution and public acceptance of full-blown, twentieth-century antisemitic ideology. While they legitimized Jewish behavior—God designated Israel to be the "torch of fire" among the gentiles, the "lion among sheep"[48]—they were also legitimizing the antisemitic assertions about the incalculable power wielded by the Jews. By fusing religious imagery with selected "facts" from the nineteenth-century industrial world, they made antisemitism relevant to the present. They updated the garb of the Jew, but whether he took the form of Satan, Rothschild, Spinoza, or Marx, his threat remained constant: the Jew conspired to destroy Christianity and Christian civilization.

The Populists did not care about conversion of the Jews but they too coupled religious imagery with references to Jewish conspiracy and money power. Indeed, how better than in Bryan's Cross of Gold metaphor could that fusion have been expressed? In the election of 1896 many political speakers talked of Christian principles and deicide while blasting the Jewish gold conspiracy and the Republican party. The GOP, some said, had clearly sold out to the Jews, for why else would a rabbi have been selected as chaplain of the Republican convention. Mary Ellen Lease summed it up this way:

The aristocracy of gold . . . despises government, it tramples upon the rights of individuals, it scoffs at justice, it sneers at everyone, makes the golden rule subservient to the golden calf, and has made the Christian nations of the earth collecting agents for the house of Rothschilds, who have sent their agents to our shores to open up the national Republican convention with prayer and draw up the platform of the National Republican party.[49]

. . . Populists did not come up with any new ideas about the Jews; they purveyed traditional images in a common idiom. Similar to Kellogg and Woolfolk who antedated them, their Jew-baiting, albeit in secularist terms, consisted of identifying the Jew with the current devil or anti-Christ, in this case the gold interests.

On the other hand, Populist antisemitism was more than the equating of goldbug with Jew. Insofar as they singled out Jewish bankers and flung stock religious charges against them, Populists were harnessing the ever-present level of anti-Jewish sentiment to an economic and political campaign. Probably those who spread the antisemitic line were antisemitic, apart from the Populist cause.[50] It is doubtful that they made Jew-haters of any who were completely untouched by the Shylock myth or by Christian religious beliefs about Jews. Their achievement was to vent the latent antipathy and popularize it. By linking Jews with serious and immediate economic issues, they made the "Jewish menace" more palpable and credible to an increasingly secularist society. . . .

Just because Populist rhetoric meant only more of the same, contemporary Jews were less concerned about the free silver campaign than the recent controversy over Populist antisemitism might lead one to expect. Jewish defensiveness, which usually climbed in direct proportion to the gravity of the situation was generally absent.[51] Although the Jew-baiting situation which accompanied the convention and the electioneering was discussed, particularly by the midwestern Jewish papers, Jews never dreamed of mobilizing the community in a united stand on the "Jewish issue." There was no concerted effort to appeal to or threaten the Democrats, or to ally with the Republicans. Indeed, much more discussion came from Jewish quarters in 1868 when Grant, the general who had expelled the Jews during the Civil War, was running for office.[52] In 1896, Jewish leaders saw no reason to lift the long-standing self-imposed community ban on bloc voting and on injecting Jewish interests into American politics. The *Jewish Voice* of St. Louis was the most extreme; it campaigned *against* Populists but *for* McKinley.[53] Rabbi Wise, a confirmed Democrat, allotted much space in his paper to the various antisemitic slurs, and he suggested that the Democratic National Committee repupdiate them. Ultimately, however, he voted for Bryan.[54] In the East, the conservative *Jewish Messenger* said "to God be the praise," when McKinley was elected, but its prime concern was the injurious effect that cheap money would have on the nation's credit and honor.[55] The *American Hebrew*, which for the most part ignored the entire campaign, would only go so far: ". . . may be necessary for Jewish voters to emphasize their abhorrence of religious intolerance by the way they cast their votes; but that will be in their sovereign right as citizens and not as Jews.[56] Apparently the Democrats did lose Jewish votes because of the antisemitic overtones of their campaign, but there was at least one "Hebrew Populist" club as well as Jews in the East and West who stood with Bryan.[57]

In short, the antisemites among the Populists were written off as annoyances, unpleasant but relatively harmless. The *American Israelite*

called them "ignoramuses, fanatics and demagogs [*sic*]" who "fortunately in our country . . . are after all only a very small minority." That
paper also reported how Jews were attacked by the other side—i.e., the
coinage of silver at the ratio of 16:1 was "an old Jewish swindle"—and
it fell back on the scapegoat theory as the only possible explanation:

> In fact whatever does not suit the world is nowadays laid upon the shoulders of
> the Jews. Just as in times of old they were charged with being the cause why
> pestilence, famine, drought, floods and other calamities came upon communities,
> so to-day, the belief in the supernatural having declined, all troubles in the
> financial and commercial world, all disturbances between capital and labor are
> laid upon the back of the Jew.[58]

Populism may have encouraged Jew-baiting and sectional receptivity to
later "ignoramuses" or "fanatics," but it would take a Henry Ford,
abetted by pseudo-scientific race findings and the circulation of the
Protocols of the Elders of Zion, before agrarian-based antisemitism
could command a significant national following.

Jews did not fail to see factors other than religious influences that could
incite social discrimination. Envy of Jewish affluence on the part of the
nouveaux riches was one such cause. More significant, the rising middle
class—ill-bred, with pretentious pseudo-aristocratic values—was using
the trappings of exclusiveness in its scramble for social prestige.[59] (Isaac
Mayer Wise called the women of that class worse offenders than men,
for they were the ones more directly influenced by the Church. For a
while he insisted that discrimination was the fault of easterners whose
caste-like distinctions could not take root in the freer West.)[60] Since
many Jews spoke with foreign accents and retained their foreign manner-
isms, that also roused suspicion and disdain.[61] Jew-baiters doubtless
drew support too from the antisemitic ideas then fashionable in Germany, Austria, and Russia.[62]

   Jewish commentators agreed that ostentatious Jews, the loud and
flashy parvenus and their jewel-bedecked women, were responsible for
feeding the distaste which was directed against an entire group. Since
popular ignorance about the Jew and his tradition was rife, and since
Jews never bothered to dispel that ignorance, the gravity of their faults
was compounded in the popular mind.[63] Leading Jews called for self-
improvement within the community. The *Jewish Messenger* in particular, which timidly cautioned its readers not to exaggerate the prejudice

or to consider it different from hostility directed against other minority groups, frequently urged Jews to look to their manners.[64]

Nevertheless, most observers argued that boorishness was more an excuse than a cause. Vulgarity cut across class, religious, and ethnic lines; Christians also gambled and bet at races, and Christian women also "disport themselves at the seashore in indecent bathing costumes." Yet why was one entire people punished for the behavior of some? Self-improvement was not the surest solution for discrimination. This was an imperfect world, Judge Mayer Sulzberger of Philadelphia wrote, and "if all Jews behaved themselves properly there would be more prejudice than ever."[65]

As they pondered other reasons, writers in the Jewish press consistently held the position that religious hostility remained the source of the infection. The *American Hebrew,* a New York weekly begun in 1879 under the editorship of Philip Cowen, was perhaps the most outspoken on that score.[66] Even the *Jewish Messenger,* more fearful of arousing controversy than its New York rival or Wise's *American Israelite,* could not deny the connection:

The persistency of popular prejudice against the Jew is due to many factors . . . but the most fruitful . . . has been the religious training of the Christian. As most Christians have capacity to understand only the material elements in the crucifixion, they take a grim religious pleasure—a sense of duty done—in crucifying the Jew.[67]

To argue that many who discriminated against Jews were not church-goers did not alter the case, for their prejudices had been instilled at an early age by religious training in schools and by a traditional Christian environment.[68] Therefore, it was futile to look to churches and schools to end the discrimination, even though, as a few articles pointed out, Jesus and the apostles would also have been barred from the summer resorts.[69]

Writing in the *North American Review* in 1881, Nina Morais pointed to a history of civil disabilities, Jewish manners, and ignorance about Jews as the causes contributing to prejudice. At least equally culpable, however, were the antisemitic Christian teachings repeated in the nursery rhymes, the public schools, and missionary exhortations. As long as Christianity refused "further enlightenment," the results in society were inevitable.

Under the circumstances, it is not wonderful that the ardent church-member should bestow some act of hatred upon the criminal, or that an involuntary aversion to the Jew should become a mental habit in the most indifferent Christian. To dislike the Hebrew *per se* is natural, whatever the causes of the dislike may be. . . . [The prejudices against him] have been wrought in the very woof of Christianity.[70]

For their part, many Christians denied that age-old doctrines could be faulted for what was transpiring in the last quarter of the nineteenth century.[71] Some said discrimination was a question of racial antagonism analogous to American hostility to the blacks and Chinese.[72] While a good number blamed Jewish manners (especially among the "lower" types) for awakening hostility, others pointed to the vulgarity of those who discriminated against Jews.[73] On separate occasions writers in the *New York Times* and *New York Herald* suggested that Christians turn to prejudice because they fear the superiority of Jews.[74]

On the other hand, many agreed that religious hostility was a primary cause, even though it might have been reduced to residual or even unconscious significance.[75] George W. Curtis, editor of *Harper's*, wrote about the absence of true "soul liberty" in the United States; the root of anti-Jewish discrimination was the charge of deicide, "a terrible retribution" for what a "Syrian" mob did over two thousand years ago.[76] The fact that some Christians pointed to Jewish violations of Christian sensibilities—such as disrespectful behavior on Sunday—also attested to the importance of the religious factor.[77]

In the 1880s, what with antisemitism rife in both western and eastern Europe and social ostracism more widespread in the United States, the "Jewish question" and the issue of Jewish/Christian relations became favorite topics of discussion. At that time, a new note was increasingly heard from Christians who spoke out on the reasons for discrimination. The fault lay, they said, in the exclusiveness and separatism practiced by the Jews. In a symposium conducted by Philip Cowen in 1890 on the causes and the nature of antisemitism, prominent clerics and public figures cited the clannishness of the Jews and their feelings of superiority as the Chosen People. Jewish behavior showed, some respondents said, that Jews were just as prejudiced as Christians.[78]

"How singular," wrote Rabbi Gustav Gottheil, "that, when the Jew attempts to . . . mix freely with his neighbors, he is repelled and unceremoniously shown back to his own tribe; and if he keeps there, he is accused of hereditary and ancestral pride!" The *American Hebrew* echoed that sentiment and argued that those who raised the charge were motivated by a religious animus. Despite centuries of Christian proselytism, Jews retained their "religious autonomy" and refused to merge with the dominant faith. The *Jewish Messenger* added a bitter comment: other groups set up their separate social institutions, but only Jews were criticized for behaving that way.[79]

Nevertheless, just because it was less crude than the charge that Jews as a group were vulgarians, and just because it was voiced by friends of Jews as well as by their critics, the argument was more troubling. For one thing, it contradicted the claim that the religiously observant Jew was accorded greater respect than his irreligious brother.[80] More important still, it meant that social amenities and cultured tastes alone did not make the Jew acceptable to society, that Jews who held on to religious practices like dietary laws and the ban on intermarriage were still beyond the pale of respectability. The choice was theirs—traditional Judaism or social acceptance—when in fact they wanted to combine elements of both. Jews knew too that some critics who attacked Jewish separatism (or "tribalism") went on to suggest that clannishness inhibited the Jew from showing proper civic loyalty. The views of one such antisemite, Goldwin Smith, an expatriate professor of history from England, were hotly debated in the United States at this time. Should Americans ever agree with Smith that Jews could not be patriots, the future of American Jewry would indeed look bleak.[81]

The charge of separatism made some Jews more self-conscious about separate Jewish associations and "self-ghettoization."[82] Since established American Jews were in no way growing increasingly exclusive, however, the argument suggests that popular pressure for conformity to the Anglo-Saxon cultural mold, cutting across liberal-conservative lines, was hardening. Jewish religious practices confined to the synagogues were acceptable, particularly if the houses of worship, the style of the service, and the religious functionaries resembled their Protestant counterparts, but customs which impeded free social intercourse with gentiles were undesirable.

The issue of Jewish exclusiveness perforce dashed the hopes of those Jews who called upon the Christian community to shoulder the responsibility for ending the "un-American" discrimination.[83] Although the overwhelming body of church and lay leaders, if asked, would have repudiated prejudice, few had actively campaigned on behalf of the victims.[84] Now the latter were faulted and the responsibility was shifted to them. After all, why should Christians extend themselves without evidence of Jewish goodwill or, in this case, of a desire for total assimilation?

Neither social discrimination nor Populism prompted American Jewish spokesmen to deep socioeconomic analyses of the causes of antisemitism. They persisted in holding Christian religious doctrines responsible for hostility against the Jews, and this in turn led to their focus on the potential dangers of religious activism and the fusion of "priestcraft" with politics. The evidence indicates that their worries were grounded in facts. Moreover, they rightly saw that constitutional guarantees alone were not enough of a safeguard for a minority. They recognized two countervailing forces that vitiated the influence of narrow Christian reforms and reformers—America's loyalty to Jeffersonian principles as well as the multiplicity of sects which precluded an effective Protestant union—but they overestimated the drawing power of Christian social activism in a society turning increasingly secularist.

Explaining antisemitism in terms of religious bigotry provided one measure of comfort. It linked the nineteenth-century experience with a long history of persecution, saying in effect that Jews had suffered and survived the same hatred before. Yet, even if familiar hostility was better than a new kind, the explanation could generate a resigned, passive, or even fatalistic mood. Nothing the Jews did could change matters radically; in a sense their persecutors too were blameless, since they were merely carrying out the logic of an omnipresent ideology. . . .

NOTES

1. The best-known works are Oscar Handlin, "American Views of the Jew at the Opening of the Twentieth Century," *Publications of the American Jewish Historical Society* (hereafter called *PAJHS*), 40 (1951), 323–44; and his *Adventure in Freedom* (New York, 1954), pp. 174–91; Richard Hofstadter, *The Age of Reform* (New York, 1955), pp. 77–81; John Higham, "Social Discrimination against Jews in America, 1830–1930," *PAJHS*, 47 (1957), 1–33; and his "Anti-Semitism in the Gilded Age: A Reinterpretation," *Mississippi Valley Historical Review*, 43 (1957), 559–78. Higham's

articles have been revised and reprinted in his *Send These To Me* (New York, 1975). On antisemitism as ethnic prejudice, see Handlin and Higham; see also, Barbara M. Solomon, *Ancestors and Immigrants* (New York, 1956), Ch. 8. For religious typing, see for example, Seymour Martin Lipset and Earl Raab, *The Politics of Unreason* (New York, 1973), pp. 92–95. Imagery and ideological antisemitism are also treated in: Sol Liptzin, *The Jew in American Literature* (New York, 1966); Louis Harap, *The Image of the Jew in American Literature* (Philadelphia, 1974); Michael Dobkowski, "Ideological Anti-Semitism in America, 1877–1927" (unpublished Ph.D. dissertation. New York University, 1976). Higham emphasizes status rivalry in "Social Discrimination," and Hamlin and Hofstadter make a case against the Populists. Other studies blaming or defending the Populists are listed by Higham. *Send These To Me*, pp. 118 n. 5, 119 n. 7. See also Michael Dobkowski, "Populist Antisemitism in U.S. Literature," *Patterns of Prejudice*, 10 (1976), 19–27.

2. See,for example, Salo W. Baron, "Changing Patterns of Antisemitism," *Jewish Social Studies*, 38 (1976), 20.

3. See for example, *Asmonean*, 5 June 1857.

4. Liptzin, *Jew in American Lit.*, pp. 72–73; Lee M. Friedman, *Jewish Pioneers and Patriots* (Philadelphia, 1942), pp. 274–75.

5. *Jewish Messenger* (hereafter called *JM*), 16 Sept. 1864.

6. *Ibid.*, 6 July 1866.

7. Naomi W. Cohen, *A Dual Heritage: The Public Career of Oscar S. Straus* (Philadelphia, 1969), p. 10.

8. Matthew Hale Smith, *Sunshine and Shadow in New York* (Hartford, 1868), p. 452.

9. Higham, *Send These To Me*, pp. 150–53.

10. *Ibid.*, pp. 144–45.

11. *Occident* (hereafter called *Occ*), 20 (1863), 486.

12. *Ibid.*, 23 (1865), 319.

13. *American Israelite* (hereafter called *AI*), 29 June 1877.

14. Edward Eitches, "Maryland's 'Jew Bill,' " *American Jewish Historical Quarterly*, 60 (1971), 273; Morris U. Schappes, ed. *A Documentary History of the Jews in the United States, 1654–1875* (Third ed., New York, 1971), pp. 239–42; *Occ*, 6 (1848), 36–40, 186–93.

15. Cf. Bertram Wallace Korn, "The Know-Nothing Movement and the Jews," *Eventful Years and Experiences* (Cincinnati, 1954); *Occ*, 11 (1853), 224–25; 12 (1855), 558–60; 13 (1856), 565ff.

16. *Occ*, 7 (1850), 563–67; *Israelite*, 17 Oct. 1856, 19 June 1857; *Asmonean*, 27 Oct. and 3 Nov. 1854; Oscar and Mary F. Handlin, "The Acquisition of Political and Social Rights by Jews in the United States," *American Jewish Year Book*, 56 (1955), 60–61.

17. Handlin, "Acquisition," p. 61; Schappes, *Documentary History*, pp. 122–25, 126–27, 169, 170, 235–46; *Occ*, 6 (1848), 39–40, 273–74, 403, 405;

14 (1856), 310–11; 16 (1859), 535; 17 (14 Apr., 13 July 1859); *Asmonean*, 16 Aug., 27 Dec. 1850; *Israelite*, 22 Dec. 1854, 9 May and 21 Nov. 1856; Eitches, "Maryland's 'Jew Bill,' " pp. 265, 267–68.

18. Bertram W. Korn, *American Jewry and the Civil War* (Philadelphia, 1951), Chs. 4 and 6; *Occ*, 20 (1863), 457–62; *JM*, 21 Nov. 1862.

19. *Occ*, 20 (1863), 485, 493.

20. *Ibid.*, 22 (1864), 368–69; 23 (1865), 313–19.

21. *Proceedings of the National Convention to Secure the Religious Amendment of the Constitution of the United States*, 1872, p. iii; *Occ*, 21 (1863), 219–22; 22 (1865), 433–45, 481–91; 23 (1865) 318–19; *JM*, 6 Mar. 1863, 16 Dec. 1864, 3, 10 Mar. 1865; Board of Delegates of American Iraelites (hereafter BDAI), Minutes (Archives of the American Jewish Historical Society), 14 Mar., 21 Dec. 1864.

22. *Occ*, 22 (1865), 481–91, 529–33; *JM*, 17 Feb., 10 Mar. 1865; BDAI, Minutes, 26 Mar., 12 June 1865; BDAI, *Proceedings*, 1865, pp. 6–8.

23. *Proceedings of the National Convention*, 1872, pp. viii–xvi; 1873; pp. 46, 54–55.

24. *Ibid.*, 1872, pp. 66–67; *JM*, 25 Feb., 11 Mar. 1870, 27 Jan., 10 Feb., 22 Dec. 1871, 1 Mar. 1872, 27 Feb. 1874; BDAI, *Proceedings*, 1867, p. 8; 1871, pp. 9–10; 1872, pp. 8–9; 1874, p. 7. The Board noted its dissatisfaction with Strong's appointment to the Supreme Court. BDAI, *Proceedings*, 1870, p. 8. See also *JM*, 7 Jan., 11 Feb. 1870.

25. *AI*, 21 Apr., 12, 19 May 1876, 12 Jan. 1877.

26. See for example, Dwight L. Moody, *Glad Tidings* (New York, 1877), pp. 264, 289, 293ff., 401–403.

27. *JM*, 7, 14, 21 Jan. 1876; *AI*, 6 Jan.–17 Mar., 25 Mar. 1876.

28. *AI*, 26 Dec. 1884; Richard K. Curtis, *They Called Him Mister Moody* (Garden City, New York, 1962), p. 280. Moody stated that he did not believe the newspaper reports about Adolf Stoecker. Moody was also criticized publicly when he blamed the Jews for influencing the Freemasons of France to give up the Bible. See *JM*, 18 Dec. 1896.

29. *AI*, 6 Jan. 1876; James F. Findlay, *Dwight L. Moody, American Evangelist* (Chicago, 1969), p. 297.

30. Barnard A. Weisberger, *They Gathered at the River* (Chicago, 1966), Ch. 7; Findlay, *Moody*, pp. 277–89.

31. *AI*, 1 July 1881.

32. Arthur M. Schlesinger, "A Critical Period in American Religion, 1875–1900," *Massachusetts Historical Society Proceedings*, 64 (1930–1932), 533–36; A. E. Thompson, *A Century of Jewish Missions* (Chicago, 1902); *Congressional Record*, 50 Cong. 1 Sess., p. 4455; 51 Cong. 1 Sess., p. 124. Both the National Association for Amending the Constitution and the National Reform Association called for Christianizing the schools and other civic institutions as well as for amending the Constitution. *Proceedings of the National Convention*, 1872, p. xv; 1873, pp. 9, 54; constitution of the

National Reform Association and pp. 71–87 in "Annual Meeting and National Conference, Philadelphia, April 24–26, 1888," *National Reform Documents*, II.

33. Isaac Mayer Wise, *A Defense of Judaism versus Proselytizing Christianity* (Cincinnati, 1889). For continuing Jewish opposition to amending the Constitution, see *JM*, 24 Feb. 1888, 2, 30 Mar. 1894, 13, 27 Mar., 24 Apr. 1896; *American Hebrew* (hereafter called *AH*), 16 Mar. 1894 (E. Calisch); *AI*, 8 Feb., 1, 15 Mar. 1894, 12, 26 Mar. 1896; Union of American Hebrew Congregations (hereafter called UAHC), *Proceedings*, 1890, p. 2636; 1894, pp. 3354–57; 1896, pp. 3648–50. For opposition to a national day of rest, see *JM*, 15 June 1888, 4 Oct. 1895; *AH*, 25 Jan., 21 June 1889, 7 Mar. 1890; *AI*, 7 Dec. 1888, 3 Jan., 14 Mar., 26 Dec. 1889, 6 Feb. 1890; UAHC, *Proceedings*, 1892, p. 3013. For opposition to prohibition and its connection with Sunday laws, see *AI*, 14 Oct. 1887, 16 Mar., 20 Apr., 14 Dec. 1888, 11, 25 July 1889; *JM*, 16 Aug. 1895.

34. *AI*, 20 Sept. 1878, 26 Nov. 1880, 26 Nov. 1896; *AH*, 3 Nov. 1882; *JM*, 23 Mar. 1877, 30 Mar. 1894.

35. *AH*, 16 Jan. 1891; *AI*, 5 May, 21 July, 29 Dec. 1892; UAHC, *Proceedings*, 1892, pp. 3079–80.

36. *AI*, 18 Apr. 1884, 6 Apr. 1888; *JM*, 7, 21; Mar. 1884; UAHC, *Proceedings*, 1884, p. 1563.

37. *AI*, 7 May 1880; *Congressional Record*, 46 Cong. 2 Sess., pp. 2325, 2360, 2630–31.

38. A personal account of alienation in the classroom was written by Rabbi Henry Berkowitz, *AI*, 5 Dec. 1889.

39. The Anglo-Jewish press frequently denied that the United States was a Christian country. See also Louis Marshall, "Is Ours a Christian Government?" (1896 article in *Menorah*), reprinted in Charles Reznikoff, ed., *Louis Marshall, Champion of Liberty* (Philadelphia, 1957), II, 936–49.

40. *AI*, 15 Apr., 14 Oct. 1887.

41. *Ibid.*, 12 July, 14 Nov. 1894, 4 June 1896; *AH*, 11 May, 15 June 1894, 12 July 1895, 7 Oct. 1898; *JM*, 23 Feb. 1894, 6 Mar., 22 May, 12 June 1896.

42. See for example, *JM*, 9 Aug. 1889; *AI*, 15 Sept. 1892.

43. Schappes, *Documentary History*, p. 552; *JM*, 30 May 1879.

44. *AI*, 16 Feb. 1877.

45. *Ibid.*, 18 June 1896.

46. Samuel H. Kellogg, *The Jews, or Prediction and Fulfilment* (New York, 1883 and 1887).

47. L. B. Woolfolk, *Great Red Dragon or London Money Power* (Cincinnati, 1889). The second edition, published in New York in 1894, was entitled *London Money Power, The Great Red Dragon*. See also, *AI*, 22 Feb. 1894.

48. Cited in Kellogg, *Jews, or Prediction*, p. 188.

49. *JM*, 21 Aug. 1896; *AI*, 13 Feb., 25 June, 9, 23 July, 1, 15 Oct., 12 Nov.

1896; Edward Flower, "Anti-Semitism in the Free Silver and Populist Movements and the Election of 1896" (M.A. thesis. Columbia University, 1952), Ch. 4.

50. Senator John Morgan of Alabama, who attacked the Jews in the free silver campaign, had an earlier record of antisemitism. *AI,* 27 Dec. 1878, 7 Mar. 1879, 23 Jan., 20 Feb. 1896.

51. One article appeared in the *AI,* 30 July 1896, on how the Jews were not represented among the trusts, or oppressors, and how Jews who serviced the farmer and the worker through small business depended on those classes for their own well-being.

52. *JM,* 15 May, 5, 26 June, 3, 10, 24 July, 7 Aug., 4, 16 Sept., 30 Oct. 1868.

53. Flower, "Anti-Semitism," p. 51.

54. *AI,* 1 Oct., 12 Nov. 1896.

55. *JM,* 6 Nov. 1896 and editorials almost weekly from July through October; see also Jesse Seligman, "The Silver Question Again," *North American Review* (hereafter called *NAR*), 152 (1891), 204–208.

56. *AH,* 10 July 1896.

57. *Ibid.,* 6 Nov. 1896; *AI,* 2 Aug. 1894, 15 Oct., 12 Nov. 1896.

58. *AI,* 25 June 1896.

59. *Ibid.,* 16 June 1876, 29 June 1877, 1 Aug. 1879 (Wolf), 7 Sept. 1883, 23 May 1889, 22 Oct. 1896 (Sulzberger); *JM,* 22 June 1877, 20 June 1879, 3 Nov. 1899 (Morais).

60. *AI,* 16 June 1876, 29 June 1877.

61. *Ibid.,* 25 July, 1 Aug. 1879, 25 Aug. 1882; *JM,* 22 June 1877; Alice Hyneman Rhine, "Race Prejudice at Summer Resorts," *Forum,* 3 (1887), 527. Although some Jews liked to blame the Russian immigrants, who began arriving in great numbers after 1881, for arousing prejudice, the Jewish press did not think the accusation was just. *AI,* 8 July 1887 (Leucht); *AH,* 31 Dec. 1887, 31 July 1896.

62. *AI,* 10 Oct. 1879, 24, 31 Aug., 7 Sept. 1883, 24 Jan. 1895; *AH,* 2 May 1884; Marcus Jastrow, *The Causes of the Revived Disaffection against the Jews* (New York, 1890), pp. 9–10.

63. *JM,* 29 June 1877, 15 Aug. 1884, 14 Aug. 1885, 6 May 1887 *(Jewish Exponent),* 19 Apr. 1889, 12 Mar. 1892, 17 Mar. 1899; *AH,* 28 May 1884; *AI,* 16 June 1876, 29 June 1877; Nina Morais, "Jewish Ostracism in America," *NAR,* 133 (1881), 270–71.

64. *AH,* 4 July 1884 (Sulzberger), 22 Feb. 1889 (Blumenthal); *AI,* 25 Aug. 1882; *JM,* 29 June 1877, 14 May 1880, 15 Aug. 1884, 19 Apr. 1889, 18 Apr. 1890, 12 Feb., 16 Dec. 1892, 15 Sept. 1899, 5 Oct. 1900 (Moise).

65. *AH,* 28 May 1894, 10 Sept. 1896; *JM,* 4 Aug. 1876; 22 June, 6 July 1877, 20 June 1879, 5 Sept. 1890; Rhine, "Race Prejudice," pp. 526–27; *AI,* 29 June 1877, 6 Aug. 1880, 22 Oct. 1896 (Sulzberger).

66. See for example, editorials of 13 May 1881, 26 July, 23 Aug., 13 Sept. 1889, 4 Apr 1890, 30 Sept. 1898.

67. *JM*, 31 Aug. 1888.
68. *Ibid.*, 15 Jan. 1887 (Furth); *AI*, 6 June 1889. Austin Corbin, when interviewed by the *New York Herald*, said that discrimination was a matter of social esthetics and not religion. To this the *AI* rejoined: "The man would be too consummate an ass in the estimation of every intelligent individual, if he, in 1879, and in the United States, would talk of religious persecution," 1 Aug. 1879.
69. *JM*, 22 June 1877; *AI*, 29 June 1877, 23 May 1889.
70. Morais, "Jewish Ostracism," pp. 271–72. Alice Hyneman Rhine, from an old and prominent Jewish family, also maintained that "the refusal of the Jews to accept the divinity of Christ, with their terrible responsibility for the crucifixion, is an ever-present ground of dislike in the Christian mind. The antipathy felt toward the Jews as deicides is hardly less strong to-day than it was in the times when the Hebrew was . . . under the ban of state and church. Hatred and contempt for the Jew the infant imbibes with its mother's milk, and it is intensified by the teachings of governesses, Sunday-schools, and church." Rhine, "Race Prejudice," p. 529.
71. That was the opinion of most clergymen polled in a symposium on antisemitism in 1890. Philip Cowen, *Prejudice against the Jew* (New York, 1928), *passim*.
72. *JM*, 1 Aug. 1879 *(New York Evening Post)*, 21 July 1882 *(Boston Transcript)*.
73. *AI*, 29 June 1877 (Harrisburg *Daily Telegraph*); *AH*, 8 Oct. 1880, 13 Aug. 1887 *(New York Times)*, 28 Apr. 1893 (quote from *New York Evening Post*), 31 July 1896; Cowen, *Prejudice*, pp. 38, 51, 62–64, 68–70, 86, 94, 101–102, 106, 117, 122, 129, 131.
74. *JM*, 3 Dec. 1880 *(New York Herald)*, 30 June 1893 *(New York Times)*.
75. Cowen, *Prejudice*, pp. 40, 61, 67, 76, 133–35; *JM*, 5 May 1882 (Savage), 11 Apr. 1890 (Toy).
76. *JM*, 26 June 1877, 26 Sept. 1879; *AI*, 18 Nov. 1881.
77. *JM*, 4 Aug. 1876 (quote from *Christian-at-Work*); *AH*, 1 Aug. 1887; *AI*, 6 June 1889; Rhine, "Race Prejudice," p. 525.
78. *JM*, 13 July 1877, 5 May 1882 (Savage), 15 Sept. 1899 *(Independent)*; *AI*, 31 Aug. 1883, 30 Nov. 1888, 24 July 1890; *AH*, 11 Oct. 1889; Cowen, *Prejudice*, pp. 46, 54, 75, 83, 86–88, 93–94, 97, 102, 104–105, 116–17, 127, 132.
79. Gustav Gottheil, "The Position of the Jews in America," *NAR*, 127 (1878), 86; *AH*, 17 May, 23 Aug. 1889, 11 Apr. 1890; *JM*, 30 Aug. 1894.
80. See for example, *JM*, 22 Nov. 1872; *AH*, 3 July 1896.
81. Naomi W., Cohen, "American Jewish Reactions to Anti-Semitism in Western Europe, 1875–1900," *Proceedings of the American Academy for Jewish Research*, 45 (1978), 52–57.
82. See for example, *JM*, 12 Feb., 3 June 1892, 5 Oct. 1900 (Moise).

83. *Ibid.*, 20 July 1877, 17 May, 12 July 1889, 5 Sept. 1890; *AI*, 16 May 1889; *AH*, 23 Aug., 13 Sept. 1889.
84. One notable exception was Rev. Madison C. Peters who lectured and wrote on the injustice done to the Jew. *JM*, 7 Feb. 1902; *AH*, 1 Sept. 1899; Madison C. Peters, *Justice to the Jew* (London, 1897).

7

Christian Sources of Anti-Semitism

Harold E. Quinley and Charles Y. Glock

For centuries, Christianity was a principal force behind the segregation and persecution of Jews. It was the official religion of much of the Western world, and its followers displayed little tolerance or mercy toward those not accepting Christian teachings. To many Christians, furthermore, Jews were not just religious heretics, but Christ-killers. They were held personally responsible for the Crucifixion of Jesus and believed to have brought down upon themselves the wrath and vengeance of God. In murdering the Redeemer, they had supposedly sealed their fate and that of their children for eternity. This charge of deicide served as the inspiration for the medieval segregation of Jews and for the bloody pogroms—officially sanctioned massacres—that have recurred throughout Western history.

The Christian roots of anti-Semitism are thus strong; Jews have been stigmatized as religious heretics, defilers, and murderers. Indeed, such images have been so powerful that they have often been invoked even when religious issues have not been directly at issue. Adolf Hitler—who otherwise had little to say about religion—found it convenient to evoke Christian symbols in justifying the confinement and execution of more than six million Jews.

While all this is true of the past, what is its relevance in America today? Heretics are not being burned at the stake, and no respected Christian leader refers to the Jews as "accursed." It is an age of *rap-*

prochement between Jews and Christians, a time of mutual acceptance and even of cooperation. American history is not without examples of religiously inspired prejudice and bigotry, of course, but over time the nation has learned to live with its religious differences reasonably well. The differences have made necessary a quest for ways to minimize disagreement and to emphasize the values of religious tolerance and pluralism.

Americans are thus understandably puzzled when it is suggested that they are religiously prejudiced. Religious intolerance is admitted to exist in the backwoods—or perhaps within untutored sections of the country —but not among the majority of Christians.

It is certainly true that Americans do not actively persecute one another on religious grounds and that Christian and Jewish religious bodies now work with one another openly and positively in a variety of ways. Yet there remain reasons to doubt that Christians are entirely free from anti-Semitic prejudice. Once a social pattern becomes deeply entrenched within a culture, it does not easily die out. In the past, Christianity was a prominent source of anti-Semitism, and it seems unlikely that there are no remaining vestiges of this legacy. Further, while the official position of Christian churches is one of tolerance, this does not mean that such a norm will necessarily be observed by all church members or, indeed, by all church leaders. Numerous examples can be cited of discrepancies between an institution's formal norms and the informal practices of its members.

Because such doubts were entertained, it was decided to make religion a subject of special investigation in the series of studies on anti-Semitism in America. If anti-Semitism is nourished by certain interpretations of Christian faith or by some forms of Christian worship, this fact ought to be known so that remedial steps might be taken. By the same token, if modern Christianity proves to be a positive force helping people to transcend their old prejudices, this too should be understood so that it can be made even more effective.

... three studies were undertaken to explore the interconnections between religion and anti-Semitism. One study involved the participation of a sample of 3,000 church members residing in the San Francisco Bay Area. A second study, designed to assess whether the findings from the Bay Area study would hold true for the adult population of the country as a whole, involved 2,000 interviews with a sample of that population.[1] A third study focused on clergy rather than laity and was based on 1,580 questionnaires completed by a sample of Protestant pastors serving parishes in the state of California.[2] The results of the two studies of laity were highly concordant. Consequently, this report on the findings is restricted to the more comprehensive of the two lay studies— the one based on Northern California churchgoers—and the study of clergy.

CHRISTIAN BELIEFS AND ANTI-SEMITISM: A MODEL

The basic propositions tested in these three studies can be stated rather simply (see Figure 7-1). They are that certain interpretations of Christian faith are conducive to producing religiously based hostility toward Jews, and that this religious hostility makes those who harbor it especially prone to secular anti-Semitism.

The beginning of this postulated causal chain is orthodox Christian belief, a commitment to those doctrines which historically have been central to the Christian religion. These include beliefs in an omnipotent, all-knowing God who imposes certain requirements of man; in Jesus Christ as the Son of God, sent to earth so that men could be forgiven for their sins and receive the blessing of eternal life; and in the existence of Hell, to which those who turn their backs upon such Christian beliefs will be sent.

As will be seen, not all church people today—clergy or laity—accept these doctrines in such literal terms. Those who do it, it was predicted, would be especially likely to be caught up in the second link in the chain leading to anti-Semitism, a disposition to see Christian truth as the only religious truth and to view all other faiths as fallacious and misguided.

The importance of such a particularistic religious orientation is that it may lead to hostile feelings toward those not accepting traditional Christian doctrines. If only right-thinking, orthodox Christians are saved, non-Christians are by definition damned. This imputation can extend to Buddhists, Hindus, Satanists, or other religious outsiders. Historically, however, Jews have been a special object of Christian invectives, and in this country Jews are by far the largest and most conspicuous non-Christian group. For these reasons, if hostile feelings flow from particularistic religious conceptions, it is likely that they will most often be directed against Jews. This can take the form of *hostility toward histori-*

Figure 7–1
Causal Sequence: Orthodoxy to Anti-Semitism

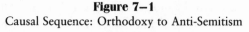

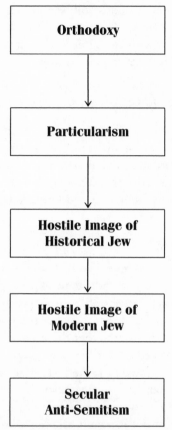

Source: Rodney Stark et al., *Wayward Shepherds: Prejudice and the Protestant Clergy* (New York: Harper & Row, 1971), p. 12. Copyright © 1971 by the Anti-Defamation League of B'nai Brith. Reprinted by permission of Harper & Row, Publishers, Inc.

cal Jews—the renegades from the Christian faith and the crucifiers and revilers of the Son of God. It can also take the form of a *hostility toward the modern Jew*—the heretic and in the nonbeliever in essential Christian truths. That *particularistic* Christian belief does lead to religious hostility toward both historical and modern Jews is the next link in the postulated causal chain.

The final link in the causal model is the crucial one—the linkage between religious hostility toward Jews and *secular anti-Semitism*. The idea here is rather simple and straightforward, namely, that ideas have consequences. It is proposed that people who maintain hostile attitudes toward Jews on religious grounds will be especially vulnerable to hostile secular stereotypes of Jews. In effect, if it is believed that Jews are heretics or out of favor with God, it is a small step to also believing that they are wicked or evil in other ways as well.

CHRISTIANITY AND RELIGIOUS HOSTILITY TOWARD JEWS

This causal sequence provided the theoretical framework used to investigate and explain the existence of anti-Semitism among American Christians. In order to determine its accuracy, it was necessary to devise ways to measure the various critical components of the theory—orthodoxy, particularism, religious hostility toward Jews, and secular anti-Semitism.

Orthodox Christianity

The measurement of commitment to orthodox Christian belief was approached through asking respondents to express their degree of acceptance of such traditional articles of Christian faith as belief in God, the divinity of Jesus, the devil, life after death, and the Biblical accounts of Jesus' miracles. It was discovered that there are considerable differences in what church people believe about these central tenets of Christianity. The differences are illustrated in Table 7–1, which shows the proportion of Protestant and Roman Catholic laypersons and Protestant clergy who responded in an orthodox way to a sample of the questions asked. The range is from 86 percent of Roman Catholics who expressed unequivocal belief in the divinity of Christ to 38 percent of Protestant laypersons who acknowledge without qualification the existence of the devil. On most questions the majority give orthodox responses, but the majority is rarely overwhelming, and it is clear that there are many Christian church members and clergy who do not subscribe to traditional tenets of faith.

That there is variation made it plausible to develop a summary measure of it. To this end, an index of orthodoxy was constructed based on lay answers to the questions asking them about the existence of a personal God, the divinity of Christ, the authenticity of Biblical miracles, and the existence of the devil. In the construction of the index, a respondent received a score of 1 for each of these belief questions on

Table 7–1
Christian Laypersons' and Protestant Ministers' Acceptance of Orthodox Religious Beliefs

	Laypersons		Protestant Ministers
	Protestants	Catholics	
"I believe in God and I have no doubts about it." (percentage agreeing)	71%	81%	67%
"Jesus is the Divine Son of God and I have no doubts about it." (percentage agreeing)	69	86	61
"There is life after death." (percentage accepting as completely true)	65	75	79
"The Devil actually exists." (percentage accepting as completely true)	38	66	41
100% (N) =	(2,326)	(545)	(1,580)

Source: Adapted from Charles Y. Glock and Rodney Stark, Christian Beliefs and Anti-Semitism (New York: Harper & Row, 1966), pp. 5, 7, 12; and Rodney Stark, Bruce D. Foster, Charles Y. Glock, and Harold E. Quinley, Wayward Shepherds: Prejudice and the Protestant Clergy (New York: Harper & Row, 1971), pp. 17, 19, 23.

which he or she expressed certainty about the truth of the Christian position. Respondents received a score of 0 for each item on which they acknowledged doubt or disbelief about the orthodox response. Thus a person could score as high as 4 by being certain in his faith on all four items, or as low as 0 by reporting doubt or disbelief on all four. Following the same procedure, an index of orthodoxy was also constructed for Protestant clergy.

Table 7–2 reports the proportion of laypersons and clergy who scored 4 on the orthodoxy index; that is, respondents who gave an orthodox response to each of the four items included in the index, and therefore can be considered highly orthodox. In this table results are presented not only for Protestants taken as a whole but also broken down to show the figures for members of different faiths. Overall, Roman Catholic laymen are much more likely to score high on orthodoxy than Protestants. The figure for total Protestants, however, masks great variations by denomination. At the one extreme are the members of the United Church of Christ, where only 4 percent score as highly orthodox. At the other

Table 7–2

Orthodox Religious Beliefs of Laypersons and Protestant Ministers

	Percentage Scoring High in Religious Orthodoxy	
	Laypersons	Protestant Ministers
United Church of Christ	4% (141)	7% (137)
Methodist	10 (381)	6 (350)
Episcopal	14 (373)	19 (204)
Disciple of Christ	18 (44)	a
Presbyterian	27 (457)	24 (225)
Lutheran Church in America	43 [b] (195)	39 (86)
American Lutheran Church		59 (115)
American Baptist	43 (76)	65 (144)
Missouri Synod—Lutheran Church	66 (111)	89 (131)
Southern Baptist	88 (76)	95 (167)
Sects	86 (247)	—[a]
Catholic	62 (500)	—

[a] None included in this study.
[b] Figure is for L.C.A. and A.L.C. combined.

Source: Adapted from Glock and Stark, *Christian Beliefs and Anti-Semitism*, p. 13; and Stark et al., *Wayward Shepherds*, p. 33.

extreme are the Southern Baptists and sect members, where respectively 88 percent and 86 percent score as highly orthodox. This variation by denomination also holds true, as can be seen, for Protestant clergy. (Catholic priests, it will be recalled, were not surveyed in these studies; thus there is no figure for the degree of their orthodoxy.)

Particularism

The main interest in these inquiries lay not with religious orthodoxy *per se*, of course, but with the consequences it has for other beliefs in the causal chain leading to secular anti-Semitism. The first of these, it will be recalled, was religious particularism—the belief that one's own religion is the only true one and that all others are false and even pernicious. Particularism can be viewed as a kind of religious chauvinism. It is a dismissal of all religious perspectives different from one's own.

Within Christianity, particularistic attitudes have historically centered on the question of salvation: Who will and who will not receive God's grace and be rewarded with eternal life. One traditional answer has been that one must accept Jesus Christ as savior in order to be so saved. In recent years, this definition has been liberalized in many denominations so that salvation is a possibility for Jews, Moslems, and other non-Christians.

However, as has been observed already in the discussion of orthodoxy, the gap between official pronouncements and individual attitudes —whether among the clergy or the laity—is often a large one. So it is with religious particularism. Two-thirds of the Protestant laypersons and half of the Catholics agreed that a belief in Jesus Christ as savior was "absolutely necessary" for salvation. Among Protestant clergy, this figure reached 69 percent. The majority of Christians clearly continue to hold beliefs that would condemn non-Christians to damnation (as well as those Christians not accepting Jesus as the Son of God).

As above, this "total" statistic is something of a fiction, varying greatly from denomination to denomination. Among Protestant laity, the percentage holding to such a belief ranges from a low of 38 percent among United Church of Christ to a high of 97 percent among Missouri Synod Lutherans and Southern Baptists. Among clergymen, the figures similarly vary from 29 percent of the United Church of Christ ministers to 97 percent among Missouri Synod Lutherans and 99 percent among Southern Baptists. The belief that non-Christians are damned is thus virtually unanimous in some churches, while a minority viewpoint in others.

Since these denominational distributions correspond to those found above for orthodoxy, it seems likely that orthodoxy and particularism are closely linked (as the model suggested they would be). In fact, they are. Among clergy and laity alike, an orthodox theological worldview leads to the belief that those rejecting Jesus Christ as the savior of mankind are personally doomed.

The potential importance of such particularistic attitudes for anti-Semitism lies in what they may imply for how persons of the Jewish faith are responded to. In the past, particularist beliefs have led to a missionary zeal to convert those not believing in orthodox Christian truths and, on frequent occasions, to the persecution of those rejecting such conversion. Christianity today has lost much of its previous fervency but perhaps not all of its righteousness. Orthodox, particularistic Christians may continue to have feelings of hostility toward nonbelievers and, because of their visibility, especially toward Jews.

Images of the Historical Jew

Undoubtedly the most pernicious and sinister of all Christian images is that of Jews as Christ-killers—the murderers of Jesus Christ, the Christian Redeemer. The principal source of this epithet is a passage in the Book of Matthew describing the trial of Jesus before the Roman Procurator of Judea, Pontius Pilate. According to Matthew's account, Pilate thought Jesus to be innocent of any wrongdoing and sought to avoid his execution. A long-standing Jewish custom allowed a condemned prisoner to be pardoned at feast time, and Pilate gave the Jewish multitude the choice of releasing Jesus or another prisoner, Barabbas, who had been found guilty of murder and sedition. Instead of Jesus, however, the crowd was persuaded by their priests and elders to pardon Barabbas. When Pilate protested Jesus' innocence, the Jewish multitude cried out, "His blood be on us, and on our children."

The charge that Jews are collectively responsible for the execution of Jesus has been repeated through the centuries and has been used to justify continued Jewish persecution. In a 1939 pastoral letter, for example, Konrad Grober, the Roman Catholic Archbishop of Freising, Germany, wrote that the Jews were entirely responsible for the Crucifixion of Christ and that "their murderous hatred of Him has continued in later centuries."[3] Bishop Hilfrich of Limburg echoed this viewpoint, adding that for their murder of God the Jews have been under a curse since the original Good Friday.[4] Such religious attitudes were fairly typical of the German Roman Catholic hierarchy—and to a lesser extent of Protestant church leaders—at the time. In this country much the same charges were being made by Father Charles E. Coughlin and revivalist preachers such as Gerald B. Winrod and Gerald L. K. Smith.

Following the destruction of European Jewry, the Roman Catholic Church and most of the major Protestant churches recanted their previous positions on this issue. They denounced the doctrines of Jewish guilt for the Crucifixion and taught that all mankind is responsible for the death of Jesus. Today only a few denominations—most notably the

Missouri Synod Lutherans and Southern Baptists—have failed to condemn the age-old charge of deicide.

Official church actions, however, can hardly be expected to change people's minds overnight. Indeed, research has shown that most Protestants remain completely unaware of their denominations' official pronouncements and that in many issue areas Catholics openly reject their church's stands (such as in relation to birth control).[5] Thus it felt that some church members might continue to hold Jews responsible for the Crucifixion, even though their church's official teachings were otherwise.

The presence among contemporary Christians of a belief that Jews were responsible for the Crucifixion was explored somewhat differently in the lay and clergy studies, although both studies confirm that such a belief continues to be widely held. In the lay study, which dealt with the subject more comprehensively, an effort was made to assess not only Matthew's account of Jewish responsibility for the Crucifixion but also the themes that Pilate tried to prevent the execution and that the Jewish multitudes, stirred up by their priests and elders, forced the Crucifixion to be carried out.

Seventy-nine percent of the laity (Catholics and Protestants alike) agreed that Pilate "wanted to spare Jesus from the cross." Forty-seven percent of the Protestants and 46 percent of the Catholics acknowledged that "a group of powerful Jews wanted Jesus dead." When given a choice of choosing the Romans, the Greeks, the Jews, the Christians, or none of these as the group most responsible for crucifying Christ, 58 percent of the Protestants and 61 percent of the Catholics chose the Jews.

At least as an historical interpretation, it is evident from these figures that many Christians continue to hold Jews responsible for the Crucifixion. Further, many of them assign questionable or evil motives to the Jewish rejection of Jesus. When asked why the Jews rejected Christ as the Messiah, 44 percent of the Protestants and 39 percent of the Catholic supported the assertion that the Jews "couldn't accept a Messiah who came from humble beginnings," 21 percent of Protestants and 16 percent of Catholics charged that "the Jews were sinful and had turned against God."

Protestant clergy were asked only the question about which group was most responsible for crucifying Christ, but the option "all mankind" was added to those made available to the laypersons. Given that option, the majority of clergy—54 percent—chose it, but 32 percent still chose the Jews. Thus, even among clergy there is a substantial minority who blame the Jews for Christ's death.

Hostile Religious Conceptions of the Contemporary Jew

The persistence of specifically religious, as distinct from secular, hostility toward Jews was also investigated with respect to the modern Jew. Is it believed that Jews today continue to bear the stigma of their rejection of Jesus? To measure this dimension of belief two propositions were put to the lay and clerical respondents. The first suggested that Jews are still to be blamed for the Crucifixion: "The Jews can never be forgiven for what they did to Jesus until they accept him as the true savior." In the lay study, 33 percent of the Protestants and 14 percent of the Catholics agreed with this statement, while another 27 percent and 32 percent, respectively, were uncertain in their beliefs. All together, then, 60 percent of the Protestants and 46 percent of the Catholics at least acknowledge the possibility that Jews are unforgiven for their treatment of Jesus. Clearly, for many Christians the Crucifixion remains a salient point of reference in their judgment about Jews.

The second statement was even more strongly worded. It asked, in effect, whether the contemporary Jew is "cursed by God": "The reason the Jews have so much trouble is because God is punishing them for rejecting Jesus." To agree with this statement is tantamount to viewing the mistreatment of Jews today as divinely ordained. It was accepted by 13 percent of the Protestants and 11 percent of the Catholics in the lay study. If we add to these figures those who were uncertain in their views, 39 percent of the Protestants and 41 percent of the Catholics allowed the possibility that Jews were under God's curse.

Many rank-and-file church members thus hold hostile religious images of Jews. Considerably fewer clergy subscribe to such images, although the number, particularly with respect to the view that "the Jews can never be forgiven for what they did to Jesus until they accept Him as the true savior," is not insubstantial. Nineteen percent of the clerical respondents agreed with this statement, while another 6 percent were uncertain of their position. On the more strongly worded statement—that Jews are being punished for rejecting Jesus—8 percent agreed, with another 4 percent uncertain.

Feelings of religious hostility toward Jews thus also exist among the clergy, albeit at a lower level than among the laity. The anomalous nature of these attitudes can be better appreciated if they are compared with the way in which Americans characteristically think about other ethnic or population groups. With very few exceptions, judgments are made about them in contemporary terms and not from the perspective of past history. For example, the atrocities of the Romans are virtually never considered in present-day conceptions of modern-day Italians, or the vicious raids of the Vikings in thinking about Scandinavians. Those are simply past events holding little relevance to contemporary values or beliefs. Even an occurrence as recent and as murderous as World War II is today of small consequence to the images held of our former adversaries. The Germans and the Japanese of contemporary times are seldom equated with the hated enemies of forty years ago.

To make such judgments of Jews is thus a rare and peculiar practice. Even if Jewish leaders were active agents in the execution of Jesus some 2,000 years ago, it is odd that Americans would consider this fact to have any bearing on their evaluations of Jews today.

Orthodoxy, Particularism, and Religious Hostility

But are these tendencies among Christians attributable to their religious beliefs? More specifically, is religious hostility toward the contemporary Jew a product of an orthodox and a particularist vision of Christian faith? The answer is yes, but not absolutely. Not all Christians whose faith is highly orthodox and particularistic exhibit religious hostility. In turn, not all Christians whose faith is other than orthodox and particularist are entirely free of such hostility. There exist, however, rather strong tendencies for the beliefs and hostilities to go together.

Among Protestant laity, 86 percent of those who are highly orthodox and highly particularist, and who attributed Christ's death to the Jews, feel that Jews still cannot be forgiven for rejecting Jesus. In contrast, only 1 percent feel this way among those low on both orthodoxy and particularism and who did not blame the Crucifixion on the Jews. Fewer Catholics than Protestants harbored a negative religious image of the modern Jew in the first place, and thus the actual percentage differences for them are smaller. However, a majority of Catholics holding the negative image scored high on particularism and orthodoxy and also blamed the Jews for the Crucifixion.

The same pattern of relation holds for Protestant clergy. Among clergy who are highly orthodox and highly particularist, and who attribute the Crucifixion to the Jews, 89 percent agreed either that the Jews can never be forgiven until they accept Christ or that the Jews are being punished by God or both. In comparison, such agreement is only 18 percent among nonorthodox, nonparticularist clergy who reject an image of the Jews as responsible for Christ's death.

As a consequence of these patterns, anti-Jewish feelings are found largely within those denominations where religious views of an orthodox and particularist nature are most commonly taught. In the clergy study, 69 percent of the Southern Baptists and 53 percent of the Missouri Lutherans agreed that Jews would remain unforgiven until they accept Christ as savior, as contrasted with only 3 to 4 percent of the United Church of Christ, Methodist, and Episcopalian clergy. A similar range of opinions was found among laypersons. Eighty percent of the Southern Baptists and 70 percent of the Missouri Synod Lutherans agreed that the Jews remain unforgiven. Among members of the United Church of Christ, Methodist, and Episcopalians, the figures were respectively 10, 12, and 11 percent.

In summarizing these findings, it must be pointed out exactly what is involved in the holding of such beliefs. To consider Jews to be unforgiven and an object of God's punishment is an unmistakably hostile attitude. It represents a highly damaging conclusion—one that is almost certain to affect the holder's general feelings toward Jews. To entertain such notions is thus a form of religious bigotry and prejudice.

From the perspective of traditional Christianity, this judgment may seem unfair or overly harsh. For conservative Christians it is often an article of faith that Jews—a group not accepting Jesus as the Son of God —remain unforgiven and unsaved; it may not seem that such a position involves any hostility or prejudice. This argument, for example, was made by the Reverend Wayne Dehoney, then president of the Southern Baptist Convention, in criticizing the results just reported. He was quoted in *Newsweek* magazine:

Christians do believe that all Jews who reject Christ as the Messiah are therefore lost from God's redeeming love—as are all men of all races who have not personally responded to God's grace through faith in Jesus Christ. This is not racism; this is the Christian doctrine of personal salvation.[6]

A similar position was taken by a Missouri Synod Lutheran minister respondent in the clerical study:

I feel sorry for all Jews who have rejected Jesus and thus have no God. There is only one God (Father-Son-Holy Ghost). "He that knoweth not the Son honoreth not the Father," said Jesus. The unrepentant Jew is unsaved. God loves the Jews and chose them, and my Savior is a Jew. But they have chosen to reject Him. What more could they have wanted from the Messiah?

While such statements might seem perfectly reasonable from an orthodox point of view, they amount to a demand that Jews renounce their own religious convictions and heritage and accept Christianity; if they do not, they will be punished for eternity.

CHRISTIAN BELIEFS AND ANTI-SEMITISM

The first four stages of the model have thus been substantiated. A commitment to an orthodox and particularistic version of Christian faith does indeed lead to the holding of hostile religious feelings toward modern-day Jews. It does so through a cognitively related chain of beliefs; once certain basic assumptions are made about religious reality, it follows logically that Jews will be viewed as religious outsiders or heretics.

It is time now to present evidence on the final and most controversial step in this model. The central purpose of these investigations was to determine whether religious convictions play any part in contemporary anti-Semitism. It was thought that people who held hostile religious conceptions of Jews might tend also to develop anti-Jewish feelings of a more general or secular nature—simply put, that people who disliked Jews on religious grounds would easily fall prey to disliking them in more secular ways as well.

Anti-Semitism among Church Members

A long battery of questions was included in the study of laity for the express purpose of measuring various forms of secular anti-Semitism.

These items included . . . belief statements . . . , as well as questions designed to measure the respondents' feelings toward interacting with Jews and their reaction to Jews under certain hypothetical conditions. Since little difference was found among these various indicators of anti-Semitism, attention here will be limited to anti-Semitic beliefs.

First, how anti-Semitic in their beliefs are churchgoers? Are the values of Christian brotherhood reflected in a greater acceptance of Jewish people? Or do the religious feelings outlined above produce greater hostilities towards Jews? Speaking generally, the level of anti-Semitism found among church members is about the same as that found among the general public. The proposition of respondents in this study accepting negative stereotypes of Jews was almost identical to that in the national study cited in Chapter 1 of our book *Anti-Semitism in America*. For example, 33 percent of the Protestants and 29 percent of the Catholics agreed that it was true or somewhat true that "Jews are more likely than Christians to cheat in business." Thirty-one percent and 26 percent, respectively, felt that "Jews, in general, are inclined to be more loyal to Israel than to America." And 57 percent and 55 percent agreed that "Jews want to remain different from other people and yet they are touchy if people notice these differences."

Such figures indicate that church members are not much different from anyone else when it comes to anti-Semitic prejudice. In the national study it was estimated that a third of the American people were highly prone to hold anti-Semitic beliefs; in the present study the figure was set at 33 percent for Protestants and 29 percent for Catholics.[7] Again, it should be pointed out that such percentages do not refer to the virulent form of anti-Semitism associated with Nazi Germany or with certain hate groups in this country. Anti-Semitic feelings of this type are relatively rare in present-day America. These figures do, however, refer to individuals who are highly disposed to stereotype Jews in negative ways, including stereotypes of an overly belligerent and hostile nature.

Anti-Semitism can thus be found within the churches as well as outside of them. This in itself is hardly a surprising finding; there are few knowledgeable observers who believe that organized religion is entirely free from prejudice. To what extent, however, are such anti-Semitic beliefs a product of distinctly religious convictions rather than of something else?

Previously, four distinct sets of Christian beliefs were identified, and their causal connections demonstrated. Orthodoxy was seen to produce a particularistic worldview in which only right-thinking Christians were subject to salvation; theological beliefs of this nature, in turn, were associated with hostile religious images of both the historical and modern Jew. Upon examination, *all four of these religious beliefs were found to be strongly associated with secular anti-Semitism.* Indeed, taken together, they prove a powerful predicator of secular anti-Semitism. This is indicated in Table 7–3, which combines these four dimensions of Christian belief into a single composite index of "religious bigotry." As this table indicates, the respondents' anti-Semitism varies in direct relation to their positions on this measure. Among Protestants, the proportion of anti-Semites ranged from 10 percent among those low in religious bigotry to 78 percent among those high on this dimension; among Catholics, the range was from a low of 6 percent to a high of 83 percent. These variations are among the greatest of any encountered in the studies in this series. Moreover, these variations are sustained when such controls as age, education, and socio-economic background are taken into account. That is to say, whether persons are young or old, educated or uneducated, rich or poor, the more the religious beliefs are subscribed to, the greater the anti-Semitism.

It is important to recognize, however, that the process through which this occurs is not directly from orthodox and particularist belief to secular anti-Semitism. Believing that salvation is possible only through Christ, for example, does not lead believers to be disposed to accept the additional belief that Jews are more likely than Christians to cheat in business. Rather, what the religious beliefs do is generate hostility to

Table 7–3
Percentage of Christian Laypersons Scoring High in Anti-Semitic Belief at Each Level of Religious Bigotry Index

Percentage Scoring High and Medium High on Index of Anti-Semitic Belief	Index of Religious Bigotry						
	Low						High
	0	1	2	3	4	5	6
Protestants	10%	15%	28%	37%	46%	57%	78%
	(216)	(233)	(206)	(146)	(159)	(124)	(97)
Catholics	6%	17%	19%	39%	40%	58%	83%
	(31)	(54)	(78)	(59)	(33)	(21)	(6)

Source: Adapted from Glock and Stark, *Christian Beliefs and Anti-Semitism*, p. 136.

Jews as religious outsiders. For those believing that Jews are damned on religious grounds, it is apparently a small step to believing that Jews are also avaricious, unethical, clannish, and unpatriotic.

The significance of the linkage of Christian orthodoxy and particularism to secular anti-Semitism should not be underestimated. A large proportion of churchgoers in this country are orthodox and particularist in their religious outooks, and in this respect *most Christians are susceptible to such religious sources of anti-Semitism*. It is not a small or deviant perspective in Christianity that contributes to anti-Semitic sentiments among people; it is the theological convictions of a large part of the religious mainstream of America.

Anti-Semitism among Protestant Ministers

Anti-Semitism among Protestant ministers is less prevalent than among Protestant laity. For example, while 53 percent of the Protestant laity agreed that it was at least somewhat true that "Jews were more likely than Christians to cheat in business," only 10 percent of the California ministers answered this way. Similarly, while 31 percent of the laity accepted the possibility that Jews were more loyal to Israel than to America, only 19 percent of the ministers agreed. Overall it was estimated that 17 percent of the Protestant clergy surveyed were anti-Semitic, as against 33 percent of the Protestant laity.[8]

This difference is attributable in part to the fact that clergymen, on the average, are better educated than lay persons. When clergy are compared with laity who have had more than a college education, which most clergy have had, the difference in anti-Semitism rates is considerably less—the clergy's 17 percent is measured against 22 percent for highly educated Protestant laity. However, among lay persons it was found that, to a large extent, the lower anti-Semitism of the more-educated was the result of their being less likely than the less-educated to subscribe to orthodox and particularist beliefs. When the more-educated did subscribe to such beliefs, they were as likely as the uneducated believers and considerably more likely than uneducated nonbelievers to be anti-Semitic.

Besides being less anti-Semitic, clergy also differ from laity in that their religious convictions are less likely to produce anti-Semitism. Among highly educated Protestant laity, for example, 86 percent are anti-Semitic of those who are highly orthodox particularists and feel some religious hostility toward Jews. Only 9 percent are anti-Semitic among those without the religious convictions and the hostility. Among clergy, the range is from 9 percent to 47 percent. Thus among both laity and clergy it is clear that religious convictions are a source of anti-Semitism, but the relation is considerably stronger for laity than for clergy. This is attributable to the clergy's greater ability than laity, while believing in the eternal damnation of the Jews, not to permit this to spill over into secular anti-Semitism.

That the links in the causal chain leading from religious convictions of the kind specified to anti-Semitism are not inexorable affords some promise that the chain can be broken without asking people to abandon their religious convictions. It would appear, however, that the clergy who are able to do this for themselves are not helping their parishioners to follow suit. Such clergy may well proclaim that Christian doctrines of love, brotherhood, compassion, and forgiveness erase any potential for prejudice contained in their Christian convictions. For themselves this may indeed hold true. The evidence suggests, however, that relatively few of the laity whose religious convictions are conservative are receiving the message.

SUMMARY

The model set forth at the beginning of this chapter proved to be accurate. The acceptance of orthodox Christian beliefs leads to a particularistic religious orientation in which only right-thinking Christians are seen as saved and all others are damned. These views, in turn, are associated with hostile feelings toward Jews—which have both a historical dimension (Jews being held responsible for the Crucifixion) and contemporary effects (Jews being condemned for their rejection of Jesus as savior). Such religious beliefs, finally, are associated with secular forms of anti-Semitism. Christian laypersons and ministers holding these religious conceptions are disproportionately prejudiced in their attitudes toward Jews.

The churches today, then, may not openly preach anti-Semitism, and their official position may be one of reconciliation and rapprochement. In reality, however, orthodox Christianity continues to serve as an agent of anti-Semitic prejudice in America. It does so by introducing a set of cognitive assumptions that provide people with reasons to dislike Jews. Not everyone who accepts these assumptions draws from them the same hostile conclusions about Jews, but the majority of theologically conservative churchpeople do make such connections. Thus, despite the liberalization of American religion, Christianity continues to have a strong impact upon what people think about Jews. Indeed, of the various factors examined in the entire series of studies, religious beliefs were second only to a lack of education as a primary source of anti-Semitic prejudice among Americans.

NOTES

1. The full report of these studies is contained in Charles Y. Glock and Rodney Stark, *Christian Beliefs and Anti-Semitism* (New York: Harper & Row, 1966).
2. The report of this study is in Rodney Stark, Bruce D. Foster, Charles Y. Glock, and Harold E. Quinley, *Wayward Shepherds: Prejudice and the Protestant Clergy* (New York: Harper & Row, 1971).
3. Pastoral letter of January 30, 1939, *Amtsblatt für die Erzdiözese Freiburg,* February 8, 1939, quoted in Guenter Lewy, "Pius XII, the Jews, and the German Catholic Church," *Commentary,* February 1964, pp 23–35.
4. Quoted in Lewy, "Pius XII."
5. Charles Y. Glock, Benjamin B. Ringer, and Earl R. Babbie, *To Comfort and to Challenge* (Berkeley: University of California Press, 1967), and Andrew M. Greeley, *The Denominational Society* (Glenview, Ill.: Scott, Foresman, 1972).
6. Wayne Dehoney, letter to the editors of *Newsweek,* May 23, 1966, in response to a story on "Christian Beliefs and Anti-Semitism."
7. Catholics have often been the objects of religious prejudice themselves, and this apparently contributes to their somewhat lower levels of anti-Semitism. Catholics, however, do not appear to be any more tolerant than Protestants on atheists. About a third of each religious group, for example, would not allow an atheist to teach in a public high school.
8. These two studies were based upon slightly different samples, of course, and the two estimates are thus not drawn from comparable populations. If anything, however, the lay sample (based upon the San Francisco Bay Area) should comprise more disproportionately unprejudiced respondents than the clergy sample (based upon the state of California as a whole).

8

American Protestantism and Antisemitism

Franklin H. Littell

For the purpose of this discussion it will be assumed that antisemitism encompasses any action, verbal or physical, that denigrates the Jewish people and/or threatens the survival of Jews. Since the emergence of the gentile church, and especially in the millennium and a half between Constantine the Great and the Enlightenment,[1] antisemitism in Christendom has been expressed in three levels of thought, speech and action. These levels are as distinguishable as levels of rock or clay in geological formations.

The three levels of antisemitism to which we refer are (1) the theological, (2) the cultural, and (3) the political.[2] At the time of the gentile church fathers, theological antisemitism was already an ideology. In its political form we see antisemitism used as an ideological weapon—first to conquer men's minds, and finally to shape their souls (i.e., to determine the patterns of the millennium to come).

When we address the current question of "American Protestantism and Antisemitism" we are not, then, directing attention to overtly and deliberately antisemitic groups. There are such, but they are politically much more marginal than in the years when Henry Ford and Father Coughlin commanded a considerable following as antisemitic propagandists.

Of course if such groups come to power, as the record of the Third Reich amply documents, the analytical and political fronts change com-

Reprinted in part by permission of The Vidal Sassoon International Center for the Study of Antisemitism, The Hebrew University of Jerusalem. Originally published in 1985.

pletely. So too do the rules as to what measures are permissible by way of resistance to decisions of government. A terrorist movement that has become a criminal dictatorship will never become legitimate, and will never be entitled to the basic loyalty due a democratic government— even when the latter makes serious blunders or acts for a time in ways that totter on the edge of illegitimacy (e.g., in President Lincoln's suspension of *habeas corpus* in Copperhead territory during the Civil War, or in President Roosevelt's internment of Japanese-American citizens after the attack on Pearl Harbor).

Terrorist movements of the NSDAP and "Aryan Nations" type are not our topic today. Our topic, "American Protestantism and Antisemitism," concerns more subtle issues. Our question is raised against the background of awareness that the Nazi war against the Jews not only actualized the ideology of Nazi true believers: it also exposed the endemic antisemitism which had been a malaise of Christendom for centuries.[3] That malaise, although somewhat modified by the religious liberty guaranteed also to Jews by the Federal Constitution and by the popular acceptance of religious pluralism as a viable social concept, still corrupts a good deal of the preaching and teaching in American pulpits and Sunday Schools.[4]

This paper is by way of being a preliminary discussion of some of the issues, for major research projects have been launched in 1984 to explore antisemitism in the primary sectors of American Christianity in depth. Under the auspices of the International Center for the Study of Antisemitism, associated with the Institute of Contemporary Jewry at the Hebrew University, self-study teams have been formed in three areas relevant to our present topic: "Liberal Protestantism and Antisemitism," "Conservative Protestantism and Antisemitism" and "Black Churches and Antisemitism." The fourth self-study group, on "American Catholicism and Antisemitism," lies outside our immediate concerns. In each area there have been gathered teams of scholars who identify themselves with a certain theological grouping, and who share the common concern to analyze and deal with the problem of antisemitism at all levels.

At first glance this might seem a task beyond human capacity, simply because of the extraordinary variety of Protestant churches in America. The ordinary viewer, having read tales of various exotic denominations, is under the impression that there are hundreds of churches—far too many for any scholar or team of scholars to survey. And, in fact, J. Gordon Melton's massive two-volume work, *The Encyclopedia of American Religions,* lists well over 800—most of which, after the Jews and Roman Catholics are subtracted, fall into that amiable category: "Protestants and Other." [5]

The fact is, however, that to the student American Protestantism affords a much more coherent picture than often assumed. Partly as a result of half a century of union movement, the twelve largest Protestant denominations comprehend approximately 85 percent of all Protestants. Most of the dozens of smaller denominations number from one to ten congregations, and most of them are splinters from the Wesleyan or Baptist communities. We are therefore initiating, as part of the study, studies within each of the twelve—as well as topical studies cutting across the lines.

We should also be clear as to what we mean by "conservative" Protestantism. Out-groupers are seldom aware of it, and the media take no notice of distinctions in reporting incidents, but within conservative Protestant ranks there are many variations and not a few controversies. These are the most significant traditional groupings: *Orthodox*—chiefly consisting of churches influenced by the older hard Calvinist theology; *Fundamentalists*—chiefly consisting of churches associated with the publication and dissemination of a tract series called *The Fundamentals;* and *Evangelicals*—churches and individuals chiefly influenced by the older Wesleyan emphasis upon individual conversion and personal holiness. Here again the lines have become blurred between groupings, as well as in the minds of newspaper and magazine reporters, and nowhere more than through the rise of Dispensationalism.

Causing additional confusion to the observer is the fact that recent studies show a marked difference in belief between church executives and prominent preachers and the rank and file membership. Nevertheless, among the dozen largest Protestant denominations in the United States it is possible to make some generalizations.

The major conservative denominations are these (figures are approximations):

Lutheran Church, Missouri Synod—3.0 million
Southern Baptist Convention—8.5 million adults
Church of Jesus Christ of Latter Day Saints ("Mormons")—3.5 million

The major liberal denominations (marked i.a. by affiliation with the
National Council of Churches and the World Council of Churches):

American Baptist Churches—1.0 million adults
American Lutheran Church—2.8 million (uniting with LCA)
Christian Church (Disciples of Christ)—1.5 million adults
Episcopal Church—3 million
Lutheran Church in America—3.1 million (uniting with ALC)
United Church of Christ—2 million
United Methodist Church—9.2 million
United Presbyterian Church—3.4 million

In addition, two of the largest denominations in America consist of
black Baptists: the National Baptist Convention (unincorporated) and
the National Baptists Convention, USA, Inc. The set of studies spear-
headed by Professor Locke will give us more information in this area.[6]
In the meantime it can be said that the black churches have been deeply
rooted in the Scriptures, especially the Hebrew Scriptures (OT), and that
the highly publicized antisemitic utterances of some of their educated
leaders are within the parameters of the more privately expressed prejudices of white denominational leaders.

American Protestantism is not, then, as elusive of generalizing studies
as might at first be supposed. It is the frank acceptance of religious
liberty and pluralism that may mislead. In American Protestantism there
is more likeness between churches than at first appears. And established
churches are less coherent and unified than they appear at first glance.
For example, German Protestantism is divided into 28 *Landeskirchen,*
most of them dating back to the Napoleonic period and divided theologically and structurally as well as politically.

Finally, it must be noted that there are in America some smaller
denominations that exercise in specific areas an influence far out of
proportion to their numbers. Cases in point would be the influence of
the so-called "Peace Churches"—the Mennonites, Brethren and Quak-
ers, the Unification Church, the Seventh Day Adventists, and numerous
smaller churches grouped under the general rubric "Pentecostals."

Of all the small beginnings that have exercised a profound and per-
vading leaven in American Protestantism, none has been more important
on the matter of the attitude of Jewish survival and well-being than that

launched by John Nelson Darby. Although the denominational bloc that claims lineal descent from Darby, the "Plymouth Brethren" or "Christian Brethren," numbers less than 100,000, vast numbers of Protestants have been affected by Darby's interpretation of the continuing place of the Jewish people—and of a restored Israel—in the province of God. As we shall shortly see, any discussion of the relationship of Christians and Jews, in doctrine or in practice—for example, on "American Fundamentalism and Antisemitism"—must begin with Darby, certainly the most underestimated religious teacher in the last two centuries of British and American Christianity.[7]

Before going into limited sectors, we should have a common understanding of some of the basic terms of reference. There have been major studies of American antisemitism before. One such study, which resulted in several widely sold books, received a subvention of $700,000. Unfortunately, the study was of limited value from its inception because of two grave conceptual errors. First, like all good children of the Enlightenment, the primary organizers were convinced that antisemitism is a sub-category of "prejudice," and that "prejudice'" is a general category of behavior—an emotional response that education and the triumph of the informed mind will eliminate. To acquire "toleration" is to divest oneself of particularism.[8] Second, although the books make reference occasionally to mysterious emotional and irrational factors, the primary focus of attention is devoted to antisemitism of the traditional kind. The shadow of Auschwitz, the weight of structures, the momentum of power —in sum, the tragic dimension of human life and history escape the attention of these and most other earlier studies of antisemitism.

They miss the main problem. Unless political antisemites come to power, the main problem is the "good people"—the theological and cultural antisemites who keep the fire smouldering under the surface. The question, to illustrate, is how a committee sponsored by the American Friends Service Committee ("liberal" Protestant) could, in the name of "even-handedness," release a book on peace in the Middle East that makes the refugee problem the main issue. Not that the refugee problem is not an issue: the question is why it never occurred to them that there were Jewish refugees in the Middle East as well as Arab refugees. The question is how an annual church convention ("conservative" Protestant) can pass in a single sitting two strong resolutions—the one supporting Israel's right to existence and well-being, and the other supporting a vigorous missionary program that targets Jews.

In stark and broad outline, the problem is this: classical Christianity has since the generation of the gentile Church Fathers taught the superseding myth: that with the life and works of Jesus of Nazareth God's use for the "old Israel" was played out. This line of thought twisted both Exegesis and Theology. At the level of popular superstition, the deicide calumny was more deadly. This myth also derived from the period of the gentile Church Fathers, for "god" could not be killed until the teachers, ignorant of Hebrew, but schooled in Greek ways of thought and Roman notions of triumphant power, apotheosized the one they called "Lord."

Most students of Jewish history are well aware of Martin Luther's maledictions in the last years of his life, although they seldom note his equally biter pronouncements on the Mennonites, Baptists and Schwenkfelder. Articles and even books have been written to prove Nazi antisemitism a legitimate offspring of Luther's hateful tracts. The truth, as Heiko Obermann has shown in a recent study of antisemitism,[9] is much more grim: what Luther wrote and taught about the Jews was written and taught by all his contemporaries—virtually without exception.

From the age of the gentile Church Fathers, both Greek and Latin Christendom was infected with a theological antisemitism that has yet to pass away. The record of the Latin church is better known. But the Eastern record is also representative of the problem throughout Christendom. After the fall of Constantinople (1453) the center in the Eastern churches shifted to Moscow. Under the last of the Romanovs, with the counsel of Konstantin Pobiedonestzev, the first deliberate use of antisemitism as a political weapon was made. Since the revolutions of 1917, a cultural antisemitism has persisted in the Marxist establishment. In Marxism, which Paul Tillich called "a Christian heresy," the superseding myth is vigorously present, albeit in modified form. In sum, throughout all major sectors of Christianity there are centuries-old teachings upon which all traditional churches agree, and which involve what Jules Isaac called "the teaching of contempt."[10]

More serious than denigration, however, they preach and teach an interpretation of history that has no place or purpose for a surviving

Jewry. The single exception to this generally dark picture was for centuries the argument that—since the Jews had inexplicably survived in spite of everything—God must be permitting their survival in order that in their suffering and homelessness all peoples might see the judgment visited upon a reprobate people.[11] Clearly, the resentment which Israel arouses in church bureaus in Europe and America is related to the fact that for centuries Christianity had a minor theme that explained the survival of Jews as losers in the game of history.

Nothing so aroused these traditional Christian centers of power as the Israel of the Six-Day War. It was threatening enough that the existence of the State of Israel became a pledge of Jewish survival. But that a successful and winning Israel should reverse the whole understanding of "the Jew" as "loser," a picture so carefully maintained in one strand of Christian antisemitism was simply ideologically unmanageable. The very event of the Six-Day War that means so much for American Jewish self-confidence, that changed so radically the pattern of Jewish living in the galut [exile] was the event that in America unleashed a new rush of hostility from the liberal Christian establishment.

But on the other side of the tracks, out of the midst of a conservative Protestantism that had been previously largely silent, a new and vocal public support for Israel and Jewish concerns generally was evident. Leaders who had been known only to "in-group" conservative Christian circles suddenly became prominent radio and television preachers, household names among Church members and in the public at large. Religious circles that had been known to specialists for their quiet docility and inconspicuous obedience to political authority, after 1967 became vocal—and sometimes even demonstrative. The conservative Protestantism that now stood forth not only gave voice to solid blocs of constituents in conservative denominations: it was discovered to have strong following in all of the major "liberal" denominations as well.

The present political situation in American Protestantism is radically different from what it was just twenty years ago. Progressive Jewish agencies are lamenting the breakup of the old "liberal alliance" that dominated the national scene from FDR through LBJ. The "liberal" churches and their cooperative agencies seem to have become wide open channels for anti-Israel and pro-PLO propaganda, while conservative forces—both Jewish and Protestant—are taking up exposed positions in public life. These positions affect both foreign and domestic issues, and the conservatives are acting with a zeal that seems totally to reverse their previous style of quietism and docile obedience to the powers that be. And however soft the old liberal "mainline" churches seem to be on terrorism and Communism and Russian expansion in the Middle East, the conservative Protestants, perhaps especially the most prominent TV preachers, seem to be unqualifiedly pro-Israel and Judaeophile.

How then, in this apparent reversal of public roles and influence, are we to understand the present line-up of American Protestants vis-à-vis Jewish survival and well-being?

There are two events which provide a kind of litmus test by which to determine whether Christians are beginning to excavate and examine their true attitude to Jewish survival. The question of Jewish survival is the red thread that binds the two events together in theological thought. Those events are the Holocaust and a restored Israel. By the way in which a Christian individual or group handles these two events you can tell whether his world is static or in the process of being mended.

Initially, the Holocaust might seem to verify the stereotype of the Jew as a loser. And, as a matter of fact, Jews who have a ghetto-mentality seem to nurse the Holocaust as a precious possession even as Christian triumphalists cherish the Holocaust as another occasion for sympathy with victims. There are, of course, small groups in both the Jewish and the Christian communities that interpret the Holocaust in traditional terms, as an expression of God's righteous wrath upon a disobedient people, but they are few in number. By far the largest numbers who miss the point, both Jews and Christian, succumb to the temptation to flatten it out into meaninglessness—the Jew by burying it in a long list of incidents of gentile perversity and murder, the gentile by burying it among numerous murderous cruelties suffered by multitudes of peoples in the twentieth century. The misuse of the Holocaust by Christians comes to a grinding halt, however, when the professing Christian realizes that this monstrous set of crimes was committed by dues-paying Roman Catholics, Protestants and Eastern Orthodox—never rebuked, let alone excommunicated.

The "liberal alliance," which included the realization and development of a Jewish homeland in its interfaith support of worthy programs, held together during the difficult years of Jewish pioneering and reclaiming the land, of snatching a piece of flesh from the bear's mouth during the Holocaust, of launching a new nation and defending it against awesome odds. Such affirmative support was developed in the American Christian Palestine Committee, and is associated in our memory with such prominent leaders as Reinhold Niebuhr, Carl Hermann Voss and Martin Luther King, Jr.—leaders who struggled valiantly against the latent religious antisemitism of the Christian churches and for a time kept the ship tacked against the wind. But the National Council of Churches and its affiliates shifted almost overnight when the designated object of pity and sympathy became "the poor Palestinian" instead of "the poor Jew." Nineteen hundred and sixty-seven was the fatal year, the year in which those Christians whose religious sentiment required an object of pity turned away from Israel.

The major strain in traditional Christian theology had always found Jewish survival undesirable and inexplicable. The minor strain was now confronted by a type of Jew who did not fit the ideological framework, and by an Israel that did not need or care for pity. The shift was made to someone else to practice pity on. The Holocaust could be discussed so long as no question was raised about Christian responsibility. But a victorious Israel was too much to conceptualize.

The credibility crisis induced by awareness of the meaning of the Holocaust in the history of Christianity is so grave, and the shock produced by the existence of a viable restored Israel is so heavy, there are as yet comparatively few Christians who have accepted the double challenge to their inherited ideological biases. In looking back over 25 years of Holocaust study and instruction and writing, and 15 years of work under the banner of "Christians Concerned for Israel," I can find no significant evidence that the meaningful lines can be drawn between "liberal" Protestants and "conservative" Protestants.

A general resistance to facing the Holocaust cuts across denominational lines, and it is imbedded in a Christian triumphalism that is more than a millennium and a half old. The attitude to a restored Israel—the other key test for assessing Christian attitudes on Jewish survival—is, so far as the main streams of "liberal" and "conservative" Protestant thought are concerned, controlled not by repentance and a turning from contempt to fraternity. In "liberal" circles the controlling factors are the abstract generalizations; in "conservative" circles, including the Dispensationalists provisionally friendly to Israel, the controlling factors are the propositions.

Marginality is as much a clue as precise denominational alignment. For example, the editorial council of *The Review of Historical Revision* not only numbers not a single historian: it has only one Christian who makes anything of his avowal, and he is an itinerant Roman Catholic teacher.[12] The slowly growing number of scholars and churchmen who are taking the knife to antisemitic preaching and teaching include Roman Catholics, black Christians and white Protestants of churches and seminaries both "liberal" and "conservative." This suggests that the dividing line which will eventually show between our schools and churches will not follow the pre-Holocaust course: rather the attitude to Jewish survival will be the watershed between the old and the new rivers of Christian thought.

In the last decade or so it has become possible in conversation to place a seminary graduate who has studied with one of the teachers who is trying to carve a path through the thicket of the antisemitic theology that has flourished since the era of the gentile Church Fathers. The names of these teachers, their articles and books, are becoming well known. But they are still few, and the overwhelming number of individuals filling our pulpits and teaching posts are still pre-Holocaust and pre-Israel in their frame of mind and style of action.

The American church members' support for Israel is very general and is found in churches of every stripe, due in large part to a traditional emotional attachment to "the Holy Land" and the memorized portions of the Scriptures. It owes a great deal to the Puritan sub-stratum in major blocs of American Protestantism, a sub-stratum from which the liberal educated leaders have largely freed themselves but which is still central to the piety of the members of the congregations. So far, no American church body has undertaken the self-education over years of committee work and parish study, and no judicatory has taken a binding position in affirmation of Jewish survival to compare with that adopted by the Synod of the Protestant Church of the Rhineland in January of 1980.[13]

This means that both in its affirmative aspects and in its negative aspects the great body of American Protestantism has been formed by the traditional teachings. The bedrock of theological and cultural antisemitism is still there, modified only where a Puritan and Judaeophile strain is still alive. The secret of the new conservative Protestantism is precisely this: to a very large extent its values and teachings, and even its historical origins in the Puritan penetration of the Appalachian highlands generations ago, are derived from Puritanism—the radical Protestantism of the seventeenth century.

As the new shape of the American Protestant attitude to the Jews is emerging, it is clear that two utterly different but powerful personalities have shaped the thinking of those who affirm the importance of Jewish survival.

Usually counted on the "liberal" side, although he came out of the German Evangelical tradition (now joined with German Reformed and Congregationalists in the United Church of Christ), and although he was generally associated with the re-discovery of Biblical theology which is called "the Theology of Crisis" or "Dialectical Theology," is my teacher, Reinhold Niebuhr (1892–1971). Certainly his influence has been felt chiefly among the liberal Protestant denominations.

During the Third Reich, Niebuhr wrote more editorials and articles on the plight of the Jews trapped in Hitler's *Festung Europa,* and on the fate of those Christians who resisted, than any other American teacher or churchman. A professor at the interdenominational Union Theological Seminary in Manhattan, he was constantly active "downtown" in committees for refugee relief, in the American Christian Palestine Committee, etc.[14] His two articles in support of a Jewish state, written during the war, were perhaps his most famous statement on Jewish survival.[15] His students have been prominent in the so-called "mainline" churches on behalf of Israel and in teaching the Holocaust and its lessons.

Believing in the Jewish right of self-definition, Niebuhr was the first prominent American theologian to come out against Hebrew Christian missions. He said that he had learned that lesson from his brother Richard. In any case, he called publicly for a moratorium on Protestant missions to Jews.[16] He adjudged "a collective survival impulse as legitimate a 'right' as an individual one," and criticized the "provisional tolerance of liberals purchased by Jews through assimilation."[17]

Niebuhr was not a Christian Zionist, that is, one whose understanding of history requires a return of the people to the land of their fathers.

Rather he was a Christian pragmatist, who saw that the insensitivity of Christendom and the murderous program of Nazism left no alternative. Moreover, he respected Jewish communal initiative and was educated by his friendship with men like Felix Frankfurter and Abraham Joshua Heschel. Heschel, especially, taught him the importance of the Land in Jewish thought.

Most of all, Niebuhr did not believe that the Jews should be consigned to role-playing in someone else's passion play. His own work was completed before the importance of the Holocaust as an event in Christian history came to the fore. The "forty years in the wilderness" was not yet up. According to Ursula Niebuhr, the chief source of what he called his "long love affair with the Jewish people" was the teaching of the prophets. His copies of A Theology of the Social Gospel and Christianity and the Social Crisis, the classics by Walter Rauschenbusch which were so influential in the beginnings of the Social Gospel movement, were heavily marked in sections which indicated the contributions of the Hebrew prophets.[18]

If Niebuhr was the major figure in bringing about some Christian reconstruction of theology in liberal Protestant circles, and several of the most radical reconstructionists in the mainline churches were students of his, the major figure in shaping conservative Protestant thought about the Jewish people and Israel was of another century and another stamp. Niebuhr was internationally known in the World's Student Christian Federation and the World Council of Churches. He gave the Gifford Lectures in 1939. The very name of the man who more than any other shaped conservative Protestant thought vis-à-vis the Jewish people is unknown even to the millions of Baptists, Presbyterians, Congregationalists, Methodists and others who accept his view of Biblical prophecy. His name is John Nelson Darby (1800–1882).

Actually, the direct channel through which Darby's views reached masses of ordinary members of congregations was not in anything that he wrote or said—although he made a number of trips to America from England and spent a total of several years carrying on his work in the New World. The channel of primary influence was The Scofield Reference Bible, which by red-lettering and notes explained the special function in holy history provided by Divine Providence to a restored Israel.

Prepared by C. I. Scofield (1843–1921), the Reference Bible schematically related each part of Scripture to a time-table of "dispensations"—

past, present, and future. Through the enormous popularity of his Bible, and through an annual series of conferences on Bible Prophecy that met from 1876 on, Darby's views penetrated denominations, came to dominate certain Bible colleges and seminaries, and became a major force in the Fundamentalist movement which rose in opposition to the "Social Gospel," in "Social Creed of the Churches," and the Federal Council of Churches.

In 1895 Scofield and his colleagues formulated the "five points of Fundamentalism," and in 1909 two wealthy laymen financed the publication of 12 small volumes entitled *The Fundamentals: A Testimony to the Truth.* At this point in time the older orthodox teaching of the literal inerrancy of the text was welded to the "prophetic" interpretation of history, providing the powerful double impact of the authority of the Bible and a chiliastic emotional appeal. This was radical Puritanism reborn.[19]

These little books, like the *Reference Bible,* went into millions of homes; and where they went they carried a certain "prophetic" view of the future which required the return of the Jews to their homeland, the restoration of the state of Israel, the triumph of a reborn Solomon's kingdom over the armies of the heathen, and—in due course—a return of Christ in glory. And in that dispensation the faithful Christians—a considerably smaller company than the official church statistics, and the blessed of Israel, also a remnant, will join in obeisance to Him, who is King of Kings and Lord of Lords, namely Jesus Christ. In the meantime they do not engage in Hebrew Christian missions.[20]

The runaway best-seller, Hal Lindsey's *The Late, Great Planet Earth* (1970), is built on this schematization. In eight years it went through 62 printings and sold over 8 million copies. It is still selling. The number of books coming from the same school of thought, including many that sell in quantity, today eludes reckoning. One of them announces its basic political themes in the title: *Israel—America's Key to Survival* (1981). The author of the book (Mike Evans) stands squarely behind the most conservative positions of Israel's most conservative parties. Another, by David Lewis, interprets the significance of the IDF military action in Lebanon in the summer of 1982. Entitled *Magog 1982 Canceled,* it advances the thesis that Israel's action prevented, or at least forestalled, World War III. For these "prophetic" writers "Gog" is Russia and Israel is fulfilling a concrete political and religious mission in the Middle East

—one that is of central importance to every American and also to every Christian who has eyes to see the future.

Fundamentalism and Bible prophecy are thus motors propelling a politics of Christian Zionism. And here we enter the universe of Jerry Falwell, probably the best known of contemporary conservative Protestant preachers. He has a huge TV audience. He has a burgeoning college and an expanding seminary. His publishing program of books, pamphlets and study units is massive. He is a force in all of the conservative denominations and penetrates the grass roots level of the liberal denominations as well.

In Falwell's program book for his native land, entitled *Listen, America!* (1980), there is a chapter headed "That Miracle Called Israel." The chapter opens with a number of affirmative statements: "Israel still stands as shining testimony to the faithfulness of God. Israel is a bastion of democracy in a part of the world that is politically unstable . . ." After a discussion of Jewish suffering and survival, amply sprinkled with related Scriptural texts, he concludes: "The Jews are returning to their land of unbelief. They are spiritually blind and desparately in need of their Messiah and Savior. Yet they are God's people, and in the world today Bible-believing Christians in America are the best friends the nation Israel has. We must remain so."[21]

It does not seem unfair to say that the friendship which is so intensely pledged is provisional.

Where then do we emerge in a preliminary appraisal of American Protestantism and antisemitism?

Where are the "liberals"? For many years the most consistently antisemitic Protestant periodical in North America, and the one with the largest circulation, was the "liberal" *United Church of Canada Observer*. Its editor was A. C. Forrest, whose book *The Unholy Land* (1971) was a veritable compendium of the most snide and vicious attacks upon Jews and upon Christians friendly to Israel. The leading "liberal" Protestant journal in the USA, *The Christian Century*, has a long record of opposition to rescue work during the Holocaust, of attacks upon American Zionists for "double loyalty," of attacks upon Jews because they fail to assimilate and become good Americans, and of suppression of information about Christian action in Holocaust education or in support of Israel. The dreary record of *The Christian Century* has been documented *ad nauseam* by Carl Hermann Voss, Robert Ross,

A. Roy Eckardt and others. In a recent magazine interview, the author of the best-selling *The Abandonment of the Jews* (1984), David Wyman, himself a descendant of two minister grandfathers, speaks of his pain in becoming aware of *The Christian Century*'s record of decades of anti-Jewish politics.

Liberal antisemitism in America is essentially banal and uninteresting. By and large it follows the theological lines of traditional Christian antisemitism, intellectually elevated on occasion by nineteenth-century German "higher criticism." Its liturgies and preaching notes are subtly antisemitic; its better books are emancipated from the particular. Structurally, as Bernhard Olson concluded after his classic study, the American liberal *Kulturprotestantismus* suffers from a "predisposition toward abstraction," an aversion to "the specificity of each intergroup situation."[22]

Liberal Protestantism slides into hostility to Jews down the same slope as Humanism and Marxism, through inability to handle the dialectic of universalism and particularism.[23]

Where are the "conservatives"? The old, openly antisemitic conservatives of the period of Gerald Winrod and Gerald L. K. Smith have virtually disappeared from the American scene.[24] Conservative Protestantism today is dominated by a school of thought which thinks to affirm Israel, which tries to be helpful to Jewish causes—and which is nevertheless triumphalist. The Christian Zionists are in place, and they expect "the Jews" to be in their appointed place too.

There is some controversy between evangelicals who still sponsor Hebrew Christian missions and dispensationalists who eschew missions, but the latter seem to be dominant today. The former believe the Jews must be converted and returned to the land of their fathers. The latter believe that when the Lord returns he will gather up in glory together, the elect of Israel and the elect of the gentiles.

In meditating upon the simple belief of those who trust in the "prophecy" that Darby launched 150 years ago, it seems like laying profane hands upon sacred things to ask the simple question: "What happens if 'the Jews' don't keep their appointed rendezvous?"

The Fundamentalist dispensationalists know more about the future than the rest of us. With their propositions they seem rather evenly matched to the abstractions of the liberals. But neither the majority of liberals nor the main body of conservatives has purged itself of the patronizing style of Christian triumphalism. They are, in short, pre-Auschwitz in manner and in content. They have not yet crossed the mountain and reentered real history.

In America today, neither liberal Protestantism nor conservative Protestantism has yet mastered the chief lesson of the Holocaust: namely, that the Jewish people has paid the price to be permitted the self-definition that every other people, not burdened by the resentment of the heathen,[25] is accorded as a matter of course.

NOTES

1. "These are my preliminary propositions; after very deep historical research, I say and maintain that the fate of Israel did not take on a truly inhuman character until the 4th century A.D. with the coming of the Christian Empire." Isaac, Jules, *Has Anti-Semitism Roots in Christianity?* (New York: National Conference of Christians and Jews, 1961), p. 45.

2. Cf. the writer's 1973 Israel Goldstein Lecture at the Hebrew University, published in X *Journal of Ecumenical Studies* (1973) 3:483–97, 492f.

3. Cf. the writer's *The Crucifixion of the Jews* (New York: Harper & Row, 1975); Eckardt, A. Roy and Alice E., *A Long Night's Journey into Day* (Detroit: Wayne State University Press, 1982); Ruether, Rosemary R., *Faith and Fratricide* (New York: Seabury Press, 1974).

4. The most sound analysis of this phenomenon, based on thorough study of thousands of items—conservative and liberal, denominational and non-denominational—remains Bernhard E. Olson's classic study; *Faith and Prejudice* (New Haven: Yale University Press, 1963). The Olson study was supplemented by one covering the subsequent decade: cf. "The Strober Report," IX *Journal of Ecumenical Studies* (1972) 4:860–62.

5. Melton, J. Gordon, *The Encyclopedia of American Religions* (Wilmington, N.C.: McGrath Publishing, 1928), 2 vols.

6. Updating such discussions as Joseph Washington's *Black Religion* (Boston: Beacon Press, 1964) and James Baldwin, ed., *Black Anti-Semitism and Jewish Racism* (New York: Richard W. Baron, 1969).

7. Geldbach, Erich, *Christliche Versammlung und Heilsgeschichte bei John Nelson Darby* (Wuppertal: R. Brockhaus Verlag, 1975), 3d ed.

8. By way of illustration, from volume 1 of the study: "Most simply put, religious particularism is the belief that only one's own religion is legitimate." Glock, Charles Y., and Stark, Rodney, *Christian Beliefs and Anti-Semitism* (New York: Harper & Row, 1966), p. 20.

9. Obermann, Heiko, *Wurzeln des Antisemitismus* (Berlin: Severin & Siedler, 1981).

10. Isaac, Jules, *The Teaching of Contempt* (New York: Holt, Rinehart & Winston, 1964).

11. Flannery, Edward H., *The Anguish of the Jews* (New York: Macmillan, 1965), pp. 49–51.

12. App, Justin J., *Autobiography* (Takoma Park, Md.: Bonniface Press, 1977); cf. my paper, "A Report on Historical 'Revisionism,' " in the Yad Vashem Council Report for 1981.

13. Cf. the translated Declaration in XVII *Journal of Ecumenical Studies* (1980) 1:211–12.

14. Cf. Genizi, Haim, *American Apathy* (Tel Aviv: Bar-Ilan University Press, 1983); Fishman, Hertzel, *American Protestantism and a Jewish State* (Detroit: Wayne State University Press, 1973), pp. 72, 77, 195, 230–31; Ross, Robert W., *So It Was True: The American Protestant Press and the Nazi Persecution of the Jews* (Minneapolis: University of Minnesota Press, 1980), pp. 14, 91.

15. Niebuhr, Reinhold, "Jews after the War," reprinted from *The Nation* (21 & 28 February 1942) in Robertson, D. B., ed., *Love and Justice* (Philadelphia: Westminster Press, 1957), pp. 132–42.

16. Rice, Dan(iel F.), "Reinhold Niebuhr and Judaism," XVL *Journal of the American Academy of Religion* (March, 1977), Supplement 1, F:101–46, 104.

17. *Ibid.*, p. 109.

18. Letter to the writer, 3.8.84.

19. Cf. Toon, Peter, ed., *Puritan, the Millenium, and the Future of Israel: Puritan Eschatology 1600 to 1660* (Cambridge & London: James Clarke 1970).

20. "Dispensationalism" is presented in clear outline in Malachy, Yona, *American Fundamentalism and Israel* (Jerusalem: Institute of Contemporary Jewry, 1978), pp. 125ff.

21. Falwell, Jerry, *Listen, America!* (New York: Bantam Books, 1980), pp. 93, 98.

22. Olson, Bernhard E., *op. cit.*, p. 80.

23. This was precisely the point where the *Deutsche Christen* lost their moorings; cf. the writer's essay, "The Protestant Churches and Totalitarianism (Germany 1933–1945)", in Friedrich, Carl J., ed., *Totalitarianism* (Cambridge: Harvard University Press, 1954), pp. 108–19.

24. Such as described in Ralph Lord Roy's *Apostles of Discord* (Boston: Beacon Press, 1953) and in the writer's *Wild Tongues: A Handbook of Social Pathology* (New York: Macmillan 1969).

25. Eckardt, A. Roy, *Elder and Younger Brothers* (New York: Charles Scribner's Sons, 1967), p. 22: *"Antisemitism is the war of the pagans against the people of God." "Antisemitism is in addition the war of Christians against Jesus the Jew."* [Emphasis in original.]

III

THE HOLOCAUST

The Nazi war against the Jews, evolving through different phases from 1933 to 1945, has spawned all sorts of literature, from scholarly studies of the administrative apparatus that the Germans developed for the destruction of European Jewry to memoirs and biographies of survivors and individual rescuers. The perpetrators and the victims alike have been analyzed from many points of view—political, economic, sociological, psychological; they have been incorporated into fiction, poetry, and drama. The bystanders and witnesses have also been scrutinized. Whatever the focus and in whatever literary form, elemental and haunting questions accompany the horror of the story—where was God, what happened to man's compassion for fellow men, why didn't someone do something. The questions are still raging forty-five years after the fall of Nazi Germany. They are asked by Jews and Christians of themselves and of each other, and they overshadow the entire range of American interreligious encounters.

For the past twenty years Christian as well as Jewish writings on the Holocaust have proliferated rapidly. (The theme is central to A. Roy Eckardt's bibliography, "Recent Literature on Christian-Jewish Relations," *Journal of the American Academy of Religion,* 1981. See also listings in the bibliography by Eugene J. Fisher, "A New Maturity in Christian-Jewish Dialogue: An Annotated Bibliography 1973–1983, *Face to Face,* 1984.) Foremost Christian thinkers generally acknowledge that it is a Christian no less than a Jewish problem. On one level the genocidal policy of the Nazis was a blatant repudiation of Christian values and beliefs. Elie Wiesel summed it up in one sentence: "Auschwitz represented a failure, a defeat of 2,000 years of Christian civilization." Father Edward Flannery said: "The fact remains that in the twentieth century of Christian civilization a genocide of six million innocent people was perpetrated in countries with many centuries of Christian tradition and by hands that were in many cases Christian. This fact in itself, stands, however vaguely, as an indictment of the Christian conscience." (Quotations from Henry James Cargas' fine collection of essays, *When God and Man Failed*, pp. 176, 179.)

Christianity must also face up to a related issue. Why, in Franklin Littell's words, were millions of the baptized "silent accomplices in the murder of most of the European Jews." (In Geoffrey Wigoder, *Jewish-Christian Relations Since the Second World War*, p. 39.) Just as Jews have leveled bitter indictments against the American Jewish community and its leadership for failing to confront and foil the unfolding Nazi blueprint, so have Christians (as well as Jews) made similar accusations against non-Jews. In the case of the Christians the argument appears stronger—after all, as the majority and as the power-brokers they were in a better position to influence American, European, and even Nazi policy. David Wyman, the grandson of two ministers, despairingly called public inaction *The Abandonment of the Jews*. Professor John R. Hinnells of the University of Manchester is one of many who concludes that "the Christian world was deafeningly silent at the Holocaust." (Introduction to *Jewish-Christian Relations since the Second World War* by Wigoder.)

Robert W. Ross, a Protestant professor of religion, documents and analyzes the "Silence" on the part of American Protestants vis-à-vis the Nazi policies toward the Jews. The first essay in this section is from his book on the reaction of the Protestant press to persecution and extermination. Ross' research leads him to the charge of moral culpability. Protestants can't plead ignorance; they had the information but did not act on it. A similar silence characterized the Catholic hierarchy. John F. Morley, in *Vatican Diplomacy and the Jews during the Holocaust, 1939–1943*, concludes that morally the Vatican failed itself as well as the Jews. An analysis of the Catholic press in the United States adds: "By and large, ... the tenor of the Catholic press response to the Holocaust was more defensive than anguished" (Esther Yolles Feldblum, *The American Catholic Press and the Jewish State, 1917–1959*, p. 57). Some Christian defenders retort with accounts of those individuals who risked their own lives to save Jews (see, for example, Eugene J. Fisher,

"The Holocaust and Christian Responsibility," *America*, 14 Feb. 1981), but the charge of overall silence cannot be refuted.

Others, like Deborah E. Lipstadt in *Beyond Belief: The American Press and the Coming of the Holocaust, 1933–1945*, have documented aspects of the overall silence within America that extended far beyond the churches. Lucy Dawidowicz, author of the major study, *The War Against the Jews*, examined one facet of silence in *The Holocaust and the Historians* (1981). There she shows that serious discussions of the subject are absent from American and foreign history books. One of her conclusions explaining why writers have ignored that cataclysmic event is a sad commentary on the continued preference for silence: "Anti-Semitism, like the Holocaust itself, it would seem, is a subject of merely parochial interest. The Nazi era notwithstanding, Jew hatred still appears to be of interest only to its victims" (p. 42).

Why the churches kept silent exposes yet another dimension of the Holocaust as a Christian problem. The question asks about Christianity rather than Christians: Did the very nature of Christianity predispose the churches to an acceptance of Nazi persecution, or, more extreme, was Nazi inhumanity linked to the antisemitic component of Christian theology? In 1933 Hitler reportedly told a meeting of Catholic prelates that Nazi antisemitism "was only continuing the 1500-year-old policies of the Church." (Quoted in David G. Singer, "From St. Paul's Abrogation of the Old Covenant to Hitler's War against the Jews: The Responses of American Catholic Thinkers to the Holocaust, 1945–76," *Anti-Semitism in American History*, edited by David A. Gerber, p. 405.)

The question follows logically from the previous discussion in our section on antisemitism, where Littell's piece illustrates the acceptance of what Alice Eckardt calls the "genocidal germ" in Christian theology. Actually, a connection between Nazism and Christianity was seriously suggested some forty years ago by Jules Isaac, a French Jewish historian. Isaac postulated that Christianity's tradition of hostility and contempt for Jews helped prepare the way for the policy of genocide. The thesis received wide attention, and it was one influence that moved the Vatican, under Pius XII and more importantly John XXIII, to amend the church's official stand on the Jews. (See, for example, chapter 3 in Wigoder, *Jewish-Christian Relations since the Second World War*.) Protestants like Littell and the Eckardts readily recognized the culpability of

Christian doctrine. Rosemary Ruether, a Catholic, stoked the fire further. Her book, *Faith and Fratricide* (1974), develops the oft-quoted proposition that antisemitism is "the left hand of Christology." Today, it is no longer radical to say as Professor Eva Fleischner does: "I believe there is ample evidence that the centuries-old Christian anti-Judaism prepared the soil for modern anti-Semitism and the Holocaust; that the Holocaust could not have happened if Christians of Germany, Europe, the world, had taken an unequivocal stand against the Nazi program of persecution and eventual extermination of the Jews. The reason why no such stand was taken . . . is the strong anti-Semitism of the West, one of the roots I perceive to be in Christian teaching." (In Cargas, *When God and Man Failed*, p. 33.)

Alice L. Eckardt's essay is a pioneer study of Jewish and Christian theological responses to the Holocaust until 1973. Although the issue is universal and not confined to the United States, Americans have been in the forefront of the theological debates, and Eckardt's focus is primarily on them. Much has been added since then, as other writers have entered the field. (Some newer material is analyzed in Steven T. Katz, *Post-Holocaust Dialogues: Critical Studies in Modern Jewish Thought* and in Abraham J. Peck's book of essays, *Jews and Christians after the Holocaust*. See also listings in the Eckardt and Fisher bibliographies.) Emendations were also made after Eckardt's article. For example, Father Gregory Baum in his introduction to Ruether's book explains why he changed his mind on the culpability of the church. Compelled to admit that Jew-hatred was central rather than peripheral to Christianity, he writes that the church produced "an abiding contempt" for Jews, a legacy that aided Hitler's design. Alice Eckardt's piece stands, however, for the outline of major issues that have continued to trouble both Jews and Christians.

Wrestling with fundamental challenges to their traditional beliefs, students of the Holocaust expatiate on philosophies or embark on novel directions dictated by their self-examination and self-criticism. Christianity may face a more difficult task than Judaism. In a valuable new book *(Jews and Christians)*, Professor A. Roy Eckardt describes the moral quandary in which Christianity finds itself. Christianity's vulnerability because of its link to the Holocaust, Eckardt says, explains why most Christians are still unable to face up to the reality of the trauma.

Indeed, once the "moral credibility" of the church is on trial, the final irony of the Holocaust might yet be a threat to the survival of *Christianity*.

The Holocaust radically and permanently altered the relationship of Jews and Christians, and church and synagogue have yet to reformulate their views of each other. Some, like Fleischner and Professor John Pawlikowski, suggest that parallel theological probing by the two faiths may encourage mutual understanding (essays in *When God and Man Failed*, edited by Henry James Cargas). And, they imply, if a seared Christianity finds a way to excise the malignancy of antisemitism, a new level of dialogue between the groups may be reached.

9

"Too Long Have We Christians Been Silent"

Robert W. Ross

Men are always accomplices to whatever leaves them indifferent.—
George Steiner, "Jewish Values in the Post-Holocaust Future"

The editor of *The Hebrew Christian Alliance Quarterly* wrote an article
for the winter 1943 issue. His title was "Hitler Plans to Destroy European Jewry." His article was based on information provided to President
Roosevelt, the reports of the Jewish Telegraphic Agency, and a Polish
underground newspaper.[1] After rehearsing the details, including a coun-
try-by-country assessment of the fate of Jews in occupied Europe, the
author wrote, "What do these revelations of German atrocities do to
you? Are you sick at heart? Are you indignant? You should be. Too long
have we Christians been silent. Our voices of protest should have been
heard long before this happened."[2] The phrase "we Christians" should
be noted. The editor, David Bronstein, was an ordained minister; he was
also a Jew and a convert to the Christian faith who was associated with
an organization and a periodical whose purpose was to carry on a
Christian witness and missionary effort among American Jews. His indictment of the silence of Christians has in it a very personal, even
despairing note; he was writing as a convert to Christianity but his
empathy was with the suffering Jews of Europe. His central message was
the indictment of Christians for their silence, a silence before not only

Reprinted in part by permission of the University of Minnesota Press, Minneapolis, from
Robert W. Ross, *So It Was True: The American Protestant Press and the Nazi Persecution
of the Jews*, 285–301. Copyright © 1980 by the University of Minnesota.

the growing knowledge of what was happening to Jews in Poland in 1942 and early 1943, which he reported in his article, but what seemed to him to be the longer silence that had been evident since 1933, when the Nazi persecution of the Jews under Adolf Hitler's dictatorship had begun.

Another comment also written in 1943 heightened the significance of Bronstein's indictment. In "The Observer," edited by R. Paul Miller, in *The Brethren Missionary Herald* for November 20, 1943, there appeared a news note, "The Greatest War Casualties." One paragraph read:

But the staggering loss of this war is among Jews. With a world population of not more than sixteen million, they have already been tortured to death and murdered to the extent of close to four million. This is practically twenty-five percent of all—the most tremendous loss of all the peoples of the world. And Israel is not at war with anybody.[3]

Indeed, the Jews (the meaning of *Israel* in this context) were not at war with anybody. No Jews were fighting as Axis soldiers. Rather, the Jews were the victims, suffering the most "staggering loss of this war." When the war in Europe ended, the final assessment of the total of number of Jews who were victims of the Nazi terror and extermination policy was fixed at 6 million, just under 27 percent of the Jewish population of the world.[4] A statistic? As Malcolm W. Bingay, then the editorial director of the *Detroit Free Press,* said to the Economic Club of Detroit, as reported in *The Churchman,* "Statistics are utterly impossible." He was answering a question as to whether the stories of the death camps were true or not.[5] Bronstein's indictment of "we Christians" and "the silence" was not an indictment of a silence before a figure, the statistic that 6 million, or 27 percent, of the Jews of the world had been victims of the Nazis. Rather, it was the indictment of a silence of Christians when 6 million human beings were being murdered by methods of torture, terror, massacre, disease, starvation, experimentation, and gas chambers. The persecution that culminated in the Final Solution was reported in the American Protestant press from the very beginning. About this there can be no question.

THE SILENCE, THE FAILURE OF INFORMATION TO PERSUADE

What then is the nature of the silence that Bronstein wrote about and that has now been raised in the postwar period to a central place in all discussions of the meaning of the Holocaust? The Silence was not a silence of ignorance or of lack of information. Based on what was published about the Nazi persecution of the Jews in the American Protestant press alone, an argument for a silence based on lack of information would not hold up. This is even more true when the information that was given in the daily press, by the radio, in the news and picture magazines is taken into account. Indeed, these sources were sometimes cited as the basis for the information being published in the American Protestant press.

What is called the Silence in a post-Holocaust context must be something other than lack of information. Elie Wiesel, in an address at the annual Bernhard E. Olson Scholars' Conference on the Church Struggle and the Holocaust, referred to the abundance of reported information specifically citing the daily press. He stated that the problem was not information but persuasion.[6] One meaning of the Silence, then, can be defined, in Wiesel's terms, as having the information but the information by itself was not persuasive in the sense that no significant action or intervention took place by governments or by large groups of influential people that slowed or halted the extermination of 6 million European Jews.

THE SILENCE, THE FAILURE OF CONCERTED EFFORT

In the sense of not being persuaded, American Protestant Christians can also be said to have been silent since what they read from their own religious periodicals over a period of twelve years about the Nazi persecution of the Jews did not result in massive actions or interventions that might have halted the destruction of Europe's Jews or saved large numbers of them from extermination. That prominent churchmen—leaders of denominations, editors and writers, officers in the Federal Council of Churches of Christ in America, and clergymen—here and there did attempt to arouse American Protestant Christians about what was happening to Jews under the Nazis is clear. That they were basically unsuccessful in arousing Christian support on behalf of the Jews is also clear.

The programs and plans that were put forward were often modest, focusing on non-Aryan Christians to the exclusion of all other Jews or emphasizing assistance to those fleeing the persecution to the exclusion of those who remained under the Nazis and who did not or could not flee. It is in this context of a failure to intervene using the full weight of American Protestant Christian opinion and resources that a second definition of the Silence can be found, the failure of concerted effort.

THE SILENCE, THE FAILURE OF MODEST ACTIONS

American Protestant Christians gave money; held rallies or participated in rallies; wrote, approved, and signed statements of protest; sent representatives to Germany, some of whom met with Hitler and other leading Nazis; petitioned President Roosevelt, the United States State Department, and the United States Congress; formed committees within denominations and interdenominationally; cooperated from time to time with concerned Jewish organizations and Jewish leaders; and offered petitions of prayer. As an individual effort and as a combined effort judged in the aggregate, never was this activity or any part of it sufficient enough to do anything beyond slightly delaying the Nazis' movement toward Hitler's often-stated goal—destroying the Jews of Europe. Hitler's calculations of the risks involved proved correct. Massive protest and massive outcry against what the Nazis planned and carried out did not happen, from the early pogroms, through manipulated laws, through the restructuring of the legal system and the political system and the creation of a Nazi totalitarian state, and through the systematic elimination of the "enemies of the state," including Jews. The Nazis carried out these actions for years, with no fear of interference from the nations of the West.

Only after the policy of *Lebensraum* had been instituted and Western Europe had fallen victim to Nazi occupation did intervention come in the form of war and even then the United States did not become a part of the "fighting war" until the nation itself was attacked on December 7, 1941. This gave Hitler from January 30, 1933, to December 7, 1941, seven years and ten months to mount successive challenges to world opinion and intervention, short of war itself, on behalf of the persecuted. None came, at least none of enough force to persuade Hitler to give up or seriously modify the planned extermination of Jews and others. Rather, in the negotiations following Kristallnacht in late 1938 and in early 1939, Germany's Jews became pawns, hostages in a plan of international blackmail, the plans for which were not a failure because they were never instituted but because they were dropped, scuttled, abandoned. Jews could not even be ransomed by their own money.

American Protestant Christians, a significant voice in the United States, did little or nothing to change any of this. Whether through refugee aid, hope for small successes put forward in relation to the Schacht plan, or larger successes expected from the conference held at Evian-les-Bains, nothing even modestly substantive resulted, but Rufus M. Jones writing in *The Christian Century* and in *The Friend* in early 1939 could and did write with a note of hope that, finally, some sort of intervention on behalf of Germany's Jews had been achieved. His hopes proved misplaced.[7] J. Hoffman Cohn, by March 25, 1939, could state flatly that Evian was a failure, if not an outright farce.[8] So yet a third definition of the Silence is suggested. There was not only the failure to be persuaded and the failure of concerted effort, there was the failure of modest attempts. What things that were tried did not work or worked so modestly as to make little or no impression. Nothing changed for the majority of Germany's and Europe's Jews, save that more of them became victims as the persecution and extermination of the Jews was extended to all Nazi-occupied countries.

THE SILENCE, THE FAILURE OF WORLD WAR II AS AN INTERVENTION FOR JEWS

Even the one great intervention, World War II, did nothing for the Jews and those classed as "subhumans" by the Nazis. The war effort was against Hitler and nazism, against Mussolini and fascism, against the Japanese and its Imperial Army and Navy; World War II was not *for* the saving of Jews who were being gassed or shot in massive numbers, which remain to this day incomprehensible. It was not *for* the bombing of the rail lines that led to Auschwitz and Chelmno and Treblinka and Buchenwald and Sobibor, the known "death factories"; it was not *for* the bombing of the great Buna factory system, or the aircraft and missile factories of Doranordhausen, or the slave-labor-run quarries near Mauthausen (that is, it was not against the slave-labor system of the Nazis.) The purpose of World War II, as stated by President Roosevelt and by the military leaders, was to win the war and in this way only help the Jews and others held prisoner in the slave-labor system and in the concentration camps.

The American Protestant Christian denominations went to war along with the nation, fully in support of the goal to defeat Hitler and all forms of fascism, German, Italian, and Japanese. Even the traditionally pacifist churches, consistent in their stance, provided a form of alternate service for their young men affected by the prosecution of the war and the need to interact with a war stance and a wartime economy. The concern for Jews as victims of German-Nazi persecution receded into the larger and inarguably correct need to win the war. The existence of a plan for the extermination of the Jews and the existence of "death factories" for this purpose remained a nagging, persistent news item reported from 1942 on in the American Protestant press, which was held under the cloud of suspicion about "more atrocity stories." But the rumors would not go away. Quite the contrary, as the prosecution of the war increased the possibility of an Allied victory, more substantive information appeared to indicate that such extermination camps did exist and that they were functioning successfully.

What intervention might have been undertaken on behalf of the concentrated, doomed Jews at this point? George M. Kren and Leon Rappaport raised an interesting point. Their subject was the survivors of the concentration and death camps and how some had managed to survive through all or part of the interminable ordeal. But, they also noted, those who survived the first few weeks in a camp often died after seven or eight months through a loss of will and a loss of hope. All their psychic energy was used up. Kren and Rappaport then wrote:

Virtually every survivor memoir contains descriptions of persons who gave up the struggle for life when they finally lost all hope of rescue. A few propaganda broadcasts or leaflet raids directed at the camps might have made a great difference, for if there is anything more crushing than the burden of an atrocious captivity, it is the sense of being forgotten in that captivity.[9]

The question is a haunting one. Could such raids or bombardments with leaflets or broadcasts have been undertaken? More to the point, could exerted, persistent pressure have been brought to bear at the proper levels to institute such a program? The effects of propaganda by print media, both in a positive and in a negative sense, were both known and used. Dropping propaganda leaflets was a known practice, but it was not done for the inmates of the Nazi camps. World War II and the prosecution of the war was not an intervention on behalf of the Jews. Only the final victory by the Allied forces brought their deliverance, six years and 6 million Jewish victims after World War II had begun in Europe. The fourth definition of the Silence can then be stated as the failure *within* the prosecution of World War II, the final and massive intervention against nazism and Hitler, to do anything specifically aimed at informing Jews held in the concentration, slave-labor, and death-camp system that they had not been forgotten. Leaflets, broadcasts, and bombings of rail lines, the barracks of the SS, even the camps themselves would have been a welcome sign that the Allies knew what was going on and that they cared. The masses of Jews and others held in these camps never received such a sign.

THE SILENCE, THE FAILURE TO SPEAK IN "MORAL PASSION"

Majdanek was overrun by the Russians in July 1944, and the world received the first eyewitness stories of an actual "death factory" not told by an escapee-survivor. But the continuation of the fighting and the somewhat unexpected delay of the end of the war served to blunt the full force of the discovery of Majdanek. Only during the final weeks of the war were the extermination centers liberated and then somehow comprehended as being a part of a very large, long-existing system of camps in which thousands of human beings had been held as slave laborers and other multiplied hundreds of thousands had been systematically put to death. Yet, in spite of the eyewitness accounts of chaplains, service personnel, military officers of high rank and distinction, prominent visitors invited by General Eisenhower to see for themselves, in spite of the motion pictures and still photographs exhibited throughout the world, in spite of the accounts of survivors, these camps remained almost incomprehensible.

It is in the context of the discovery of the death camps and the response to them that a fifth definition of the Silence can be proposed. J. H. Oldham was the editor of a newsletter published in England. Selections from his newsletter were published in *The Living Church* on May 20, 1945, under the headline, "Sees Lack of Moral Passion Helping Growth of Barbarism." As printed, the article read:

Asserting that "our own lack of moral passion contributed to the rank growth of barbarism" in the world, Dr. J. H. Oldham said in the Christian News-Letter of which he is editor that "even for the infamy of German concentration camps we cannot wholly divest ourselves of responsibility."

"The inhumanity and torture being practiced in them were known in this country in the years before the war," he declared. "A few courageous individuals raised their protest and did what they could to succour the victims, but the public as a whole was apathetic and the disposition in influential quarters was to hush things up."

"The web of sin is all of one piece," he wrote. All pride, selfishness and callous indifference to needs of others are a siding with the enemies of Christ.

"We especially need to remind ourselves of this," he added, "when we encounter revolting wickedness. We are then more than ever in danger of externalizing and localizing evil by identifying it with those guilty of these particular abominations."[10]

Oldham raised the central question, which remains in any assessment of the response in the American Protestant press to the discovery of the death camps. The subjects are two, lack of "moral passion" and a sense of complicity for failure to act, but not only for failure to act but a more direct charge of complicity through apathy, "the disposition in influential quarters . . . to hush things up," pride, selfishness, and "callous indifference."

The reaction was shock, horror, disbelief, or finding a prophetic meaning in the events, and it was silence. But there was no indignation or moral passion, words of moral outrage at such evidence of human degradation and utter disregard for human life.[11] Further, there were very few words specifically addressed to Jews, either survivors or Jews in America, addressing this sense of moral outrage that the Jews of Germany and Europe had become the victims of the Hitler and the Nazi-planned extermination and that the world, particularly the Christian world, had "passed by on the other side" in the classic sense of the parable of the Good Samaritan.[12] The fifth proposed definition of the meaning of the Silence, then, is the silence in the absence of moral outrage and moral indignation. As resigned or as compassionate as Maxwell's "So It Was True!" editorial may have been or as overcome with horror as Charles Clayton Morrison professed to have been almost to the point of not writing and then saying, "What can be said that will not seem like tossing little words up against a giant mountain of ineradicable evil?" or Caswell's "in condemning the Germans, we must remember that we are condemning the human race . . . , 'Buchenwald is only a new entry in a long list of crimes for which all mankind must inevitably take the blame, ' " they still do not seem to have said what needed to be said.[13]

Guy Emery Shipler in *The Churchman* did center his editorial on the Jews, but only in part. The central theme of the editorial was the American prisoners of war whose bodies had been found among those in the "charnel houses, along with the bodies of Russians, Poles, Frenchmen, Czechoslovaks, and Jews." Shipler went on to state that the Christian world failed to protest in any significant degree when the Nazis first began their persecution of the Jews "years ago." He also said that the Nazi intention had been not to destroy Jews only but to destroy "the dignity and humanity of the whole human race."[14]

Opinion, a Jewish monthly magazine, brutal as its condemnation may now seem, may have come closest to the realities of the spring of 1945 and the finding of the death camps as the final chapter in the program of the extermination of the Jews by the Nazis. Even this *Opinion* article would have escaped the attention of Christians if it had not been quoted at length in "Happenings in Israel" in *The Hebrew Christian Alliance Quarterly.*

The most shocking of the war, indeed of all history, is the extermination of close to five million European Jews! Almost equally shocking is the indifference of the civilized world. If the Nazis had murdered five million dogs or cats under similar circumstances, the denunciations would have risen to the high heaven, and numerous groups would have vied with one another to save the animals. Jews, however, has created hardly a stir! Hitler certainly has scored a superlative success in at least one field in the war on the Jews.[15]

That the original article in *Opinion* also went on to blame American Jews only compounds the fact that American Christians, with or without their Jewish "elder brothers," did not intercede or intervene effectively or respond in indignation and outrage when the full story of the extermination of the Jews became known. It is this silence, the silence of moral indignation, that may be the closest definition of the Silence in the meaning in which the Silence is now used in post-Holocaust times. In truth, the Silence may best be defined as having a multiple, comprehensive meaning, in the context of what was published over a period of almost twelve years in the American Protestant press. First, American Protestant Christians knew, but they were not persuaded to take significant action. Second, the Silence may also be defined as the failure of a concerted effort by a unified American Protestantism to do anything for Germany's or Europe's Jews during the Nazi years. Those attempts to assist or intervene that were undertaken, even on a modest scale, failed. Third, yet another definition of the Silence, then, may be the failure of modest attempts to intervene on behalf of Jews.

A fourth meaning of the Silence concerns the failure to encourage the concentrated, slave-labor and death-camp populations through bombings, broadcasts, dropping leaflets, or other assistance, thus leaving the camp's inmates with a sense of hopelessness born of the seeming indifference of the world, particularly the Western and Christian world. In this sense, then, World War II as an act of intervention on behalf of condemned Jews was a failure for those who died without hope. To those Jews who did survive and were rescued by Allied forces, those who had lived through the horrors of concentration camps, the deliverance was bittersweet. They knew the seeming miracle of their own survival amidst the terrible memory of those who had not survived, compounded by the added knowledge of how they had died. Finally, there was the awful silence when the death camps were found, the silence of a morally indignant and outraged world of Christians, including American Protestants, who failed to speak out about the death camps and who in subsequent years failed even to remember. These five meanings of silence —knowing but not being persuaded; the failure to act in concert; the failure of modest actions; the failure of World War II as "containing" specific intervention for Jews; and the failure to speak in words of moral indignation, confession, or moral outrage in the face of the death camps —these together are the Silence against which the voice of survivors and of Jews alike cries out "remember."

A CONTRAST, THE DEATH CAMPS AND HIROSHIMA/NAGASAKI

In reading and rereading the articles in the American Protestant press (through the late spring, summer, and fall of 1945 and on into 1946 and 1947) used in this study, I looked in vain for a lucid, burning prophet's message. Where is the profound, soul-searching, seering condemnation-confession of a man of Christian faith, an American Protestant, a Poling, a Morrison, a Shipler, a Fosdick, or any of a host of other such Christian leaders who would step forward to say in our blindness, in our preoccupation with ourselves, that we have failed at the very heart of the most fundamental of all Christian commandments, to love our neighbors as ourselves. In this, by ignoring the most basic of Christian responsibilities, we have sinned against our "elder brother." No such statement was found.

Such moral outrage or moral indignation and a sense of culpability by American Protestant Christians was felt later, and it was widely reported in the American Protestant press. The subject, however, was not the Nazi persecution of the Jews or the death camps, but the dropping of the atom bomb on Hiroshima and Nagasaki, Japan. . . .

THE DEATH CAMPS AND THE ATOM BOMB, A SUMMATION

So the American Protestant press spoke out on the atom bomb and the dropping of the bomb as an act deserving shame. As for the moral and ethical consequences of this action, the evidence was clear. By the use of the atom bomb to end the war with Japan, America had lowered itself in the eyes of the world. A democracy proud of its moral strength by this single action had undone its reputation as a moral leader and a guide among nations. If nothing else, at least the continuance of an effective missionary outreach in the Orient would be much less possible because of the immoral action taken, the dropping of atom bombs on Hiroshima and Nagasaki.

Not so on the death camps. On March 9, 1944, just over a year before the end of the war in Europe, a meeting was held in Washington, D.C., attended by leading Protestant, Roman Catholic, and Jewish leaders, some of whom were members of Congress. Vice-President Henry A. Wallace was present, and at the dinner a telegram from President Franklin D. Roosevelt was read. The meeting had been called by the American Palestine Committee in conjunction with a number of other groups. The papers, resolutions, and the list of delegates to the conference were published as *The Voice of Christian America: Proceedings of the National Conference on Palestine.* One of the speakers was William B. Ziff. He spoke on "Palestine in the Present Crisis." He referred to what was happening to Jews under the Nazis, saying:

As a result of the current phase of the Nazi brutality almost three million Jews, men, women and children have been wantonly butchered under conditions of savagery and lust scarcely equalled anywhere in the long, sad history of man's faithlessness and inhumanity to his own kind.

One is compelled to stand aghast, not only at the brutishness which created these acts, but at the indifference and apathy of the Western world which lifted no hand to save these people. . . . They were hermetically sealed in with the full desperate knowledge that their death sentence had been written. These three million lie in nameless graves together, poets, dreamers, businessmen, scientists, grimy-handed workers, housewives and little children. Many were said to have been buried even before they died. Eye witnesses have stated that the very earth in these mass graves shook with the last convulsive breathing of these tragically broken people.

The stark measure of this crime and the irreparable loss it has cost humanity can never be plumbed, but even more terrible has been the silence of the West. . . . If this silence is a symbol of that inner demoralization for which Hitler has prayed, it represents a subtle alteration of standards which should well make the West tremble.[16]

Just two months before the meeting in Washington, D.C., Alfred Kazin had written an article published in the *New Republic*. His article was a commentary brought about by the death of Shmuel Ziegelboim, a Polish Jew, who committed suicide in his London apartment on May 12, 1943, leaving a letter addressed to the president of Poland and the premier of Poland. The entire letter was included in Kazin's article. Among the things Kazin wrote were comments on the failure of the world to comprehend what was happening to the Jews. "Shmuel Ziegelboim came from a ghetto-driven, self-driven, but spiritually generous culture; and I honestly think he was thinking not only of his own people at the end, but of the hollowness of a world in which such a massacre could have so little meaning." A few sentences later, he wrote:

I do not speak here of the massacre of the Jews, for there is nothing to say about it that has not already been said. . . . For the tragedy is in our minds, in the basic quality of our personal culture. . . . The tragedy lies in the quality of our belief —not in the lack of it, but in the unconsciousness or dishonesty of it; and above all in the merely political thinking, the desperate and unreal optimism, with which we try to cover up the void within ourselves.

Kazin's article closed with an indictment of those

—not liberals, not radicals, certainly not reactionaries—who want only to live and let live, to have the good life back—who think that you can dump three million helpless Jews into your furnace, and sigh in the genuine impotence of your undeniable regret, and then build Europe back again. . . .

For I know that the difference . . . is far more terrible than physical terror and far more "tangible" than conscience. Something has been set forth in Europe. . . . That something is all our silent complicity in the massacre of the

Jews (and surely not of them alone; it is merely that their deaths were so peculiarly hopeless). For it means that men are not ashamed of what they have been in this time, and are therefore not prepared for the further outbreaks of fascism which are deep in all of us.[17]

Ziff and Kazin, in 1944 and separate from each other, spoke of silence, the "silence of the West," and "the silent complicity in the massacre of the Jews."

THE SILENCE, A CLOSING WORD

It is now time to go back to that first year of the Hitler era, to September 21, 1933. On that date, Robert A. Ashworth, who was associated with the National Conference of Jews and Christians and who was a former editor of *The Baptist,* had his letter to the editor to *The Reformed Church Messenger* published. He was responding to an article by Dr. E. G. Homrighausen, "Behind the German Jewish Problem," and disagreeing substantially with Homrighausen's analysis. "Germany's treatment of the Jews," Ashworth wrote, "is an offense against humanity, a violation of the most basic human instincts, a revival of sadism on a wide scale, and from a Christian point of view, a denial of all that we hold most sacred." He concluded his lengthy letter with the following statement:

As Hilaire Belloc says in the article from which we have quoted, "As it seems to be a particular and flagrant injustice of this kind affects not only the individual who suffers from it, nor only the unhappy men who perpetuate the outrage, but also those who are silent in the presence of it. They themselves will be poisoned if they do not protest, for it is their duty to protest."[18]

Ashworth, quoting Belloc, was right. What the Nazis, Hitler, and Germany did to the Jews was an offense against humanity, and American Protestant Christians stood witness in the presence of it, from 1933 to 1945. The American Protestant press did report what was happening to the Jews in Germany. As had been shown, the press reported far more extensively than has generally been thought to be the case. The accepted view has been that the press had said little or nothing. Clearly, this was not true. It must be said, then, that American Protestant Christians did know, for, if the people read, the people knew. But the editors and writers of the American Protestant press tried to deal with the mass extermination of the Jews of Germany and Europe as if it were a part of an ordered, stable, normal world. In fact, it happened in a world gone mad. In the end, editors and writers seemed unable to cope with something as unreal, even unimaginable, as the mass slaughter of millions of people, among them 6 million Jews, in an organized, bureaucratic, planned extermination. They could report this madness, this unreality, but, beyond the reporting and even beyond the expressed shock and horror over the discovery of the death camps, there remains the awful pall that hangs over this entire episode in modern history.

NOTES

1. The editor, "Hitler Plans to Destroy European Jews," *The Hebrew Christian Alliance Quarterly* (Winter 1943), 25–26. A delegation of Jewish leaders visited President Roosevelt on December 8, 1942. The statement left with President Roosevelt was later published by the American Jewish Committee as *Hitler's Black Record: The Documented Story of Nazi Atrocities against the Jews*, New York, American Jewish Committee, 1943.
2. The editor, "Hitler Plans to Destroy European Jewry," *The Hebrew Christian Alliance Quarterly* (Winter 1943), 26.
3. R. Paul Miller, ed., "The Greatest War Casualties," *The Brethren Missionary Herald* (November 20, 1943), 712.
4. 16 million divided by 6 million equals 26.666 percent.
5. *The Churchman* (August 1945), 56.
6. Elie Wiesel, "Solitude and Madness," an address given at the Annual Bernhard E. Olson Scholars' Conference on the Church Struggle and the Holocaust, March 5, 1975, New York City.
7. Rufus M. Jones, "The Visit to Germany," *The Friend* (January 12, 1939), 256; "Rufus Jones Back from Germany: Reports Tentative Plans for Refugees," *The Christian Century* (January 18, 1939), 99.
8. J. Hoffman Cohn, "The Jews of Europe," *The Brethren Evangelist* (March 25, 1939), 14–15. (The conference was held July 6–15, 1938, at the Hotel Royal, Evian-les-Bains, France.)
9. George M. Kren and Leon Rappaport, "Victims: The Fallacy of Innocence," *Societas* (Spring 1974), 111–29.
10. "England: Sees Lack of Moral Passion Helping Growth of Barbarism," *The Living Church* (May 20, 1945), 10.
11. The "Jewish sufferings of the past few years" of prophetic interpretation of the death camps and their meaning were from "The Jewish Problem," *The Watchman-Examiner* (October 25, 1945), 1032–33.
12. Luke 10:29–37, for the parable of the Good Samaritan.

13. Editorial, "So It Was True!" *The Signs of the Times* (May 22, 1945), 3; editorial, "Gazing into the Pit," *The Christian Century* (May 9, 1945), 575–76.

14. Editorial, "Think on This," *The Churchman* (May 15, 1945), 4.

15. Victor Buksbazen, "Happenings in Israel," *The Hebrew Christian Alliance Quarterly* (Spring 1945), 24–26.

16. William B. Ziff, "Palestine in the Present Crisis," *The Voice of Christian America: Proceedings of the National Conference on Palestine*, Washington, D.C., March 9, 1944, 13–14.

17. Alfred Kazin, "In Every Voice, In Every Ban," *New Republic* (January 10, 1944), 44–46.

18. Robert A. Ashworth, letter to the editor, *The Reformed Church Messenger* (September 21, 1933), 13–14. (The Belloc article quoted by Ashworth was published in part in *The Voice of Religion: The Views of Christian Religious Leaders on the Persecution of the Jews in Germany by the National Socialists*. New York, the American Jewish Committee, 1933, p. 7, and was taken from Hilaire Belloc, "The Persecution of the Jews," *America* [July 22, 1933], 367–69.)

10

The Holocaust: Christian and Jewish Responses

Alice L. Eckardt

The Holocaust is, by itself, such an enormity in the questions it raises that this survey of Christian and Jewish responses cannot possibly do complete justice to any of the views represented. However, we may benefit more from considering this wider range of views than if we were to concentrate on a narrower spectrum.

Perhaps the first factual observation that must be made is that there is simply no comparison between the responses and reactions of the Christian and Jewish communities to the reality of Hitler's Final Solution. Whatever aspect of response one looks at—historical, theological, psychological, existential—it is overwhelmingly that of Jews, individually and collectively. If we say that this is to be expected and is quite normal, we are only giving away the very problem: that nothing normal should prevail after the most fearful abnormality in human history. It further assumes that the Holocaust is primarily a *Jewish problem*—whereas in fact it is, in far deeper respects, a *Christian problem*.

Christianity has failed to grasp the crucial nature of the questions raised by the Holocaust for its own theology and future, just as it generally has refused to admit any responsibility for the death camps.[1]

Those Christians who have grappled with the reality and implications of the Holocaust see a church in vast apostasy, involved not only in the murder of Jews but also of God through his people, still linked to a

Reprinted by permission of Scholars Press from the *Journal of the American Academy of Religion* 42 (Sept. 1974): 453–69.

supersessionist theology that bears the genocidal germ, in danger of repeating its complicity in criminal actions, and without credibility because of its failure to understand that everything has been changed by Auschwitz.[2]

If the Jewish community as a whole has only recently begun to try to come to terms with the implications of the Holocaust, it has not been because of a lack of awareness, but because of an all-too-devastating appraisal of the catastrophe. It has been stunned by the accomplishment of the unthinkable, and has been fearful of looking more closely at the face of evil. Yet despite having suffered its greatest tragedy, and being uniquely aware of its still terrible vulnerability, the Jewish people have experienced resurrection in history—through the rebirth of the State of Israel and a new vitality in its various Diaspora communities (including the long-presumed "lost" Jews of Russia). Judaism's tradition involves questioning and challenging God. Its history encompasses long periods of God's apparent absence as well as numerous revelations of his divine presence. Its understanding of God's silence allows for his presence-in-suffering with the guiltless, even while the people cry out in non-understanding and despair. Because of all this, perhaps Judaism is better equipped to survive the Holocaust than a Christianity that continues to insist that the world's redemption has already occurred, while accommodating itself to the vilest forms of culture religions; a Christianity that by and large maintains a triumphalism and which strives if not for racial genocide for Jews, then for religious genocide through conversion; and a Christianity that interprets human affairs as having little significance other than "spiritual" in the parenthesis between the resurrection and the parousia, while having sold its soul to the sword of Constantine.

For both communities nothing can be the same as before the Holocaust, though most of Christendom remains unaware of this. Though Jews as victims suffered the agonies and deaths, paradoxically the death-of-God theology has had little impact among Jewish circles. Moreover, Judaism is not faced with the same threat to its integrity with which the church is faced as perpetrator of, or complicitor in, the genocidal program. Franklin H. Littell is one of the most vocal and concerned Christian theologians on this aspect of the subject. The Holocaust "remains the major event in recent church history—signalizing as it does the rebellion of the baptized against the Lord of History. . . . Christianity itself has been 'put to the question' "—by the apostasy of millions of the baptized, by being witting or silent accomplices in the murder of most of the European Jews, by being more concerned for real estate and institutional privileges than for persons, and by failing to confess or profess. "Among large numbers of the misled laity—especially the youth and students—both the 'God-talk' and the organized efforts of the churches have simply lost their credibility. . . . Christianity is bleeding to death intellectually [whether we are aware of it or not], and we shall not return to the path of health until we have worked our way through the difficult thickets of the meaning of the Holocaust and the Church Struggle." After the death camps, who can speak most authentically for the theology of suffering? Certainly not the churches. In fact, "perhaps the question put to us by the Holocaust and [the State of] Israel is *whether we [Christians] are still able to grasp the meaning of crucifixion and resurrection.*"[3]

A Roy Eckardt writes in a similar vein: "the church that collaborated in the Nazi 'final solution' dealt itself mortal blows. From that Jewish crucifixion and Christian self-crucifixion there could and did come a Jewish resurrection—the State of Israel—but not a Christian resurrection. For the church has nowhere to go now."[4] Considering the church from without, Emil Fackenheim has "no doubt that if masses of Christians in Hitler's Europe had voluntarily put on the yellow star there would today be no doubt or confusion in the Christian churches, no talk of the death of God. I also have an uncanny feeling that Christians might find the renewal they presently seek if . . . their souls were to enter into the despair and the hope-despite-despair of Auschwitz."[5]

Can a theology of a responsive and saving God survive the test of the Holocaust? Is the reality of evil, especially the reality of Auschwitz, consonant with traditional Jewish and Christian teachings? Can God be held accountable for evil? Is history a divine-human encounter moving toward a messianic climax, or is it a meaningless tragedy? Is the voice of God discernible amidst the horror of Auschwitz?

Theological response among Jews has been undertaken especially by Emil Fackenheim, Eliezer Berkovits, Arthur Lelyveld, and Richard Rubenstein (not to mention a host of others). More existential or mythological responses have come particularly from Elie Wiesel and other survivors of the camps, such as Alexander Donat. Yet, as Nora Levin points out, there is still no body of thought that provides religious or philosophical answers to the terrible questions posed by the Passion of the Six Million—and perhaps there never will be. But this "incompleteness . . . is of a piece with Jewish religious tradition"—a tradition that across the centuries has not only contended with God, but has even considered the idea that God can sometimes sin. Judaism generally has refrained from pursuing "the unknowable and the limitless, [and] does not insist on answers when there are none."[6]

This may be more difficult for many contemporary Jews than it was for their grandfathers, yet it remains a dominant strand in Jewish religious thought, in contrast to Christianity which has proclaimed that it has the final certainties, whether in the most complex theological systems, or simplistic piety, fundamentalism, or the current charismatic movement. Perhaps one of the results of Holocaust studies by Christians will be a greater awareness of the unknowable and the mysterious, and a lesser willingness to accept dogmatic or abstract answers to existential questions.

For almost all those—Christians and Jews—trying to wrestle with the problem of evil as exemplified by the death camps, there is a realization that few of the old concepts and arguments can be the same after Auschwitz. Among some there is a conviction that "the Holocaust is not a dilemma of God, but a dilemma of man. The Holocaust proved not that God was dead, but that man's humanity to man was dead. Man is given the freedom to choose"—and most of mankind chose unbridled evil, silence, or indifference.[7] Omnipotence and omniscience must yield to a new understanding. The meaning of life may have to be found in man's response, even to incalculable suffering, rather than in his fate.

In a recent study that is a response to a new awareness of antisemitism and its genocidal consequences, Father Gregory Baum sums up the traditional Christian view of divine providence as insisting that God is not responsible for evil. Yet, as Baum says, the church's view of God as Lord of history necessarily implied that somehow human sins and crimes are in keeping with God's permissive will. God was thought of as permitting evil in the present, for the sake of a greater good to be achieved in the future. Even Auschwitz, according to this theology, had a place in divine providence. Does not such a view make a monster out of God,[8] as Richard Rubenstein has concluded from the Jewish side?

Baum finds he must reject the traditional concepts of providence, omniscience, and omnipotence.

God is not provident . . . in the sense that as ruler of the world he has a master plan for human history by which he provides help for the people in need, especially those who ask him for it, and by which he guides the lives of men, while acknowledging their freedom. . . . [or] in which God has permitted evil and . . . calculated its damaging effects and compensated for them in the final outcome. . . . [But] God is provident in the sense that in whatever trap man falls, a summons continues to address him and offer him new life that makes him more truly human.

This leads Baum to conclude that

God is omniscient [only] in the sense that there exists no human situation, however difficult, however obscure, however frightening, in which God remains silent or . . . in which a summons to greater insight is not available. . . . [Similarly], God is omnipotent [only] in the sense that there is . . . no situation, however destructive, in which an inner strength is not offered to man, allowing him to assume greater possession of his humanity.

With this understanding, "we are able to affirm the radical opposition between God and evil." Evil is not permitted by him. Rather, "God is constantly at work among men, summoning them . . . to discern the evil in human life, to wrestle against it, to be converted away from it, to correct their environment, to redirect history, to transform the human community. The death that destroys is never the will of God. On the contrary, God is the never-ending summons to life." [9]

The expression "This is God's will" must never be taken to mean that God wants or even permits terrible calamities or injustices to happen. But it can mean, on the part of a person of great faith, a continuing trust that God will summon forth new insights, and will create life out of death in new ways.

Jewish men and women on the way to the extermination chambers may have said to themselves that this incomprehensible and groundless evil was in some mysterious way God's will—in the sense that they continued to trust in God. But on the lips of an observer such a statement would be a dreadful blasphemy.

God's power over the world is not the miraculous action by which he makes things happen as he pleases, but the redemptive action by which he enables men to deal with their own problems and by which he calls people to "resist evil and find ways of conquering it." [10]

Rabbi Arthur Lelyveld also agrees that the "problem of evil cannot be solved as it stands—something has to give . . . usually . . . some aspect of divine omnipotence." We must say that "*evil* is there—gargantuan evil—uncontrolled by [God]. We cannot pretend to know why—we can only cling stubbornly to the conviction that there is meaning . . . in spite of everything. In the cosmic scope . . . there is that which is demanded of us." Jews must acknowledge that "the God of Judaism is the God who *demands* . . . 'Thou *shalt* be' . . . '*Choose* life' . . . The covenant obligation that is central in Judaism calls upon the Jew to be God's co-worker in perfecting the world—not to *be* saved, but to *participate* in the redemption of mankind." Therefore, "I must interpret my responsibility as it is defined by the covenant task—to battle evil and to perfect the world. . . . [As] I hear it, the greater the evil, the more insistent and the more intense, even to the point of anguish, is the demand."[11]

If the Final Solution was indeed the "greater evil," was it *uniquely* evil? Rabbi Lelyveld says no. Auschwitz was a "new phenomenon only in a quantitative and technological sense." The more efficient instruments for carrying out human destruction "give the problem of evil new dimensions, but [they do] not change its essential nature."[12]

What of God, then, in making a demand that Jews, and mankind in general, engage this ever-increasing efficiency of evil? Lelyveld points to the "sympathy at the heart of the universe"—sympathy for the very men on whom these demands are made: "God 'wept' over Auschwitz." It is this sympathy that "enables man to enter into 'partnership' with God."[13]

Lelyveld, like Baum, is convinced that to say God "willed" the death of the six million is "a repelling, blasphemous idea." But he cannot withdraw from them "the dignity that lies in recognition that there existed among them a willingness to die in fulfillment of a distinctive role"—whether it was the incredible courage to fight with "the certainty of the futility of resistance," or the courage to march to the freight cars that were to carry them to hell with the "*Ani Ma-amin*" on their lips.[14]

"We have said that Hitler's victims were offered no alternative. This is not wholly so. They had the alternative of dying as cravens, of cursing God and their identity. All the evidence says that in overwhelming numbers they died with dignity."[15]

Lelyveld believes we can assert *general* providence: meaning and purpose in the whole, and a thrust of cosmic evolution toward greater

love, harmony, and justice. However, he insists we reject *special* providence: the childish notion of God as a personal protector and coddler.
Such a view is "asking the impossible of the universe. Life is contingency
and risk. . . ." In the "relationship of Covenant responsibility, when God
is the guarantor of value and the source of demand, then the confrontation of evil elicits . . . the response 'What does God ask of me?' " [16]

Viktor Frankl, himself a survivor of the death camps, complements
Baum's and Lelyveld's theological views by his own experiential and
psychiatric conclusions which are, at the same time, very attuned to the
above strand of Jewish tradition: We camp inmates had to stop asking
about the meaning of life and instead think of ourselves "as those who
were being questioned by life—daily and hourly." The inmates' usual
question was, "If we don't survive, what meaning will all this suffering
have?" Frankl responded by reversing the query. If all this suffering and
dying have no meaning, then what meaning has life itself? After all, a
life whose meaning stands or falls on such a happenstance as whether
one survives ultimately would not be worth living at all. So Frankl
concludes that "life's meaning includes even suffering and death." Potentially we can give meaning to our lives by suffering as well as by creating
and loving; "by the way and manner in which we face our fate, in which
we take our suffering upon ourselves." In the final analysis, man should
"realize that it is not up to him to question—it is he who *is* questioned,
questioned by life; it is he who has to answer, by answering for life. His
role is to respond—to be responsible." [17]

In *Faith after the Holocaust*, Eliezer Berkovits reminds us that the
Hiding of the Face has two biblical meanings: the first caused by man's
guilt which brings *merited* suffering; the second, where man is guiltless
and therefore the suffering is *unmerited*, and yet God remains hidden
and apparently indifferent. This is the supreme challenge—to faith as
such but also specifically to theodicy. Is God in fact salvationally present
and active in history? The experience of God's absence amidst suffering
is not new; each generation of Jews had its "Auschwitz experience" and
its "radical theology." Auschwitz does not "stand by itself," even though
it is both the "most horrifying manifestation of divine silence" and the
greatest crime in human history because of the Germans' "planned
destruction of the human status of their victims." In all of the radical
abandonments by God, the people of faith continued to insist on a Judge
and Judgment. They insisted that God's attributes as Redeemer and

Resurrector in history were true—if not now, then yet in the future. One can only speak of the "silence" of one who is present.[18]

God is incapable of evil, but he is also long-suffering—

with the wicked as well as with the righteous. . . . This is the inescapable paradox of divine providence, [and] the ultimate tragedy of existence: God's very mercy and forebearance, his very love for man, [including his direct concern for the wrong-doer] necessitates the abandonment of some men to a fate that they may well experience as divine indifference to justice and human suffering. . . .[19]

"God took a risk with man and he cannot divest himself of responsibility for man." God is caught in a paradox:

If man is not to perish at the hand of man, . . . God must not withdraw his providence from his creation. He must be present in history. That man may be, God must absent himself. . . . The God of history must be absent and present concurrently. . . . He is present without being indubitably manifest; he is absent without being hopelessly inaccessible. . . . Because of the necessity of his absence, there is the "Hiding of the Face" and suffering of the innocent; because of the necessity of his presence, evil will not ultimately triumph; because of it, there is hope for man.[20]

The Nazi crime against Israel is "the most tragic testimony to this presence-in-absence." It was the Nazis' "metaphysical fear of . . . God's 'powerless' presence in history as 'revealed' in the [mysterious] continued survival of Israel" that led to the "satanic idea of the Final Solution. If the symbol of this presence-in-absence were eliminated, if the witness were destroyed, God himself would be dead." Then the irrational, the reversal of all human values, the satanic, could prevail.[21]

Nevertheless, "while God is long-suffering, he is not so forever. That would not be divine mercy, but divine indifference. Were there no judgment in history over power history, faith history would have no chance of survival," nor could Israel itself have survived.[22] Yet a world ruled only by a *just* God could not exist. Because God's mercy and love delay judgment, man may indulge in rebellion and become guilty of hubris and may get away with it—for a while. But judgement is only delayed. "The man of hubris does not escape nemesis. There is judgment and there is a Judge in world history."[23] As far as Christian responsibility for the Holocaust and other massacres of Jews is concerned, Professor Berkovits does not hesitate to accuse: Had Christianity concerned itself with homicide, which is the *real* capital crime, instead of preoccupying itself with what it chose to consider an act of deicide, "mankind would have

been spared much horror and tragedy." Neither Auschwitz nor Treblinka could ever have happened.

God suffers not on account of what man does to him. . . . He suffers because of
what man does to himself and to his brother. He suffers the suffering of his
servant, the agony of the guiltless . . . who carry the burden of his long-suffering
patience and mercy. . . . The status of [God's dilemma with man] at any one
moment in history is revealed by the condition of Israel at that moment. . . . God
who leads man 'without might and without power' sent his people into the
world without the might of power. This is the essence of the confrontation
between Israel and the world [in which] Western man had to prove himself. God
has pushed Israel right across the path of Christianity. Israel was God's question
of destiny to Christendom. In its answer, the Christian world failed him tragically. . . . This gruesome failure of Christianity has led the Western world to the
greatest moral debacle of any civilization—the Holocaust.[24]

At the same time, Professor Berkovits insists that one must not question God over the Holocaust because of its vastness; this is not the
essential point. In fact, "the Holocaust was only possible because mankind was quite willing to tolerate less than the Holocaust." The question
after the Holocaust is that of how long God will tolerate man as a
failure. "God's dominion over the world is not a dominion of justice. In
terms of justice, he is guilty. He is guilty of creation. But is he guilty of
indifference or is he guilty of too much long-suffering?" When will he
decide to "intervene and call a halt to misused freedom?"[25]

Related to this are the questions of whether, after Auschwitz, the
Jewish people may still be witnesses to God's elusive presence in history,
and how we are to understand the nemesis of history and Jewish survival. The ultimate in hubris—Nazism—was "overtaken by its complete and inescapable nemesis"; nor was this nemesis limited to Nazi
Germany—but "has overtaken Western civilization itself."[26] Berkovits
shares the conviction with the Austrian Catholic, Friedrich Heer, that

it is no mere coincidence that having countenanced the Final Solution to the
Jewish problem, . . . the world is now confronted with the serious possibility of
a Final Solution to the entire problematic existence of man on this planet. . . .
This post-Holocaust era is charged with the nemesis of history. This is the
ignoble twilight hour of a disintegrating civilization.[27]

What then of the Jewish people? They have already paid a "terrible
price for the crimes of mankind," and now, as part of mankind, are also
involved in the world-wide human crisis. Yet, "the Final Solution in-

tended for [this people] is far from being final. Though truncated, Israel survived this vilest of all degradations of the human race [and] has emerged to new dignity and historic vindication in the state of Israel."[28]

Even while making this affirmation, Berkovits wonders whether the State perhaps came too late, arising after the wholesale slaughters, in the atomic age, and in the midst of a disintegrating civilization. Moreover, in a world of giant states and power blocs, a state such as Israel may be as "homeless" as the individual Jew during his long exile.[29]

But Berkovits, like others, is convinced that post-Auschwitz is a totally new era. The very surfeit of power is breaking the vicious circle of force being met by greater force. "Power has overreached itself and, thus, it has defeated itself." Consequently, he sees mankind as having the choice of "entering upon its 'Jewish era' or else upon an era of self-immolation." Under the Lord of history, mankind and the nations of power will have to "survive as Jews have survived to this day—by the renunciation of force as the arbiter of human destiny!" The meaning of the new era was tragically dramatized by Auschwitz, for it has shown "that man's lack of moral force is sufficient to bring about a 'final solution.' " The Holocaust proved "not what man was capable of doing to the Jew, but what man is capable of doing to his fellow. The bomb has rendered the final solution on a universal scale a practical possibility; Auschwitz has demonstrated it to be morally feasible."[30]

Are these attempts to grapple with the enormity of evil experienced in the Holocaust radical enough? Do they go sufficiently to the depth of the mystery of such iniquity? Not for some of our contemporaries in the two communities.

Richard Rubenstein testifies how his own theological "point of no return" came about, paradoxically, as a result of a conversation with one of the very few German Protestant pastors who had consistently risked his own life and that of his family during the Hitler era by opposing Nazism on *Christian* grounds and by extending all possible aid and comfort to Hitler's chief victims. Dean Heinz Grüber of Berlin insisted on the "very special providential relationship between Israel, what happened to it, and God's will," not just in biblical times but continuing to this very day. Unlike other German clergy and church members who had withdrawn, at least partially, from this theological position when Rubenstein pressed them on whether this meant that the Nazi slaughter of Jews was somehow God's will, Dean Grüber relent-

lessly and candidly followed the logic of his convictions by quoting
Psalm 44:22: ". . . for Thy sake are we slaughtered every day. . . ." Then
he continued, "For some reason, it was part of God's plan that the Jews
died. God demands our death daily. He is the Lord, He is the Master, all
is in His keeping and ordering." In the same conviction, Grüber was
willing to have his own life taken when God willed it (which almost
happened at Dachau). Rubenstein realized then that "as long as Jews are
thought of as special and apart from mankind in general, they are going
to be the object of both abnormal demands and . . . decisive hatreds," as
well as of the sort of theology that holds "God wanted Hitler to punish
them." Consequently, Rubenstein has rejected any notion of chosenness,
or special vocation, or peculiar responsibility as a "thoroughly distaste-
ful pill to swallow" after the Final Solution.[31]

Rabbi Rubenstein is convinced that the problem of God and the death
camps is the central problem for Jewish theology in the twentieth century.

The catastrophe of 1939–45 represents a psychological and religious time bomb
which has yet to explode fully in the midst of Jewish religious life. . . . God really
died at Auschwitz [in the sense that] nothing in human choice, decision, value or
meaning can any longer have vertical reference to transcendent standards. We
are alone in a silent, unfeeling cosmos. . . . Morality and religion can no longer
rest upon the conviction that divinely validated norms offer a measure against
which what we do can be judged.[32]

Despite such cosmic emptiness, Rubenstein is not in despair. "Death
and rebirth are the greatest moments of religious experience," and Jews
have known both in this century. In Europe

we Jews tested the bitterest and most degrading of deaths. Yet death was not the
last word. . . . Death in Europe was followed by resurrection in our ancestral
home. We are free as no men before us have ever been. Having lost everything,
we have nothing further to lose and no further fear of loss. . . . We have passed
beyond all illusion and hope. We have learned . . . that we were totally and
nakedly alone, that we could expect neither support nor succor from God or
from our fellow creatures. . . . We have lost all hope and faith. We have also lost
all possibility of disappointment.[33]

For Rubenstein, tragedy has liberated Jews. Yet here we must challenge his premise. Having regained the land of Israel, and national
sovereignty, have Jews not also made themselves vulnerable again? Have
they not reappropriated hope, and hence exposed themselves to the

possibility of even greater disappointment, even unto despair? The very fact that Israel's Finance Minister Pinhas Sapir would advise the Knesset, in April 1973, that Israel "should openly admit [that it has] a Warsaw Ghetto complex" reveals this new vulnerability. Sapir went on to say that "it would show a lack of responsibility if Israel tried to rid itself of that complex," [for the] "world has not properly learnt the lesson of the Jewish Holocaust. . . ."[34]

Mr. Sapir specifically made reference to the failure of nations to learn that appeasement will not save them from evil and chaos, and that while Jews may be the first victims of violence, they are not the last. We may suggest other lessons: "In some mysterious way the appreciation accorded the Jewish people is a measure of a civilization's devotion to humanity."[35] "The absence of morality generates its own laws of conduct."[36] To forget or ignore the past is to invite a repetition of it.

The refusal to learn such lessons, combined with the ingrained Christian conviction that the "new Israel" entails the death of the "old Israel," helps to explain for Professor Fackenheim why the Christian world "failed to recognize the danger of a second Holocaust [in 1967], for it still cannot face the fact of the first." Hitler widened the gulf between Jews and Christians. To the extent that it remains unbridged, Hitler has his posthumous victories.[37]

Though Fackenheim is at many points diametrically opposed to Professor Rubenstein's convictions, there are points on which they agree, especially about the nature of the Holocaust. Both are aware, along with Berkovits and Alfred Kazin, that for Nazism, the only war that really counted was that waged against defenseless Jews.[38] For Berkovits, it was "the ultimate of irrationality. The conscious and radical removal of every vestige of moral restraint on subhuman passions, . . . the extirpation of all human feelings, . . . the religion of brutality . . . was not 'of this world.' " It was metaphysical barbarism. It was not just inhuman— it was satanic.[39] For Kazin, "The Holocaust was 'unaccountable,' yet in some way . . . the most 'irrational' side of the war was somehow at the heart of it."[40] For Fackenheim, Nazism's *essence* "was the murder-camp . . . a demonic, nihilistic celebration of death . . ." Auschwitz was "the scandal of evil for evil's sake."[41] There is no other way to explain the self-defeating emphasis and energies devoted to the annihilation of Jews when these energies were needed elsewhere to win the other war. Nor is there any other way to comprehend the zeal with which Hitler and his

henchmen, including above all Eichmann, welcomed the total destruction of Germany while gloating over the success of their Final Solution
of the Jewish question. Furthermore, Fackenheim and Rubenstein are
equally convinced that with a German victory, the death machines would
have been self-perpetuating.[42]

This intersecting of convictions about the Holocaust, and about aspects of life and faith as a result of the Final Solution, strikes one
repeatedly as one reads the literature of those most deeply involved.
Alexander Donat rejects Rubenstein's radical theology, Fackenheim's
"learned theodicy," and Wiesel's "passionate *din-Torah* with God"
(lawsuit before a religious court) as a failure to "come to grips with the
immanent meaning of the Holocaust." Nevertheless, he believes with
them that the "far-reaching religious implications have by no means
been explored nor . . . completed."[43] Elie Wiesel says that "perhaps
some day someone will explain how, on the level of man, Auschwitz was
possible; but on the level of God, it will forever remain the most disturbing of mysteries."[44] Donat, like Rubenstein, Wiesel, Berkovits, Eckardt,
and Heer, is convinced that "the Holocaust was the beginning of an era,
not its end—an era of turmoil and upheaval, of irrationality and madness . . ."[45] Just as Rubenstein sees the Jewish building of the State of
Israel partly as a result of "the massive refusal of the survivors of
Auschwitz ever again to live as a part of Christian Europe,"[46] so Donat
asserts that "the legacy of the Warsaw ghetto can be epitomized in
'Never again!' Never again ghetto, never again Treblinka and Auschwitz, never again defenseless martyrdom." And paralleling Rubenstein's
conviction that Jews have passed beyond all illusions and hope, Donat
adds that the "never again" also means: "no more faith in hollow terms
like humanity, culture, conscience of the world, proletarian solidarity."[47] Dr. Fackenheim hears God's voice in the midst of Auschwitz not
as a redeeming voice, but as one of *command,* issuing a new, a 614th
commandment to all Jews: Survive. Survive as Jews, lest my people
perish; remember the victims of Auschwitz, lest their memory perish; do
not despair of man and his world, lest you cooperate in delivering the
world over to the forces of Auschwitz; and do not despair of the God of
Israel, lest Judaism perish. Above all, do not give Hitler a posthumous
victory.[48] From the British Christian community Dr. Colin Morris responds to this reaction to the death camps with a call for Christian
identification with the extraordinary act of faith demonstrated by Jews

in bringing up their children as Jews in the post-Auschwitz age. Christians are to rejoice at such embodiment of hope based, necessarily, on survival.[49] Alan Davies also hears a new commandment from the crematoria *for Christians:* a command never again, "either through silence, speech, or act . . . to involve themselves in a second Auschwitz . . ." Implicit in this command is the Christian responsibility to eliminate antisemitism and the obligation to preserve the people and State of Israel.[50]

While Donat tells his grandson that "a new apocalyptic calendar may well start with a new Genesis: 'in the beginning there was Auschwitz . . .,' "[51] Wiesel echoes, "In the beginning there was the Holocaust. We must therefore start all over again. We have to write a new Talmud, just as we did after the destruction of the Second Temple . . . in order to accentuate the new beginning" since the Torah was taken back in the Kingdom of Night.[52] Indeed, Wiesel has been described as one who is already writing a new Bible.[53] Emil Fackenheim writes that perhaps the Jewish theologian must create a new Midrash. In any case, he asserts that this is "the heroic age par excellence *in all of Jewish history.*" For the survivors of the two-work-permit custom, which "robbed [the individual Jew] of his soul and made him forever innocently guilty of the murder of all his family except one member, did not, by and large, commit suicide, go insane, or reject their Jewishness. Rather they reaffirmed their Jewishness and raised new Jewish children."[54] Speaking from a Christian perspective, A. Roy Eckardt also thinks in terms of a new age: "The dispensation of the first Torah is ended. . . . This is the epoch of the incarnation of the Jews. B.F.S. [the age Before the Final Solution], is past."[55]

On the question of the uniqueness of the Holocaust, Franklin Littell has this to say:

in the convulsion of history which was the Holocaust, Christendom stands exposed in rebellion and betrayal of the most awful measure. For the Holocaust was not another illustration of "man's inhumanity to man." . . . The Holocaust was the final blasphemy of the baptized Gentiles, an open revolt against the God of Abraham, Isaac and Jacob—and the Jewish people who still kept the terms of their covenant, while the Christians had betrayed their own mandate. . . . The Jews who suffered and perished in Hitler's Europe suffered and perished for what the baptized would have testified had they remained Christian: for being a counter-culture, a sign to the One who is the True God, the Author and Judge of history. The Holocaust is the major event in recent centuries of *Christian* history precisely because it exposed the thinness of the veneer which covered with a sham Christianity the actual devotion of the European tribes to other gods.[56]

Fackenheim pointedly notes that "Christians cannot yet face the fact that the returning Christ would have gone to Auschwitz. . . . Still less can they face the fact that he would have gone involuntarily if not voluntarily."[57]

Is Christianity all that is on trial? Or is God himself? In his writings, Elie Wiesel has put God on trial (as did the Berditchever reb in the past) —"not to chastise," but to beg that "He at least offer a plea on His own behalf. . . . Despite [Wiesel's] yearning for God and for an answer, he must condemn God for the most unforgiveable crime—useless murder."[58]

Roy Eckardt also says that God is among the major defendants at the trial now under way. "The excruciating question is whether, if God lives and is not helpless, he ought to go *on* living, he who has permitted the death of the six million." Can God live with himself? "For even after Auschwitz, God does not seem to be exactly working hard to present a recurrence. . . . Must not the words be flung at him . . . 'I accuse'? . . . What kind of a Father are you, God?"[59] Eckardt asserts radically that the "ultimate responsibility for evil in the world is God's, for the simple reason that it is he who created the world and it is he who permits monstrous suffering to take place. . . . The new charge against God is no less than that of Satanism." Pleas of weakness and absence from the scene are not applicable; "if . . . in the Holocaust are 'the flames of God's ever-burning love for his chosen people,' then the Lord of life and love becomes the Lord of death and hate. He is transmuted into the Devil."

Eckardt asks how God is to defend himself from such a charge? Or do penance for the "unspeakable injustices for which he is plainly culpable?" There is only one way he can express his sorrow and never again be responsible for such suffering: by abrogating the Covenant. "For the Covenant is the blameworthy divine instrument of Jewish oppression. . . . God's original sin was to insinuate the divine powerlessness, the divine perfection, into the life of ordinary human beings." Thus Eckardt surmises that Wiesel's proclamation that God took back the Torah and abrogated the Covenant reflects God's awareness that his "soul was in imminent danger of going to hell." Consequently, now we have a "total reversal of the doctrine of Jewish election. For the first time in the history of the people of God, their existence becomes an unqualifiedly normal, human reality. ... Chosenness now [must come] to mean election-beyond-suffering, election to life. The covenant is fulfilled and yet transcended through a 614th commandment: the command to survive."[60] As Emil Fackenheim insists, after Auschwitz Jewish martyrdom is only an encouragement to potential criminals. Today a Jew "is commanded to descend from the cross and in so doing ... suspend the timehonored exaltation of martyrdom."[61] Indeed, adds A. Roy Eckardt, Jewish martyrdom in the age After the Final Solution would not sanctify God's name but only blacken it. The 614th commandment is not really a commandment but "an end to all commandments." It is "the *free choice* and right of Jewish existence as such."[62]

Here we are obliged to ask some questions of Eckardt and Fackenheim. Professor Eckardt asserts that this free choice of survival is a *declaration* of independence. But if it is indeed the voice of God that issued the new commandment on which the choice is made, then is it not in fact a *gift* of independence from God? On the other hand, if the commandment Fackenheim hears the voice from Auschwitz utter is not simply "Survive!" but "Survive *as Jews*," then are Jews really liberated? Or are they not still inextricably linked to God, and thus exposed to the fury of all those who wish to kill God and pursue their own idolatrous interests? *Has* God taken back the Torah? Or has He simply reasserted the binding of his people through, and despite, the Holocaust?

Has God begun to repent? Perhaps—a little. Jews now have a place, "the only defense against the international spatiality of antisemitism."[63] If that place does not survive, we must conclude, in Professor Eckardt's terms, that God has not repented enough, and that his Satanism has prevailed.

What are the consequences of the Holocaust for Christianity? After the wholesale apostasy of Christendom, Professor Littell sees a desperate need for Christians to "recover the language of events, especially as they begin to internalize the lessons of the *Kirchenkampf,* the Holocaust, and a restored Israel." This will necessitate "a major change of [Christian] spiritual condition" which in turn will require "a miracle as astonishing, as awesome, as the events which have transformed the life and hope of the Jewish people." The possibility of a healing process and the possibility of Christian future are utterly dependent on Christians coming to terms with these major events of recent Jewish history, and appropriating them in their own symbols and liturgies.[64]

In turn A. Roy Eckardt asks, if the Torah has been taken back by a kind God in the new era of the Final Solution, has the Cross and the Empty Tomb also been taken back? He responds with another question: Since the church of the Final Solution simply worked out the ultimate consummation of its own theology, and hence its own fate as Cain, a fugitive on the face of the earth, how else can Christian antisemitism ever die unless a new birth and resurrection of God take place? He believes that Professor Heer implied the answer in his book, *God's First Love,* a conclusion which Eckardt himself endorses: Christians who wish to be faithful may now only commit themselves to the burial of the faith that men transmuted into a cancer, lest worse crimes be done in God's name. Faithfulness may require denying God *for his sake,* that is, for the sake of his other children. If God dies in this way, "perhaps then he will live once more, . . . because he is 'the coming God: A God of the present and the future, in which he will submerge the brutal past.' "[65]

Bryon Sherwin attests that "any word about the Holocaust is inadequate. But there is the paradox. The Holocaust imposes silence yet demands speech. It defies all solutions but calls for responses."[66]

The responses are beginning to come. Will they be listened to? Will they come in time? Above all, will we remember? Elie Wiesel confided that though he could not explain an inner certainty, "I only know philosophically that for the first time man's fate and the Jewish fate have converged. That means it is impossible to try again another Holocaust without committing the collective suicide of the whole world."[67] In the spirit of Wiesel's own conviction that questions are far more important than answers, let us end with one: How is the world different, if it is, because Auschwitz happened?[68]

NOTES

1. CF. William Jay Peck, "From Cain to the Death Camps: An Essay on Bonhoeffer and Judaism," *Union Seminary Quarterly Review* 28 (Winter 1973), pp. 160, 162: ". . . one can either have God and his people or no God and no people. . . . to retain God and destroy his people is to murder God . . ." In a "structural sense, the whole of Christianity was responsible for the death camps. The denial of such involvement will doom the message

of the Church to remain at the level of shallow and impotent argumentation."

2. Cf. Elwyn Smith, "The Christian Meaning of the Holocaust," *Journal of Ecumenical Studies* 6 (Summer 1969), pp. 421–22: "Was not the holocaust a terrible test—which the church failed? . . . It may be . . . that the question whether Christianity is to remember the holocaust or dismiss it is a question of the ability and the right of Christianity to survive in a form in any way conformable to the Scripture." Arthur C. Cochrane, "Pius XII: A Symbol," in *The Storm Over the Deputy*, ed. Eric Bentley (New York: Grove Press, 1964), p. 158: "No church, especially in our age can be expected to be taken seriously as the 'representative' of God on earth unless she acknowledges her solidarity with the sin of the world. . . . Indeed, what is at stake . . . is the very possibility of faith in the face of man's frightful inhumanity and the Church's indifference" during the Holocaust. Friedrich Heer, "The Catholic Church and the Jews Today," *Midstream* 17 (May 1971), p. 27: "The actions and sacrifices of some ordinary people did not redeem the church, but exposed her guilt all the more clearly. . . . Christianity cannot continue to exist unless Christians are constantly aware of their responsibility for the continued existence of Jews on this . . . earth." William Jay Peck, "From Cain to the Death Camps," pp. 159–60: "After Auschwitz, everything has changed subtly but genuinely. The old agendas have become partial, if not sterile. The central problem for theology in our time is . . . the problem of murder. In the West, . . . it is not only human survival which is at stake, the very being of God is also somehow tied up with the problem of murder."

3. Franklin H. Littell, "The Meaning of the Holocaust: A Christian Point of View," address at the University of Michigan, Nov. 3, 1971 (unpublished manuscript; italics in original). See also Littell, "Christendom, Holocaust, and Israel," *Journal of Ecumenical Studies* 10 (Summer 1973), pp. 483–97.

4. A. Roy Eckardt, "The Nemesis of Christian Antisemitism," in *Jewish-Christian Relations in Today's World*, ed. James E. Wood, Jr. (Waco, Texas: Baylor University Press, 1971), pp. 59–60.

5. Emil L. Fackenheim, "The People Israel Lives," *The Christian Century* 87 (May 6, 1970), p. 568.

6. Nora Levin, "Life over Death," *Congress Bi-Weekly* 40 (May 18, 1973), pp. 22–23.

7. Shraga Arian, "Teaching the Holocaust," *Jewish Education* (Fall, 1972), p. 44.

8. Gregory Baum, *Man Becoming: God in Secular Experience* (New York: Herder and Herder. 1971), pp. ix, 245.

9. Ibid., pp. 242–44.

10. Ibid., pp. 248–49.

11. Arthur J. Lelyveld, *Atheism Is Dead* (Cleveland: World Publishing 1968), pp. 158, 176, 177.

12. Ibid., pp. 172, 174–75.
13. Ibid., pp. 181, 183.
14. Ibid., pp. 178–79. The "Ani-Ma-amin" is part of synagogue liturgy: "I affirm, with unbroken firmness, that the Messiah will come. And even though He tarries, even so, I affirm it."
15. Ibid., p. 179.
16. Ibid., pp. 183–84.
17. Viktor Frankl, *From Death Camp to Existentialism: A Psychiatrist's Path to a New Therapy* (Boston: Beacon Press, 1959), pp. 77, 105, 107.
18. Eliezer Berkovits, *Faith after the Holocaust* (New York: KTAV Publishing House, 1973), pp. 78, 94–101, 135.
19. Ibid., p. 106.
20. Ibid., p. 107.
21. Ibid., pp. 117–18.
22. This insight points up the intrinsically self-destructive nature of the other-worldly emphasis of so much of the Christian tradition, and the way in which it plays into the hands of evil.
23. Ibid., pp. 119–20.
24. Ibid., pp. 126–27; see also p. 136.
25. Ibid., pp. 130–31.
26. Ibid., pp. 131–33. Nazi hubris sought "the conscious extirpation from human nature of the last remainder of the fear of God in any form. It was the ultimate rebellion of nihilism against all moral emotion and all ethical values" (ibid., pp. 131–32).
27. Ibid., pp. 132, 133. Cf. Friedrich Heer. "The Catholic Church and the Jews Today," p. 29: "There is a straight line from the Church's failure to notice Hitler's attempt at a 'final solution of the Jewish problem' to her failure to notice today's and tomorrow's endeavors to bring about a 'final solution of the human problem.' The murder of millions of Jews during the Hitler era anticipated the murder of millions and perhaps hunreds of millions of human beings who would die if the Great War returned—a war that could only end in mass murder and genocide." See also Friedrich Heer, *God's First Love* (New York: Weybright and Tatley, 1967), p. 392.
28. Berkovits, *Faith after the Holocaust*, p. 133. The issue of the State of Israel and its relationship to the Final Solution is only mentioned in passing in this paper. A proper discussion would entail another article.
29. Ibid., pp. 137–38.
30. Ibid., pp. 141–42.
31. Richard L. Rubenstein, *After Auschwitz* (Indianapolis: Bobbs-Merrill, 1966), pp. 52–54, 56, 58, 69. By contrast, Rabbi Lelyveld retains the concept of election, as meaning a special task (Lelyveld, *Atheism Is Dead*, pp. 177–78).
32. Rubenstein, *After Auschwitz*, pp. x, 223–25.

33. Ibid., p. 128.
34. Pinhas Sapir, in *The Jerusalem Post* (overseas airmail edition), April 30, 1973. Rubenstein partly acknowledges this condition when he refers to the Israeli determination that there will never be another Auschwitz, though there may be another Masada (Richard L. Rubenstein, Foreword to Alan T. Davies, *Anti-Semitism and the Christian Mind* [New York: Herder and Herder, 1969], p. 11). Nora Levin sees the Holocaust as having shattered Jewish illusions about their indestructibility as a people, and made them aware of their total vulnerability ("Life over Death," p. 23).
35. Littell, "The Meaning of the Holocaust."
36. Ernst Pawel, "Fiction of the Holocaust," *Midstream* 16 (June/July 1970), p. 21.
37. Emil L. Fackenheim, *Quest for Past and Future* (Boston: Beacon Press, 1968), pp. 24–25. The Rev. Edward Flannery goes even further than Fackenheim after considering Christian reactions to the Holocaust and to the emergence of the State of Israel: "there is a strong probability that many Christians harbor a deeply repressed death-wish for the Jewish people." See his "Anti-Zionism and the Christian Psyche." *Journal of Ecumenical Studies* 6 (Spring 1969), p. 182.
38. Despite Fackenheim's claim that Rubenstein's "more recent spoken utterances have characterized the Nazi murder camp as simply the extreme technological nightmare" (see Fackenheim, "The Human Condition after Auschwitz," B.G. Rudolph Lectures in Judaic Studies [Syracuse: Syracuse University, 1971], p. 7), Rubenstein has written: "The Nazis often seemed far more intent upon achieving irrational victories over defenseless Jews and Gypsies than a real victory over their military opponents. They won the war that really counted for them, the war against the Jews" (*After Auschwitz*, p. 2). Fackenheim has dealt with the irrationality of Hitler's Final Solution in "The People Israel Lives," "The Human Condition after Auschwitz," *Quest for Past and Future*, and *God's Presence in History* (New York: Harper and Row, 1970).
39. Berkovits, *Faith after the Holocaust*, p. 117.
40. Alfred Kazin, "Living with the Holocaust," *Midstream* 16 (June/July 1970), p. 6.
41. Fackenheim, "The Human Condition after Auschwitz," p. 8; *Quest for Past and Future*, p. 18.
42. Fackenheim, "The Human Condition after Auschwitz," pp. 7, 9; Rubenstein, *After Auschwitz*, pp. 35, 42–43.
43. Alexander Donat, "A Letter to My Grandson," *Midstream* 16 (June/July 1970), p. 43.
44. Elie Wiesel, *Legends of Our Time* (New York: Holt, Rinehart and Winston, 1968), p. 6.
45. Donat, "A Letter to My Grandson," p. 43.

46. Rubenstein, Foreword to Davies, *Anti-Semitism and the Christian Mind,* p. 11.

47. Donat, "A Letter to My Grandson." p. 44.

48. Fackenheim, *God's Presence in History,* p. 84. also see his *Quest for Past and Future,* p. 20.

49. Colin Morris, *The Hammer of the Lord: Signs of Hope* (London: Epworth Press, 1973); excerpts in *Christian Attitudes on Jews and Judaism* (London) no. 29, April 1973, pp. 1, 2, 6.

50. Alan T. Davies, "The Contemporary Encounter of Christians and Jews," *The Ecumenist* 10 (May–June 1972), p. 58. See also "Statement of Christian Concern about the Middle East," issued October 17, 1973 by a number of Christians in Toronto, Canada, including Davies.

51. Donat, "A Letter to My Grandson," p. 43.

52. Elie Wiesel, in A Symposium: "Jewish Values in the Post-Holocaust Future," *Judaism* 16 (Summer 1967), p. 285; *A Beggar in Jerusalem* (New York: Random House, 1970), p. 200.

53. Byron Sherwin, "Elie Wiesel and Jewish Theology," *Judaism* 18 (Winter 1969), p. 40.

54. Seymour Cain, "Emil Fackenheim's Post-Auschwitz Theology," *Midstream* 17 (May 1971), p. 74; Fackenheim, "The Human Condition after Auschwitz," pp. 10–11.

55. A Roy Eckardt, "In What Sense Is the Holocaust Unique?" unpublished manuscript.

56. Franklin H. Littell, "Particularism and Universalism in Religious Perspective," address at the 17th Annual Institute of Religion, Beth Tzedec Congregation, Toronto, Canada, May 11, 1972 (unpublished manuscript).

57. Fackenheim, "The People Israel Lives," p. 568. Fackenheim assumes that the Christ would have gone to the murder-camp voluntarily, as did Father Riccardo in Rolf Hochhuth's *The Deputy.*

58. Sherwin, "Elie Wiesel," p. 41.

59. A. Roy Eckardt, "Toward an Authentic Jewish-Christian Relationship," in Wood, *Jewish-Christian Relations in Today's World,* pp. 94–95. The trial is occasioned by the "Holocaust and responsibility for it, the rebirth of the State of Israel, and the eventuality of a second Holocaust, namely, Israel's possible obliteration" (ibid., p. 93).

60. Eckardt, "In What Sense Is the Holocaust Unique?" See Wiesel, in A Symposium, "Jewish Values" p. 281.

61. Fackenheim, *God's Presence in History,* pp. 75, 87.

62. Eckardt, "Toward an Authentic Relationship" (italics added).

63. Ibid.

64. Littell, "Christendom, Holocaust, and Israel," pp. 486, 494–496.

65. Eckardt, "Toward an Authentic Relationship." See also Eckardt's review of Heer, *God's First Love,* in *Commentary* 51 (March 1971), pp. 91–98.

66. Byron Sherwin, "The Holocaust," *Jewish Spectator* 34 (October 1969), p. 25.

67. "Conversation with Elie Wiesel," *Women's American ORT Reporter* (March/April 1970). p. 5. See also Wiesel, A Symposium, "Jewish Values," p. 287.

68. Cf. Arthur Hertzberg. "A Generation Later," *Midstream* 16 (June/July 1970), p. 9.

IV

ZIONISM AND ISRAEL

Linked to the Holocaust by history and contemporary theology, the creation of the State of Israel was the second happening of the twentieth century that forever changed the course of Jewish history. American Jews were generally spectators here too, but overwhelmingly they identified with the Jewish state. Except for the small and short-lived American Council for Judaism, former differences over the legitimacy of Zionism were eroded by the Second World War. In post-Holocaust thought a Jewish state symbolized a new hope for Jewry and a new breed of Jew —modern, proud, independent, unafraid. Since 1948, support of Israel has been the issue that most readily unites the American Jewish community. Popularly it has also become a conventional means of affirming one's Jewishness as well as measuring the Jewish loyalty of fellow Jews. (The importance of Israel to American Jewish identity has long been highlighted in sociological studies by Marshall Sklare, Charles Liebman, Steven Cohen, and Calvin Goldscheider.) Small wonder that Israel has become a Jewish barometer of Christian readiness to accept them and their faith on Jewish terms.

Theodor Herzl, the Viennese Jew who launched the Zionist movement in 1897, saw in Zionism a solution to the heightened antisemitism of the Western world during the last quarter of the nineteenth century. Although he looked for a mass following, support of the Zionist movement came principally from eastern Europe, where less assimilated Jews lived under more straitened conditions. In the United States Zionism never elicited a personal commitment except from a very few Jews. Some of its supporters may have recognized the benefits to Jewish culture or Jewish character that a state would bring, but most saw it as a philanthropic

233

scheme, a way of securing the physical and material well-being of Jews not fortunate enough to live in America. After Auschwitz Israel became more than a philanthropy, but although the entire American Jewish community now bears a self-imposed responsibility for the Jewish state, no more than a very small number considers *aliyah*. (For a short general background that traces developments from 1897 to 1967 see my book, *American Jews and the Zionist Idea*.)

For the first twenty-five years of its existence, political Zionism encountered the formidable opposition of American Reform Jews. They denounced the movement for many reasons—it cast doubt on Jewish loyalty to the United States, it incited antisemitism, it obstructed Jewish assimilation within American society. More important to the Reformers, Zionism contradicted the essence of Reform theology, their concept of the Jewish mission which was predicated on the providential dispersion of the Jews throughout the nations. To some degree, the arguments of classical Reform in America contributed to Christian anti-Zionism.

After the Balfour Declaration of 1917—issued by Britain and approved by a Presbyterian American president—officially sanctioned the establishment of a Jewish homeland in Palestine, the Zionist movement drew increased attention from Christian Americans. To be sure, the churches were long familiar with the idea of a Jewish return to Palestine. Jewish restoration to the Holy Land, usually tied to their mass conversion, figured prominently in evangelical and millenarian strands of nineteenth-century Christianity. But that support for early restorationist schemes saw a Jewish return as part of the Christian design for the second coming of Jesus. The legitimacy of a Jewish state, independent of Christian purposes, had yet to be considered. Obviously, if only because of the majority/minority equation and the powerlessness of Zionists to proceed without gentile aid, American Christian opinion would also be crucial to the actual establishment and viability of a Jewish state.

From the beginning of political Zionism, various strands of thought have shaped American Christian opinion. A few Christians, like Reinhold Niebuhr, have defended the right of the Jews as a discrete people to carve out a state and a destiny of their own. Mainstream Protestant leaders, however, have been generally cool if not opposed to Jewish nationalism. Theological considerations underly the rejection of the Zionist plea to be "like all the nations." The Jews, after their supersession by Christianity, were exiled from Zion; any positive role that remained for them in the Christian world was to be played as a people dispersed throughout the nations. An independent Jewish state flouted the terms of the divine punishment incurred by the errant people for their rejection of the true faith. Moreover, Christian associations with the Holy Land could be jeopardized by a secular Jewish Palestine. (On concrete ties between American Protestants and Palestine see Robert T. Handy, ed., *The Holy Land in American Protestant Life 1800–1948*.) Certainly, early missionaries to the Ottoman Empire who met the first Zionists objected to the Jewish nationalists. Resistant to conversionary efforts, the Jews were primarily secularists, and their success weakened the appeal of Western religion for potential Arab converts. In the aftermath of World War I, Christian religious imagery and purposes that bore upon Palestine and Jewish nationalism became increasingly entwined with political, social, and humanitarian issues. "Respectable" antisemites also found a place in the ranks of the opposition, and after 1917 anti-Zionism often masked cruder antisemitism. Thus reinforced, Christian myth became entrenched in popular as well as government reactions to the Zionist cause. (See my recent book, *The Year after the Riots: American Responses to the Palestine Crisis of 1929–30*.) Today, traditional Christian views on Jewish statehood pose a serious obstacle to harmonious relations between American Jews and Christians.

The fate of the Jews under Nazism raised the clamor for a Jewish state, but it failed to erase Christian opposition. The selection from Hertzel Fishman's important book, *American Protestantism and a Jewish State*, documents the response of two leading liberal Protestant journals to pre-state events in the 1930s. The evidence underscores the importance of anti-Jewish religious imagery in the anti-Zionist position, specifically that of the influential *Christian Century*. Fishman also considers the response of liberal Protestantism to the post-1948 realities of a Jewish state. In both time periods, he concludes, the first principles of Protestantism respecting the historic roles of both Judaism and Christianity set up weighty obstacles to an acceptance of Jewish nationalism.

The Six-Day War of 1967, as Franklin Littell described in the selection included under part two of the present volume, unleashed a new wave of Protestant hostility against the Jewish state. When annihilation again threatened the Jews, the churches, as during the Holocaust, kept silent. The Eckardts wrote that they like American Jews were shocked and disillusioned by the new silence, but they were not surprised. ("Silence in the Churches," *Midstream*, Oct. 1967.) Continued Protestant hostility since then, manifested particularly by support of the PLO from the liberal church institutions, severely strained the traditional alliance between Jews and liberal Protestants. The irony was that the conservative Protestants, those who scored highest on antisemitism, were the most supportive of Israel. Christian organizational behavior toward Israel since 1967 also proved that the Holocaust had failed to budge Christian thinking about the right of Jews to chart their national destiny.

American Catholic opinion of Zionism and Jewish statehood, following the lead of the Vatican, exhibited a similar hostility that was firmly grounded in Christian tradition. For religious as well as political reasons the church moved little from the position outlined by Pope Pius X to Herzl in 1904: "We are unable to favor this movement [Zionism]. We cannot prevent the Jews from going to Jerusalem—but we could never sanction it. . . . The Jews have not recognized our Lord, therefore we cannot recognize the Jewish people and so, if you come to Palestine and settle your people there, we will be ready with churches and priests to baptize all of you." Esther Yolles Feldblum, who reprints that entry from Herzl's diaries, examined diocesan papers and journals of Catholic organizations, religious orders, and institutions for the period from 1917 to 1959. In the chapter chosen for this section she shows how in the first years of statehood American Catholics fixed on specific issues raised by Jewish statehood (e.g., internationalization of Jerusalem) and on the theological dilemma of how to square a Jewish state with Catholic doctrine. (An approach similar to Feldblum's is used by David G. Singer in "American Catholic Attitudes toward the Zionist Movement and the Jewish State as Reflected in the Pages of *America, Commonweal,* and the *Catholic World,* 1945–1976," *Journal of Ecumenical Studies* 22[1985]:715–40.)

Despite the breakthrough of Vatican Council II on Catholic-Jewish relations, the same silence of the Protestant churches in 1967 permeated Catholic circles. (George G. Higgins's essay in *Twenty Years of Jewish-Catholic Relations* [edited by Fisher, Rudin, and Tanenbaum] recounts how Jewish-Catholic dialogue was seriously, albeit temporarily, endangered. Edward H. Flannery's article in that book explains how Israel and Jerusalem remained outside the pale of dialogue.) The Vatican still refuses to establish diplomatic relations with Israel, but writing in 1986 (*Jewish-Christian Relations since the Second World War*, p. 117), Geoffrey Wigoder concludes that "in many ways Vatican-Israel relations have improved over the past twenty years."

American Christians, both supporters and critics of Israel, are the subject of a work in progress by two prominent Protestant writers, Carl Hermann Voss and David A. Rausch. The final essay in this section presents some of the material they have amassed. The focus is primarily on organizations and individuals—clerical and lay, Protestant and Catholic, white and black—who since World War II have attempted to bend American public opinion to their views of a Jewish state. (Earlier American Christian interest in Israel is briefly considered by Lawrence J. Epstein in *Zion's Call: Christian Contributions to the Origins and Development of Israel.*) Voss and Rausch, themselves friends of Israel, end their account on a gloomy note: ". . . the Jewish state must never expect justice from American Christendom as a whole."

11

The Apparition of Jewish Nationalism

Hertzel Fishman

In the 1930s, the *Christian Century* was the only independent, nondenominational Protestant weekly in the United States. It was most effective in molding and reflecting liberal Protestant opinion on current public issues, including the subject of Jewish nationalism. It maintained a clear editorial policy on current events, but its columns were open to divergent viewpoints. It devoted considerable attention to the subject of Jewish nationalism, in marked contrast to the Protestant denominational press which had little of significance to say about the subject. The *Christian Century* may be considered as the most significant source for ascertaining the attitudes of American Protestantism during this period.

THE *CHRISTIAN CENTURY*'S CRITIQUE OF AMERICAN JUDAISM

The *Christian Century* was consistently opposed to Jewish nationalism. This opposition was compounded by the journal's view of American nationalism in which the melting pot theory played a major part. Any ethnic or religious group within American society that professed cultural pluralism was, in the publication's opinion, clearly out of step with the best interests of the nation.[1]

Quite objectively, the Jews were the one discernible ethnic-religious group within the American body politic which, from the time its members arrived in the United States, seemed to deviate blatantly from the

Reprinted by permission of Wayne State University Press from Hertzel Fishman, *American Protestantism and a Jewish State* (Detroit: Wayne State University Press, 1973), excerpts from chaps. 2, 10.

melting pot norm. Whereas other immigrant groups would gradually give up more and more of their unique ethnic characteristics, and even modify some of their "old country" religious beliefs and practices to suit their new American environment, American Jews by and large continued to view themselves as a religious and ethnic group—a faith and a culture —apart from the great majority of Americans. They wished to achieve equal rights and opportunities as individuals, but continued to perpetuate their group identity. Not all Jews were able to define the nature of their collectivity, but most of them continued to maintain an emotional and psychological, if not practical, relationship with it.[2]

The *Christian Century* clearly did not understand the unique nature of American Jewry. During the 1930s, it vigorously upheld the melting pot theory, and the principal target of its indignation was the Jews. When the Jews exercised their distinctive patterns of faith and culture outside the purview of the majority populace, they were, in the paper's view, violating a cardinal democratic principle of "majority rule."

Can democracy suffer a hereditary minority to perpetuate itself as a permanent minority with its own distinctive culture, sanctioned by its own distinctive cult forms? . . . They have no right *in a democracy* to remove their faith from the normal influences of the democratic process by insulating it behind the walls of a racial and cultural solidarity.[3]

It would appear that the *Christian Century*'s view of American nationalism confused the democratic political process with majority rule in matters of faith and culture. Yet, this conclusion seems to be ambivalent. While not denying the right of American Jews to practice Judaism—in fact, while applauding their right to do so—the paper would have liked them to practice *its* notion of Judaism. It hoped for a diminution of distinctive Jewish beliefs and practices, and an adoption by American Judaism of some distinctive Christian beliefs and practices which the *Christian Century* equated with authentic American nationalism. In this manner, Judaism would increasingly melt into the American Christian melting pot. Such melting was not to be accomplished by force or even by Christian proselytizing.[4] It would be implemented by the open competition between Judaism and Christianity, and by the mutual effects of one faith upon the other.

This contest, however, did not imply that both religions were equally valid: "Not for a moment do we consent to be misunderstood with those whose creed asserts that one religion is as good as another, your religion for you, mine for me."[5] It merely allowed the "separatist" Judaic religion to encounter the "universalistic" Christian religion in an open market, and to induce the former to become more universalistic. In this way, Judaism might become attuned to what the paper considered to be American's democratic environment. "The Jewish religion, or any other religion, is an alien element in American democracy unless it proclaims itself as a universal faith and proceeds upon such a conviction to persuade us all to be Jews."[6] The genius of American democracy was to provide an ongoing public forum for both Judaism and Christianity to engage in open "conflict looking toward a higher integration."[7]

It is little wonder, therefore, that when, in 1946, the Jewish Theological Seminary of America announced a $15 million campaign to strengthen American Judaism's distinctiveness, the *Christian Century* criticized this policy because "if the process of social assimilation is really speeding up, we cannot regard that as anything but a gain for the American future."[8]

The *Christian Century* did not comprehend the character of Judaism nor did it recognize the place of religious minorities in American society. Yet its erudite editors and its educated readers surely were not unaware of *both* the separatist and the universalist tendencies of Judaism, originating in Pentateuchal and Prophetic sources of the Bible. The laws of social justice in the Five Books of Moses were explicitly directed not only to Jews, nor did Amos and Isaiah pronounce their visions of international peace other than to a universal humanity. Still, American Jews were expected, by the American Protestant ethos, to surrender their particularistic patterns and to concentrate more potently on the universalistic elements of Judaism, in the hope of accelerating a "higher integration of social relationships" in the United States.[9] To American Protestantism, America's greatness lay in its homogeneity, not in its heterogeneity. Cultural pluralism, which contributed distinct racial, cultural, and religious strains to a common melting pot, was tolerable only until the unsettling 1930s. But such a philosophy could not be tolerated as a permanent feature of American democracy. "America's hospitality [to cultural pluralism] has already imperiled its democracy. Carried too far, this hospitality results in a society so heterogeneous that it cannot be a community: too many communities can destroy the community."[10]

The *Christian Century*'s attack on cultural pluralism was an open attack on the American Jewish community. It wrote: "When the doctrine of cultural pluralism is taken to mean religious pluralism—"Judaism is true for the Jew and Christianity is true for the Christian"—it sets itself in direct opposition to the Christian faith which cannot exist at all except on the presumption of its universality."[11] Other ethnic, religious, and racial communities in the United States proceeded to practice their unique patterns of behavior without consistent reminders of their melting pot obligations. It was taken for granted that sooner or later they would melt into the majority culture. Although the Catholic community was always considered suspect by Protestantism for its alleged dependence on Papal authority, it was still part of a universalistic Christian framework. The American-German community was not castigated for perpetuating its distinctive cultural practices. The American Negroes were not criticized for their separatist racial patterns of expression and behavior. Only American Jews were singled out for all three offenses: they retained a distinctive culture, they felt a common solidarity of peoplehood or race, and their religion was essentially separatist rather than primarily universalist.

The *Christian Century* argued that, by championing these distinctive characteristics, American Jews were perpetuating and strengthening the forces of anti-Semitism in the United States. In its view, this thesis was tantamount to a self-fulfilling prophecy: "Democracy cannot guarantee our American Jewish brethren against the emergence of a crisis in which the prejudice and anger generated by their long resistance to the democratic process will flame up to their great hurt."[12]

The periodical was clearly interested in trying to influence American Jewry to alter its pattern of religious-ethnic uniqueness. What twenty centuries of anti-Semitism and brutal physical persecution could not compel the Jews to do, the modern American Protestant weekly would have them do in a single generation. In its articles and editorials, the *Christian Century* warned the insecure Jews during the Depression that they would not be tolerated by American society if they continued to retain their unique ethnic-religious attributes. Judaism should divest itself of its "cultural fatalism"[13] and freely encourage the devotees of one religion to cross over to another. With remarkable lack of subtlety it asserted that, should Judaism remain obstinate and not allow itself to reach "a higher synthesis," the Protestant's "spirit of tolerance would shrivel up."[14]

This enforced religious liberalism was characteristic of American

Protestantism until the early 1950s. Either the religious groups in the United States were to toe the mark of liberal religion as defined by the Protestant churches, or they would be harassed and sniped at by the Protestant establishment. Either the other religions were to take on more common characteristics of a "civic," white Anglo-Saxon Protestant ethos, or they could not be acknowledged as partners in the American religious arena.[15]

The starting point for the Jewish religious group to begin its melting process into the spiritual mainstream of America could be the incorporation by Judaism of the teachings of Jesus into its liturgy and preachments.[16] "A simple gesture of [this] recognition would be the unconstrained observance of Jesus' birthday." To be sure, his place in Judaism did not have to be the same as that which is accorded him in the Christian church. Neither should Judaism feel, so the periodical said, that its interaction with Christianity must be a one-way movement in which Christianity did all the giving and Judaism all the receiving. "If the religion of Judaism is good for the Jews, it is also good for gentiles," proclaimed the *Christian Century*. "If it is not good for gentiles, it is not the best religion for Jews."[17] Whatever this simplistic and deceptive statement was meant to convey, the periodical felt it was "not fair to democracy to cherish a religious faith which provides a sanction for racial or cultural or any other form of separation."[18]

A more accurate statement of the journal's viewpoint, on the subject of who was to influence whom in the interplay between Judaism and Christianity, was explicated several years later when it quoted from a study about intermarriage. The study indicated that the total number of conversions to Judaism was relatively small. Approving this small number of converts, the paper hoped the finding "would clear away such misunderstandings as have grown out of a widespread belief that the purpose of many synagogues and rabbis has been to employ Judaism to block the normal assimilative processes of American life."[19] It was clearly the policy of the periodical to advocate assimilation, and rabbis who fought this homogenizing tendency while seeking to strengthen Jewish loyalties, were viewed as reactionary forces in America.[20]

This view prevailed in American Protestantism until the post–World War II era, when a new mutual pluralistic tolerance began to emerge among religions in America.[21] Furthermore, the international campaign to establish a Jewish state after the war substantially muted American

Protestantism's aggressive advocacy of Jewish religious assimilation in the United States by diverting its anti-Jewish thrust from the purely religious to the political arena.

OBJECTIONS TO JEWISH NATIONALISM

Despite the sharpness of the *Christian Century*'s critique of Judaism as a religion, it was mild when compared to the paper's criticism of Judaism as a way of life of a particular people. The "peoplehood" concept of American Jewry was a disturbing factor in the orderly design of American social groupings. One could grasp the meaning of a religious group, an ethnic collective entity, or even a "nationality" which was somehow associated with a modern nation. The Jews, however, were the only large group in America which was more than a religious or ethnic entity, and still less than a nationality. They had no sovereign political state, an essential prerequisite of modern nationhood.[22] Furthermore, since World War I American Jews had blended increasingly into the American political and social fabric. They were Americans by nationality. What then *were* the Jews?

While some writers have called then a "race," the latter term has been appropriated by social scientists to describe a group's visible, physical characteristics (Caucasian, Negroid, Mongoloid). The term most approximating Jewish group practices, values, and ideals—incorporating many aspects of religion, ethnicity, and even nationality—is peoplehood. The Jews are a "people," in Hebrew: *'am,* a connotation applied to them from Bible times. Some modern Jewish writers specifically add the adjective "religious" before "people," while others use the term "religious civilization" to indicate the rubric of religious peoplehood.[23]

This complicated analysis of the nature of the Jewish group disturbed the *Christian Century.* Encouraged by a very small number of Jewish Reform rabbis and laymen in the United States, who fought the concept of Judaism denoting anything more than a religion, the periodical persisted in attacking the notion of Jewish peoplehood and its nationalist manifestation, Zionism. One can detect several strains in the anti-Jewish nationalist stance of American Protestantism.

One objection to Jewish nationalism lay in its possible conflict with other nationalisms, in the United States and elsewhere. Before the establishment of the State of Israel, the sheer advocacy by Jews of such a state implied, in the eyes of the *Christian Century,* a clash of national loyalties —Jewish vs. other.

When, early in 1942, there was clamor for the formation of a separate Jewish army unit to fight against the Nazis, to be composed mostly of Palestinian Jews and European refugees, the periodical objected lest "such an army would dramatize and make official the segregation of the Jew. It might, as claimed, increase his sense of separate nationality."[24] Acknowledging its anti-Zionist bias, the *Christian Century* could not refrain from stating, "at the risk of further misunderstanding," that the formation of such an army would do world Jewry far more harm than good.[25] Three years later, it strongly advised Jews to reach a decision "whether they are an integral part of the nations in which they live or members of a Levantine nation dwelling in exile."[26]

When a representative national conference of American Jewish organizations meeting in Pittsburgh at the end of 1944 called on the United Nations to seat representatives of the Jewish people on the board of the United Nations Relief and Rehabilitation Agency, the *Christian Century* was angry.

No single factor has done more to render insecure the position of the modern Jew than the charge that he is not completely, wholeheartedly, first, last and all the time a citizen of the country in which he resides, but that he attempts to hold a dual citizenship, which in actuality works out in a divided loyalty, with his primary loyalty given to an allegiance other than the land in which he lives. We do not believe that this is true for the overwhelming majority of Jews in this and other countries. But the resolutions adopted by the Pittsburgh Convention are well calculated to revive this ancient charge.[27]

The periodical accused American Zionist organizations of operating "under the cloak of religious liberty" when in fact they were "parts of a government operating outside the law of nations."[28] In its obsessive denunciation of Jewish nationalism, the *Christian Century* even suggested insidious comparisons between German nationalism and Jewish nationalism. In June 1937 it editorialized:

The Jewish position in American democracy may be visualized in principle by imagining five million Germans held together in racial and cultural unity by the Hitler doctrine of the folkic soul, transported to America, established in our democratic land as the Jews now are, and determined to maintain their racial doctrine and their racial separateness.[29]

After the Nazis were defeated in 1945, the *Christian Century* expressed the hope that the German people would not develop a martyr complex and "become another Jewry; they have not lived long enough with their ideology of a unique and privileged race."[30] This implication that the Jews have a "privileged race" mentality analogous to the Nazi superior race ideology was challenged in the periodical by the director of the Chicago chapter of the National Conference on Christians and Jews. "I was shocked beyond words," he wrote, "and could hardly believe my eyes when I came across this sentence."[31] The periodical did not see fit to comment on his criticism.

How can one assess the almost hysterical policy against Jewish nationalism on the part of the *Christian Century?* It appears that the Protestant attitude towards the concept of Jewish nationalism was based fundamentally on theological grounds. In May 1933, after the rise of Nazism, the *Christian Century,* in a long, penetrating editorial, openly admitted that

The Christian mind has never allowed itself to feel the same human concern for Jewish sufferings that it has felt for the cruelties visited upon Armenians, the Boers, the people of India, American slaves, or the Congo blacks under Leopold imperialism. Christian indifference to Jewish suffering has for centuries been rationalized by the tenable belief that such sufferings were the judgment of God upon the Jewish people for their rejection of Jesus.[32]

The editorial proceeded to urge its readers to distinguish between Jews as Jews and Jews as nationalists. It was not the former who were guilty of Jesus' death. Jews as Jews should not be despised by the Christian world. His crucifixion was brought about by the "nationalist" Jews.

He was crucified because he had a program for Israel which ran counter to the cherished nationalism of Israel's leaders—political and priestly. He opposed their nationalism with the universalism of God's love and God's kingdom. . . . In the eyes of the Jewish rulers, he was a seditious person, a menace to their fantastic nationalism and to their vested rights and prestige. . . . It was nationalism that crucified Jesus. . . . It was because he threatened by his teaching to upset their cherished ambition to make Israel and Israel's God the dominant power of the world that he came into collision with Israel's rulers.[33]

Here then, one finds the major source of Protestant hostility to modern Jewish nationalism. By juxtaposing modern Jewish nationalism to the Jewish nationalists of the first century, the *Christian Century* took upon itself to exonerate "Jews as Jews" from the crime of the crucifixion, even as it directed the anger of its Protestant readers against modern Jewish nationalists. It is not important here to dispute the *Christian Century*'s interpretation of the events leading to Jesus' crucifixion, as did a few published letters in a subsequent issue,[34] or other analyses of the event.[35] What is important is the revelation of the theological underpinning for its contemporary anti-Jewish nationalism crusade.

The editorial draws an ironic conclusion: "Jewish nationalism crucified Christ, and Christian nationalism is now, and for centuries has been, engaged in crucifying the Jews. ... Let the Jews see themselves as suffering from the same cause as that which put Jesus of Nazareth to death."[36]

The pages of the *Christian Century* carried little criticism with regard to other nationalist groups. American nationalism is applauded, and the nationalist aspirations of colonially held societies are respected. Only Nazi nationalism and Jewish nationalism are put in the same category.[37]

The truculent attitude of American Protestantism towards Jewish nationalism in the 1930s may also be understood in implicit theological terms. As indicated in the first chapter, great numbers of Christians believed that "Old Israel" had ceased to exist as a collective national entity with the birth of Christ, its place taken by the church, the "new Israel." While liberal Protestantism sought to explain away anti-Semitism in religious, psychological, and sociological terms,[38] it never faced up to the obvious embarrassment that "old Israel," though considered theologically deceased, was nonetheless very much alive. Its descendants were promoting its resurrection as a modern sovereign nation in its ancient land of Israel. To modern Protestantism, Jewish nationalism was not just any "nationalism." It contradicted the centuries-old Christian theological myth of Jewish national demise. The apparition of "old Israel" warranted theological concern, if not outright opposition, from Protestants.

THE JEW: ENEMY OF ISOLATIONISM

As mentioned earlier, the *Christian Century*'s sharp bias against Jewish nationalism was compounded by its own concept of authentic Americanism. The periodical's notion of Americanism was not universally held by American Protestants, but it undoubtedly reflected the attitudes of large numbers of Protestants. In essence, the idea of American nationalism advocated by the paper was isolationism. To be sure, the *Christian Century* was not pro-German during the period of Nazism's rise, nor did it actively desire a German victory when war broke out in 1939. Along with other American groups and periodicals, it merely wanted the United States to keep out of the war.[39] Any group advocating United States intervention was severely criticized by the publication and, of course, American Jewry, as a collective entity identified with intervention, was a frequent target of its wrath.

During the crucial year of 1941, before America actually entered the war, the *Christian Century* was especially hostile to those who sought to influence American intervention. In early January of that year, it rejected the "doctrinaire dogma that Hitler is anti-Christ" and advised Jews "not to declare that those who are not with us in these theories are against us."[40] In June 1941, it reported the death in the House of Representatives of a Jewish Congressman from New York City who died of a heart attack after replying to a speech in which a Mississippi Congressman had charged that "Wall Street and a little group of our international Jewish brethren" were behind a prointerventionist meeting in New York City.

Ignoring the probability that American Jewry was indeed overwhelmingly for United States entry into the war on the side of the Allies, as were other ethnic groups in America, the *Christian Century* nonetheless expressed the belief "that there are plenty of Jews in the United States who are decidedly against intervention. . . . The trouble is that, with the exception of those who are Communists or members of other left-wing groups, they have generally kept silent."[41] This Protestant periodical found it inconceivable that American Jewry, like other American groups, felt that democracy was gravely threatened, or that America's best interests lay with a victory over Germany. It blatantly warned American Jewry "to keep silent no longer" if it wished to protect the American nation against the possibility of "a future racial tragedy" which was bound to make scapegoats of Jews during the projected disillusionment following the peace.[42] In September 1941, the periodical, obviously frustrated by its inability to influence American Jewry to side with its non-interventionist stand, flatly stated that

Despite all the attempts to gloss over and to conceal the tension between Jew and gentile in this land of freedom, the simple truth is that the spirit of tolerance is hardly more than skin deep. . . . The reason is that anti-Semitism . . . is an irrational passion which . . . cannot be controlled in the interest of any rational public policy. . . . The Jewish problem is not primarily a religious problem. It is a racial and social problem. . . . Its explosive possibilities do not inhere in any conflict of religious forms or creeds, but in a tragic social unassimilability.[43]

ADJUSTING TO THE RELIGIOUS REALITY OF ISRAEL

There can by now be little doubt that Protestant thought was seriously challenged by the establishment of the state of Israel. The very dynamics of a Jewish sovereign state in the Holy Land and its implications for Jews and Christians inevitably called into play new patterns of Protestant religious thinking affecting the Jewish people. Even the *Christian Century* reflected a drastic change in attitude towards the subject of Israel.[44] Such a policy shift climaxed almost two decades of that periodical's tortuous adjustment to the new Jewish reality.

The principal question facing the Christian world since the advent of the Jewish state has been: "What is 'Israel'?" As the *Christian Century* admitted in 1967, it had consistently questioned the wisdom of interpreting the terms "a faith and a folk," used throughout the centuries, to mean a political state.[45] But having made the "necessary journalistic adjustments," the periodical believed that as the word "Israel" became increasingly identified with a particular political entity, it would forfeit some of its theological mystique. "As the word moves from general, abstract meanings to a specific, concrete focus, it inevitably loses its broad and deep spiritual significance" for both Jews, and especially non-Jews. Jews might gradually tend to give up the use of the term as a literary symbol for "a heritage, a folk, a community, a faith"; Christians might slowly become deprived of the figurative meanings of the word which has been used "as a synecdoche for the Christian church, the whole Christian community."

The Protestant weekly concluded that the right of Zionists to insist that Israel be granted diplomatic recognition by her Arab neighbors was valid. On the other hand, it warned Jews that Israel would henceforth by judged by the same standards applicable to all other states "without appeals for special consideration based on . . . spiritual and non-political values." Christians, it asserted, will continue to "owe to Israel—the faith, the heritage, the community—a debt they can never fully discharge, but history has not made the state of Israel the collector of that debt."[46]

PROTESTANT THEOLOGIANS' REACTIONS TO THE NEW STATE

Not all Protestant thinkers were prepared at last to adjust their thinking to a valid dichotomy between Israel the state and Israel the faith. To the Protestant adherents of the millennial hope, the Jewish state was merely an extension of the Jewish faith. These millenarians applauded the creation of the state as a fulfillment of prophecy. William M. Smith, professor of Bible at the Fuller Theological School, told his readers in the mid-1950s: "The promise to Israel of Palestine as a permanent possession is *at no time cancelled*. Not only has the idea of Israel's permanent occupation remained unfulfilled, but . . . when has Israel ever enjoyed the permanent, uninterrupted peace and prosperity here promised? . . . If we take the unauthorized liberty of cancelling these prophecies, why may we not with equal liberty cancel any other prophecy with which a particular theory would lead us to disagree? The promises regarding Canaan were made to one nation, Israel, and to no other."[47]

The executive editor of *Christianity Today*, L. Nelson Bell, rejoiced in 1967 when East Jerusalem fell to the Jews, claiming that this event "gives a student of the Bible a thrill and a renewed faith in the accuracy and validity of the Bible. . . . If we say, as the Arabs do, that Israel has no right to exist, we may prove blind to her peculiar destiny under the providence of God."[48] And William Culbertson, president of the Moody Bible Institute, reminded his readers that though the Jews have returned to their land "in unbelief," it is only when "the Redeemer comes to Zion that all Israel will be saved" (Rom. 11:26).[49]

Less fundamentalist Protestant leaders also viewed the emergence of the Jewish state as an act of God. Edwin T. Dahlberg, president of the National Council of Churches, wrote in 1957: "If we did not believe in an omnipotent God, we might well fall into despair concerning the situation in the Middle East. . . . But of one thing we can be sure: in the land of Israel a work of God is going on that will affect the future history of the human race as truly as in the days when Moses led the children of Israel through the wilderness from the land of Pharaoh to the land of Canaan."[50]

Kyle Haseldon, maverick editor of the *Christian Century* from 1964 to 1967, upon visiting Israel in 1965 wrote: "Any one travelling through the land, looking and listening, is soon convinced that some agent—which cannot be defined as anything less than spiritual—has transformed the sea of diversity which swept into this little country into a people, a nation, and has done so in much less time than the forty years required by Moses for a similar project. This story cannot be told dispassionately. .... As a Christian, I want to believe that the people who produced the prophets and from whom came Jesus of Nazareth are still chosen to witness to all nations."[51]

A. Roy Eckardt, professor of religion at Lehigh University, found the State of Israel playing a crucial theological role in that the Jews refused "to subordinate the 'natural' domain to the 'spiritual' domain (always, though, at the risk of secularization)." He lauded the Jews' return to their land "as living refutation" of the Christian contention that Israel must be barred from its land until it fulfilled the "conditions upon which the church fancied it had a monopoly. But Israel *has* returned. It is almost as though God has deliberately said 'no' to Christian pretensions."[52]

Needless to say, not all Protestant spokesmen were equally approving of the positive theological role of the State of Israel. Some of them, especially Europeans, while not fully convinced of this role, nonetheless were prepared to have an open mind on the subject.[53]

European Protestants were far more theologically oriented than were the Americans. When their respective representatives met together, the Europeans would invariably influence the Americans' thinking: the Europeans were the teachers, the Americans the students. This pattern was demonstrated at sessions of the World Council of Churches and at other international church conferences. Robert C. Dodd, director of the Committee on Ecumenical Affairs of the National Council of Churches, placed several agonizing questions before the readers of *Christian Century* when he reported on an international conference of Christians and Jews held in England in 1966.[54] It would seem clear that the formulation of these questions was primarily due to the influence of European Protestant and Jewish participants, for prior to Dodd's report, similar penetrating queries were absent in the American Protestant press. Dodd wrote:

If the continuing existence of the people of Israel has been an embarrassment to Christianity, then the existence of a political entity known as the state of Israel may be an even more acute embarrassment. . . . Is it possible in biblical terms to comprehend the plan of God for the children of Israel apart from the land which He promised through Moses? . . . Are there any official church actions which recognize, either in support or in condemnation of, this new state? If not, why are the churches and such of their agencies as the World Council of Churches silent about its existence? . . . Is it legitimate for Christians to hope and to pray for changes in the state of Israel that might make it a light unto the nations and a faithful—yes, and suffering—servant of the Most High? Can Christians say that the existence of Israel is either outside or in opposition to the divine plan?

If there were Protestants who remained uncertain about the State of Israel's role in the drama of divine salvation, and were prepared to study it, there were others who were quite certain that the Jewish state and its nationalistic ideology was anything but part of a theological design. Immediately after the state was established, Millar Burrows, professor of biblical theology at Yale, and president of the American Schools for Oriental Research in the Near East, suggested that "the present resurgence of Jewish nationalism is a repetition of the same fatal error that caused Israel's rejection of Jesus. It is the focal point at which Christian opinion, in all brotherly love, should make clear and emphatic its disagreement with the dominant trend in contemporary Judaism."[55]

During the same period, the *Christian Century* expressed fear lest Jewish nationalism "further emasculate the *religious* contribution of the universal religion of Judaism to the spiritual purification and strengthening of Western society."[56] It direly predicted that the extent to which Jewish congregations "now become absorbed in the support of a national state which is neutral toward, and largely indifferent to, the fate of Judaism as a faith, to that extent the remarkable triumph now culminating in the emergence on history's stage of the new Israel may turn out to be one of the darkest tragedies in the record of Judaism." On the eve of Israel's tenth anniversary, the periodical still was of the opinion that the "most difficult of all" problems facing that society was "how to rescue Judaism, the religious faith, from Zionism, a nationalistic creed."[57]

Even Protestant fundamentalists were not of one mind on the theological significance of the state of Israel. O. T. Ellis, formerly professor of Old Testament at Princeton Theological Seminary, raised this question: "What other people in the world would venture to demand that the clock of history be put back two millennia for their benefit?"[58] The author maintained that God's promise to Abraham's seed to give them title over Palestine "was conditioned on obedience to the will of God," and that for the Christian, Palestine had only sentimental interest. Only "racial pride and nationalistic aspirations" make it important for a Jew "who still lives more or less in the Old Testament Dispensation" to possess Palestine. "There are many open spaces in the world, many friendly nations, in which oppressed Israelites can find a refuge and a home without imperiling the peace of the world," Ellis contended. He did not specify any such places, but instead concluded his article as follows: "Does the Israeli cause deserve to succeed? . . . We believe the verdict of history will be, No!"

NOTES

1. Both theories are attributed to Jews, the melting pot theory to an English-Jewish writer, Israel Zangwill, and the cultural pluralism theory to an American-Jewish thinker, Horace Kallen. Zangwill wrote a novel, *The Melting Pot*, in 1980. For Kallen's views and other concepts relating to minority groups in a democracy, see the summary in Samuel Dinin's *Judaism in a Changing Civilization* (New York: Teachers College, Columbia University, 1933), chaps. 1 and 2.
2. Nathan Glazer, *American Judaism* (Chicago: University of Chicago Press, 1957); Mordecai M. Kaplan, *Judaism as a Civilization* (New York: Macmillan 1934).
3. *Christian Century* (hereafter cited as CC), 9 June 1937, p. 735.
4. Ibid., 7 July 1937, p. 862.
5. Ibid.
6. Ibid.
7. Ibid., p. 863.
8. Ibid., 13 March 1946, pp. 323–24.
9. Ibid., 9 June 1937, p. 735.
10. Ibid., 7 July 1937, p. 863.
11. Ibid., 1 July 1936, p. 926.
12. Ibid., 9 June 1937, p. 735.
13. Ibid., 29 April 1936, p. 625.
14. Ibid., p. 626.
15. Reviewing the period under discussion, Will Herberg concluded (in 1962): "Until about thirty years ago, America was a Protestant nation . . . Protestantism was America's established church. . . . Non-Protestants . . . experienced their non-Protestant religion as a mark of their foreignness. . . . [The] syncretism [of the democratic society and nation] was a Protestant phenomenon exclusively. Jews and Catholics, being outsiders and foreigners, did not share in this culture-religion." (*Christianity and Crisis*, 5 February 1962, pp. 3–7.)

16. CC, 20 December 1939, pp. 1566–67.
17. Ibid., p. 1567.
18. Ibid.
19. Ibid., 17 November 1954, p. 389.
20. The *Christian Century* was not atypical in American Protestantism regarding its views on desirable assimilation. A Princeton historian, reviewing Arthur Hertzberg's *The French Enlightenment and the Jews* (New York: Columbia University Press, 1968) in *Christianity and Crisis,* justified the assimilationist tendencies of European Jewry resulting from the emancipation period. He concluded: "The truth seems to be that 'Jewish emancipation' . . . succeeds best as in 1770 when accompanied by a degree of assimilation. If this raises special problems in Judaism, the rest of us have also had to put aside ancestral traditions" (R. R. Palmer, "At the Sources of Jewish Liberty and Equality," *Christianity and Crisis,* 28 October 1968, pp. 253–56).
21. Will Herberg, *Protestant, Catholic, Jew* (New York: Doubleday 1955).
22. An exception to this general rule was found in the minority treaties after World War I which recognized the Jews of several East European states as a nationality despite their having no modern nation. The practice of the Soviet Union also is to indicate a Jewish nationality in the passports of its Jewish citizens.
23. Kaplan, *Judaism as a Civilization.*
24. CC, 11 February 1942, p. 173.
25. Ibid.
26. Ibid., 28 November 1945, p. 1311.
27. Ibid., 3 January 1945, p. 5.
28. Ibid., 25 June 1947, p. 789.
29. Ibid. 9 June 1937, p. 736.
30. Ibid., 13 June 1945, p. 702.
32. Ibid., 3 May 1933, pp. 582–84.
33. Ibid.
34. Ibid., 10 May 1933, pp. 659–62.
35. *Judaism* 20, (January 1971). The major feature of *Judaism's* winter 1971 issue is a symposium of distinguished scholars on the trial of Jesus. Robert M. Grant of the University of Chicago asserts that though the idea of kingship preached by Jesus was religious in nature, it was interpreted by Jews and Romans alike as having political overtones and, therefore, carried within it the seeds of rebellion against Rome. S. G. F. Brandon of the University of Manchester argues that Jesus was a nationalist patriot, a member, or at least a sympathizer, of the zealots. He maintains that the Gospels alter these facts in order for the early Christian church to win favor, or at least toleration, in the Roman Empire. Israel Supreme Court Justice Haim Cohen believes that at the hearings before the Jewish authorities, the

latter sought to save Jesus from execution, but his insistence on proclaiming himself the Christ rendered their attempt futile.

36. *CC*, 3 November 1937, p. 1351. The editorial arbitrarily equated Christian nationalism with German nationalism.

37. Other Protestant periodicals published similar views. Warned a leading British Protestant, the principal of New College, Oxford: "If Jewish nationalism were arrogant and aggressive, as it is probable it might be, it would become a danger to the world as German communities dominated by Nazi sentiment are proving to be" (A. E. Garvie, "The Jewish Problem," *International Review of Missions*, 30 [1941], p. 222).

38. The religious explanation for anti-Semitism was that the Jews were responsible for Jesus' crucifixion and that they had rejected Jesus' role as the Messiah. The psychological explanation for anti-Semitism was that the Gentiles had rejected Jesus' Jewishness in favor of their pagan background. The sociological explanation was that the Jews retained their separate identity within the American society.

39. This adamant isolationist stand on the part of the *Christian Century* brought forth *Christianity and Crisis* in 1941. In December of 1940 the *Christian Century* published an article by Dr. Reinhold Niebuhr in which he analyzed the error of liberal Protestants who upheld a policy of neutrality and non-involvement in war. The thrust of Niebuhr's argument was that it was wrong for Christians to believe that Christianity would shame the enemy into goodness so that he will cease to imperil them (*CC*, 8 December 1940, pp. 1578–80). Niebuhr was particularly incensed at the *Christian Century*'s stubborn isolationist policy affecting the possible survival of Western European democracies.

40. *CC*, 8 January 1941, p. 47.

41. Ibid., 18 June 1941, pp. 796–97. In a letter published in response to this editorial, a rabbi asked: If the majority of American Jews agree with Roosevelt and Willkie "should they then give expression to a contrary view in order to forestall the possibility that otherwise they may be used as scapegoats at some future date?" (ibid., 23 July 1941, p. 937).

42. Ibid., 18 June 1941, pp. 796–97.

43. Ibid., 24 September 1941, pp. 1167–69.

44. At the end of 1964, the new managing editor of *Christian Century*, Kyle Haseldon, began to modify radically that paper's policy with regard to such subjects as Jewish nationalism, Israel, and the "melting pot" desideratum for America. Haseldon's more flexible stance on these issues was reflected in the editorials of the publication from the time he assumed his position as managing editor through the end of the period of our investigation. In late 1967, Haseldon was stricken with cancer, and died shortly thereafter.

45. *CC*, 30 August 1967, pp. 1091–92.

46. Modern Jews have not helped very much in clarifying the theological term

'Israel.' Reporting on a 1966 interfaith dialogue in England, a *Christian Century* correspondent wrote that one of the participants, Professor Uri Tal of the Hebrew University in Jerusalem, told the gathering that the character of contemporary Israel had not yet been fully articulated. Tal, personally an observant Jew, was purported to have said that though Israel appeared to be a politically secular society it was essentially a religious state and had a theological, but not an eschatological, significance. Commented the reporter, Cecil Northcott: "No messianic vision for Professor Tal! His Israel seems to be an Anglican type, church-state compromise, which perhaps explains why Anglicanism seems to be able to live so happily with Israel on the dialogic frontier" (*CC*, 31 August 1966, p. 1049).

47. *Christianity Today*, 15 October 1956, pp. 7ff.
48. Ibid., 21 July 1967, pp. 1044–45.
49. Ibid., 7 June 1968, pp. 870–73.
50. *CC*, 9 January 1957, pp. 41–42.
51. Ibid., 24 March 1965, pp. 360–61.
52. A. Roy Eckardt, *Elder and Younger Brothers* (New York: Charles Scribner's Sons, 1967), p. 147.
53. The principal question at the 1951 meeting of the German branch of the International Missionary Council's Commission on the Christian Approach to the Jews was not the *sui generis* nature of the Jewish people—which was acknowledged—but the uniqueness of the land of Israel. One reporter wrote: "The only question was whether one could now say, in the same *[sui generis]* sense, that even the land of Israel, the Holy Land, is 'no mere country among countries,' on the same plane as them, but that it had the character of a 'sacrament,' that the Land of Israel acquires 'consecrated dignity' " (Gerhard Jasper, "The State of Israel and Christendom," *International Review of Missions* 40 [1951]:313–21).
54. *CC*, 2 November 1966, pp. 1359–62.
55. Ibid., 30 March 1949, pp. 400–402. See note 35 above.
56. Ibid., 16 March 1949, pp. 327–29.
57. Ibid., 7 May 1958, p. 550.
58. *Christianity Today*, 24 December 1956, pp. 6ff.

12

New Realities: Israel in the Holy Land
Esther Yolles Feldblum

A German nun, living in Jerusalem when the State of Israel was proclaimed, recently recalled: "I well remember our firm conviction that it would never come into being."[1] James O'Gara, an American Catholic journalist, echoed the same sentiments in an autobiographical essay in which he observed, "There are those who spread the myth that the Jews were condemned to wander through the world until the end of time—a myth so strong that many Christians feared that the establishment of the State of Israel contradicted the Sacred Scriptures."[2] The incredulity and consternation felt by Catholics, laymen and religious alike, was confirmed in a scholarly article by Fr. Edward Flannery. Indeed, shock was the most pervasive immediate reaction of Catholics to the Jewish state, and this shock was rooted in a theological assumption that the dispersion of the Jews was a divine punishment of perpetual duration.[3]

The impact of the new reality was neither tempered nor allayed by official statements of the Church. At this time, a full account of Vatican diplomacy vis-à-vis the new state is still not available, and one can only conjecture the reactions of leading Vatican circles on the basis of what was officially said and what remained unsaid. Nevertheless, it seems that the Vatican, too, was in a quandary. On the one hand, it did not cherish the idea of Palestine being engulfed again in the Moslem world, and on the other hand, it could not be happy with Jewish dominion over the

Reprinted in part by permission of Ktav Publishing House from Esther Yolles Feldblum, *The American Catholic Press and the Jewish State, 1917–1959* (New York: Ktav Publishing House, 1977), chap. 5.

Holy Land. Misgivings toward the former were rooted in a history of strife; discomfiture with the latter was enmeshed in theological sensitivities. At the same time, the Vatican could not easily disregard the repentant mood of the Christian world following the Holocaust, and oppose a Jewish state. Perforce, its policy veered toward a noncommittal silence. As late as two weeks before the proclamation of the state, a papal encyclical touching on the events then transpiring in Palestine made no mention of the two proposed states in the area. The Pope only expressed his "keen anxiety" for the safety of the holy places, and alluded with masterful vagueness to a just solution to the Palestinian strife.[4] In the later allocutions and encyclicals, the political entity of Israel was deliberately and consistently ignored. When the Pope wished to refer to the territory of Israel, he used the terms *Holy Land* or *Palestine*.[5] Nonrecognition surely did not indicate a positive attitude toward the state, but neither were there *official* statements of outright condemnation.

Taking its cue from the Vatican, the American hierarchy refrained from comment on the establishment of Israel. The diocesan press, likewise, reflected a pervasive hesitation and ambivalence. Most of the papers simply ignored the existence of Israel, with its connotations for Christendom, and narrowed their attention, as the Pope had done, solely to the fighting in Jerusalem and the danger to the holy places. The notable exceptions were those papers which had been openly hostile to Zionism in the pre-state period. The Brooklyn *Tablet*, for example, published a bitter attack on the state. Its editor denounced Israel for being a wholly secular, modern, and materialistic state which would respect neither God, nor Jesus, nor the "mementos of Christ." Concluding his censure of "modern Israel," Scanlon recommended that "Christians meanwhile, must pray that God deliver the Holy Land from the blind and the wicked who know not God."[6] *Sign*'s editor waited, but after the Bernadotte truce in June 1948, sanguine confidence in the ephemerality of Israel dwindled. The July issue of *Sign* carried abrasive criticism in its news comments, in a signed editorial by Ralph Gorman, and in an article by Kermit Roosevelt, then the executive director of the pro-Arab Committee for Justice and Peace in the Holy Land.[7] Gorman deplored the mistake of the United States in permitting a Jewish state to arise in Palestine, and the news editorial decried the lavish and complimentary coverage the "self-proclaimed" state was receiving in the press and on the radio. The paper chided Christians for hesitating to criticize Israel for fear of being labeled anti-Semites.[8] Also in July, the editor of *Catholic World* spoke up. Fr. Gillis lashed out against President Truman's "unholy haste" in recognizing the Jewish state in Palestine and condemned the "special pleading" which had brought about its establishment.[9]

It should be noted that following the President's recognition of Israel, the National Catholic News Service (NC-NS) in Washington prepared a carefully worded statement which took cognizance of the fact without official comment. The release quoted, however, Senator Arthur Vandenberg's explanation of the President's action as a "logical and proper step," and readers were further informed that the new state's declaration promised to ensure religious equality and the safeguarding of the shrines.[10] Several days later, the NC-NS received bulletins from its Vatican bureau. These releases, quoting liberally from the *Osservatore Romano* and the Catholic Action daily, *Quotidiano*, denounced the fighting in the Holy Land as sacrilegious and blasphemous. While the *Osservatore* blamed Christians for "spiritually abandoning" the Holy Land, the *Quotidiano* urged the Church to take immediate action.[11] As the weeks went by, the reports streaming into the diocesan press reinforced the anxieties of the Vatican release, rather than the guarded assurances of the Washington release.

Resort to theological arguments in response to Israel was generally rare in the press. The associate editor of the *Catholic Worker* opened his May 1948 editorial with a subtle reminder that a Jewish state belongs to the "Old Dispensation," but developed the theme that the Dispensation of Jesus called for an end to "all national States as desirable entities."[12] Far more pointed was the opinion expressed in the monthly of the Catholic Central-Verein. The *Social Justice Review* turned to a Jewish convert to Catholicism for an assessment of the new state. In his article, David Goldstein emphatically denounced the validity of any theological claim to Palestine on the part of the Jews: "There was a time when such a Palestine claim was warranted; that was during the days when the Jewish religion was God's one and only religion. . . . That was when they were given the land for the purpose of carrying out Israel's divine mission. That mission they have no more."[13] Even the few papers which took cognizance of the state in more positive tones did so with ambivalent feelings. The papers . . . not unfriendly to Jewish aspirations in the pre-state period now assumed the stance of interrogators, some with barely veiled suspicions.

Typical of this distrust were the questions raised by an editorial in *Commonweal* on May 28. Entitled "In Exitu, Israel" as if it were a legal brief, the editor pummelled the new state with questions. Would Israel be able to curb its extremists? What would be its relationship to Russia? What were its expectations regarding boundaries? Explicit criticism of Israel, however, was confined to a Christian demurrer on the name of the state.

As Catholics, Israel's arrogation of a universal name for so local an habitation must distress us. It is a good example of what Prof. Toynbee has called an archaizing tendency. Israel, for every Christian, is the whole redeemed world, and all peoples, since the Incarnation, are equally chosen in fulfillment of the prophecies to be heirs to the glory. Despite our sympathy for Israeli and Jew, we must not forget that to think of the Law and the Prophets as historically given only to their physical descendants, is a minimizing and a belittling of the greatest fact in history.[14]

America's first editorial on Israel began with yet another rehearsal of Arab versus Jewish claims to Palestine, but concluded,

The recognition extended by seven governments to the new state is recognition of a fact: that the Jews have staked their claim and do not intend to abandon it. . . . The extermination or subjugation of Israel would not sit well with world opinion. And that again is a fact which should be recognized.[15]

Nonetheless, apprehensions for the safety of the holy places and the security of Christian missions in Arab lands lent a quavering tone to *America*'s support.

To sum up Catholic press reactions to the State of Israel, one may say that there are a few discordant notes in what seemed to be an orchestrated response. The majority of the papers prudently adopted a "wait and see" attitude. Only those papers with well-known anti-Zionist biases were outspoken in opposition to the state, while the papers reputedly sympathetic to Zionism were less than enthusiastic. As the months wore on, reports from Catholic functionaries and observers in the Holy Land began filing into the press, and neutrality gave way. . . .

In the early years following the establishment of Israel, American Catholic opinion crystallized around two specific issues: internationalization of Jerusalem, and the Arab refugee problem. Despite popular impressions to the contrary, internationalization was not originally a Vatican proposal. The idea of international territory in the Holy Land was first proposed by secular governments with rival interests in the Middle East. Soon after the outbreak of World War I, Sir Mark Sykes, a British orientalist, and Charles Georges-Picot, a former French consul in Beirut, prepared a draft agreement for the postwar disposition of the Ottoman Empire. Their proposed map provided that Palestine, west of the Jordan between Haifa and Gaza, be established as an "international administration." In the course of the war, this plan was superseded by other secret agreements, and the recommendation of an internationalized area did not reappear until 1937, when it was again suggested by a secular government.[16] . . .

The majority plan of the United Nations Special Committee on Palestine (UNSCOP) divided the country into three units: an Arab state, a Jewish state, and the city of Jerusalem. The latter territory was to be placed, after a transitional period, under an international trusteeship system.[17] It is interesting to note that during the UNSCOP hearings, held from June to July 1947, the representative of the [custodians] of the Holy Land, Bro. Bonaventure Simon, refrained from endorsing an international regime for Jerusalem. He addressed his concern solely to the holy places and implied a preference for a Western Commission, designed along the lines of a "protector" system, similar in role to that of France during the Ottoman period.[18] In the modification of the majority plan by the Ad Hoc Committee on Palestine, the city of Jerusalem was designated a *corpus separatum,* with a statute to be detailed and approved by the Trusteeship Council. The governor, who would be neither Arab nor Jew, was to be appointed by, and responsible to, the Trusteeship Council.[19] This latter scheme of territorial internationalization, incorporated in the majority plan, was adopted by the General Assembly on November 29, 1947. No official approval came from Rome. Yet it seems that the Vatican preferred the majority plan, which included the internationalization of Jerusalem, and in discreet diplomatic activity let that preference be known.[20]

The announcement of the United Nations decision on partition inflamed the Arab world and set off a new wave of explosive violence in Palestine. Jerusalem was attacked on January 3, 1948. On May 1, on the eve of a rumored truce for the walled city, the Pope issued an encyclical, *Auspicia Quaedam,* in which he spoke of his "keen anxiety" for the safety of the holy places. After extolling Palestine as the land which should be "most dear to every cultured person" because of its association with the life and martyrdom of Jesus, he asked the following: "We desire, therefore, Venerable Brethren, that supplications be poured forth to the Most Holy Virgin for this request: that the situation in Palestine may at long last be settled justly and thereby concord and peace be also happily established."[21] The ambiguous phrase "settled justly" is nowhere explicated, and the Pope's words contain no clearly stated advocacy for the internationalization of Jerusalem. The uneasy truce of May 2 fell apart on May 15, when full-scale war broke out in the Holy Land. By June 2, when another truce was being arranged for Jerusalem, the Arabs still held an advantageous military position in the city. Just a few days earlier (May 29), the Jewish Quarter had succumbed.[22] During the night of June 1, the Pope received word of the Israeli acceptance of a cease-fire, and the next day he addressed the College of Cardinals on "la guerra in Palestina." Again the Pope made no specific mention of internationalization for the war-ravaged city, although he intimated that the Christian world would not "look on with indifference or with barren indignation while the Holy Land . . . is still being trodden by troops at war and subject to air bombardments."[23] Concerning the holy places, the Pope displayed increasing anxiety, precipitated perhaps by the May 31 manifesto of the "Christian Union" and the letter from the Catholic priests in Jerusalem detailing the damage to churches and institutions. "We do not believe that it [the Christian world] could allow the devastation of the Holy Places to become complete, the great "Sepulchre of Christ" to become destroyed. May it be God's will that the peril of this horrendous scourge be finally dispelled."[24] Several days before this allocution, the United Nations mediator, Count Folke Bernadotte, in a conversation with French Foreign Minister Bidault, revealed his plan for incorporating Jerusalem in the Arab state. Even after June 28, when Bernadotte's recommendation was officially delivered to the United Nations, the Pope made no plea for internationalization.[25] It was not until October 1948 that the Vatican openly and specifically espoused the United Nations plan. By then, there was good reason to fear that the temporary division of the city, with Israel in control of West Jerusalem, would harden into a permanent arrangement. In the encyclical *In Multiplicibus,* Pius XII stated,

We are confident that these supplications and hopes, indicative of the value which such a large number of people attribute to the Holy Places, will deepen the conviction in the high assemblies in which the problem of peace is being discussed that it would be expedient, as a better guarantee for the safety of the sanctuaries under the present circumstances, to give an international character to Jerusalem and its vicinity. . . .

It is also necessary to assure with international guarantees both the right of free access to the Holy Places scattered throughout Palestine and the freedom of religion and the respect for customs and religious traditions.[26]

Several months later, the Pope found it necessary to issue yet another encyclical on internationalization. Since the United Nations had failed to implement its proposal on Jerusalem, the Palestine Conciliation Commission was authorized by the General Assembly to draw up a new plan which would take into account the changed circumstances in the city since the hostilities of May 1948. The commission, therefore, was entertaining suggestions which would provide maximum local autonomy for Jordan and Israel. On April 7, 1949, the Israeli government informed the commission that it would be willing to concede to a functional internationalization (i.e., international control of the holy places), though it remained adamant on the point of territorial internationalization.[27] One week later, Pius XII issued the encyclical *Redemptoris Nostri,* which restated Vatican demands for full territorial internationalization, and furthermore, exhorted Roman Catholics to pressure their respective governments to support this plan. The intensity and urgency of the papal appeal is extraordinary.

We have already insisted in Our Encyclical letter "In Multiplicibus," that the time has come when Jerusalem and its vicinity . . . should be accorded and legally guaranteed an "international" status, which in the present circumstances seems to offer the best and most satisfactory protection for these sacred monuments.

We cannot help repeating here the same declaration. . . . Let them, wherever they are living, use every legitimate means to persuade the rulers of nations, and those whose duty it is to settle this important question, to accord to Jerusalem and its surroundings a juridical status. . . .

Encourage the faithful committed to your charge to be ever more concerned about the conditions in Palestine and have them make their lawful requests known, positively and unequivocally, to the rulers of nations.[28]

U.S. Catholics responded. The American hierarchy drew up a statement on April 27 which reiterated the plea of Pius XII. Cardinal Cushing spoke out forcefully on the issue at a mass rally in Boston's Fenway Park. The entire Catholic press, both diocesan and national, carried the papal pronouncement, and some appended editorials and articles reemphasizing the Vatican view.[29] With Cardinal Spellman in command, diplomatic activity centered in New York City.[30]

Among Cardinal Spellman's monsignori, the most influential exponent of internationalization was the executive secretary of the Catholic Near East Welfare Association (CNEWA), Msgr. Thomas McMahon. During a visit to Israel in the winter of 1948–49, McMahon gave the impression of having other duties than the official charitable mission on which he came.[31] In fact, the Israeli Ministry for Religious Affairs had opened negotiations with him prior to his visit, and a member of the ministry referred to him as an "unofficial representative of the Holy See on political matters." Confirming this impression, Pius XII told James G. McDonald that he hoped McMahon would be able to work out a settlement with the Israeli government.[32] Indeed, McMahon may have been responsible for more than just implementing papal directives; he may have been instrumental in formulating the Catholic position on internationalization and in securing Vatican backing for his views.

McMahon's position on internationalization rested on concepts which went beyond the rubrics of freedom of access and safety of the holy places. He insisted on the need for the full restoration and growth of the Christian population in Jerusalem in order to save the shrines from becoming mere "museum pieces." Jerusalem must develop into a vital center of Christianity. Only territorial internationalization would provide the atmosphere for the growth of a Christian population large enough to support such a center. Anything less than full territorial internationalization would compromise the Christian stake in the Holy Land, as McMahon understood it.[33]

In September 1949 the Conciliation Commission forwarded to the secretary-general its draft for Jerusalem. According to the commission's plan, Jerusalem would be divided into two zones, an Arab zone administered by Jordan, and a Jewish zone administered by Israel. The protection of the holy places would be the responsibility of the United Nations commissioner, and a system of international courts would deal with questions involving the holy places. The plan was neither fully territorial nor fully functional in its approach to internationalization. On the first day of the United Nations debate, the Australian representative introduced a draft resolution to reaffirm the territorial internationalization provisions of the 1947 partition plan. The Vatican radio commended the Australian resolution, and all Catholic action was channeled in its support.[34] Perhaps the most heralded effort was made by Cardinal Spellman, who was later credited with garnering crucial Latin American votes in support of the Australian resolution.[35] In the final vote, on December 9, 1949, the General Assembly rejected the Conciliation Commission's plan for Jerusalem and reaffirmed full territorial internationalization. The Vatican hailed the vote, but the implementation of the decision was again thwarted by Jordanian and Israeli opposition. By the spring of 1950, the resolution was paralyzed by a stalemate in the General Assembly.[36]

Official Catholic persistence in calling for the implementation of territorial internationalization continued unabated. In the United States, the campaign was waged by the Jesuit weekly *America* and by the articulate spokesman for the CNEWA, Msgr. McMahon, who asserted that "Come what may through the politics of *fait accompli* and the ineptitude of the U.N., the Church and churchmen have by no means abdicated their just right to demand their stake in the Holy Land of Jesus Christ."[37] *America*'s editors were ever on the alert to call attention to the unrequited claim of Christianity. Time and again the paper urged the United Nations to implement its decision, even advising that sanctions be imposed to force compliance. Editorials reminded Truman of his campaign pledge to support internationalization, and both Christians and Jews were criticized for praising Israel as long as it did not abide by the United Nations order.[38] One editorial even went so far as to draw a macabre analogy: ". . . the World Jewish Congress insisted that the graves of Nazi concentration-camp victims should not be entrusted exclusively to Germans—so, too, shrines of Christians cannot be entrusted exclusively to Jews and Arabs."[39] Apprehensions lessened somewhat as the Israeli government took effective action to eliminate causes of complaint. Access to Christian shrines in Israeli territory was open, incidents of desecration were rare, and the Israeli government was paying reparations for the damages.[40] Though the official Catholic stand on internationalization remained unchanged,[41] the crusading spirit in the press ebbed. Critical reactions to Israel now turned largely on the second issue, the Arab refugees.

The Arab refugee problem can hardly be described objectively. Its history is enmeshed in polemic, news reports are charged with emotion, and most evaluations tend to disintegrate into political-moral debates. However, in order to place the Catholic response in a reasonable perspective, it is important to briefly review the "facts" and the range of their interpretation.

On the origin of the problem Arabs and Jews differ. The Arab view claims that the Jews drove out the Palestinian Arab by use of force, terror, and intimidation. The Arabs point to the Deir Yassin incident as a confirmation of Israeli guilt and responsibility.[42] The Israeli counterclaim maintains that though the Jews wished to govern their United Nations-approved state in peaceful coexistence with the Arabs, the neighboring Arab countries invaded Israeli territory from all sides. Arab nationalist leaders encouraged, and even ordered, native Arabs to leave their homes to make room for the invading armies, while assuring the fleeing Arabs a speedy return to a wholly Arab country.[43]

A dispassionate study of the problem reveals that the leaders of the Jewish state neither planned nor anticipated the Arab exodus. Much of the mass flight was voluntary, although sociological and psychological factors inhering in the 1948 situation contributed enormously to a contagious flight psychosis. Not the least of these factors was the collapse of Arab morale, the absence of native Arab leadership, and the hysteria which fed on increasing Israeli military victories. Based on the precedents of Arab warfare, the Palestinian Arabs could expect nothing less than massacres if the Jews were victorious, and an isolated incident gave credence to such fears.[44]

The United Nations struggled with the refugee problem for many years. The numerous commissions and plans attest to the complexity of the problem.[45] The first solution attempted was repatriation. Of interest is the initial Arab reaction to this proposal. Until 1949 the Arabs were opposed to repatriation, reasoning that it implied a recognition of the state and a reminder of their inability to dislodge the Israelis. In contrast, the Israeli government had no fixed position concerning the problem.[46] The tables were reversed after the signing of the armistice treaties in the spring of 1949. Now the Arabs demanded repatriation, while the Israelis moved toward categorical rejection.[47] The United Nations then turned to schemes of resettlement of refugees in Arab states, where their absorption would not only be economically feasible, but also beneficial to the host countries. These programs met with steadfast opposition from the

Arab states. Even small-scale work-relief programs failed for lack of cooperation.[48] Unsolved, the problem remains a festering sore in the Middle East.

The Catholic Church took an early interest in the refugees. It prided itself on having preceded the United Nations in care and relief activities.[49] In the United States, the New York-based CNEWA played a very prominent role in this charitable work. In August 1948, Archbishop Arthur Hughes, papal internuncio to Egypt, appealed for large-scale relief funds for the refugees. He sent one telegram to the Vatican and the other to Cardinal Spellman. In less than a month, Spellman dispatched $50,000 from CNEWA and another $25,000 from the War Relief Services of the National Catholic Welfare Conference (NCWC).[50] Shipments of food, clothing, and other supplies followed. At the Bishops Conference in November 1948, McMahon was authorized to go to the Holy Land as special representative of the American hierarchy, in order to investigate the needs of the Arab refugees and to disburse $75,000 of Emergency Relief funds. By January 1949, the diocesan press was printing appeals by McMahon to "adopt holy towns like Nazareth." McMahon returned in March, as the papers said, "Weeping at What He Saw." His report stimulated a Bishops Emergency Drive, which made a nationwide appeal for funds on March 27, at the Laetare Sunday Mass.[51]

Whether by design or inadvertently, the Catholic press presented the refugee problem largely from the Arab perspective. Phrases such as "drive out," "forced to flee," "brutally uprooted," left no doubt that the guilt lay solely with the Jews.[52] Reports detailed the misery and deplorable living conditions of the refugees, but failed to note the reluctance of the Arab states to make any provisions for their kinsmen. It was the human-interest angle, the emotional tug of the story, that seized the attention of the press, while the political background of offers and counter-offers went unheeded. More telling than the contents of the stories were the analogies employed. In some papers the Israelis were likened to, the Nazis, in others to Titus and a string of tyrants; and in still others the Arab "expulsion" was paralleled hypothetically to "shipping off all U.S. Negroes to Portugal."[53] A typical conclusion was that of the syndicated weekly, *Our Sunday Visitor:* "Israel is a state that should not exist. How can it have God's blessing, how can it flourish when it is founded on the robbery of the 900,000 innocent people?"[54] Opposition to Jewish nationalism could now be legitimately couched in moralistic terms, and there was, indeed, a high correlation between earlier denunciations of Zionism and present moral indignation.

Only a small percentage of the refugees were Catholic, yet Catholics plunged wholeheartedly into relief efforts. Over 2,000 priests and nuns ministered to their needs in refugee camps.[55] Without questioning the humanitarian impulse which inspired these efforts, for Christian missionaries have always been involved in humanitarian causes in all parts of the world, one may ask if there were other motivating factors. McMahon's own words are suggestive. "For the Catholic effort in this humanitarian endeavor illustrates the fact that the Palestine problem is not bipartite but tripartite. There is a Christian stake in the Holy Land."[56] It did the Church no harm to give visibility to its claim of historical and contemporary interest in Palestine.

Of at least equal importance was the concern of the Vatican for the safety of Catholic minorities in the Middle East. The precariousness of the position of these minorities was heightened during crises or periods of intense nationalism, when Arab was frequently equated with Moslem.[57] Moreover, Christian communities were afraid of being identified with the Western countries which supported Israel. For fear of reprisals, many Christians sought to outdo the Moslems in support of the Arab cause.[58] The solicitude of the Vatican for the Arab refugees, regardless of religion, could serve effectively to demonstrate Catholic solidarity with the Arab cause. In June 1949, Pius XII set up the Pontifical Mission for Palestine to consolidate and strengthen worldwide Catholic relief efforts in the Middle East. McMahon was appointed president of the mission, and in his report of November 1951, he announced that the Pontifical Mission had already expended ten million dollars in aid for the Palestinian refugees.[59] The magnanimity of the Church was both commendable and expedient.

To question the legitimacy and justness of a Jewish state may also have appeared as a necessity, a theological necessity. Theologians were faced with the obvious dilemma of how to fit the unexpectedly renascent Israel into Christian doctrine and eschatology.[60] And on the practical level, there were difficulties in preserving the atmosphere of a pilgrim's Holy Land in the technologically progressive and secular Jewish state.

As theologians tried to come to grips with Israel, reinterpretations evolved. At the outset, though, a conservatively traditional assessment dominated Catholic thinking. This approach assigned no positive role to modern Israel. It looked upon the state as a secular aberration, potentially inimical to Christianity. Jewish control over the Holy Land could not be lasting, for the land was promised to the "spiritual sons of Abraham," the *verus Israel,* which is the Christian Church.[61] Invoking Romans 9:6, "They are not all Israelites who are sprung from Israel," Msgr. Matthew Smith, editor of the *Register,* explained, "Therefore the present Zionist state can have nothing spiritual to contribute to the world, and on Biblical grounds it has not [sic] right to the Holy Land. If God has given any group a mandate to occupy the country, it is the Christians. . . ."[62] Speculations on the eschatological significance of the Jewish state were not lacking. *Pilot* adjured its readers to view the events and the war in the Hold Land "as something vastly different" from similar political events elsewhere, and mused upon the likelihood of its bringing about the Second Coming.[63] In line with a popular belief that the state was inherently evil, some even subscribed to the view that it would beget the Antichrist.

There is an old legend, accepted by many Christian Fathers, that the Antichrist will be of Jewish descent and from the tribe of Dan, that he will be circumcised, will rebuild Jerusalem and the Temple, in which he will set himself up as God. Likewise, he will begin his seduction among the Jews, who will accept him as the Messiah.[64]

Rev. Edward A. Cerny, in a presidential address to the Catholic Biblical Society, also spoke of the "messianic" implications of the new state. "Perhaps it is too early to say," he admitted, "but we cannot help taking notice. The question is already being put to us by our pupils." Cerny observed that there were two possible explanations for Israel's functioning again, "at least temporarily," as a nation. Either it was Divine Providence to bring back Israel to her ancient homeland as a "preliminary to that conversion and to her ultimate incorporation into the Church where she is destined to play a glorious part before the end," or it is that "*an* Antichrist, if not *the* Antichrist expected before the end, is already operating in Israel."[65]

The first possibility found echoes in other voices. *Catholic World* printed a sermon contending that the political renascence would usher in a new era of conversion. Articles reiterating this expectation appeared in influential American Catholic journals with large clerical readership.[66] An in-depth theological development was assayed by a French Dominican theologian, Yves Congar.[67] In his view, modern Israel was a stage in the fulfillment of the final promise. Political restoration was necessary in order to bring into the Holy Land a representative cross-section of the entire Jewish people, who would ultimately find, in the disappointing realities of return, the way to Jesus. The "realities" which would jar Judaism from its complacency would be the disparity between statehood and the messianic vision of the prophets, the difficulty of adapting the "laws of Moses" to a modern state, and the complications that would arise with the rebuilding of the Temple. All of these problems would force the Jews into "a blind alley of grace," that is, Jews would recognize Christianity as the only solution. The new state, then, had a "positive" mission, although the generosity of Congar and the theologians who espoused the same idea sprung from their expectations of Jewish conversion.[68] It was not until after Vatican II, when ecumenical-minded theologians began to recognize the validity of post-Christian Judaism, that an appreciation of the Jewish state, apart from missiological connotations, could emerge.

Preservation of the Christian *image* of the Holy Land was the practical problem which troubled Catholics. Not fundamental theologically, it nevertheless exerted a considerable psychological force. For Christians, the importance of the land lies primarily in its religious memories. It is the birthplace of Jesus, the land of his ministry, and the place of his martyrdom. The excitement of the land is not in its present, but in its past. Although some churches have invested heavily in establishing religious and eleemosynary institutions, the Holy Land is still primarily a place of shrines, and all Christian efforts on its behalf have been to safeguard these sacred places and to provide access to them for pilgrims. The pilgrim who comes to venerate these sites, consecrated through their association with the life of Jesus and his apostles, wants to find them in their first-century setting. He wants to be able to experience the land of the Bible and the Gospels.

Not so the Jews. While they, too, have numerous biblical and post-biblical recollections which endow the land with a sacredness, the land, in and of itself, is venerated as the home of the Jewish nation. The land is part of an ongoing and pulsating national life. The ties of the people are to its climate, to its soil, and to its growth. The country, which served a glorious past, lives very much in the present, with great expectations for the future. Therefore, technological development enhances the land for the Jews, while for the Christians, development is an intrusion which disfigures its essence. The pilgrim wants to recapture the presence of Christ's time, not a modern, bustling country! Understandably, pilgrim sympathies tend to be with the Arabs who (unwittingly) preserved that life, rather than with the Jews who (unwittingly) disturbed that image.[69] Pilgrim literature reverberates with the longing for a pilgrim's Palestine. Happy is the visitor who can write, "The Holy Land, for the most part, has changed little since the time of Christ. . . . shepherds still roam the fields, oxen still pull the plows, the fisherman's nets can still be seen drying on the shores. . . . The colorful garb of the natives provide genuine biblical atmosphere."[70]

The decade that followed the establishment of Israel brought with it an alleviation of some of the antagonisms felt toward the new state. In part, this was due to Israel's own efforts. In larger part, it was due to events outside Israel. A not insignificant factor in creating the change in perspective was the political upheaval in neighboring countries in the Middle East. The relative security of Christian institutional and personal life in Israel, vis-à-vis the growing insecurity of Catholics in Arab countries subject to leftist coups, bears close watching in the next chapter of Catholic-Israeli relations.

NOTES

1. Charlotte Klein, "Theological Dimensions of the State of Israel: A Christian Perspective," mimeographed (Address to a joint seminar of the Institute of Judaeo-Christian Studies and the American Jewish Committee, October 18, 1970).
2. James O'Gara, "Anti-Semitism: A Catholic View," In *The Star and the Cross: Essays on Jewish-Christian Relations,* ed. Katherine T. Hargrove (Milwaukee: Bruce Publishing Co., 1966), p. 84.
3. Edward Flannery, "Theological Aspects of the State of Israel." *Bridge,* 3 (1958): 304.
4. *Auspicia Quaedam, Acta Apostolicae Sedis* (hereafter cited as *AAS*), ser. 2, 15 (May 10, 1948): 171.
5. *Holy Land* is, of course, traditional usage and, indeed, was frequently used. The curious fact is that the Pope did not *always* use *Holy Land* to circumvent the term *Israel*, but did, occasionally, substitute *Palestine*.
6. *Tablet,* May 22, 1948.
7. For a description of the committee and its biases, see Hertzel Fishman, "American Protestantism and the State of Israel, 1937–1967" (Ph.D. thesis, New York University, 1971), pp. 174 ff.

8. *Sign*, 27 (July 1948): 2, 4 f., 15 ff.

9. *Catholic World* (hereafter cited as *CW*), 167 (July 1948): 289–90. Cf. the gentle chiding of *Ave Maria*, 68 (August 7, 1948): 165.

10. National Catholic News Service (hereafter cited as NC-NS) bulletin, May 17, 1948 (S), p. 4.

11. Ibid., May 24, 1948 (F), p. 1.

12. *Catholic Worker*, 15 (May 1948): 1. The next issue (July–August 1948) carried a reprint of Peter Maurin's paraphrase of Leon Bloy's "Salvation Is of the Jews." Maurin stressed that Jews were a religious, not a national, people, whose future was inextricably tied to Christian eschatology.

13. *Social Justice Review* (hereafter cited as *SJR*). 41 (June 1948): 75–78. Goldstein wrote a weekly column for the *Pilot* and was a frequent contributor to the diocesan press. His anti-Zionist bias was well known. One of the best examples of his mustering of arguments against a Jewish state is found in an earlier essay written for the Archconfraternity of Prayer and reprinted in the "News and Views" section of the Dubuque, Iowa, Catholic paper, *Witness*, October 3, 1946.

14. *Commonwealth* (hereafter cited as *CMW*), 48 (May 28; 1948): 151 f. Surely the name *Israel* must have irritated many Catholics, but I found no editorials as frank as this one on the subject of the name. Some papers substituted *Palestine* or *Holy Land* for *Israel*. *CMW*'s editorials continued the same skeptical attitude following the truce of June 11. 48 (June 25, 1948): 247 f. and (July 23, 1948): 343 f.

15. *America*, 89 (May 29, 1948): 186.

16. Texts of the Tripartite (Sykes-Picot) Agreement for the partition of the Ottoman Empire (April–October 1916) and the substituted Clemenceau-Lloyd George Agreement (December 1918) are found in J. C. Hurewitz, *Diplomacy in the Near and Middle East: A Documentary Record, 1914–1956* (Princeton, N.J.: D. Van Nostrand Co., 1956), 2:18–25. Also, Esco Foundation for Palestine, *Palestine: A Study of Jewish, Arab and British Policies* (New Haven: Yale University Press, 1947), 1:59–63, particularly the map on p. 62.

17. United Nations, *Official Records of the First Special Session of the General Assembly, Resolutions*, A/364.

18. Bonaventure cited the requirements deemed necessary for assuring protection of the holy places in the following order: freedom of access; unhampered conducting of religious services; an enclave for the holy places *in* Jerusalem and the constitution of a commission, composed of Western countries, to whom juridical recourse could be had in cases of interreligious disputes. Bonaventure was questioned closely on what he meant by "enclave," and in his explication he dismissed internationalization of the cities of Jerusalem and Bethlehem as "not in accordance with the Holy Places as such." Bonaventure stressed that Christian holy sites are dispersed throughout Palestine. The Roman Catholic Church had exclusive jurisdiction over

forty-five of these places and shared proprietorship with other religious communities in numerous other sites. Ibid., annexes, A/364/Add. 3, pp. 13–19.

19. United Nations, *Official Records of the Second Session of the General Assembly. Ad Hoc Committee on the Palestine Question,* 4th meeting, annexes 19, 19a.

20. See Edward B. Glick, "The Vatican, Latin America and Jerusalem," *International Organization,* 11 (Spring 1957): 213–19. Msgr. Thomas McMahon, in an exchange with Israeli authorities in the summer of 1949, revealed that the Pope had not opposed Jewish statehood in 1947 because he then understood that the Jews would abide by full territorial internationalization. H. Eugene Bovis, *The Jerusalem Question, 1917–1968* (Stanford: Hoover Institution Press, 1971), p. 72. The acquiescence of the Jewish Agency to internationalization has been attributed to the notice that otherwise certain Catholic countries, presumably under Vatican pressure, would be forced to withdraw their support for Jewish statehood. David Horowitz, *State in the Making,* trans. Julian Meltzer (New York: Alfred A. Knopf, 1953), p. 296.

21. *AAS,* ser 2, 15 (May 10, 1948): 169 f. Eng. trans. Constantine Rackaukas, *The Internationalization of Jerusalem* (Washington, CAIP, 1957), in pp. 68 f.

22. See Natanel Lorch, *The Edge of the Sword: Israel's War of Independence, 1947–49* (New York: GP. Putnam's Sons, 1961), pp. 182–88.

23. *AAS,* 15 (June 2, 1948): 252 f.

24. Ibid.

25. Count Folke Bernadotte, *To Jerusalem* (London: Hodder & Stoughton, 1951), p. 12. Bernadotte later revised his plan for Jerusalem and espoused a scheme of special and separate treatment, as is evident from the posthumous publication of his progress report of September 1948. United Nations, A/648. Cf. Bovis, op. cit., p. 65.

26. *AAS,* 15 (October 26, 1948): 443–46. Eng. trans. in Rackauskas, op. cit., p. 71.

27. The Jewish Agency accepted the plan of internationalization in 1947, and according to informed sources, the majority of the Jewish population was willing to implement the U.N. provision at that time. However, after the savage battles for Jerusalem, and the wholesale destruction of the synagogues in the Old City, few Israelis were still willing to seriously consider internationalization. ... Kenneth W. Bilby, *New Star in the Near East* (Garden City, N.Y.: Doubleday, 1950), p. 202; also Dov Joseph, *The Faithful City* (New York: Simon & Schuster, 1960), pp. 334–36. The Arab League, meanwhile, reversed its position on Jerusalem. ... For an analysis of the changing Arab and Israeli stands, see Bovis, op. cit., pp. 60–64, 79 ff., 113–19.

28. *AAS,* ser. 2, 16 (April 15, 1949): 161–64. Eng. trans. in Rackauskas, op. cit., p. 72.

29. Raphael Huber, ed., *Our Bishops Speak, 1919–1951* (Milwaukee: Bruce Publishing Co., 1952), pp. 364 f.

30. See n. 35.

31. McMahon came to Israel as the official representative of the National Catholic Welfare Conference (NCWC) to investigate the condition of Arab refugees and report on their needs. *Catholic Action* (hereafter cited as *Cath Action*), 30 (December 1948): 2. McMahon left for Israel in December 1948 and returned to the United States four months later, after a brief stopover at the Vatican.

32. McMahon published a disclaimer of his diplomatic mission in a pamphlet, *Hills of the Morning* (New York: CNEWA, n.d. [1954?]), pp. 17 f. However, on the basis of conversations with persons who are familiar with the Herzog (while in Israel, McMahon met with Dr. Yaakov Herzog, of the Ministry for Religious Affairs) and McMahon papers, it appears that McMahon, indeed, was a pivotal figure in American-Israeli-Vatican relations.

33. McMahon's thesis was popularized in his numerous speeches and articles for Catholic audiences. He reported on the Palestine issues in the following pamphlets published by CNEWA and contained in their files: *Job and Jacob* (n.d. [1946?]); *Only. the Meek* (1949); *The Pope and the Palestine Tragedy* (n.d. [1951?]; *Not by Bread Alone* (n.d. [1952?]; *Hills of the Morning* (n.d. [1954?]).

34. The texts of the commission proposal, the Australian resolution, and the later Netherlands-Sweden proposal for purely functional internationalization are found in United Nations, *Official Records of the Fourth Session of the General Assembly:* Ad Hoc Political Committee, annex, I, A/973; A/AC. 31/L.37. November 12 was designated by the Pope as a day of prayer for the settlement of Palestine in harmony with Christian rights. *America,* 82 (November 26, 1949): 216. On November 17 the American hierarchy reissued their April 27 statement on internationalization. Huber, op. cit. Vatican radio support for the Australian resolution was reported in the *New York Times* (hereafter cited as *NYT*), November 27, 1949, p. 27. See, also, the editorial "Catholic Thinking on the Internationalization of Jerusalem," in *Cath Action,* 31 (November 1949): 3.

35. Glick, op. cit., p. 216, noted that Spellman directed the papal nuncios in all Latin American capitals to make vigorous representations demanding the Latin American governments take an unflinching stand on *full* territorial internationalization. . . . On Cardinal Spellman's association with the Latin American countries, see Robert Gannon, *The Cardinal Spellman Story* (Garden City, N.Y.: Doubleday, 1961), pp. 122–26. On Vatican pressure in the U.N. in reference to the vote on internationalization, see *NYT,* December 13, 1949, p. 1.

36. Bovis, op. cit., pp. 78–91. Bovis gives a concise history of the meanderings of the resolution in U.N. sessions.

37. *Hills of the Morning*, p. 7. See also McMahon's letter to U.N. Secretary-General Dag Hammarskjöld, September 16, 1953, and his telegram to President Eisenhower, November 4, 1954, in which he protested the U.S. ambassador's presentation of credentials in Jerusalem, Rackauskas, op. cit., pp. 80 f.

38. *America*, 82 (December 31, 1949): 381 and (February 4, 1950): 511; 83 (June 17, 1950): 313 and (September 16, 1950): 619; 74 (November 4, 1950): 124; 86 (December 8, 1951): 275 and (December 15, 1951): 298.

39. Ibid., 83 (June 17, 1950): 313.

40. Israeli Government, *Jerusalem 1948–1951: Three Years of Reconstruction* (Jerusalem, March 1952), pp. 28 f. *Christian News from Israel* published a chronicle of government regulations and transactions relating to the Christian communities. For example, on the restitution of ecclesiastic properties and the repair of churches and religious institutions during 1949–50, see ibid., 1 (August 1949): 2, 8; (September 1949): 3; (December 1949–Jan. 1950): 4; (January–February 1950): 3; (March–April 1950): 5 f. By November 16, 1955, all outstanding claims of the Roman Catholic Church in Israel were settled. Ibid., 6 (December 1955): 21.

41. Robert A. Graham, S.J., authoritative historian of Vatican diplomacy, pointed to Paul VI's recent exhortation on internationalization (June 21, 1971) as evidence that "the pope apparently thought it appropriate to repeat what he thinks about the future status of Jerusalem, because unauthorized reports had been circulated that the Vatican is quite satisfied with the present situation." *Columbia*, 50–51 (August 1971).

42. Fayez Sayegh, *The Palestinian Refugees* (Washington: AMARA Press, 1952), pp. 9–24. Deir Yassin was an Arab village massacred by a Jewish terrorist splinter group on April 9, 1948, before the Israeli military gained control. It was a singular incident in the war.

43. Israeli Government, *The Arab Refugees* (Jerusalem, 1953), pp. 7–14.

44. Don Peretz, *Israel and the Palestinian Arabs* (Washington: Middle East Institute, 1958), pp. 4–8. See also Joseph Schechtman, *The Arab Refugee Problem* (New York: Philosophical Library, 1952), pp. 1–7. Schechtman outlines in detail the three major phases of the flight.
No accurate account of the number of refugees has been made. Relief agency figures are based on ration lists, which have been found to be inflated. Estimates range from less than a half million to over one million. Bernadotte's figures in 1948 totaled less than 4,000. The later estimate of the U.N. Economic Survey Mission for the Middle East, which is generally quoted, totaled 726,000 refugees as of September 1949. See Peretz, op. cit., p. 30, n. 2, for a discussion on the discrepancies in refugee figures.

45. For a summary of U.N. programs and their failures, see ibid., pp. 12–17. Peretz discusses each of these programs in fuller detail in subsequent chapters of his book. Among the many commissions appointed to deal with the problem were the U.N. Relief for Palestine Refugees. Technical Committee

on Refugees, Economic Survey Mission for the Middle East, and the Relief and Works Agency.

46. Schechtman, op. cit. In December 1948, the Arab states rejected a U.N. resolution which incorporated the recommendation of repatriation, only to extract the recommendation later, out of the original context of the resolution, and demand its implementation. For early Israeli offers of repatriation, see Peretz, op. cit., pp. 33, 40–50. Israel repatriated 25,000 Arab refugees, and another 8,000 returned under the "family reunion" scheme. Ibid., pp. 49, 55.

47. Israeli opposition was based on fears of harboring a fifth column as long as the insecure political situation, in which no peace treaties were signed, prevailed. These fears were amply supported by Arab rhetoric. Schechtman, op. cit., pp. 24–26.

48. Ibid., pp. 35–41; Peretz, op. cit., pp. 13, 77–94.

49. America, 80 (March 26, 1949): 677.

50. Minutes of the Executive Committee, Catholic Near East Welfare Association (hereafter cited as CNEWA), August 27, 1948. CNEWA archives. Spellman authorized McMahon to send two checks for refugee relief: One of $25,000 to Abp. Testa, apostolic delegate for Palestine, and another $25,000 to Abp. Hughes. Hughes's telegrams were reported in the NYT, August 12, 1948, p. 3. Shipment of the monies was publicized in an NC-NS bulletin, September 13, 1948 (S), 4.

51. Minutes of the Board of Trustees, CNEWA, November 18, 1948. CNEWA archives.

52. These phrases cropped up, for example, in papers as dissimilar as Catholic Mind, 47 (June 1949): 372; Columbia, 35 (October 1955): 4, Priest, 11 (December 1955): 982; SJR 48 (November 1955): 276 f.

54. Our Sunday Visitor, March 25, 1956, p. 2. On the figure cited, see n. 44.

55. Estimates generally run to approximately 150,000 Christian refugees, of which only 55,000 were Catholics. America, 80 (March 26, 1949): 677. Catholic Biblical Quarterly (hereafter cited as Cath Bib Q), 12 (January 1950): 114, estimated that one out of every ten refugees was Christian, but gave no estimate for the percentage of Catholics. The Pontifical Mission for Palestine Report of 1954 calculated that there were 268 pontifical centers for refugees in the Middle East and 31,000 refugee children enrolled in pontifical schools. Minutes of the Board of Trustees, CNEWA, Nov. 18, 1954, CNEWA archives. Catholic assistance to refugees from 1948 to 1950 climbed to over $6 million out of the total of $10,391,000 in aid given by private agencies. U.S. Congress, House, Committee on Foreign Affairs, Palestinian Refugees: Hearings on S.J. Res. 153, 81st Cong., 2d sess., February 16–17, 1950, p. 23.

56. Quoted in America, 80 (March 26, 1949): 677.

57. A. H. Hourani, Minorities in the Arab World (London: Oxford University Press, 1947), pp. 34–36.

58. *CMW*, 48 (October 8, 1948): 614 f.

59. Minutes of Board of Trustees, CNEWA. November 15, 1951, CNEWA archives. Of this amount, two million was given in cash, and the remainder in goods and services. An extensive report of the agency's founding and the scope of its activities is given in McMahon's pamphlet *The Pope and the Palestine Tragedy*, CNEWA files. See also, *Unitas*, 1 (October–December, 1949), 79 f., and *Eastern Churches Quarterly* 8 (October 1949):269–73.

60. Esther Yolles Feldblum, *The American Catholic Press and the Jewish State 1917–1959* (New York: Ktav Publishing House, 1977), pp. 9–15.

61. *Osservatore Romano*, May 14, 1948, quoted in Pinchas E. Lapide, *The Last Three Popes and the Jews* (London: Souvenir Press, 1967), p. 282. The same belief was echoed in *Sign*, 27 (January 1949): 39 f., in a homiletical piece on the inevitable failure of Zionism.

62. *Register*, March 6, 1949, p. 2.

63. "We cannot but wonder if the problem of Palestine will go on plaguing the world until there is offered with the solution of the Jews and the solution of the Arabs, a solution of the Christians of the world." *Pilot*, August 7, 1948, p. 4.

64. Editorial by Msgr. Matthew Smith in the *Register*, March 27, 1949, pp. 1, 6. In the unfolding of this theory, the Jews will eventually recognize the Antichrist as an imposter and rebel against him. War will ensue, at which time the Jews will convert to Christianity and thus bring about the Second Coming. Vladimir Soloviov, "A Short History of the Antichrist," in *War, Progress and the End of History*, trans. A. Basky (London: University of London Press, 1915), pp 224–26.

65. The address was printed in *Cath Bib Q*, 12 (April 1950): 119 f.

66. *CW*, 169 (August 1949): 326–29, and 170 (December 1949): 192–97; *Homiletic and Pastoral Review*, 51 (October 1950): 47–49; *American Ecclesiastical Review*, 124 (January 1951): 31–36. In the latter article, Nicholas Rieman, S.J., noted that a "surprising percentage of immigrants to Israel are Christian in sentiment, and at times, in belief."

67. Yves Congar, O.P., "Sens de la restauration (politique) d'Israël au regard de la pensée chrétienne," Notre Dame Sion, *Sessions d'Information*, July 1955. Congar's views reached the English-speaking public in the following articles, "The State of Israel in Biblical Perspective," *Blackfriars*, 37 (June 1957): 244–49, and "Modern Israel, Fulfillment of God's Promise?" *Theology Digest*, 9 (Spring 1961): 95 f.

68. For example, Paul Demann, "Signification de l'Etat d'Israel," *Cahiers Sioniens*, 5 no. 1 (March 1951): 32–43; Charles Journet, "The Mysterious Destinies of Israel," *Bridge*, 2 (1956): 77. Fr. Edward Flannery did much to popularize this school of thought in his article, "Theological Aspects of the State of Israel."

69. Frankly stated by an American Catholic visitor to Palestine in 1946, *America*, 74 (January 19, 1946): 428.

70. From a pilgrim's report in *Sign*, 31 (December 1951): 46–49. See also *Catholic Digest*, 26 (December 1961): 110–13, which praised Bethlehem's citizens for striving to retain the biblical image, and Richard Pattee in *Columbia*, 35 (November 1955), who noted the disappointment of Christian pilgrims to find the town of the Bible "modernized."

13

American Christians and Israel, 1948–1988

Carl Hermann Voss and David A. Rausch

Dr. Henry A. Atkinson, founder in 1942 of the Christian Council on Palestine, was the embodiment of the classic Protestant Social Gospeler: optimistic, if not quite utopian, open to sundry suggestions and solutions, possessed of singular fortitude as well as a rugged assurance that good always triumphs over evil and the "Kingdom of God on earth" will prevail.

. . . A robust, outspoken Christian statesman, Henry A. Atkinson led fellow Social Gospelers into the fray with buoyant hopes that a new world was "a-bornin'." True, the Kingdom might now be delayed; but it would assuredly come—eventually . . . So with Zionism.

One aspect of Atkinson's indomitable faith over the decades was seen in his firm belief that, at long last, Zionism would indeed be victorious. Not only was this certainty rooted in the biblical promises read aloud by his mother from his earliest childhood in the 1880s but it was confirmed afresh by his own visits to the Holy Land in his travels between the two world wars. He had come to know about the famed Fundamentalist Zionist, William E. Blackstone, whose 1891 petition to President Benjamin Harrison met with Atkinson's whole-hearted approval when he chanced upon it some years later.[1] He also was a friend of the Congregationalist clergyman, Dr. Adolf Berle, Sr., whose *The World Significance of a Jewish State* (1918) he had read at the time of publication, soon after Great Britain's promulgation of the 1917 Balfour Declaration, "view[ing] with favor the establishment in Palestine of a national home

Reprinted in part by permission from *American Jewish Archives* 40 (April 1988): 41–81.

for the Jewish people."[2] Atkinson enthusiastically endorsed Balfour's famous letter to Lord Lionel Rothschild and often quoted from it. Even though Britain might be slow to implement its League of Nations Mandate for Palestine, granted at San Remo in 1922, Atkinson believed that the British would "muddle through" and effect a satisfactory settlement. He fancifully speculated that some cantonal arrangement on the Swiss model of unity might be achieved, naively proposing a future Palestine in which Jew and Arab, Christian and Moslem would model their government "perhaps after the pattern of Lebanon," he would muse.

At one of the earliest meetings of the Christian Council on Palestine in 1943, Atkinson was taken aback by the sharp disagreements he encountered from such important members of the executive council as archaeologist William Foxwell Albright and theologian Reinhold Niebuhr. They reminded him that realism required a *Jewish* state, not a new bi-national or tri-national satrapy.

Later that fateful fall of 1943, the newly elected co-chairman of the American Zionist Emergency Council, Rabbi Abba Hillel Silver of Cleveland, listened to Atkinson's simplistic expedient of amassing Christian opposition to the 1939 British White Paper and abruptly and sternly rebuked his Christian friend. Rabbi Silver reminded him that only a "Jewish commonwealth" with a self-governing Jewish majority could achieve justice for a harassed and homeless people. Merely relaxing immigration restrictions would not be enough. When Atkinson's rabbinical preceptors—Stephen S. Wise, Philip S. Bernstein, and Milton Steinberg—echoed Silver, though in less vehement fashion, the Christian clergyman began slowly to take a new tack. Nevertheless he held back; he still retained his optimistic outlook as he continued in valiant efforts to secure much-needed Christian support for the newly organized Council on Palestine composed, as planned, almost entirely of Christian ministers.

After Henry Atkinson had gathered many influential names, he told the executive secretary of the Council, a young minister from Pittsburgh, that the work with the council would really last a very short time. He read aloud scores of outstanding names beginning with Reinhold Niebuhr of New York's Union Theological Seminary and continuing with Ralph W. Sockman of New York's Christ Church (Methodist), the doughty Methodist Bishop Francis J. McConnell, the brilliant William

Foxwell Albright of Johns Hopkins University, the rugged Daniel A. Poling of the *Christian Herald* and Philadelphia's Baptist Temple, "and many big shots like that," gloated the quintessential Social Gospeler. "You know, [Carl Hermann] Voss, it really will be a matter of only a few months. Then you'll see: the British are going to be so impressed by that letterhead of ours with all those top-notch names on it that they will realize we really do have public opinion on our side. They'll grasp the fact that the Christian world will not allow the gates of Palestine to remain closed to the Jewish refugees left in Hitler's Europe. They'll open the gates of Palestine and refugees will pour in. We'll fold up the Committee and congratulate ourselves on a job well done."

When reminded of this naive prediction fifteen years later, shortly before his death, Atkinson reflected grimly: "How wrong I was, lad . . . How wrong I was!"

Like all too many Americans, Atkinson had misjudged the trends and events. He had underestimated the lack of courage in the American government, the insensitivity of the average Christian's conscience, the power of missionary groups to quench all hope of using Palestine as a refuge. He failed to gauge correctly the silence of the Roman Catholics, as well as the hesitation of many Jews. He assessed inadequately the crippling effects of the obduracy of the British Foreign Office and the myopic-minded *Realpolitik* of the Departments of Defense and State to convince the public that any meddling in British policy in the Middle East would spell disaster for the war effort.

When, at the end of World War II, these same circumstances prevailed with scarcely any change in the hard facts of political life, the attainment of the Partition of Palestine after the vote by the General Assembly of the United Nations on November 29, 1947, and the establishment of the new State of Israel in May 1948 seemed almost a miracle. Again a mood of unreasoning optimism arose among many in the newly formed American Christian Palestine Committee (ACPC), which had from 1946 carried on the work of the combined American Palestine Committee (founded in 1931) and the Christian Council on Palestine (founded in 1942).

At a meeting in the early winter of 1949 the executive council of the American Christian Palestine Committee had to decide whether it was going to continue now that Israel's statehood had been achieved and the new nation was apparently soon to be admitted to the four-year-old

United Nations. An Episcopal minister from Westchester, the Reverend Wendell Phillips, argued that the Committee had now done its job. He maintained it should be dissolved and the information services of the embassy and consulates of the new State of Israel allowed to carry on their own programs to counter the hostile forces aligned against Israel.

Professor Paul Tillich, however, thought otherwise. As a member of the ACPC since February 1944, and as a refugee from Nazi Germany since 1933, he recalled the false optimism of his countrymen, especially among his own friends and comrades of the Religious Socialist movement in Germany in the days of the Weimar Republic (1919–1933). He argued that a prudent view of the future would demand a strong Committee, ready and willing to oppose all hostility and antagonism.

Indeed, opposition even then had begun in one organization, the Committee for Peace and Justice in the Holy Land, composed of such well-known pro-Arab supporters as former oil company executive Kermit Roosevelt, Barnard's dean Virginia Gildersleeve, Yale's archaeologist Millar Burrows, Harvard's philosopher William Ernest Hocking, Harry Emerson Fosdick of Riverside Church, Union Theological Seminary's president Henry Sloane Coffin, and Rabbi Morris Lazaron of Baltimore's Hebrew Temple and the American Council for Judaism. The rabbi's presence reflected, it was announced, "the non-partisan character" of the organization's constituency.[3]

The American Christian Palestine Committee soon discovered it would have to continue carrying on an educational and informational program among Christians. It did so in effective fashion for a number of years, only to wind down its activities in the late 1950s and early 1960s as financial support began to shrink. By that time, the Israeli government, through the embassy in Washington and consulates throughout the country, was carrying on an ever-growing number and variety of services that interpreted the new Israel to Christians and, of course, to Jews and non-Jews alike. . . .

The Evangelical publication, *Christian Herald,* with a circulation approaching 400,000 in 1948, claimed to be *inter*denominational and *un*denominational. Its editor was Dr. Daniel A. Poling, a member of the (Dutch) Reformed Church of America and honorary member of the Ohio Conference of the Evangelical United Brethren Church (his father's church, in which his own ministry had begun). A self-proclaimed "gentle

Fundamentalist," Poling was senior minister of the Baptist Temple in Philadelphia and national co-chairman of the American Christian Palestine Committee. Answering unequivocally a reader's question in October 1947, Daniel Poling declared to the *Christian Herald* readership: "I am a Christian Zionist who believes that Palestine should become, as promised, the Jewish state." Welcoming the new State of Israel, he never wavered from that position.[4]

The American Christian Palestine Committee was able to build upon the support that had been gathered through the years by this spectrum of varied minds and theologies to back the idea of a Jewish national home for many different reasons. The joint leadership in earlier decades of such men as the Mormon Senator William King of Utah and the quintessential Protestant Henry Cabot Lodge of Massachusetts were two extremes of the kinds of interest and support given by Christians to the cause of a Jewish state. In the realm of politics in the 1940s, the guidance came from the individuals as diverse as Senator Charles McNary (a Republican who was Wendell Willkie's running mate in the presidential campaign of 1940) and Senator Robert Wagner of New York, a leading Democrat and New Deal advocate and an outstanding Roman Catholic layman.

Bipartisan in representation but mostly Protestant in its constituency, the ACPC encompassed more than 20,000 Christian leaders under its standard. It carried on a comprehensive educational program into the late 1950s and early 1960s to inform the American public concerning the new Israel. The ACPC endeavored to interpret to American Christians the Jewish people's quest for nationhood as reflected in the Zionist movement, while also drawing attention to the extraordinary achievements of the Jews of the new land of "Israel." At the same time the Committee pointed to the responsibility Christians had, in light of the Hitler terror, to wipe out the evils of anti-Jewish persecution and to remedy the problem of Jewish national homelessness.

To accomplish these ends the Committee had an expansive and varied program: it sponsored seminars on a local basis and conferences on a regional scale, forming city and state chapters. A small but capable staff distributed pamphlets, reprints, and other literature. The ACPC organized a speaker's bureau, Club Program Service, which offered more than three hundred non-Jewish speakers to church groups, university forums, service clubs, and community organizations on the subjects of

Zionism, Israel's history, and Jewish-Christian understanding of Israel. Study tours, composed of Christian leaders, were organized to visit Arab lands and Israel. Each year such groups, sponsored by local Jewish communities, attained a rare kind of mutual understanding and friendship, which continued to prevail among Jews and Christians participating in such projects. Films and slides, radio and television programs were promoted, and a provocative, informative, well-edited journal, *Land Reborn*, was published to highlight the major parts of this program, mobilize support among non-Jews, and share informed opinion, usually from prominent Christians, on burning issues in Israeli-Arab affairs.[5]

In 1951 a rival organization suddenly sprang up, the American Friends of the Middle East (AFME). The AFME asserted to be "pro all nations of the Middle East" but proved to be especially critical of the new Israel. Claiming that its support came from individuals and corporations interested in the Middle East, the AFME group gathered a sizable number of Middle Eastern authorities, ranging from professors to authors, oil company executives to missionaries, archaeologists to Middle East educators, carrying on an extensive program which called for an annual budget of at least half a million dollars. Not until the early 1960s, however, was it disclosed that the greatest part of the budget—more than $400,000—came from the CIA, being dispensed in the Middle East by the so-called Dearborn Foundation.[6]

Dr. Garland Evans Hopkins, an associate editor of *Christian Century* magazine, served as executive vice president of AFME; and the president for a considerable length of time was Miss Dorothy Thompson, a famed newspaper correspondent and the daughter of a Methodist minister. Raised in a family devoted to social justice, Thompson had seen her father criticized to the point of almost losing his parish for making friends with a local Italian Catholic priest. During the 1920s, 1930s, and early 1940s Miss Thompson, by then a popular columnist and lecturer, had been an enthusiastic pro-Zionist who spoke at Zionist rallies, and, in later years, at American Christian Palestine Committee affairs on such subjects as, "I Speak as a Christian" and "I Speak Again as a Christian." In her column in the *New York Herald Tribune* and allied newspapers she sounded a recurring refrain: "The Jews Are a People," "The Jews Deserve and Need Palestine," "Jewry is Deserving of Justice and Palestine," etc.[7]

In the mid-1940s, after a trip to the Middle East, Dorothy Thompson suddenly changed her mind, following two and a half decades of single-minded support of Zionist aspiration. At that time she began to condemn Zionists in general and Israelis in particular, using her column and lecture platform as a means to berate the Jews as a people and Israel as a nation.[8] This was quite a contrast from the 1930s and early 1940s, when the New York Jewish community, for example, found strength and courage in Thompson's column as it alternated in the *New York Herald Tribune* with the writings of Walter Lippmann, a Jew who never mentioned Jews or Zionism or the Nazis' extermination of Jews.[9] Thompson's columns now became anti-Israel, and her new brand of writing appeared even in the pages of *Commentary*, the publication of the American Jewish Committee, in a widely publicized article entitled "America Demands a Single Loyalty: The Perils of a 'Favorite' Foreign Nation" (March 1950).

When her lecture engagements shrank in number and her column fell victim to cancellation in a number of newspapers, she made a prudent decision and resigned from the presidency of the American Friends of the Middle East. Thompson retained her membership in the organization, however, speaking out on its behalf and maintaining her loyalty to its principles. . . .[10]

The biblically and prophetically minded Fundamentalist-Evangelicals were quite a contrast to the liberal [William Ernest] Hocking or the anti-Semitic right-wing extremists. While acknowledging imperfection in the State of Israel and the plight of the Middle East milieu, the bottom line for Fundamentalist-Evangelicals was the Jewish right to the Land. Hocking had stated in the *American Mercury*: "Nor can any will of God be appealed to to sanction the present situation." Much to the contrary, Fundamentalist-Evangelicals concurred with the early sentences of Blackstone's Petition of 1891, i.e., "According to God's distribution of nations [Palestine] is their [the Jewish people's] home, an inalienable possession, from which they were expelled by force. . . . Let us now restore them to the land of which they were so cruelly despoiled by our Roman ancestors." . . .

Prophetically minded Fundamentalist-Evangelicals fully expected the Jewish people to occupy all of Jerusalem. As early as 1950, the Moody

Bible Institute, the "West Point" of Fundamentalist-Evangelicalism, offered a correspondence course entitled "World Crises and the Prophetic Scriptures." The series of twelve lessons was written by a famed professor in their circles, Wilbur M. Smith, who had taught at MBI from 1937 to 1947, at Fuller Theological Seminary from 1947 to 1963, and at Trinity Evangelical Divinity School from 1963 to 1968. Lesson 7 was "The Reestablishment of Israel in Her Own Land," while Lesson 8 was entitled "At the Center of the Earth—Jerusalem." To Wilbur Smith, God had not only promised the Jewish people Palestine and worked the miracle of their restored state, but would restore Jerusalem to Jewish control. He wrote:

I am not an alarmist, and I trust through the years I have never attached to any world event a prophetic significance that was not justified; but it seems to me that almost any day or night this prophecy of our Lord could be fulfilled. Already there are more Jews living in Jerusalem than there were Jews living in the whole of Palestine at the dawn of this century. Furthermore, there is a government of a newborn nation in the modern city of Jerusalem—Israel. One hundred feet of no-man's land, some barbed wire fences, and a few machine guns manned by a mere handful of Arabs—these are all that keep the Jews from fully occupying this city and setting up their government there.

"Why the Jews do not go in and take that city, I do not know," Smith interjected. "They certainly could do it." . . .

While many other Christians were calling for "internationalization" of the city of Jerusalem, Fundamentalist-Evangelicals believed that the Bible gave it to the Jewish people. These supporters of Israel also believed that the right of Jewish statehood was fair and just, totally in accord with sound protocol.

Little wonder then that 1967 found Evangelical periodicals ablaze with eschatological fervor. The Six-Day War and Israel's victory had thrilled these Christians. The October 1967 issue of *Moody Monthly* had a picture of the Wailing Wall on its front cover. This special issue on the Bible and prophecy was captioned: "The Amazing Rise of Israel!" Dr. John F. Walvoord, president of the dispensationalist Dallas Theological Seminary, began his article of the same title with these words:

The recent dramatic victory of Israel over the Arab states electrified the entire world. The stunning impact of this war of only sixty hours on the political scene was not only a great setback for Russian designs in the Middle East, but crushed

Arab hopes of destroying Israel. For students of the Bible the most significant aspect of the war lies in the fact that Israel, after 1900 years of exclusion from the capital city, Jerusalem, now possesses this holy place so rich in both history and prophecy.

Emphasizing that Israel had been attacked by Arab nations at its inception, Walvoord related to his readers the great gains Israel had made in reclamation of the Land and progress in agriculture. Other articles on Israel as the depository of divine revelation and Israel in prophecy followed.[11]

Eternity magazine (which had absorbed Our Hope) had the caption "Israel is Here to Stay" on its July 1967 cover, featuring an article by Raymond Cox, "Eyewitness: Israel." The article had been written a few months before the "current violence," but the editors explained that they found it "more timely than ever." With the Arabs stockpiling armaments for an attack on Israel, Cox noted that "many wonder whether Israel can survive a united assault." He himself, however, believed that "this is more a prophetic question than a military question. . . . Israel will survive."[12] . . .

The scholar who researches the attitudes of American Christians toward Israel is impressed by one striking reality: the same anti-Israel arguments are used decade after decade. Apart from new events and actions taken by Israel, the Arabs, the United Nations, etc., reported in the media, the basic arguments in 1988 remain the arguments from 1968 (or even 1948!). For instance, Christianity Today magazine, founded with the support of Billy Graham and Sun Oil magnate J. Howard Pew to be an Evangelical counterpart to the Christian Century, was undergoing intense upheaval during 1967. Editor Carl F. H. Henry had embarked on gaining nationwide Christian respect for the magazine, which included more "balance" on the Middle East than Billy Graham had. During 1967, Christianity Today received most of its information on the Arab-Israeli situation from its correspondent, Dwight L. Baker, chairman of the Baptist Convention in Israel. Again, the importance of the missionary movement and its anti-Israel rhetoric must not be underestimated, even in affecting the opinions and stance of Evangelicals. Pastor Baker was concerned that the position of missionaries in Arab nations was becoming "more dangerous" because of the Israeli victory in the Six-Day War. The views of Harry W. Genet, assistant executive secretary of the Arabic

Literature Mission in Beirut, were also included in the July 7, 1967 issue, as Genet related that the "slender missionary force in the Arab world" was experiencing "the hardening Arab attitude toward foreigners." [13]

The next issue of *Christianity Today* (July 21, 1967) contained a diatribe against Israel by James L. Kelso, a former moderator of the United Presbyterian Church, that was so incendiary the editors labeled his remarks an "interpretative appraisal of the Arab-Jewish conflict." Next to missionaries, Christian archaeologists (with notable exceptions, such as William Foxwell Albright) had been progenitors of the anti-Israel rhetoric, in both liberal and conservative circles. Kelso also worked with Arabs for forty-one years and had participated in a number of archaeological expeditions in Palestine. He began:

How did Israel respect church property in the fighting a few weeks ago? They shot up the Episcopal cathedral just as they had done in 1948. They smashed down the Episcopal school for boys so their tanks could get through to Arab Jerusalem. The Israelis wrecked and looted the YMCA upon which the Arab refugees had bestowed so much loving handcraft. They wrecked the big Lutheran hospital, even though this hospital was used by the United Nations. The hospital had just added a new children's center and a new research department. The Lutheran center for cripples also suffered. At Ramallah, a Christian city near Jerusalem, the Episcopal girls' school was shot up, and some of the girls were killed.

So significant was this third Jewish war against the Arabs that one of the finest missionaries of the Near East called it "perhaps the most serious setback that Christendom has had since the fall of Constantinople in 1453."

Dr. Kelso then went on to blame the Balfour Declaration as "the major cause of the three wars whereby the Jews have stolen so much of Palestine from the Arabs who have owned it for centuries." He expounded upon the Arab refugee problem, the mothers and babies that he saw suffering in the camps "in the bitterly cold winter of 1949–50," interjecting that "Mary and Christ received better treatment at Bethlehem than the Arab refugees did that winter."

Missionary and archaeologist came together in a duet of anti-Israel rhetoric in his following statements. The United Presbyterian pastor exclaimed:

A missionary who has worked constantly with Arab refugees through the long years since Israel became a state in 1948 speaks of them as "human sacrifices to political ruthlessness." It is the most accurate statement I know. Sometimes it was actual human sacrifice, as when 250 Arab men, women, and children were massacred at Deir Yassin, I know that massacre well, for one boy who was fortunate enough to escape that massacre later worked for me on my excavations. There is deep horror about all this history in the fact that great numbers of Christians in the United States applaud Israel's crimes against Arab Christians and Arab Muslims. How can a Christian applaud the murder of a brother Christian by Zionist Jews? The Arab church is as truly the body of Christ as the American church.[14]

This last question, unfortunately, came to dominate both liberal and conservative Christian propaganda against Israel. Either in blatant denouncement or a secretive whisper, the anti-Israel argument took the form of anti-Jewish thought, i.e., how can you support the non-Christian Jew against your Arab brother?

Some *Christianity Today* readers were appalled at Reverend James L. Kelso's interpretation, and their edited letters in following issues showed shock and dismay. Elias Newman of Minneapolis wrote of his "chagrin and disillusionment," while Reverend Harold P. Warren of First Baptist Church in Oak Park, Michigan, emphasized that many of Kelso's statements "are contrary to the facts as I know them." Warren's church was attempting to build a good rapport with the Jewish community in their area, and he believed that "it is time for Christians to speak out on behalf of Israel and be identified as friends of Israel." In the September 29, 1967 issue, Benad Avital, first secretary of the embassy of Israel in Washington, D.C., responded to Kelso's "emotional charges." The following year, William Culbertson, president of the Moody Bible Institute of Chicago, supported the Jewish restoration to the Land of Israel in an article citing relevant biblical passages. It was followed by James Kelso's fifteen-point response. Again, Kelso began by reminding *Christianity Today*'s readers that "10 per cent of the Arab population is Christian."[15]

Christianity Today had been striving since its inception to capture not only the entire spectrum of Evangelicals, but also to affect Christians from all walks and of all theologies. Even the letters to the editor concerning Israel underscore the great diversity in the conservative Christian community regarding Israel. Among liberal Christians, Dr. Henry P. Van Dusen, past president of Union Theological Seminary, deplored the Israeli victory in 1967 as "the most violent, ruthless (and successful) aggression since Hitler's blitzkrieg across Western Europe."

He argued that "every square mile of Arab homeland appropriated by Israel, every additional Arab subjugated or driven into exile, will merely exacerbate the smoldering resolve for revenge." The *Christian Century* called for joint administration by Israeli and Jordanian forces, while the National Council of Churches favored an "international presence" to guarantee the holy sites and security.[16]

Reinhold Niebuhr, however, graced the pages of *Christianity and Crisis* (June 26, 1967) with his famous article "David and Goliath." "No simile better fits the war between Israel and the Arabs in lands of biblical memory," the respected theologian began, "than the legend of David and Goliath. David, of course, is little Israel, numbering less than 2.5 million souls. . . . Goliath, of course, is the Arab world under Egyptian President Abdel Nasser's leadership, numbering a population of 20 to 40 million. This Goliath never accepted Israel's existence as a nation or granted it the right of survival." This time, the chairman of the editorial board, John C. Bennett, followed with his "Further Thoughts on the Middle East."

Niebuhr approved of Jerusalem's administrative reunification, asserting that "Judaism presupposes inextricable ties with the land of Israel and the city of David, without which Judaism cannot be truly herself." After his death, the magazine he founded was often unjustly critical of Israel, so much so that his widow, Ursula Niebuhr, has requested *Christianity and Crisis* to withdraw her husband's name from the journal as a "Founding Editor." Nevertheless, disciples of the great theologian, such as Franklin Hamlin Littell and A. Roy Eckardt (with his wife, Alice), have carried the message to the liberal Christian community. Franklin Littell was active first in the American Christian Palestine Committee as a young graduate student fresh out of Yale with his bright new Ph.D. He then became extremely important in successor organizations to the ACPC, including the Christians Concerned for Israel (CCI) and the National Christian Leadership Conference for Israel (NCLCI). The latter included both Fundamentalist-Evangelical and Pentecostal Christians as well as members of the liberal Christian tradition.

On the fortieth anniversary of the liberation of Europe and the rescue of the survivors of the concentration camps, the NCLCI, in a press conference at the Church Center for the United Nations, urged the UN to reconsider "the falsehood promulgated in its 1975 resolution declaring Zionism to be a form of racism" and called on the Christian community to appreciate the centrality and importance of the State of Israel for the Jewish people. The statement, "Forty Years Later: Christians Speak Out on Israel and Zionism," was delivered at the UN in May 1985, and later appeared in newspapers. "We see it as urgent that Christians speak out against the vicious anti-Semitism that hides under the cloak of anti-Zionism," the ad continued. Similar newspaper advertisements have been paid for by Christians for Israel as well as those whose oppose Israeli actions.

While the signers of the above declaration include "Reverend Franklin H. Littell, President Emeritus," the leading signature is that of Father Edward H. Flannery, president of the NCLCI in 1985. Sister Rose Thering is listed as one of the three vice-presidents of the organization. This underscores the fact that there are a number of eminent American Catholics who have been supporters of the State of Israel and its right to exist. This is phenomenal when one considers that the Vatican was not only opposed to the establishment of the State of Israel, but has carefully refrained from recognizing the Jewish state. After the Six-Day War in 1967, Pope Paul VI proposed the internationalization of all holy places in Jerusalem. Pope John Paul II stated in 1980 that in the establishment of the State of Israel "a sad condition was created for the Palestinian people who were excluded from their homeland. These are facts that anyone can see."

On the American scene, the National Conference of Catholic Bishops in 1975 declared that because "Jews see this tie to the land as essential to their Jewishness," Christians "should strive to understand this link between land and people which Jews have expressed in their writings and worship throughout two millennia as a longing for the homeland, holy Zion." Nevertheless, this official statement on Catholic-Jewish relations added the caution that this affirmation was not "meant to deny the legitimate rights of other parties in the region, or to adopt any political stance in the controversies over the Middle East, which lie beyond the purview of this statement." A Roman Catholic theologian, Rosemary Ruether, who has been very active in Christian-Jewish relations, wrote in the *National Catholic Reporter* (September 14, 1984) that Zionism was a "form of nationalism that most Americans regard as unacceptable and, ironically, a Fascist state if settlements continue to be established in the West Bank or annexation takes place." She concluded that if Israel is to remain a democratic state it must cease to be a Zionist state. Similar diatribes by Ruether appear in the *Christian Century*.[17]

Father Edward Flannery deplores such attitudes among Christians— including Catholic Christians. In the essay "Israel, Jerusalem, and the Middle East," he wrote:

The Middle East (Arab-Israeli) conflict has proven a grave distraction for the Jewish-Christian dialogue and for Jewish-Christian understanding generally. Numerous Christians, unaware of any bias on their part, see the establishment of the State of Israel very simply as a serious injustice inflicted upon the Palestinian Arab population by the Israelis. Through this prism they fail to perceive much significance, historical or theological, in the new state, and direct their attention exclusively to problems of Arab refugees, a Palestinian state, and other socio-political aspects of the problem. The peril in which Israel continuously exists and the problem of its security and survival become in this way secondary considerations, if they are considered at all. The simplicity and one-sidedness of this approach, for one thing, stems in most cases from inadequate information and uncritical acceptance of Arab or anti-Zionist propaganda. The United Nations can serve as a large-scale sample of this way of approaching the Middle East problem. It is imperative, in any case, for the health and survival of the Jewish-Christian embrace that the misinformation and mythologizing that have engulfed the conflict be dispelled.[18]

Recognizing that one must not be insensitive to the Palestinian Arab, Father Flannery identified the root problem in the Arab-Israeli conflict as "the refusal of many of Israel's enemies to accept or respect Israel's right to live in peace and security." Answering the question, Is anti-Zionism in its various degrees and forms anti-Semitic? he answered: "Not necessarily, but almost always."

The pro-Israel, Fundamentalist-Evangelical biblical and prophetic interpretations made great inroads into the black church in the twentieth century. To these black Christians, the newly formed Jewish state of Israel was part of God's plan and purpose. Support from the remainder of the black community, however, was slow in developing all through the years from 1948 onward. A number of blacks, prominent in their local communities, often accompanied study tours sponsored by the American Christian Palestine Committee to the Middle East, returning with positive and favorable reports of what they had seen. Many times this occurred because these black leaders encountered immigrants of a darker hue, such as the people from India, the B'nai Zion, and the

Falashas from Ethiopia, and heard them report that they had been well received and were being accommodated into the stream of economic and political life in Israel.

Walter White, well-known executive director of the National Association for the Advancement of Colored People, visited Israel in 1949; and Vernon Jordan, executive vice-president of the National Urban League, visited the land in the 1960s. Both returned with favorable reactions, but neither with startling reports nor with enthusiastic championing of the Zionist achievements. They had other responsibilities on their own civil rights agendas, and these came first.

In May of 1967, Dr. Martin Luther King, Jr., joined seven other prominent Christian clergymen, including Franklin Littell, Reinhold Niebuhr, and John Sheerin (editor of the *Catholic World*), in issuing a statement urging all Americans to "support the independence, integrity and freedom of Israel in the current crisis." The clergymen declared that "men of conscience must not remain silent at this time" and warned that the Egyptian blockade of the Straits of Tiran "may lead to a major conflagration." Shortly before he was assassinated in 1968, Dr. King made his definitive statement on Israel at a meeting before the Conservative rabbis' Rabbinical Assembly at Kiamesha Lake, New York. There, the great black leader spoke of Israel as a democratic force in the Middle East, as a creative factor in the life of Jewry, and as a potent force for good Jewish-Christian relations. These assertions he firmly believed and resoundingly affirmed.

The left wing among the civil rights groups, both black and white, was tinctured with anti-Semitism. This directly fostered anti-Zionism, as Israel was often viewed as an imperialist force in the Middle East. Black militants supported the Arab nations in their struggle with Israel, at times condemning Israel as part of a world conspiracy against blacks. Animosity between blacks and Jews resulted in a *Time* magazine cover story (January 31, 1969) entitled "Black vs. Jew: A Tragic Confrontation." Moderate black leader Whitney M. Young, Jr., executive director of the National Urban League, criticized *Time's* "unfortunate, almost irresponsible reporting of the current tensions between the black and Jewish populations." In a letter published February 14, 1969, Young pointed to the significant positive relationships between the two groups, and "the masses of black people who are obviously not anti-Semitic."

Indeed, even in regard to Israel, well-known black leaders such as A.

Philip Randolph of the AFL-CIO, Bayard Rustin, civil rights activist and publicist, and Whitney Young had given their unqualified support. Their names were among sixty-four black leaders who signed a page-length *New York Times* advertisement, "An Appeal by Black Americans for United States Support to Israel" (June 28, 1970). Christian clergymen, such as Martin Luther King, Sr., Gardner Taylor (past president of the Progressive National Baptist Convention), and William J. Walls (bishop of the African Methodist Episcopal Zion Church), joined black publishers, editors, congressmen and women, political and judicial leaders, union representatives, businessmen, and organizational representatives in calling upon the United States to uphold the ideals of democracy and social justice in the Middle East by "unequivocally guaranteeing Israel's security."

It is an important fact that the opposing *New York Times* advertisement (November 1, 1970), "An Appeal by Black Americans against United States Support of the Zionist Government of Israel," was filled with left-wing signatories, but notably lacked black Christian leaders. In fact, Reverend Albert B. Cleage of Detroit's Shrine of the Black Madonna was the only black Christian clergyman listed—a less than overwhelming sign of Christian support. Loaded with extremist rhetoric, this proclamation began: "We, the Black American signatories of this advertisement are in complete solidarity with our Palestinian brothers and sisters, who, like us, are struggling for self-determination and an end to racist oppression."

Early in 1975, Manhattan Borough president Percy Sutton took a trip to Africa and Israel, returning with an enthusiastic response. Writing in the nation's largest black newspaper, the New York *Amsterdam News,* Sutton praised "the genius of a dedicated group of agronomists, technicians and scientists who have turned Israel's roadsides, mountains and deserts into fertile and productive land." Later that month, an editorial acknowledged the role of the Jewish people in the civil rights movement, declaring that blacks could not adopt a position of "benign neutrality" when Jews needed support. In April 1975, the Black Americans Supporting Israel Committee (BASIC) was formed.

As there is much debate about the state of black-Jewish relations today, so also there are many questions surrounding black Christian attitudes toward Israel. While Reverend Charles Mims, Jr., Evangelical black pastor of the 1,500-member Tabernacle of Faith Baptist Church in the heart of Los Angeles' Watts district, is indicative of millions of blacks who are supportive of the Jewish people and of Israel, Reverend Jesse Jackson's sharp criticism of Israel and uncritical attitudes toward the Palestine Liberation Organization are indicative of a segment of the black community with little compassion toward the Jewish state.

Perhaps the complex state of affairs in the black community today only reflects the historic ambivalence that has dominated Christendom as a whole. The World Council of Churches has often uttered expressions of "effective international guarantee" for the territorial integrity and political independence of Israel and the Arab nations, while repeatedly criticizing Israeli policies and calling for "an international presence" over Jerusalem. With so many Christian denominations fearful of losing their missionary agencies and institutions in Arab lands, their animosity toward the Jewish state has steadily increased.

And forty years of Arab and Christian propaganda have certainly taken their toll. In 1980, the National Council of Churches of Christ in the USA endorsed a pro-Arab commission report which stipulated that the Palestine Liberation Organization, with Yasser Arafat as its leader, was the accredited agency of those opposed by Israel. The Middle East agenda of the seventeen-member commission was so biased at its inception that major Jewish organizations, including the American Jewish Committee, the American Jewish Congress, and the Anti-Defamation League of B'nai B'rith, refused to present testimony—the pro-PLO findings were a foregone conclusion. The recent defeat of positive statements on Israel in both the 199th General Assembly of the 3.1 million member Presbyterian Church (USA) and the 1.7 million member United Church of Christ in June 1987 underscores the political ploys, stereotypes and caricatures, and fears of divisiveness over Israel that plague even the best of intentions in Jewish-Christian relations.

Significant in this study is the fact that American Christians were not silent concerning the State of Israel from 1948 to 1988. There are American Christian movements for and against the Jewish state that in fact predate that state. Those who oppose the Jewish state today, however, continue to use the same arguments and comparisons that were formulated forty years—and more—ago. Arguments concerning refugees, internationalization, bi-national and tri-national states, United States "bias" against Arabs and the harm threatening American interests, have changed little. Comparisons of the Israelis to Adolf Hitler and the Nazis, to sophisticated warmongers in a well-armed bastion, to internationally funded parasites, to Arab haters and denigrators, have been used by anti-Israel Christians for four decades. Yet, throughout these years there has been a segment of the American Christian community that has loved and supported Israel. This essay has underscored the conclusion that Israel may well count on a strong core of Christian supporters in America, but at the same time the Jewish state must never expect justice from American Christendom as a whole.

NOTES

1. Henry A. Atkinson, "William E. Blackstone," *Land Reborn* 6, no. 1 (February–March 1955):6–7.
2. In the June 23, 1922 issue of the *New Palestine*, Adolf Berle, Sr., wrote a brief article, "The Jew: Barometer of Civilization," describing the Palestine he had recently visited: "I who had set out as a pilgrim and had been captured by the way by interests that appeared to be anything but pilgrim interests, discovered that I had not gone astray when I found myself on the highways and in the camps with men and women who had come to Palestine with love in their hearts and as day laborers were the purest idealists" (p. 405). Berle, professor of Christian ethics at the Crane School of Religion at Tufts University, looked upon the Jew as "a permanent intellectual and moral asset of mankind, [a great fact which] has made the natural ally of culture and the development of the intellectual life." . . .
3. The founding of the Committee for Peace and Justice in the Holy Land is described in the autobiography of Barnard's dean, later president, Virginia Gildersleeve, *Many a Good Crusade* (1954). Of special interest are the accounts of her support of the Christian educational institutions of the Near East College Association and her activities in the spring of 1945 at the San Francisco Charter Conference for UNO (United Nations Organization), where, as a member of the United States delegation, she cast a baleful influence on any individuals or organizations favoring the Zionist cause. She singled out among the delegates the graduates of the American Universities of Beirut, Aleppo, Cairo, Assuit, Istanbul (Robert College), etc., for briefing sessions and special conferences, never reluctant to manifest her anti-Zionist views. See especially pp. 177 ff. and 400 ff.
4. "Dr. Poling Answers Your Questions," *Christian Herald* 70 (October 1947): 4. Cf. Poling's columns in the July 1947 issue (p. 4) and the June 1948 issue (p. 5). In this latter issue, Poling expounds: "CHRISTIAN HERALD is inter-denominational and undenominational. Its managing editor is a Meth-

odist, its publisher a Presbyterian. Practically every Protestant Evangelical denomination is represented on its roster, and all races and colors as well." Dr. Daniel A. Poling was also treasurer for the Children's Memorial Forest in Palestine; cf. Joyce Van Patten and Richard Tyler, "Children's Memorial Forest in Palestine," *Christian Herald* 70 (August 1947): 32.

5. See Carl Hermann Voss, "The American Christian Palestine Committee," in *Essays in American Zionism 1917–1948*, edited by Melvin I. Urofsky, *Herzl Year Book*, vol. 8 (1978), pp. 242–262.

6. In a book unfortunately marred by inaccuracies and omissions, *American Protestantism and a Jewish State* (1973), Hertzel Fishman deals in a scholarly way with the origin and purposes of the American Friends of the Middle East. He documents definitely and precisely the matter of the CIA sponsorship and financing of AFME.

7. Dorothy Thompson's articles of the 1930s included "Refugees: A World Problem" (*Foreign Affairs*, April 1938); "Nazi Rule of Terror Described" (*Pro-Palestine Herald*, 1933); and "The White Paper on Palestine" (*New York Herald Tribune*, May 19, 1939); and in the early "American Opinion Denounces Land Regulations in Palestine: Blood and Soil under the Union Jack" (March 1, 1940); "The Future of the Jews" (National Conference on Palestine, Philadelphia, Pa., 1943); "The Jews Are a People" (*Our Voice*, May 1, 1943); "I Speak As a Christian" (Balfour Day, November 2, 1943, New York City); "To Whom Does the Earth Belong?" (Madison Square Garden, New York City, March 21, 1944 and *Jewish Frontier*); "There Is Only One Answer" (*Palestine*, American Zionist Emergency Council, November 1942); "The Jews in the Family of Nations" (Jewish Agency Publications, 1943–44); "Let the Promise Be Fulfilled: A Christian View of Palestine" (*New Palestine*, December 1944); "I Speak Again As a Christian" (January 1945, American Christian Palestine Committee, St. Louis, Mo., ACPC Reprint); and "Why the Zionists Are Right" (February 1945, *Palestine*, American Zionist Emergency Council).

8. By the summer of 1946 Dorothy Thompson had begun to change her viewpoint, and her pro-Zionism abated, giving way to anti-Zionism with increasing intensity until by 1948–49 she was quite anti-Israel.

9. Ronald Steel, *Walter Lippmann and the American Century* (1980), esp. pp. 186–195, 330–336, 372–390.

10. A sympathetic, accurate, but somewhat limited biography, *Dorothy Thompson: A Legend in Her Time* by Marion K. Sanders (1973), gives no clue to the mystery of her sudden, inexplicable change of mind in 1946. Her July 9, 1946 column in the *New York Post*, "The Palestine Tragedy," was the first indication of her altered views; in subsequent weeks and months she focused her attacks on "Jewish acts of terrorism" and "Zionist zealotry." By 1952 her distinguished journalistic career began to wane; her influence declined and she died in 1961.

11. John F. Walvoord, "The Amazing Rise of Israel!" *Moody Monthly* 68

(October 1967): 22–25. A sidebar on pp. 24–25 by Richard Wolff is entitled, "Why Did God Choose Israel?" It underscores the fact that the Bible stresses that God's choice is the Jews and that their covenant with God has not been nullified. Hal Lindsey, the director of Campus Crusade for Christ at UCLA, who would become a millionaire through his book, *The Late Great Planet Earth,* in the 1970s, also has an article entitled "The Pieces Fall Together" (pp. 26–28) in this issue. "For centuries Christians have pondered over the prophetic puzzle," the caption to his article asserts. "Now in this mid-twentieth century they are seeing the pieces fall together."

12. Raymond Cox, "Eyewitness: Israel," *Eternity* 18 (July 1967): 6–8.

13. Note "Mideast: Weighing the Effects," *Christianity Today* II (July 7, 1967): 31. Cf. "Middle East Crisis: A Biblical Backdrop," *Christianity Today* II (June 9, 1967): 38–40; and "Jews in Old Jerusalem!—A Historic Re-Entry," *Christianity Today* II (June 23, 1967): 37–38. On the magazine's history and turmoil, see Carl F. H. Henry, *Confessions of a Theologian: An Autobiography* (1986).

14. Rev. James L. Kelso's "interpretive appraisal of the Arab-Jewish conflict" follows the special news report of Dr. Dwight L. Baker, "Jerusalem: A Third Temple?" *Christianity Today* II (July 21, 1967): 34. The quotations from Kelso are on pp. 35–36.

15. "Perspectives on Arab-Israeli Tensions," *Christianity Today* 12 (June 7, 1968): 7. Dr. William Culbertson's views are found on pp. 6 and 8. Before becoming president of the Moody Bible Institute, he was bishop of the New York and Philadelphia synod of the Reformed Episcopal Church. A graduate of Temple University and of the Reformed Episcopal Seminary, Culbertson mentioned the Arab refugee problem at the end of his article, his "heart" going out to them. But, in face of the fact that "Israel has incorporated hundreds of thousands of refugees" into its economic and social life, he asks: "Why have not Arab countries (especially those rich in oil) done more to help their own?" (p. 8). Cf. "Letters to the Editor" August 18, 1967 (p. 24) and Benad Avital's letter, September 29, 1967 (pp. 18–19).

16. *Christianity Today* even reports these views in its editorial, "Casting Lots for Jerusalem," II (August 18, 1967): 29–30.

17. Father John T. Pawlikowski, professor of social ethics at the Catholic Theological Union in Chicago, singled out Dr. Ruether in his September 1986 address to the delegates of the Zionist Organization of America (ZOA) in Baltimore as one of his colleagues who, while sensitive to the pain suffered by Jews for centuries from anti-Semitism, apparently "considers Zionism roughly equivalent to Fascism." "This reaction by a scholar who has spoken out so strongly against anti-Semitism in all its other forms," Father Pawlikowski underscored, "shows how urgent is the need for a serious, *sustained* and comprehensive conversation between Zionists and Christians." See *Christianity and Zionism: A Necessary Dialogue,* a booklet

of speeches sponsored by the Jacob Goodman Institute of the ZOA (1986), pp. 10–14.

18. Father Edward H. Flannery, "Israel, Jerusalem, and the Middle East," in *Twenty Years of Jewish-Catholic Relations,* edited by Eugene J. Fisher, A. James Rudin, and Marc H. Tanenbaum (1986), p. 79. The following quote is on page 82.

V

DIALOGUE

There were American Christians, like Congregationalist minister Ezra Stiles, who in the eighteenth and nineteenth centuries showed an interest in the religion of their Jewish neighbors or visited their synagogues. However, dialogue between Jews and Christians, other than the "disputations" between Jews and missionaries, was unreal to both synagogue and church. At the end of the last century, hints of mutual regard and even ecumenism accompanied the World Parliament of Religions in 1893 and the Congress of Liberal Religious Societies, a body compromised of left-wing Protestants and a few Reform Jews. But despite occasional pulpit exchanges and parallel activities (e.g., the social gospel movement which in Jewish circles became the social justice movement), no serious attempts at sustained interfaith activities were mounted until the goodwill movement of the 1920s. Until then, suspicion if not hostility generally governed the views that the major religions held of one another.

Less than fifty years ago, a Jewish writer in the *Congress Weekly* (20 Feb. 1942) denounced the goodwill movement as a "phoney." " 'Goodwill' is apologetics," he said, "it is professional Jew-loving on the one hand; it is perpetual fawning on the other." Therefore, it was both "demoralizing and humiliating." The goodwill movement he referred to was the early organized effort at interreligious amity and harmony that dated from the establishment of the National Conference of Christians and Jews. It ran into opposition from both sides. Christians feared a watered-down theism that would gloss over the fundamental essence of their faith; Jews, very much the junior partners, feared the insidious penetration of Christian dogma into joint ventures.

But by the 1960s the movement had radically changed. Spurred on by

Christian awakening to the Holocaust, religious groups moved beyond Brotherhood Weeks and conventional platitudes that denounced prejudice to a new level of encounter, that of dialogue. (See, in Arthur Hertzberg, Martin A. Marty, and Joseph N. Moody, *The Outbursts that Await Us,* the thoughtful comments by Marty on the evolution of the dialogue and post-dialogue stages.) Not only do interfaith meetings now address issues likely to expose differences among the faiths, but increasingly religious leaders have dared to examine the core beliefs of their own faith in light of the needs of their neighbors and of society at large. Indeed, all of the issues illustrated in this reader are in one fashion or another on the contemporary interfaith agenda.

Skeptics remain in all groups—Orthodox Jews and other fundamentalists hold serious doubts and reservations about interfaith activity— but dialogue has forged ahead. Interreligious encounters between Christians and Jews involve some evangelical groups as well as the mainstream "liberal" churches (see, for example, *A Time to Speak: The Evangelical-Jewish Encounter,* edited by A. James Rudin and Marvin R. Wilson), and interfaith configurations on specific matters can and do supersede the liberal alliance that often joined Jews and Protestants on secular, socioeconomic issues. The Jewish-Christian dialogue is highlighted in all sorts of periodicals, and new journals have been established to record developments as they occur. (See the chapter on Journals in Michael Shermis, *Jewish-Christian Relations: An Annotated Bibliography and Resource Guide.*)

The most dramatic breakthrough in dialogue between Jews and Catholics came from Vatican Council II. (Two lucid and detailed accounts are Judith Hershcopf's "The Church and the Jews: The Struggle at Vatican Council II," *American Jewish Year Book,* 1965 and 1966, and Arthur Gilbert's *The Vatican Council and the Jews.*) The Declaration on the Jews in 1965, part of *Nostra Aetate,* stated that Jews were not accursed or rejected by God; it acknowledged the Jewish roots of Christianity, it "deplored" antisemitism, and it commended dialogue between the two faiths. To be sure, as Jewish, Catholic, and Protestant critics pointed out, fundamental negative images, like the deicide charge and the truncated role of Judaism after Jesus, were left untouched. Antisemitism was not forthrightly condemned, nor was any mention made of the Holocaust and the State of Israel. But, as Geoffrey Wigoder maintains, the Declaration was more important for the new attitudes it initiated:

"A completely new vocabulary was now employed in referring to the Jews and this contributed to the creation of a fresh atmosphere conducive to mutual understanding and dialogue." Additional progress, albeit with qualifications, was made by two other Vatican documents, one in 1975 and one in 1985. (For the texts of the major documents and for a recent insightful analysis see Wigoder, *Jewish-Christian Relations Since the Second World War*.) As a direct result of Vatican policy, cooperative ventures between Catholics and Jews were launched in areas like social ethics and textbook revision.

Dialogue as defined by its present-day protagonists testifies to the inner logic of a democratic society. Predicated on the reality of religious pluralism which effectively destroyed the nineteenth-century dream of a homogeneous Christian America, it affirms the legitimacy of diversity among the faiths. Since it permits meetings among equals, it has served to redress significantly the numerical imbalance between Jews and Christians.

The rank and file have not always followed church leadership on matters of doctrine or social policy. In the area of dialogue, leadership itself has been divided. Egal Feldman examines three outstanding Protestant figures of the twentieth century who, of the minority, have broken new ground in Christian understanding and acceptance of Judaism. In all three cases—Moore on post-exilic Judaism, Niebuhr on Zionism and on mission to the Jews, and Eckardt on Christian responsibility for anti-semitism and the Holocaust—respect and sympathy for Jewish beliefs involved a break from mainline Christian thought. The words and actions of each one challenged long-held myths and images that had contributed over the centuries to Christian persecution and Jewish suffering. Upholding the integrity and independence of Judaism in the post-Biblical world, each wrestled with the Christian axiom of supersession.

Of the three, George Foot Moore is probably least well-known. Unlike the other two, he spoke to a limited audience of scholars. His was a solitary voice that disputed the conclusions of Christian "higher criticism." Critical study of the Bible, entwined with the social application of Darwinian thought, purported to offer "scientific proofs" of the superiority of Christianity over Judaism. Jewish scholars of the early twentieth century noted how Christian animus worked in tandem with those ideas; Solomon Schechter said that higher criticism was but higher antisemitism. Intent on divorcing the two faiths, and totally ignoring Jewish scholarship on the intertestamental period, Biblical critics advanced some radical notions—i.e., that Christianity owed nothing to Judaism, and that Jewish history ended with the rise of Christianity. In that fashion they challenged the basic theological premise for Christian toleration of the Jews. For if Judaism was not the mother of Christianity, or if Christianity developed independently of rabbinic Judaism, Jews had no claim on Christian sufferance. (See my article, "The Challenges of Darwinism and Biblical Criticism to American Judaism," in *Modern Judaism*, 1984.) George Foot Moore rescued rabbinic literature for Christian scholars. The thrust of his work, which adumbrated Christian acceptance of the integrity of post-Biblical Judaism, was furthered by both Niebuhr and Eckardt.

Contemporary religious thinkers of the major faiths continue to measure how far dialogue has gone. The literature on the subject grows more voluminous each year. One worthwhile study is John T. Pawlikowski, *What Are They Saying about Christian-Jewish Relations?* For books that contain Protestant as well as Catholic documents pertaining to the Jews, see Eugene J. Fisher, "A New Maturity in Christian-Jewish Dialogue: An Annotated Bibliography, 1973–1983," *Face to Face*, 1984.

Some frankly question how far dialogue can or should go. Does fruitful dialogue necessitate a readiness on the part of each faith to heed the criticisms of its fundamental beliefs or even to admit that its creed is no "truer" than the others? Over twenty years ago, theologian Abraham Joshua Heschel asserted that dialogue required neither Christians nor Jews to deny that their religion was the "ultimate truth." At bottom, Heschel said, they shared areas of common moral and spiritual concern that transcended their separate legitimate commitments and that gave each religion a stake in the survival of the other. (Heschel's classic essay, "No Religion Is an Island" is reprinted in *Disputation and Dialogue: Readings in the Jewish-Christian Encounter*, edited by Frank Ephraim Talmage.)

In 1978 Rabbi Henry Siegman, then of the Synagogue Council of America, addressed a related question: who needs dialogue more, Jews or Christians? On theological grounds, he said, there was a qualitative distinction between their needs. Christians could not escape dialogue, for Christianity's very *raison d'être* was inextricably bound up with

Judaism. On the other hand, Judaism, an autonomous faith, was independent of Christianity. Thus, whereas Christians might be prompted to dialogue by theological concerns, Jews were impelled rather by historical reasons—e.g., issues of antisemitism and the Holocaust, Christian missionizing, the land of Israel. Siegman's analysis, applying to Protestants and Catholics alike, theoretically gave Jews the greater latitude, but the urgency of the historical agenda has proved at least as crucial as theological concerns in efforts to maintain dialogue. (Siegman, "A Decade of Catholic-Jewish Relations—A Reassessment," *Journal of Ecumenical Studies*, 1978.)

David Berger, an historian and ordained rabbi, picks up the discussion. He finds that although the historical or Jewish agenda has prevailed in interreligious exchanges, theological issues will inevitably come under scrutiny. Berger explains his misgivings about the possible success of theological interchanges, and he elucidates the developments, and problems, that beset the different areas on the interfaith docket. Providing a fuller account than is generally given of Orthodox Jewish opinions, he offers a well-balanced summary of the state of the field as well as its immediate prospects.

14

American Protestant Theologians on the Frontiers of Jewish-Christian Relations, 1922–1982

Egal Feldman

From the very beginning of American history a degree of ambivalence marked Protestant attitudes toward Jews.[1] Admired at times as descendants from and inheritors of a biblical tradition, at other times they were resented for their resistance to conversion. Despite American Protestantism's evangelical and missionary outlook, its relationship with Jews, especially with individual Jews, evolved harmoniously. . . .

American Protestants did, however, share with universal Christendom a common outlook toward Judaism. The Jewish rejection of Jesus as the Messiah and and its alleged responsibility for the Crucifixion were matters strongly imbedded in American Protestant teaching. The conviction that the "New Israel" had superseded the "Old" and that Judaism was a religion of "Laws" which had achieved their fulfillment with the coming of Jesus were not debatable matters. These notions were accepted by many of the most prominent leaders of American Protestantism throughout the nineteenth and early twentieth centuries. Lyman Abbott, for example, one of the most respected voices of late nineteenth-century Protestantism, recognized little value in Judaism except insofar as it provided mankind a bridge to cross "from paganism . . . to Christianity."[2] The Jews, he was convinced, were responsible for the death of

Reprinted in part by permission of Egal Feldman and the University of Illinois Press from David A. Gerber, ed., *Anti-Semitism in American History* (Urbana: University of Illinois Press, 1986), 363–85.

the Savior. "The Jewish church was corrupt . . . and the corrupt church hates the reformer and the purifier," he wrote in 1903.[3] Even Walter Rauschenbusch, the most important Protestant theologian in the early twentieth century, attributed any lingering anti-social elements in Christianity to the influence of Judaism. Like his co-religionists, Rauschenbusch presented Jesus as a leader who challenged the authority of the Jews, a people whose "piety was not piety," whose "law inadequate." The Jews, he observed in 1918, "were the active agents in the legal steps which led to the Christian Savior's death."[4]

The studies of Charles Glock and Rodney Stark, published in 1966, suggest that such thinking continued in Protestant circles well into the twentieth century. Their discovery that Sunday School texts repeat the deicide myth and the ancient Christian idea that Jewish suffering for this act will persist until its collective conversion surprised them. "We expected that this religious process had become more or less vestigial," remarked the authors of *Christian Beliefs and Anti-Semitism*. "We were entirely unprepared to find these old religious traditions so potent and so widespread in modern society."[5]

Three Protestant theologians have challenged such thinking: George F. Moore, Reinhold Niebuhr, and A. Roy Eckardt. While each one represents a different era in our recent past—Moore, the decade of the 1920s; Niebuhr, the time of Nazism, World War II, and its aftermath; and Eckardt our own post-Holocaust generation—insofar as their vision of Judaism is concerned, none speaks for the Protestant majority. Centuries of persecution, not to mention the cataclysmic and historic events that have overwhelmed the Jewish people in recent years—their almost total destruction and political rebirth—have as yet done little to alter Christian thinking about Jews. In this sense the works of Moore, Niebuhr, and Eckardt are exceptional and stand as reminders that, at least in selected cases, traditional attitudes are capable of significant transformation.

Few eras in American history have been more justifiably disassociated with progress in the area of ethnic, racial, and religious relations than the decade of the 1920s. Remembered primarily for its religious fundamentalism, the Ku Klux Klan, and the immigration restriction movement, which among other things unabashedly singled out Jews as a threat to the stability of American institutions, it was also the decade in which George F. Moore (1851–1931) offered a significant challenge to anti-Semitic thinking. His attack was indirect, for he did so by producing a series of studies which enabled Christian biblical scholars to view Judaism from a fresh and more sympathetic perspective.

A graduate of Union Theological Seminary in 1877 and ordained a Presbyterian minister in the following year, Moore taught at Andover until 1902 and later at Harvard as a professor of Hebrew, Bible, and Rabbinics.[6] A careful, meticulous, and dedicated scholar, he did more than anyone of his generation to disabuse his co-religionists of the accumulated misinformation about the Jewish religious heritage. Although he was not an active crusader against anti-Semitism, Moore was sympathetic toward those who sought to eradicate it. Jews "have small reason to admire Christian ethics in application, whether ecclesiastical, political, social, or individual," he wrote in 1923. "Judging the tree by the fruit it has borne in eighteen centuries of persecution, they not unnaturally resent Christian assertions of its preeminence."[7]

Moore was chiefly a scholar, a student of Talmudic literature, who labored a lifetime to disengage the Jewish historical record from Christian sources and interpretations. His primary effort was to convince the historians of early Christianity that their vision of Judaism was faulty since it was based upon a foundation of ignorance of Rabbinic literature. He complained in 1921 that Christian writing about Jews has been primarily "apologetic or polemic rather than historical."[8] He was critical of Catholic and Protestant scholarship which for centuries saw little else in Rabbinic literature beyond a mine in which to search for superstitions, "unholy rites," and blasphemies against Christianity.[9] Moore lamented that even recent and contemporary scholars found little else beyond arid "legalism" in the sacred Jewish sources. The argument that runs consistently throughout his work is that Judaism can be understood only on its own merits, by a study of its own sources, and not by an attempt to find its relationship to the Christian faith.[10] He urged his readers to approach Rabbinic literature with the same reverence accorded to the Synoptic Gospels.[11]

He was also critical of Old Testament scholarship; here, too, Moore recognized the inability of Christian biblicists to accept the Jewish scripture on its own terms, but only as they believed it to be related to the Gospels. He was appalled, for example, at Christian efforts to seek in the Old Testament and its commentaries "a figure corresponding to the

Son, or the Word (Logos)" or "a divine being, intermediary between God the Father and the world."[12] It was clear to Moore that no such figure or symbol could be discovered in sacred Jewish literature and urged Christians not to spend their time searching for it.

Moore's two-volume work, *Judaism in the First Centuries of the Christian Era* (1927), continues to stand among the clearest expositions of Rabbinic Judaism produced by an American Christian scholar. His stress upon the formative years of modern Judaism stands in sharp contrast to the traditional practice of Christian scholars to disregard post-biblical Jewish history. He was not disturbed by the thought that "the completion of the New Testament" was of no significance to the early rabbis; that it had no impact on their own achievements. He recognized that any meaningful comprehension of "the creation of a normative type of Judaism" will fail to materialize without a thorough study of the creative accomplishments of the early Talmudic age.[13]

Moore's view of the Pharisees, as the most significant religious body in the Judaism of the early Christian Era, grew out of his familiarity with the Rabbinic sources. Unlike other Christian writers (even Reinhold Niebuhr, as will be seen, was uneasy with the Pharisees) Moore does not capitulate to the deprecation of the Pharisees found in the Gospels. He understood that Jewish survival depended upon their intelligent guidance, that because of the groundwork which they established, "unity of belief and observance among Jews in all their wide dispersion has been attained in later centuries."[14]

Aware of the differences which have evolved between Christians and Jews, Moore warns his readers that "Judaism must be allowed to speak for itself" and not be viewed as "a background, an environment" or "a contrast" to Christianity.[15] Christian ignorance about Judaism has invariably resulted in confusion and misunderstanding about such important designations as "law," a term which Moore considers "a poor English rendering" for *Torah*, or "original sin—an alien doctrine" for believing Jews. Its employment, Moore insists, has served no useful purpose in enhancing Jewish-Christian relations.[16]

Moore represented a lonely voice in a generation captivated by the idea of triumphant Christianity when he suggested that both Judaism and Christianity, each in its own unique way, represented a valid road to God. "Both Rabbis and Church Fathers," he writes, were "convinced that they were showing men exactly how to conform to the revelation of

God." [17] Moore stopped short of demanding a reevaluation of Christian theology in regard to its treatment of Jews, a task which would be left to others of a later generation.

It is difficult to gauge precisely the extent of influence that Moore's scholarship had upon American Protestant thought. The noted biblical scholar Samuel Sandmel believed that Moore's "eminence has been such that it has created a new tone in the Christian assessment of Judaism" but that its influence has been most pronounced among "Christian Biblical scholars." [18] How far it extended beyond this exclusive circle or filtered down from it, is another question; it was probably not very far. Moore's writings, found primarily in specialized journals with small circulations, possessed limited popular appeal. Still, as a Christian student of Judaism, Moore towered above his contemporaries.

In Reinhold Niebuhr (1892–1971) we meet a much more popular figure; unlike Moore, he was not a systematic theologian but a prolific and influential author. His writings grew primarily from his observations of the troubled world about him. "I must confess," he remarked in 1939, "that the gradual unfolding of my theological ideas has come not so much through study as through the pressure of world events." [19] In 1929, after serving thirteen years as a pastor in Detroit, he accepted a professorship at the Union Theological Seminary, where he remained until his retirement. His life was characterized by an active involvement in a variety of social and political issues of the day. [20]

Early in his career Niebuhr became disenchanted with the views of Christian liberals, especially with their belief of the inherent goodness of human beings. He concluded that the fundamental assumptions of the eighteenth-century Enlightenment and the Social Gospel of the nineteenth, especially as these related to the moral decisions which individuals made about social and political matters, were unrealistic. He recalled in 1941 that "between Versailles and Munich I underwent a conversion which involved rejection of almost all the liberal theological ideas with which I first ventured forth." [21]

Niebuhr's name soon became associated with the idea of "Christian Realism," a point of view which enabled him to better grasp and cope with the discordant and complex issues of the 1930s and 1940s. His keen observation and extensive reading convinced him of at least two things: first, that democratic institutions were not capable of altering the self-seeking behavior of individuals,[22] and, second, that "a sharp distinction must be drawn between the moral and social behavior of individuals and of social groups, national, racial and economic." As Niebuhr saw it, human behavior was most brutal in its collective form. To him "the perennial tragedy of human history is that those who cultivate the spiritual elements usually do so by divorcing themselves from . . . the problems of collective man."[23] His was a new social gospel, rooted not in confidence but in suspicion of collective behavior. Indeed, it was the striking social consciousness of the Jewish people that attracted him to them. "The glory of their religion is that they are really not thinking so much of "salvation' as of a saved society," he wrote while still a pastor in Detroit in 1928. It was a thought to which he would return repeatedly.[24]

By 1930 Niebuhr already sensed the ominous potential of German Nazism.[25] His periodic visits to Germany as a special correspondent confirmed his initial anxiety. "With unexampled and primitive ferocity," Jews were being "arrested, beaten and murdered, with no public protest," he reported back to the *Christian Century*.[26] The capitulation of the German churches, Protestant and Catholic, to Nazism and Jew-hatred disturbed him greatly. He was appalled at the Reichbishop's insistence "that Jesus was the first anti-semite and that he lost his life in his fight against Judaism."[27] Niebuhr traced to Luther's teaching German Protestantism's rapid fall to the dark forces of "blood and race."[28]

He also found inexcusable the indifference of American churches to the German atrocities of the 1930s. He urged his fellow Christians to issue "public pronouncements," organize public meetings, and "apply pressure upon the Washington government." "We must," he wrote in 1933, "in spite of our own sins, do what we can to inform the German people of the impression which their actions make upon sane people."[29] He rejected a style of Christianity "which transcended the whole sphere of sociological relationships" and ignored the evil around it.[30] It is therefore understandable why he deplored and viewed as heretical the Roman Catholic tilt toward Nazism as a defense against Communism. The rationalization that "fascism does not intend to destroy the Church while Communism does" he considered spurious.[31] . . .

Observing Germany's anti-Semitic fury, Niebuhr became convinced that the United States must ultimately adopt a pluralistic social ideal. The melting-pot concept, he became increasingly convinced, was an illusion. He argued that ethnic and racial groups have not only a right, but a duty, to remain different from the majority, to be themselves. "There is a curious, partly unconscious, cultural imperialism in theories of tolerance which look forward to a complete destruction of all racial distinctions," he wrote in 1942.[32]

A logical outgrowth of Niebuhr's rejection of the assimilationist ideal was his disdain for Protestant efforts to convert Jews to Christianity. With its large Jewish population, New York City was not the place for Billy Graham's crusade, he declared on one occasion.[33] He was particularly annoyed with Gentile hypocrisy which practiced tolerance toward Jews "provisionally in the hope that it will encourage assimilation ethnically and conversion religiously." He warned that proselytizing will invariably end in disappointment as it always had in the past.[34] "It is not our business to convert Jews to Christianity," he told a group of worshippers on Palm Sunday in 1962.[35] Like Moore, Niebuhr rejected the Christian claim that it had a monopoly on salvation. He countered such assertions with his belief that there was more than one way to God, more than one road to salvation.[36] He believed that efforts to convert the Jews were not only unnecessary but socially and psychologically disruptive. The symbol of Christ might be spiritually uplifting for Christians, but it could not induce a similar emotion for Jews, he told his co-religionists. "We are reminded daily of the penchant of anti-Semitic . . . groups claiming the name of Christ for their campaign of hatred."[37]

Niebuhr recognized that anti-Semitism was rooted in an ancient legacy of Christian misrepresentation of the meaning of the Jewish heritage. Like Moore he challenged the prevailing tendency to reduce the difference between the two belief systems to "a religion of the law and a religion of the spirit,"[38] or of viewing the New Testament as the embodiment of a "religion of the spirit" in contrast to the Old Testament as a "religion of the law."[39] The "Love Commandment," which Christianity claimed as its invention," he wrote in 1958, "is taken from the Old Testament and the Rabbis have taught consistently that love is the fulfillment of the law."[40]

As a proponent of pluralism, it followed that Niebuhr would emerge as a vocal supporter of the Zionist movement. He entertained little sympathy for the liberal, universalistic presuppositions prevalent among Christians and some Jews, who rejected a national solution. Niebuhr became aware of the ethnopolitical realities of life sooner than most of his co-religionists. "A collective survival impulse is as legitimate a 'right' as an individual one," he wrote in 1942.[41]

Even before knowledge of the European Holocaust dawned on the public imagination, Niebuhr recognized the inappropriateness of the European environment for postwar Jewry. This realization reinforced his conviction about a Zionist solution. Jews, he argued in 1942, were a "nationality and not merely a cultural group" and were entitled to a homeland, a place where they could be neither "understood nor misunderstood . . . appreciated nor condemned, but where they could be what they are."[42] In 1944 Niebuhr helped initiate the pro-Zionist American Christian Palestine Committee, serving as its first treasurer and for many years as a member of its executive committee.[43] Like Supreme Court Justice Louis D. Brandeis, whom he admired, Niebuhr saw no incompatibility between Zionism and loyalty to the United States.[44] He viewed the Zionist solution not only as a way to alleviate the plight of postwar Jews, but also as an opportunity, denied Jews for centuries, for an uninhibited cultural and religious expression.[45] Neither did he detect a contradiction between a two-thousand-year dispersion and the Jewish claim to nationality. On the contrary with its biblical roots "grounded in a religious covenant experience" he saw Jewish nationhood as one of the oldest and most legitimate in history.[46] "No nation," he wrote, "has ever been 'so conceived and so dedicated' by such a variety of social, moral, and religious forces and factors."[47]

As the Jews of Palestine, the *Yishuv*, prepared for statehood, Niebuhr's voice was conspicuous among American Protestants in offers of encouragement and support. He testified on Zionism's behalf in Washington and publically criticized British bungling and callousness.[48] In the years that followed Israel's independence in 1948, his support for the new state remained consistent. For example, he applauded Israel's refusal to evacuate captured Egyptian territories following the Suez War of 1957, in defiance of both the United Nations and the United States, before it was assured of substantive guarantees for its security. Israel, he declared, had every right to suspect the "legalistic logic which asserted that its security could not be guaranteed until it had purged itself of defiance." Instead of censure, Niebuhr requested from Washington "an unequivocal" voice that it "will not allow the state to be annihilated" by its Arab neighbors.[49] It was more than sympathy that drew Niebuhr to Israel's cause. He also saw in its survival a "strategic anchor for a democratic world" and an asset to America's national interests in the Middle East.[50]

Although disabled by a long illness, Niebuhr mustered sufficient strength in 1967, as six Arab armies prepared to obliterate the Jewish state, to write, "No simile better fits the war between Israel and the Arabs . . . than the legend of David and Goliath." Israel's preemptive strike, he declared, was fully justified. "A nation that knows it is in danger of strangulation will use its fists."[51] These remarks appeared in *Christianity and Crisis,* a journal Niebuhr founded in 1941 "to rally American Christians against Nazism," and which he edited for many years. Nevertheless, because of its intolerance toward Israel following the 1967 victory, Niebuhr broke his association with the magazine. Shortly after his death, when the magazine printed an article charging Israel's annexation of East Jerusalem as immoral, Niebuhr's widow requested that *Christianity and Crisis* remove her late husband's name from the masthead of the journal.[52] The gesture was in keeping with Niebuhr's long and dedicated support for the Jewish states.

Steeped primarily in Christian sources and lacking the profound knowledge of early Judaism attained by Moore, Niebuhr's writings were not totally free, however, of signs of ambivalence about Judaism. This was especially true of his earlier works which reflected for example, an acceptance of the Christian story of the Crucifixion[53] and were interspersed with deprecations of the Pharisees and their "Judaistic-legalistic tradition."[54] Even his strong support for the State of Israel was on occasion weakened by an exaggerated concern about its theocratic potential.[55] Too close in time to the extermination of Europe's Jews, Niebuhr also represented a generation of Christians not yet ready to formulate a theological reaction to the Final Solution. Nonetheless, when measured against the support and understanding he offered Jews during one of the most difficult periods of their history, these lapses fade into relative unimportance.

How the Holocaust and the rise of the Jewish state are molding contemporary Christian thought about Jews can be seen in the writings of the theologian A. Roy Eckardt.[56]

Inspired by his mentor Niebuhr, Eckardt, a Methodist clergyman, was among the first to probe the Christian roots of the European catastrophe.[57] From his post at Lehigh University, where he served for many years as professor and chairman of the Department of Religion, Eckardt has conducted a relentless attack on Christian responsibility for anti-Semitism. "Opposition to Jews is the one constant of Christian history," its one unifying theme throughout the centuries. The Christian world, he believes, is responsible for the invention of anti-Semitism.[58] No other prejudice, racial or ethnic animosity, can be compared to it. What is more, recourse to historical explanations alone or to the theories of the social sciences will explain neither its character nor its persistence.[59]

For Eckardt, the attack upon the Jewish people mirrors the ambivalence with which Christians view their own faith. Envied for their chosenness, hated for their alleged rejection and murder of the Christian Savior, the Jews emerge as the only group through which the Christian is able to " 'get back at' Christ" for the challenge he makes upon his life. Unable to divest himself of the Christian burden, the Christian strikes out at God's chosen people, the Jews, who are accessible and vulnerable.[60]

Neither does Eckardt find the rhetoric of the New Testament blameless. Indeed, he is among the first Christian theologians to trace the origin of anti-Semitism to the "word of God."[61] "To shut our eyes to the antisemitic proclivities of the Christian Scripture is indefensible," he wrote in 1971.[62] Within this context, the false and evil charge of deicide, flung at the Jewish people for centuries, and accepted even today by leading representatives of Christendom, is understandably high on his list of Christological myths marked for elimination.[63] The charge of deicide, according to Eckardt, cannot be viewed merely as an historic event, for its power is such that it continues to haunt Jewish-Christian relations.[64] For this reason Eckhardt is deeply disappointed at the Second Vatican Council's Declaration of 1965 which purportedly absolved the Jewish people of the charge of deicide. He finds the document weakly worded, even declaring that some Jews were guilty of the Crucifixion. Its puny efforts came too late to have genuine meaning, lacking "the slightest mark of Christian contrition." "Could there be a more damning judgment upon the church of our century than this one—that not until after the day of Auschwitz did Christians see fit to fabricate a correction of the record?"[65]

Like Niebuhr, but with less hesitation, Eckardt challenges the Christian denigration of Jewish "law." Juxtaposing *Torah* and Christian love, according to Eckardt, can only result in the strengthening of the foundation of Christian anti-Semitism.[66] Similarly, Eckardt's assault upon the notion that the "New Israel" has displaced the "Old" goes far beyond what is seen in traditional theological texts. Eckardt views the theology of displacement as an "affront to the Ruler of the Universe."[67]

It is understandable why Eckardt's repudiation of the "supersession-ist-triumphalist Christology of the Crucifixion and Resurrection"[68] leads him to an emphatic rejection of Christian missionary activity among Jews. Like Niebuhr, but more strongly, he acknowledges that Jews need no Christian guidance along the road to salvation.[69] Most importantly, Eckardt believes that the end of anti-Semitism will begin only when Christians refrain from missionary activity. In this, the post-Holocaust age, Eckardt equates any attempt to convert Jews with a "spiritual Final Solution."[70]

Like other thoughtful Christians of recent years, Eckardt's imagination has been captivated by a search for meaning in the European catastrophe, the *Shoah* (Hebrew: Holocaust). Because of this event, he wonders about, and on occasion despairs of, the possibility of a future genuine relationship between Christians and Jews.[71] He admits sadly that the Nazi gas chambers represented the logical outcome of centuries of Christian teaching about Jews,[72] and for that reason believes that the Final Solution has also altered forever the central meaning of the Christian faith.

In one of his boldest assertions Eckardt declares, "After Auschwitz, the Crucifixion cannot be accepted as the determinative symbol of re-demptive suffering"; it cannot be seen anymore as the ultimate and "absolute horror upon which the Christian faith can and should, dialec-tically, build its hope." In the face of burning Jewish children "the death of Jesus upon the Cross fades into comparative moral triviality."[73]

Christians must henceforth accept the Final Solution as a central event in their own lives, an event which could not have occurred without their complicity.[74] "Many of the Nazi executions of Jews," Eckardt repeat-edly reminds his readers, "were carried out by believing Christians." Neither should the *Shoah* be reduced to "an aberration," "a nightmare," or a peculiar historical mutation, he warns; on the contrary, it should be seen as the culmination of Christian history.[75]

So that this singular act of inhumanity, described by Eckardt as one of "transcending uniqueness," be permanently implanted upon the Christian memory, Eckardt marks the year 1941 as the dividing time between "two epochs": "B.S." being "the age before the *Shoah*" and "A.S." "the age of the *Shoah* and its aftermath." The division, Eckardt explains, will serve also to separate humanity into those "who take the *Shoah*-event with absolute seriousness" and "those who do not."[76] Without a genuine expression of repentance Eckardt sees no future for Jewish-Christian relations.[77]

Eckardt is not oblivious to the risk involved in reminding Christians of their complicity. He admits that it may evoke resentment, give sadistic pleasure to sick minds, and even serve to perpetuate anti-Semitism. "In gazing down the abyss, may we not open the abyss within ourselves?" The risk, he is convinced, is worth taking, for he sees a much greater danger in silence and ignorance about the most tragic event in the history of Western civilization.[78] It is the latter that concerns him most, for too few have as yet pondered the meaning of the Holocaust. Most Christians, Eckardt laments, continue to live as if there had never been a Final Solution. Anti-Semites even deny that the event ever occurred. In its own way, such a denial, by robbing the victims of their tragedy, underscores further the transcendent singularity of the Final Solution.[79]

Like Niebuhr, Eckardt is a staunch supporter of the Jewish state and, even more so than his mentor, probes for meaning in its emergence and impact upon the Christian world. He sees the two events—Holocaust and national rebirth—as altering forever the relationship of Christians and Jews. Jewish statehood, he believes, has put a final end to "the dreadful epoch of Jewish martyrdom."[80]

He has little sympathy for Christians perplexed by the theological meaning of the birth of the Jewish state, who believe that the Jewish return to their ancestral home is a dreadful miscalculation, a "violation of Christian eschatology."[81] Eckardt, on the contrary, sees the birth of Israel as a repudiation of the "Christian fantasy" that Jews are doomed to perpetual dispersion and rootlessness.[82] What is more, Christian support for Israel's survival, he believes, constitutes the only meaningful gesture of atonement for their past mistreatment of the Jewish people.[83]

Throughout the years Eckardt has repeatedly challenged the Arab denial of Israel's right to a sovereign existence.[84] "To contend that Jews have a right to exist as an ethnic . . . or a religious community . . . but not as a sovereign nation . . . is an example of antisemitism," he recently stated, for it denies the Jewish people a basic human need accorded to all other collective groups.[85]

The Arab world's yearning for Israel's demise and its repeated efforts to destroy the Jewish state Eckardt views as politicide, another form of genocide.[86] He is, therefore, skeptical about the future relationship of Israel and her neighbors. He is convinced that in the Arab mind, peace with Israel is equated with the abolition of Israel. Israel's aspiration for survival is matched by Arab dreams of its extinction. "No reconciliation or compromise is possible," he notes, "between antagonists one of whom rejects the reality of the other."[87] Eckardt sees hatred of the Jewish state as another form of anti-Semitism. *"It is impossible to separate Arab anti-Israelism and anti-Zionism from antisemitism. They are mutually reinforcing."* What is more, Arab hatred of the Jewish state has much in common with Nazism, from which the Arabs have borrowed heavily.[88] Only hatred of Israel has been able to unite the Arab world, as it has for centuries united the Christian. Islam, with little discouragement from the West, has inherited Christianity's animosity toward Israel and the Jewish people.[89]

Neither does Eckardt absolve the Western world, including the United States, for duplicity in their dealings with the Jewish state. Western deceitfulness manifests itself by a "general schizophrenia which judges Israel at one moment by superhuman standards . . . and at the next moment by subhuman standards." In the United Nations Israel is condemned repeatedly for defending herself, while her Arab and terrorist aggressors escape even mild rebuke.[90] Even more regrettable, according to Eckardt, is that in regard to Israel, American church organizations and their leaders have adopted a similar double standard. He points to the American Friends Service Committee, a Quaker organization, the World Council of Churches, and the editors of the widely read *Christian Century* as examples of Christian groups ever ready to "lecture Israel" on the slightest pretext, but who are quick to tolerate and forgive the most heinous acts of Arab terror. Why is it, he asks, that no other nation but Israel "is told to practice universal sainthood?"[91] "Why is it that the Christian world has challenged no other nation's right to exist in the way it has Israel's?"[92] Is it possible, he wonders, if the Church conceals a hidden desire, "a secret wish for the demise of Israel?"[93]

In the hours of her peril, while the Arab world stood ready to annihilate the Jewish state, first in 1948, then in 1967, and in 1973, American Protestants and Catholics, as did world Christianity in general, looked on with passive indifference. Assaulted by Egyptian and Syrian forces on the Day of Atonement, October 1973, Father Daniel Berrigan accused Israel of behaving like a "criminal" and "racist state," while Henry P. Van Dusen, former president of the Union Theological Seminary, compared the Jewish commonwealth to Nazi Germany. It appears, Eckardt notes perceptively, that "whenever Israel is assailed, certain suppressed, macabre elements in the Christian soul are stirred to sympathy with the assailants."[94] He is left to conclude that in the Christian mind, the State of Israel, repeatedly reproached for its militancy, aggressiveness, inflexibility, vengefulness, and irreligiosity, has replaced the mythical Jew.[95] Clearly, the Christian world has drawn few lessons from the Holocaust.

Eckardt also views Christian attempts to read theological meaning into the founding and history of Israel as a form of anti-Semitism, perhaps even a more sinister strain because it is disguised. He agrees with Niebuhr that the "theologization of politics is a guarantor of immorality," for it makes unnatural demands upon Jews and invests their misfortunes with biblical meaning. He warns Christians against the temptation to lecture Israelis "as if they were biblical prophets."[96]

For this reason Eckardt finds the theology of "Christian Zionism" disturbing. Despite the guise of friendship that the conservative wing of Christendom assumes toward the Jewish state, its adherents see little value in its emergence except as it might serve as a preparation for the "second coming." Christian Zionists invest Israel with a divine importance, theologize its political existence, and in the process rob it of its humanity and its dignity.[97]

This is not to say that Christianity's liberal Left has not also erred in its view of Jewish nationalism. Unlike the "evangelicals," who picture Israel as a "political church," the liberal Left views Judaism exclusively in religious rather than in cultural and national terms, and consequently, it sees no need for a Jewish state at all. Because of their attitudes, both wings of Christianity, the right and left, are guilty of anti-Semitism, for each, in its own way, denies the Jewish people a basic human requirement: the need to pursue a normal collective and political existence.[98]

Tension between the two faiths will continue, Eckardt believes, until Christianity acknowledges the self-sufficiency of the Jewish system of belief, that Christianity is not for the Jews, and that the two faiths, each in its own inimitable way, are separate and complete.[99] "Exodus-Sinai is for Israel what the life, death, and resurrection of Jesus Christ are for the Church." Indeed, the Jewish people deserve praise for their centuries of resistance and stubborn refusal to succumb to the pressures of Christianity. "Jewish non-acceptance of Jesus," Eckardt declares, "remains the most sublime and heroic instance of Israel's faithfulness to her Covenant with God."[100] Christians must know that for Jews Christianity "is in essence false."[101]

Christianity's inability to sever its ties with the Jewish faith, out of which it was born and with which it feels intertwined, has made it difficult for it to accept Jews "simply as people, ordinary people." Since for understandable reasons this Christian perspective will continue to create uneasiness among Jews, Eckardt wonders if a permanent parting of the ways may not be the best solution. Like Jews, Christians must also learn to accept their autonomy and disassociate their identity and eschatological thinking from that of the living Jews. "I do know," he has recently written, "that loved ones part from one another and go their different ways—though they need not thereby cease their loving or their caring."[102] This latter admission must have been difficult for Eckardt to make. Certainly his willingness to re-think some of the most sacred assumptions of his own belief places him today in the forefront of the Christian crusade against anti-Semitism. . . .

With Eckardt we meet a contemporary figure whose work is still unfolding. He represents a growing circle of American Christians stunned by the Final Solution, and awed and challenged by the rise of Jewish sovereignty.[103] He is a leading participant in a quiet revolution, the impact of which has yet to be felt. It has been suggested that because of his work and of others like him, writers of Sunday School tracts must now proceed with greater caution. The stereotypical images of old and modern Judaism have been severely cracked because of such efforts.[104] More so than his predecessors and most of his contemporaries, Eckardt's writings raise penetrating questions about Christian responsibility for the *Shoah,* and his call for a reevaluation of long-held Christian beliefs about Jews has opened new vistas for thoughtful Christians and all concerned persons as well.

NOTES

1. In this connection see Michael N. Dobkowski's *The Tarnished Dream: The Basis of American Anti-Semitism* (Westport, Conn., 1979), pp. 11–15.

2. Lyman Abbott, "Paganism, Judaism, and Christianity," *Outlook* 40 (Jan. 14, 1899): 107.

3. Lyman Abbott, "Was Jesus Christ a Jew?" *Outlook* 70 (June 6, 1903): 311.

4. Walter Rauschenbusch, *A Theology for the Social Gospel* (New York, 1918), pp. 31–32, 248–52.

5. Charles Y. Glock and Rodney Stark, *Christian Beliefs and Anti-Semitism* (New York, 1966), pp. 207–8.

6. "Moore, George Foot," *Encyclopaedia Judaica* 12 (Jerusalem, 1972): 294.

7. Quoted in Samuel Sandmel. *We Jews and Jesus* (New York, 1965), pp. 115–16.

8. George Foot Moore, "Christian Writers on Judaism," *Harvard Theological Review* 14 (July 1921): 197.

9. Ibid., pp. 198, 213–14, 221, 230.

10. Ibid., pp. 239–40.

11. Ibid., p. 253.

12. George Foot Moore, "Intermediaries in Jewish Theology, Memra, Shekina, Metatron," *Harvard Theological Review* 15 (July 1922): 41.

13. George Foot Moore, *Judaism in the First Centuries of the Christian Era* (New York, 1971 ed.), pp. vii–viii, 3, 39.

14. Ibid., pp. 110–11. The English biblical scholar R. Travers Herford, a contemporary of Moore, also defended the Pharisees in his *The Pharisees*, first published in 1913 and reissued in a larger edition in 1924.

15. Moore, *Judaism in the First Centuries*, pp. 128–29.

16. Ibid., pp. 263, 479, 483.

17. Ibid., p. 60.

18. Sandmel, *We Jews and Jesus*, pp. 100–101.

19. Reinhold Niebuhr, "Ten Years That Shook My World," *Christian Century* 56 (Apr. 26, 1939): 542–46.

20. For biographical information, I have relied upon June Bingham, *Courage to Change: An Introduction to the Life and Thought of Reinhold Niebuhr* (New York, 1961), pp. 49, 51; Nathan A. Scott, *Reinhold Niebuhr* (Minneapolis, 1963), pp. 10, 12–13; Reinhold Niebuhr, "Some Things I Have Learned," *Saturday Review* 48 (Nov. 6, 1965): 21.

21. Quoted in *Time* 37 (Mar. 24, 1941): 38.

22. Niebuhr, "Some Things I Have Learned," p. 21.

23. Reinhold Niebuhr, *Moral Man and Immoral Society. A Study in Ethics and Politics* (New York, 1932), pp. ix, 256.

24. Quoted in Reinhold Niebuhr, *Leaves from the Notebook of a Tamed Cynic* (New York, 1930), p. 187. See, for example, his *Moral Man and Immoral Society*, p. 61; *Reflections on the End of an Era* (New York, 1934), pp. 132–33; *Man's Nature and His Communities* (New York, 1965), pp. 17–19, *Christianity and Power Politics* (New York, 1969 ed.), p. 199; and *Pious and Secular America* (New York, 1958), pp. 91–94.

25. Reinhold Niebuhr, "The German Crisis," *Nation* 131 (Oct. 1, 1930): 360.

26. Reinhold Niebuhr, "Germany Must Be Told!" *Christian Century* 50 (Aug. 7, 1933): 1104. See also his "The Germans: Unhappy Philosophers in Politics," *American Scholar* 2 (Oct. 1933): 411–12.
27. Quotation from Niebuhr, "Germany Must Be Told!" p. 1015. See also his "The Catholic Heresy," *Christian Century* 54 (Dec. 8, 1937): 1524.
28. Reinhold Niebuhr, "Church Currents in Germany," *Christian Century* 50 (June 28, 1933), pp. 843–44, and "The Churches in Germany," *American Scholar* 3 (Summer 1934): 348–49. For a discussion of the political implications of Lutheranism, see Niebuhr, *Christianity and Power Politics*, pp. 49–51.
29. Niebuhr, "Germany Must Be Told!" p. 1015.
30. Reinhold Niebuhr, "Barthianism and Political Reaction," *Christian Century* 51 (June 6, 1934): 757, 759.
31. Niebuhr, "The Catholic Heresy," p. 1524.
32. Reinhold Niebuhr, "Jews after the War," Pt. 1, *Nation* 154 (Feb. 21, 1942): 215.
33. Reinhold Niebuhr, "Proposal to Billy Graham," *Christian Century* 73 (Aug. 8, 1956): 921; Patrick Granfield, "An Interview with Reinhold Niebuhr," *Commonwealth* 85 (Dec. 6, 1966): 319; *New York Times*, June 2, 1957, p. 38.
34. Niebuhr, *Pious and Secular America*, p. 88; *New York Times*, Apr. 5, 1958, p. 10.
35. Reinhold Niebuhr, "The Son of Man Must Suffer," in *Justice and Mercy*, ed. Ursula M. Niebuhr (New York, 1974), p. 85.
36. Reinhold Niebuhr, *The Children of Light and the Children of Darkness* (New York, 1944), pp. 134–35, and *Pious and Secular America*, pp. 98–99, 105.
37. Niebuhr, *Pious and Secular America*, p. 108.
38. Reinhold Niebuhr, "Rosenzweig's Message," *Commentary*, 15 (Mar. 1953): 312.
39. Reinhold Niebuhr, *The Self and the Dramas of History* (New York, 1955), p. 88.
40. Niebuhr, *Pious and Secular America*, p. 102. Niebuhr, however, was not always consistent in these assertions; see, for example, ibid., pp. 105–6.
41. Niebuhr, "Jews after the War," Pt. 1, p. 216. See also his "Toward a Program for Jews," Part 1: "Survival and Religion," *Contemporary Jewish Record* 7 (June 1944): 241.
42. Niebuhr, "Jews after the War," Pt. 1, pp. 214–16.
43. Bingham, *Courage to Change*, pp. 284–85.
44. Reinhold Niebuhr, "Jews after the War," Pt. 2, *Nation* 154 (Feb. 28, 1942): 352–54.
45. Niebuhr, "Toward a Program for Jews, Part 1," p. 245.
46. Reinhold Niebuhr, *Discerning the Signs of the Times: Sermons for Today and Tomorrow* (New York, 1946), pp. 75–76; Niebuhr, *The Self and the*

Dramas of History, pp. 40, 87; Niebuhr, *The Structure of Nations and Empires* (New York, 1959), pp. 161–62.

47. Niebuhr, *Structure of Nations and Empires*, pp. 161–62.

48. Hertzel Fishman, *American Protestantism and a Jewish State* (Detroit, 1973), pp. 78–80; Reinhold Niebuhr, "Palestine: British-American Dilemma," *Nation* 136 (Aug. 31, 1946): 239.

49. Reinhold Niebuhr, "The U.N. Is Not a World Government," *Reporter* 16 (Mar. 7, 1957): 32, and "Our Stake in the State of Israel," *New Republic* 136 (Feb. 4, 1957): 11–12.

50. Niebuhr, "Our Stake in the State of Israel," p. 12; *New York Times*, May 18, 1951, p. 26.

51. Reinhold Niebuhr, "David and Goliath," *Christianity and Crisis. A Journal of Christian Opinion* 27 (June 26, 1967): 141.

52. A. Roy Eckardt, "A Tribute to Reinhold Niebuhr" *Midstream* 17 (June/July, 1971): 16, *New York Times*, May 8, 1972, p. 9.

53. See, for example, Niebuhr, *Leaves from the Notebook of a Tamed Cynic*, p. 28, and "At Oberammergau," *Christian Century* 47 (Aug. 13, 1930): 984.

54. See Niebuhr, *Christianity and Power Politics*, p. 19; Niebuhr, "Religion and Action," in University of Pennsylvania Bicentennial Conference, *Religion and the Modern World* (Philadelphia, 1941), p. 93; Niebuhr, *The Nature and Destiny of Man: A Christian Interpretation* (New York, 1949), pp. 41, 58, 215–16.

55. Niebuhr, "Toward a Program for Jews, Part 1," p. 242, and "Our Stake in the State of Israel," p. 10.

56. Other theologians, both Protestant and Catholic, whose thinking has been affected by these events and whose work I have found impressive, include Alan T. Davies, Eva Fleischner, Franklin H. Littell, Bernard E. Olson, John T. Pawlikowski, and Rosemary Ruether.

57. Eckardt also acknowledges his debt to the historians Salo W. Baron and James Parkes. See A. Roy Eckardt, "Theological Approaches to Anti-Semitism," *Jewish Social Studies* 33 (Oct. 1971): 272, Robert Evans' review of A. Roy Eckardt's *Your People, My People: The Meeting of Christians and Jews* (New York, 1974) in *Jewish Social Studies* 37 (Jan. 1975): 90. As will be evident in the notes below, a few of Eckardt's books have been co-authored with his wife, Alice L. Eckardt. For the sake of stylistic consistency my references through the text are to "Eckardt."

58. Eckardt, *Your People, My People*, p. 79, and "The Devil and Yom Kippur," *Midstream* 20 (Aug./Sept. 1974): 70.

59. A. Roy Eckardt, *Christianity and the Children of Israel* (New York, 1948), pp. 3–13; Eckardt, "Christian Faith and the Jews," *Journal of Religion* 30 (Oct. 1950): 239–40; Eckardt, "Can There be a Jewish-Christian Relationship?" *Journal of Bible and Religion* 33 (Apr. 1965): 122. Following the suggestion of James Parkes ("the noted British historian, Anglican Clergyman, and pioneering scholar in Jewish-Christian understanding"), Eckardt

concludes that the spelling "anti-Semitism" is inappropriate. Since most of the people of Southwestern Asia are "Semites," the term implies far more than Jew-hatred. The non-capitalized and non-hyphenated version, "antisemitism" (in actuality a new word) is more appropriate. Parkes and Eckardt assert that the spelling "anti-Semitism" is " 'pseudo-scientific, mumbo-jumbo.' " It implies " 'that the phenomenon in question is somehow a movement directed against an actual quality' " called Semitism. On the other hand, since the word antisemitism makes no pretense to a scientific designation, "it is entitled to neither a hyphen nor a capital." See Eckardt, "The Nemesis of Christian Antisemitism," *Journal of Church and State* 13 (Spring 1971): 227. In spelling "antisemitism," I had wished to follow Eckardt's suggestion, but have used the conventional spelling for the sake of consistency with common usage.

60. Eckardt, *Christianity and the Children of Israel*, pp. 43–45, 50–56; Eckardt, "Theological Approaches to Anti-Semitism," 275–77, 283; Eckardt, *Your People, My People*, p. 80.

61. Eckardt, "Can There Be a Jewish-Christian Relationship?" pp. 126–27; Eckardt with Alice L. Eckardt, *Long Night's Journey into Day; Life and Faith after the Holocaust* (Detroit, 1982), p. 114; Eckardt, "The Nemesis of Christian Anti-Semitism," pp. 231–32.

62. Eckardt, "Theological Approaches to Anti-Semitism," p. 282, and *Your People, My People*, p. 38.

63. Eckardt, *Christianity and the Children of Israel*, pp. 1–2; Eckardt, *Elder and Younger Brothers: The Encounter of Jews and Christians* (New York, 1967), pp. 116–17.

64. Eckardt, *Elder and Younger Brothers*, pp. 118–19, and *Your People, My People*, p. 12.

65. Eckardt, "Can There Be a Jewish-Christian Relationship?" pp. 123–24, and *Your People, My People*, pp. 42–45.

66. A. Roy Eckardt, "Jürgen Moltmann, the Jewish People and the Holocaust," *Journal of the American Academy of Religion* 44 (Dec. 1976): 681.

67. Eckardt, "Can There Be a Jewish-Christian Relationship?" p. 127, and *Long Night's Journey into Day*, p. 118; see also his *Elder and Younger Brothers*, pp. 51, 129–30, 158.

68. A. Roy Eckardt, "Contemporary Christian Theology a Protestant Witness for the Shoah," *Shoah: A Review of Holocaust Studies and Commemorations* 2 (Spring 1980): 11.

69. Eckardt, *Elder and Younger Brothers*, pp. 141, 152–53.

70. A. Roy Eckardt, "Christian Responses to the *Endlösung*," *Religion in Life* 48 (Spring 1978): 39; see also his "Christians and Jews; Along a Theological Frontier," *Encounter* 40 (Spring 1979): 98, 126.

71. Eckardt, "Can There Be a Jewish-Christian Relationship?" p. 122.

72. Eckardt, *Elder and Younger Brothers*, pp. 12–14.

73. Eckardt, "Jürgen Moltmann," pp. 686–87; Eckardt, "The Recantation of

the Covenant?" in *Confronting The Holocaust: the Impact of Elie Wiesel,* ed. Alvin H. Rosenfeld and Irving Greenberg (Bloomington, Ind., 1978), pp. 102–4; Eckardt, *Long Night's Journey,* pp. 99–104.

74. Eckardt, "Christian Responses to the *Endlösung,*" pp. 34–35; Eckardt, "Christians and Jews: Along a Theological Frontier," p. 92.

75. Eckardt, *Long Night's Journey,* pp. 17, 23.

76. Eckardt, "Christians and Jews: Along a Theological Frontier," p. 95, and "Contemporary Christian Theology," pp. 12–13; see also his *Long Night's Journey,* pp. 45–47.

77. A. Roy Eckardt and Alice L. Eckardt, *Encounter with Israel: A Challenge to Conscience* (New York, 1979), p. 256.

78. Eckardt, *Long Night's Journey,* pp. 28–30.

79. Eckardt, "Christian Responses to the *Endlösung,*" pp. 34, 41; see also his "Christians and Jews: Along a Theological Frontier," p. 95.

80. A. Roy Eckardt, "Eretz Israel: A Christian Affirmation," *Midstream* 14 (Mar. 1968): 12, and "Toward an Authentic Jewish-Christian Relationship," *Journal of Church and State* 13 (Spring 1971): 271.

81. A. Roy Eckardt and Alice L. Eckardt, "Silence in the Churches," *Midstream* 13 (Oct. 1967): 28.

82. Eckardt, "Eretz Israel: A Christian Affirmation," p. 11, and *Encounter with Israel,* p. 261.

83. A. Roy Eckardt, "The Fantasy of Reconciliation in the Middle East," *Christian Century* 48 (Oct. 13, 1971): 1202.

84. Eckardt, *Christianity and the Children of Israel,* p. 170, and *Encounter with Israel,* p. 194.

85. Eckardt, *Encounter with Israel,* p. 231.

86. Ibid., pp. 200–202; see also his "The Fantasy of Reconciliation in the Middle East," p. 1200.

87. Eckardt, "The Fantasy of Reconciliation in the Middle East," p. 1199.

88. Eckardt, *Encounter with Israel,* pp. 219, 222, Eckardt's italics.

89. Eckardt, "The Devil and Yom Kippur," p. 69.

90. Eckardt, "Eretz Israel: A Christian Affirmation," p. 10, and *Encounter with Israel,* pp. 184, 205.

91. Eckardt, *Encounter with Israel,* p. 208, and "The Devil and Yom Kippur," p. 72.

92. Eckardt, *Your People, My People,* p. 141.

93. Eckardt, "Christians and Jews: Along a Theological Frontier," p. 121.

94. Eckardt, "Silence in the Churches," pp. 28, 32; Eckardt, "The Protestant View of Israel," *Enyclopaedia Judaica Year Book,* 1974 (Jerusalem, 1974), p. 162; Eckardt, "The Devil and Yom Kippur," pp. 67–68, 71, 73–74; see also, *New York Times,* Oct. 11, 1972, p. 44.

95. A. Roy Eckardt, "Christian Perspectives on Israel," *Midstream* 18, (Oct. 1972): 40–41, and "The Nemesis of Christian Antisemitism," p. 239.

96. Eckardt, "The Nemesis of Christian Antisemitism," p. 237; Eckardt, *Long*

Night's Journey, p. 106; Eckardt, "Christian Perspectives on Israel," pp. 44–45.

97. Alice and Roy Eckardt, "The Achievements and Trials of Interfaith," *Judaism* 27 (Summer 1978): 320; see also his "Toward a Secular Theology of Israel," *Religion in Life* 68 (Winter 1979): 462, 466.

98. Eckardt, "Toward a Secular Theology of Israel," p. 467.

99. Eckardt, *Christianity and the Children of Israel*, p. 46; see also his "The Mystery of the Jews' Rejection of Christ," *Theology Today* 18 (Apr. 1961): 55.

100. Eckardt, *Elder and Younger Brothers*, pp. 105, 135, 242, and "Christians and Jews: Along a Theological Frontier," p. 96.

101. Eckardt, *Elder and Younger Brothers*, p. 160, and "A Response to Rabbi Olan," *Religion in Life* 62 (Autumn 1973): 404.

102. Eckardt, *Long Night's Journey*, p. 122, and "A Response to Rabbi Olan," p. 404.

103. This circle includes such names as Alan T. Davies, Eugene J. Fisher, Franklin H. Littell, and Paul M. Van Buren.

104. The suggestion comes from a conversation with Father John T. Pawlikowski, July 26, 1982.

15

Jewish-Christian Relations:
A Jewish Perspective

David Berger

Our generation has seen some fundamental, even revolutionary changes in the official position of many Christian churches toward Jews and Judaism. Antisemitism has been denounced, contemporary Jewish responsibility for the crucifixion denied, missionizing reexamined, textbooks revised, and dialogue encouraged. These changes, though welcomed by most Jews, have left many lingering problems unresolved, and, especially in the case of dialogue, they have raised new, complex questions about the propriety and character of interfaith relations.

The most famous Christian statement on the Jews in recent years is, of course, the widely heralded and much debated document issued by Vatican II in 1965 (*Nostra Aetate 4*), which spoke of a special bond between Christians and Jews. Since then, a series of Catholic statements both in Rome and in various national churches has attempted to grapple with the ambiguities and omissions in *Nostra Aetate 4,* and in January 1975, official guidelines were issued for the implementation of the council's declaration and the encouragement of continuing contacts between Catholics and Jews.

Protestant churches have also moved toward a reassessment of their attitudes concerning Jews and Judaism in a number of statements by the World Council of Churches, international conferences of individual denominations, and national organizations. Although the decentralized character of Protestantism makes generalization difficult, most of the

Reprinted by permission from the *Journal of Ecumenical Studies* 20 (Winter 1983): 5–32.

major trends in the Catholic declarations appear among Protestants as well, and here, too, the call for interfaith dialogue is a prominent and recurring feature.[1]

To further such contacts, both Christians and Jews have set up institutional mechanisms whose primary function is interfaith relations. The Pontifical Commission for Religious Relations with the Jews and the Consultation on the Church and the Jewish People of the World Council of Churches are major examples of Christian bodies which function on a worldwide scale. In the United States, the Catholic Secretariat for Christian-Jewish Relations, the Committee on Christian-Jewish Relations of the National Council of Churches, and a substantial number of national officials of individual Protestant churches deal primarily with Jewish issues. Jews reciprocate with significant programs for interreligious affairs at the American Jewish Committee, Anti-Defamation League, American Jewish Congress, Synagogue Council of America, Union of American Hebrew Congregations, and elsewhere, while the National Conference of Christians and Jews continues to expand its longstanding efforts. Though the scope and intensity of such activities vary greatly from country to country, some increase in interfaith contacts is noticeable in virtually every Western nation with a significant Jewish population.[2]

This essay will concentrate on some of the substantive issues raised by these contacts: the problem of dialogue itself, mission and covenant, Antisemitism, the State of Israel, and moral questions affecting public policy. These topics may not exhaust the Jewish-Christian agenda, but they play a central role in defining both the progress and the continuing problematic of a relationship which is nearing the end of its second decade and its second millennium at the same time.

THE PROBLEM OF DIALOGUE

At first glance, the case for dialogue is self-evident, straightforward, and deceptively simple. Communication is preferable to isolation; friendship and trust can be established only by people who talk to one another. Nevertheless, although dialogue is often initiated by the Jewish side, the history of Jewish-Christian relations has bequeathed to many Jews a legacy of mistrust and suspicion which makes them perceive the Christian advocacy of such discussions as a subtle and more sophisticated expression of the missionary impulse. We shall have to examine the question of mission later on, but to the extent that this perception could be defended, the argument for dialogue—at least in the eyes of many Jews—would be severely undermined.

The conviction that the motivation for dialogue is a sincere desire for mutual understanding is indispensable for the legitimation of such conversations, but it does not define their content. The most interesting questions, in fact, arise only in the context of a favorable decision about the fundamental enterprise. What should be discussed? Are some subjects too sensitive, or does the exclusion of such topics contradict the essential objective of interfaith dialogue? Should discussants direct their efforts toward the solution of clearcut problems in Jewish-Christian relations, or should they address essential matters of faith as well? If a separation between such issues is desirable, is it in fact possible?

In a thoughtful and perceptive article, Henry Siegman argued that Jews and Christians bring different agendas to what is essentially an asymmetrical discussion.[3] Since Jews can understand their faith without reference to Christianity, there is no internal Jewish need to engage in theological discussion with Christians; Christianity, on the other hand, confronts Judaism the moment it "searches into the mystery of the Church."[4] The Jewish agenda is historical rather than theological and focuses on such issues as Antisemitism, the Holocaust, and the State of Israel. Although each side may recognize some value in the other's agenda, the basic impulses leading to dialogue are profoundly different.

Since no one can compel the discussion of any particular issue, inhibitions about the content of interfaith exchanges are likely to be respected. While Christians may be more interested in theology, they have no fundamental objections to a discussion of the "Jewish" themes, and considerations of conscience make a refusal to confront such topics both morally questionable and politically awkward. Many Jews, on the other hand, regard certain theological discussions very warily, and the Jewish agenda has generally prevailed.

A striking example of this Jewish "victory" is the agenda proposed by a Christian writing in the middle of the last decade. Though he expressed hope that "the frequency and scope" of purely theological discussions would be increased, the major elements of his list were the establishment of study groups, recognition that Jews can be saved without conversion, renunciation of missionary work, more effective denunciation of Antisemitism, curricular changes in Christian seminaries and congregational schools, liturgical revisions, and joint social action.[5] The primary emphasis of this proposal is self-evident.

Some Christians, however, have been more assertive. One leading ecumenist, though referring to Siegman's article as a "now classic" statement, has argued that Jewish theology can be aided by Christian insights on "covenant, mission, peoplehood, [and] the Kingdom," while Jewish "self-articulation" in the Christian period was deeply affected by its relationship with Christianity.[6] Another Christian response to Siegman's analysis put the issue even more sharply: "Full attention to theology and ultimate questions can wait. The point is, can they wait forever?"[7]

A look at some very recent Christian proposals for discussion reveals a combination of "historical" and "theological" issues. A German Catholic working paper lists belief in the wake of the Holocaust, the meaning of the State of Israel, the problem of combining belief in salvation and political action, a variety of ethical issues, and the diminishing of the supposed conflict between a religion of law and a religion of grace.[8] In a statement that has aroused considerable attention, the Evangelical Church of the Rhineland suggested a similarly "mixed" agenda: the Holocaust, a common Bible, the standing of Jesus, "the one people of God," justice and love, and the problem of mission to the Jews.[9]

In the eyes of many Jews, these lists present a minefield of sensitive issues. Dialogue is by definition a two-way street, and, if Jews expect Christians to revise certain longstanding perspectives on Judaism, they cannot expect Christians to refrain from entertaining reciprocal expectations. This development emerges with striking clarity in the German Catholic working paper. The Christian, it says, cannot regard the Jew as merely a surviving witness of the period of the "Old Testament" and early Christianity. "Conversely, the Christian partner cannot be satisfied if the Jewish partner thinks that only he has something to say to the Christian which is essential to the Christian's faith, while that which the Christian has to say to the Jew has no essential meaning for the faith of the Jew." The Jew cannot know how Abraham became the father of a multitude of nations without an understanding of Christianity; indeed, dialogue can take place seriously only when Jews assume that Christianity was caused by God and when Christianity interests them "for God's sake." Moreover, "Jews can acknowledge that, for the Christians, Jesus has become the way in which they find Israel's God," and one example of a possible "Jewish interest in Christianity" is Franz Rosenzweig's statement that "whether Jesus was the Messiah will be shown when the Messiah comes." This sort of expectation—closer to a hope than to a demand—is also reflected in a recent book by the Swiss Catholic scholar, Clemens Thoma, who quotes David Flusser's very similar remark that "I do not think many Jews would object if the messiah when he came again was the Jew Jesus."[10]

Even with respect to the core issues of trinity and incarnation, Thoma attempts to show from biblical, midrashic, and mystical sources that "a Christological perception of God—apart from its historical realization—is not un-Jewish." On similar grounds, another Christian theologian wants Jews to recognize that the doctrine of the trinity "acquired its depth" from the Jewish Scriptures.[11] In a more oblique fashion, the question was raised by John Sheerin in an article whose major thrust is to persuade Christians to modify their preconceptions about Judaism; dialogue, he says, is made difficult if not impossible by some of these Christian ideas. "Likewise, many Jews feel that they cannot engage in dialogue with Christians because they see the adoration of Jesus as sheer idolatry and they simply cannot bring themselves to discuss it with Christians."[12] Since Sheerin's article is not concerned primarily with this problem, he does not say explicitly what Jews should do about it or whether or not this makes dialogue impossible from a Christian perspective. Nevertheless, it is clear that some Christians are beginning to expect a measure of theological reciprocity if meaningful dialogue is to progress.

Can Jews offer such reciprocity? In most cases, I think the answer is no. Statements like those of Rosenzweig and Flusser about Jesus and the Messiah are thoroughly atypical in the Jewish community, and there is little prospect that this will change; indeed, aside from the subtle pressures of the "dialogue" relationship, there is no moral or intellectual reason for such change. Though many Jews are prepared to say that classical Christian theology does not constitute idolatry for Gentiles, there is a consensus that it is idolatry for Jews. Efforts to make the combined doctrines of trinity and incarnation more acceptable to Jews by citing the *Sefirot* of the kabbalists or the *shekhinah* of the rabbis are not likely to bear more fruit today than they did in the late Middle Ages.

It is therefore a matter of considerable importance for the future of dialogue that Christians not maintain illusory expectations about significant modifications of such theological positions.[13] At the same time, this situation points up an even more troubling asymmetry in interfaith discussions. Many Christians involved in dialogue have been prepared to modify venerable attitudes toward mission, covenant, the significance of Judaism, and even the historicity of Matthew's account of the crucifixion. Jews are not in a position to make gestures nearly as significant, and this creates a situation in which Jews appear to be demanding change without offering very much in return.

There are, of course, valid reasons for this state of affairs. As Siegman has noted, the fundamental factor that gives Jews the "standing" to suggest certain changes in Christian theology is "the price that [they] have paid for such theology in history."[14] As we shall see in our discussion of Antisemitism, a modification of those elements in Christianity which may lead to hatred of Jews requires at least a careful look at beliefs which come uncomfortably close to the core of the faith. On the other hand, although there is no denying that a pejorative perception of Christians and Christianity exists among many Jews, such perceptions have not led to any significant Christian suffering in the last millennium; moreover, some of them result at least as much from Antisemitism itself as they do from Jewish theology. Consequently, the relative absence of a Jewish *quid pro quo* is in a certain sense justified.[15]

Notwithstanding this justification, there is an uncomfortable imbalance in the structure of Jewish-Christian discussion, and one can only admire those Christian participants who are genuinely interested in revising certain elements of Christian theology without expecting much change on the Jewish side. One way to correct this imbalance, at least to some extent, is for Jews to resist as much as possible the temptation of telling Christians what to believe. This is an extremely delicate question which we shall encounter in specific cases later on, and there are several fine lines on the road from hope to suggestion to expectation to demand. Often Jews are simply responding to Christian questions about the effect of certain doctrines, and on such occasions they are acting as what one prominent rabbi has described as a resource for the Christian community. Nevertheless, there is no obligation to answer every question; silence is still sometimes "a hedge around wisdom" (*Mishnah Avot* 3:13).

The classic, extreme formulation of this position, which has theoretically governed official Orthodox involvement (and non-involvement) in dialogue, is Rabbi Joseph B. Soloveitchik's argument that matters of faith are not an appropriate subject for interreligious discussion, because they are rooted in profoundest recesses of the religious experience of both the individual and the faith community.[16] Such Orthodox reservations about dialogue are reflected to a somewhat lesser extent in the attitudes of many Christian fundamentalists and evangelicals. The dangers of dialogue for these Christians emerge with striking clarity from an assertion by two liberal Christians whose devotion to the Jewish people and interfaith discussion is unsurpassed. Alice and Roy Eckardt have argued that insistence on "the divine inspiration of all Scripture . . . cannot escape a proclivity to antisemitism" and makes interfaith dialogue very difficult.[17] Their theoretical goal is presumably to persuade fundamentalists to abandon fundamentalism, though the realistic objective is to prevent their "achieving forms of political power and influence." To the extent that this approach to dialogue envisions significant changes in the basic beliefs of the participants, it can appear especially threatening to both Christian fundamentalists and Orthodox Jews.

The issue of Jewish relations with fundamentalist evangelicals has become particularly acute in the United States as a result of the meteoric rise of the Moral Majority and related groups. Jewish reactions have varied widely, because the positions espoused by these groups can arouse both enthusiasm and deep suspicion when examined from the perspective of Jewish interests. On Israel their stand is exemplary. On theological issues, they are oriented toward mission and Christian triumphalism, and denials that they seek a Christian America, while welcome, do not always appear consistent with the policies and behavior of local activists. Remarks by the head of New York's Moral Majority (for which he later apologized) asserting that Jews control the city and the media and possess a supernatural ability to make money show not so much conscious Antisemitism as staggering naiveté and unthinking acceptance of anti-Jewish stereotypes; incredibly, the statement was genuinely intended to demonstrate support and admiration. (Jerry Falwell, who knows better by now, reacted immediately by denying that "you can stereotype any people."[18]) On social issues, most Jews are considerably more liberal than the Moral Majority, but there is no unanimity on these questions; still, school prayer is an example of a major goal of the politically oriented evangelicals which is opposed by virtually the entire spectrum of the Jewish community. Hence, the perceived dangers to pluralism and liberalism have led Jewish leaders such as Alexander Schindler to denounce this movement with exceptional vehemence; the vigorous support of Israel has led some Zionist groups to express enthusiastic approval in a world where offending Israel's friends appears suicidal; and the conservative position on moral issues has led some hasidic figures, for whom interfaith discussions are usually anathema, to support an alliance in the face of a deluge threatening all traditional morality.[19]

With respect to dialogue between Jews and evangelical groups in general (not necessarily the political activists), there has been real progress, and some voices have been raised questioning the general view that Jews are "safer" holding discussions with Christian liberals than with conservatives and fundamentalists.[20] The challenge here will be to establish communication and friendly relations without the expectation of much theological flexibility in the Christian position. In light of the potential tensions in the standard dialogue, this is a situation that deserves to be explored with interest. From the perspective of the "Jewish agenda," the prospect of improving relations without theological change was put forcefully by Yosef Yerushalmi: "After all that has happened, do we still have to await a reformulation of Christian theology before the voice of Jewish blood can be heard crying from the earth? Is our common humanity not sufficient? In any case, Christian theology is an internal affair for Christians alone."[21]

Nevertheless, most Christian and some Jewish participants in dialogue remain interested in "internal" theological issues, and the inner dynamic of the interfaith process may lead inexorably in the direction of such discussions. The historical agenda does not lead to new frontiers, so that some Christians involved in dialogue for many years have begun to complain of discussions that review the same issues again and again. To the extent that such a perspective is correct, progress can be made by either involving new people or exploring new topics, and even though reaching out to new participants is an essential goal of interfaith programs, there remains the inexorable impulse to keep the dialogue vibrant on all levels. Since the frontier appears to be in the theological arena, there is reason to expect—or to fear—that the "victory" of the Jewish agenda will turn out to be ephemeral. To some extent this development is already evident: Clemens Thoma's book, which demonstrates a genuine, sympathetic understanding of Judaism, has been the focus of a major dialogue; the March, 1981, meeting of the National Conference of Christians and Jews dealt with a Christian theology of Judaism and a Jewish theology of Christianity; recently published discussion on monotheism and the trinity was held some time ago in Europe; and, on a practical level, the National Council of Churches and the Union of American Hebrew Congregations have prepared guidelines for joint worship.[22]

The dialogue, then, for all its accomplishments on the intellectual and especially human levels, is facing a major challenge. The historical agenda may be losing its freshness and vitality; the theological agenda is fraught with problems of the most serious sort, especially from the Jewish perspective. Advocates of dialogue will have to display a remarkable combination of creativity and caution. An interesting decade lies ahead.

MISSION AND COVENANT

Perhaps the most vexing question with a direct bearing on the feasibility of dialogue is the status of the traditional Christian desire to convert the Jews. The point was made with exceptional vigor in a recent article in *The Christian Century:* "Dialogue can never be an attempt at conversion, nor can it occur if one party assumes an objective ultimacy or a superiority for his or her point of view. Dialogue must be an interaction in which each participant stands with full integrity in his or her own tradition and is open to the depths of the truth that is in the other."[23] The last sentence is an exaggeration (a person cannot be entirely open while standing with full integrity in a religious tradition), and if the assumption of objective superiority makes dialogue impossible, then most believers will find it impossible. What is, however, indubitably true is that dialogue cannot be an attempt at conversion; if it is, it automatically becomes disputation or polemic, which is precisely what dialogue is intended to transcend.

What is less clear is whether dialogue is impossible with people who run a missionary program to convert you, provided that this particular discussion is not geared to that objective. What if they hope that you will be converted but have no missionaries? And what if that conversionary hope applies only to the end of days? Answers will differ, but there is certainly something uncomfortable about religious discussions with a partner who is working actively toward the elimination of your faith. Consequently, the "dialogue" relationship has played a role in a reassessment by some Christians of the applicability of the missionary ideal to the Jewish people.

Three approaches characterize Christian attitudes on this question: missionize everyone, including Jews; missionize everyone, especially Jews; missionize everyone except for Jews.[24] The first approach requires no explanation. The second argues that since Jews were the original chosen people, since Jesus was of their flesh and was originally sent to them, and since their conversion is singled out as part of the eschatological drama (Rom. 11:25–26), they should be the special targets of the Christian mission. The third approach is the most recent and the most interesting. No one, it is true, can reach the Father except through Jesus (John 14:6), but Jews are already with the Father. The covenant with the original Israel has never been abrogated (Rom. 11:28–29); hence, there is no theological necessity for Jewish conversion, at least not before the end of history.

This so-called double-covenant theory has played a major role in Christian discussions of the standing of the Jewish people and the propriety of missions to the Jews. The central text in Romans leaves room for divergent interpretations and deserves to be quoted in full: "As concerning the Gospel, they [the Jews] are enemies for your sakes, but as touching the election, they are beloved for the fathers' sake. For the gifts and calling of God are without repentance." All this text says clearly is that the *Jews* are in a certain sense still chosen; it says nothing unequivocal about Judaism. Hence, when a Christian writer says that the Vatican II declaration "makes clear that the Jewish religion has a continuing validity" because of its paraphrase of this Pauline passage,[25] he goes beyond the evidence. On the whole, official and semi-official Christian documents have avoided a clearcut assertion of the double-covenant theory in a way that would ascribe anything like religious equality to contemporary Judaism; such documents tend to remain ambiguous or to acknowledge frankly the existence of divergent views on this question.[26] Explicit recognition that Judaism remains binding for Jews, with its implication that Jewish conversion is not even desirable, remains confined to a relatively small group of interfaith activists.

May Jews legitimately tell Christians that they must abandon the belief that Christianity supersedes Judaism? One Jewish leader has recently described Christian supersessionism as "vainglory (and) a kind of religious arrogance that must be labelled a sin. And that sin . . . needs to be purged from the soul of Christianity."[27] This is an exceptionally strong statement which seems to deny any religion the right to declare its own beliefs true and those of another religion false. As Siegman put it, "Judaism constitutes a denial of the central Christian mystery and its notion of salvation; it cannot at the same time demand that Christianity be reformulated to accommodate the 'equality' of Judaism."[28] Nevertheless, it is exceptionally interesting that the World Council of Churches' most recent draft guidelines for Jewish-Christian dialogue discuss supersessionism under the rubric of Antisemitism and come very close to the sort of affirmation that most official documents have so far avoided:

We must be especially attentive to those traditional convictions that have furthered antisemitic stances and attitudes on the part of Christians. Attention should therefore be given to the following points: Judaism should not be presented as a kind of anachronism after the coming of Christ: the Jews are a living people, very much alive in our present time as, for instance, the establishment of the State of Israel shows. Neither should the impression be given that the Church has superseded the Israel of old. The Jewish People continues to be God's People, for God is not unfaithful to those whom he has chosen (Rom. 11:29). As long as Christians regard Israel only as preparation for Christianity, as long as Christians claim the validity of God's revelation to them by negating the validity of God's revelation to the Jewish People, Judaism is denied any theological validity, and it becomes impossible to maintain a common ground for our common hope.[29]

Even this carefully formulated statement does not say that the conversion of Jews is not desirable, and in a later paragraph the document acknowledges differences among Christians concerning the obligations to "bear witness . . . to the Jews." It is when the discussion shifts from the abstract level of covenant to the more concrete plane of "witness" and mission that matters become particularly difficult for both Christians and Jews.

Christian witness is a rather important element in most forms of Christianity, and, in the absence of a fairly extreme position on the covenant question, it is difficult to see why Judaism should be excluded as the object of such witness. At the same time, not only is dialogue made difficult by an affirmation of missionizing, but the consciences of many Christians are troubled by the unsavory history of missionary efforts directed at Jews. The solution has been a distinction between witness, which is obligatory, and proselytism, which is forbidden. What is the difference? In the most important Catholic paper on this subject, Tomasso Federici describes "unwarranted proselytism" as any witness or preaching involving "a physical, moral, psychological or cultural constraint on the Jews ... that could ... destroy or even diminish personal judgment, free will, full autonomy to decide, either personal or communitarian." This excludes the offering of "legal, material, cultural, political, and other advantages" and certainly rules out any form of coercion. Finally, since conversion must involve the free religious conscience and come only after inner distress and spiritual transformation, no organization should be set up for the conversion of the Jews.[30]

Now, it is perfectly clear that the reasoning in this last sentence does not apply to the Jews any more than it applies to any other group, and its use in this context points up an important ambiguity in the paper. In an early passage, Federici refers to the survival of God's covenant with the Jews, and he later concludes by encouraging study of the "history and mission of Israel, ... her election and call, her privileges recognized in the New Testament"; nevertheless, these observations do not appear at the heart of his argument. With the exception of a reference to the unpleasant history of Christian mission to the Jews, the central arguments against "unwarranted proselytism" of Jews appear to be arguments against unwarranted proselytism of anyone. Such a position is naturally commendable, but the impression given by Federici that Jews have special standing in this matter appears more rhetorical than substantive when the concrete arguments are examined.

Catholic reactions to the Federici paper have varied widely. Some conservative figures have condemned it outright and defended the necessity of missionizing Jews.[31] While one account reports that Federici rejected "high pressure evangelism,"[32] another cites his paper along with other Catholic statements as evidence that proselytism, apparently meaning all missionary efforts with respect to Jews, has been rejected.[33] The truth is that some of those other statements speak of rejecting proselytism in the context of dialogue, which is not the same as total rejection, though one or two—particularly a 1973 declaration by the bishops of France—do make the point quite vigorously and in a more general context. In a recent paper, Eugene Fisher attempted to read Federici's work in the most liberal way possible and to go beyond it toward a position in which the permanent value of Judaism would rule out any of the traditional forms of mission to the Jews.[34]

Needless to say, Protestant views reflect at least as wide as a range of opinion as those of Catholics. Back in 1968, the World Council of Churches denounced crude missionizing ("cajolery, undue pressure or intimidation") and reported the belief of some Protestants that "service" rather than "explicit words" might be the best way to testify to the Jews. On the whole, the document recognizes the goal of conversion quite frankly and does not renounce active missionary efforts. The Lutheran World Federation in 1973 placed mission to the Jews on an equal footing with mission to all other groups, while the position of the German Evangelical Church in 1975 is a striking example of the studied ambiguity often generated by this question: "We have now come to understand mission and dialogue as two dimensions of one Christian witness. ... Mission and dialogue as descriptions of Christian witness have an ominous sound to Jewish ears. Christians must therefore reassess the meaning with regard to the Jews of their witness to Jesus Christ as salvation for all mankind, the terms by which to identify their witness, and the methods of procedure."[35]

We have already seen that the most recent draft guidelines of the World Council of Churches continue to report disagreement about the need to witness to the Jews. The guidelines, however, do "reject proselytism both in its gross and refined forms. This implies that all triumphalism and every kind of manipulation are to be abrogated. We are called upon to minimize the power dimension in all encounters with the Jews and to speak at every level from equal to equal." At the same time, the guidelines say that "future work" includes "reaching a common understanding of the nature of divine revelation and thus healing the breach which exists between the Jewish people and the Church." While the precise meaning of these remarks is unclear, they are hardly likely to allay Jewish suspicions about the persistence of missionary intentions in an age of dialogue.

Among American evangelicals, Jews continue to be considered appropriate targets of missionary activity, although Billy Graham noted in 1973 that he has never singled out Jews as Jews and is opposed to "coercive proselytizing."[36] Jews for Jesus and other groups whose *raison d'être* is missionizing Jews receive considerable support from evangelical

Christians. Here even Jews who hesitate most about intervention in the internal affairs of Christianity have some mixed feelings. Henry Siegman argues that Jews have no right to demand that Christians abandon such missionary activity but notes that "an active Christian mission to the Jews precludes serious dialogue."[37] Jacob Petuchowski maintains that telling a Christian not to missionize is "an illegitimate attempt by one faith to dictate to the other"; nevertheless, he cannot refrain from going beyond Siegman and adding that he would argue that such efforts are unwise and that perhaps the Jews' conversion should be left to God.[38]

This issue, which is a deeply emotional one for many Jews, can be viewed as a matter of simple self-defense. When Marc Tanenbaum persuaded President Carter's sister not to address a group whose purpose was converting Jews, this was not an assertion of the "subordination of Christianity to Judaism," as the *National Review* described it in a remarkably insensitive editorial, but a reaction to a direct spiritual threat.[39] The Jewish mandate to protect Jews from conversion is no less a religious requirement than any Christian mandate to convert them, and, although my basic sympathies are with the "non-interventionists," in the case of aggressive missionizing aimed specifically at Jews the overriding principle of *pikkuah nefesh,* or danger to life (including spiritual life), may well prevail.

Active missionaries are in any case rarely dissuaded from pursuing their task, and the Jewish response must often take the straightforward form of replies to missionary argument. Such exchanges run the risk of acrimony; in fact, however, they need not be strident or disrespectful. Several years ago, the Jewish Community Relations Council (J.C.R.C.) of New York asked Michael Wyschogrod and me to write a booklet addressing the central issues raised by Jews for Jesus; our fundamental objective was to produce a work that would combine frank argumentation with a respectful tone.[40] Whether or not we succeeded is not for me to judge, but the angry denunciation that sometimes marks the Jewish response to this challenge is sometimes inappropriate and usually self-defeating.[41] Even more recently, the New York J.C.R.C. has set up a hotline to advise Jews faced with this problem, and a variety of Jewish organizations have recognized the need for a low-key but carefully prepared program to counter missionary efforts.[42]

The counter-missionary act which has aroused the most resentment among Christians is a recent Israeli law which makes illegal the offering of material inducements to convert. At the same time, several mainline churches have supported American Jews in opposing the misleading propaganda of various "Hebrew Christian" groups which attempt to give the impression—at least initially—that they are simply Jews. Finally, a leading Reform rabbi has recently suggested that *Jews* begin to proselytize. Although he has carefully restricted this proposal to "unchurched" Gentiles, the idea remains unpalatable to most non-Reform Jews, partly because of religious principle, but also because it appears to undercut the moral basis for Jewish opposition to Christian missionizing. Like most issues in Jewish-Christian dialogue, the question of mission is one in which significant progress has been made but which remains extremely sensitive, profoundly difficult, and ultimately unresolved.

ANTISEMITISM

Condemnations of Antisemitism are by now routine in the declarations of most major churches. For some time, the linguistic nuances of such statements were examined with exquisite care, so that it became a *cause célèbre* when Vatican II "decried" but did not "condemn" Antisemitism, when it avoided the word "deicide" in declaring contemporary Jews free of responsibility for the crucifixion, and, more seriously, when it refrained from any recognition of Christian guilt for Jewish suffering. On the whole, these nagging points are no longer a problem. At least one official Catholic statement now "condemns" Antisemitism, and various quasi-official or local declarations speak of Christian guilt.[43] Among Protestants, the first assembly of the World Council of Churches in 1948 denounced Antisemitism as a sin; a 1968 statement by its Faith and Order Commission followed the lead of Vatican II by rejecting the ascribing of responsibility for the crucifixion to most Jewish contemporaries of Jesus or to any Jews living today; and the latest draft guidelines speak of an "ashamed awareness of Christian antisemitism." In the United States, even conservative churches have no hesitation in declaring Antisemitism an unchristian phenomenon that must be combatted.[44]

This, however, is not the end of the issue. It is here that the "historical" and "theological" agendas become disturbingly, perhaps inextricably, intertwined. Rosemary Ruether has coined what has developed into a classic phrase in this discussion; Antisemitism, she says, is "the left hand of Christology." In Alan Davies' paraphrase, "The question of anti-Judaism is more than a question of a few notorious Matthaean, Pauline, and Johannine passages, but deals with the basic structure of New Testament theology itself." The problem, he says, is whether or not Antisemitism is a fundamental part of the essential Christian heritage.[45]

Ruether's own view is that Antisemitism can be purged from Christianity only by a rather fundamental revision of Christian theology. If she is right, then Jews participating in dialogue face a stark dilemma. On the one hand, the right of self-defense would appear to justify demands for such revision;[46] on the other hand, Jews who ask Christians to respect Judaism cannot at the same time demand that classic Christian beliefs be dismantled.[47] Moreover, the problem cannot be easily avoided even if Ruether is wrong, because there still remain those "few notorious passages" in the New Testament which have undeniably bred Antisemitism in the past. If, for example, the Jews really said that Jesus' blood would be on them and on their children, and if Matthew's report of this statement is read as a theological endorsement (Matt. 27:25), anti-Jewish consequences could not easily be avoided.

Concerned Christians have addressed this problem in various ways. Some are prepared to deny that such passages are binding at all; the solution is to develop a "hermeneutic . . . that is not slavishly dependent on accepting the New Testament *in toto* as the Word of God."[48] A somewhat different formulation is that though the text is divinely inspired, on a certain level it must reflect the political and polemical concerns of its time; nevertheless, when read as a whole, the New Testament cannot be regarded as antisemitic.[49] Finally, there are Christians who refuse to reject even one line of the Gospels but nevertheless argue that no antisemitic implications need emerge.

What position should Jews take on these questions? Since the ideal answer is clearly that Jews should not prescribe the nature of Christian faith to their partners in dialogue, the only justification for taking a position is, as we have seen, the need for self-defense. If, however, that objective can reasonably be sought in more than one way, Jews, I think, should choose the approach which requires the least intervention in matters of Christian theology. Thus, Jews should encourage efforts to break the link between certain New Testament passages and anti-Jewish consequences but should avoid instructing Christians not to believe what the Gospels report. Needless to say, Jews do not have to become fundamentalist Christian missionaries, and the position of Christians who have rejected certain of those "notorious passages" can be welcomed. But Jewish preaching against the historicity of the Gospels is not only unseemly in the context of dialogue; it is probably also unwise from a purely pragmatic standpoint. Fundamentalist Christians are not about to reject the historicity of Matthew because Jewish ecumenists tell them to, and all that will be accomplished is the transformation of dialogue into polemic with all the resentment—and perhaps even Antisemitism —which this can generate.

The best example I have seen of a sensitive, yet vigorous approach to these problems is the recommendations made by two Christian scholars for changes in the Oberammergau passion play. At the request of the Anti-Defamation League, Leonard Swidler and Gerard Sloyan produced a commentary on the play which, with one or two exceptions, avoids any proposal based on the rejection of the Gospel crucifixion accounts.[50] For example, when dealing with the passage in Matthew wherein the Jews say, "His blood be on us and on our children," they do not insist on deletion, even though that is the solution they would no doubt prefer. Instead they suggest an alternative more palatable to the people of Oberammergau: the crowd should say it once, as in Matthew, and not four times, as in the play, and the choir, which now responds, "It will come on you and on your children," should change just one word: "It will come on you—not on your children."

None of this means that Jewish scholars who are convinced that such a passage is unhistorical should censor their scholarly work. These considerations of restraint apply only to the context of religious dialogue, where respect for the other's faith commitment is the essential element that separates dialogue from disputation. There are, furthermore, certain scholarly issues which belong under the rubric of Antisemitism that do not address the most sensitive matters of faith and can appropriately be raised in dialogue. These issues were addressed by Charlotte Klein in an excellent study of *Anti-Judaism in Christian Theology*,[51] in which she examined the treatment of Judaism in scholarly works used in European seminaries and universities.

The results were profoundly discouraging. Judaism in the time of Jesus continues to be depicted as a legalistic faith concerned primarily with trivialities; the Jewish people in first-century Israel is described as the Jewish religious community; and the term "late Judaism," with its implication that the religion came to an end with the rise of Christianity, remains in vogue. Klein's chapter on "Jewish Guilt in the Death of Jesus" is especially depressing. It is not the defensible assertion that Jews were involved in the crucifixion; it is, rather, the motives ascribed to them and to their descendants throughout the generations for their rejection of Jesus. This rejection allegedly results not from understandable or even honest error but from obstinacy, the desire to remain the chosen people, culpable blindness, and the like. Nothing in the Gospels really requires such assertions, and Jewish indignation need not be restrained when confronted with this sort of antisemitic pseudo-history. It is worth noting that the 1975 Vatican guidelines specifically state that "the Old Testament and the Jewish tradition founded upon it must not be set against the New Testament in such a way that the former seems to constitute a religion of only justice, fear, and legalism, with no appeal to the love of God and neighbor." [52] Though the Pope himself violated this guideline in the recent encyclical, *Dives in Misercordia*, it remains an important statement, and the one encouraging finding in Klein's book is that Anglo-American scholarship displays far greater accuracy and sensitivity on these issues.

All the ringing denunciations of Antisemitism and progressive reassessments of Judaism have little importance if they are confined to an activist elite and have no resonance among ordinary Christians. Liturgical reform and textbook revision are, therefore, key elements in the effort to exorcise the impact of historic Christian anti-Judaism. With respect to liturgy, the most serious problems in at least some churches arise in connection with Holy Week in general and Good Friday in particular, when biblical passages commemorating the crucifixion are read. Some of these passages inevitably convey an anti-Jewish message, and, although thoughtful proposals for retranslation, judicious omissions, and substantial corrective commentary have been made, they all raise serious difficulties and face considerable obstacles. [53] The Good Friday "Reproaches" hymn, which is perhaps the most disturbing single prayer, has now been made optional for American Catholics. In 1976, the Liturgical Commission of the Episcopal Church recommended that the hymn be adopted; [54] eventually, the proposal was rejected, but the very suggestion indicates that movement on these matters is not always in the direction that Jews would like.

On the textbook issue, there has been considerable progress, at least in the United States. Though various problems remain, the depiction of Jews and Judaism in both Protestant and Catholic texts has shown marked improvement. The Pharisees are no longer simply hypocrites, and there are some indications that Judaism has remained a living religion despite the advent of Christianity. Since there is a movement away from standardized texts, it is now especially important that teachers and preachers be trained to appreciate and transmit these changing perceptions. This is a gargantuan task, but it is crucial if declarations about Antisemitism are to have a significant impact in the real world.[55]

The most terrible manifestation of Antisemitism has taken place in our own time, and the vexing question of Christian responsibility for the Holocaust is a brooding presence hovering over all discussions of anti-Jewish elements in Christianity. Inevitably, assessments of this question vary widely. Some would assign primary responsibility to the legacy of Christian teachings; others absolve Christianity with the argument that Nazism was a neo-pagan revolt against the Christian past; while others take a middle position. My own view is that Nazi Antisemitism achieved such virulent, unrestrained consequences because it stripped away the semi-civilized rationales which had been given in the past for persecuting Jews and liberated the deepest psychic impulses which had been partly nurtured but partly suppressed by those rationales. The Nazis utilized the standard political, economic, and sometimes even religious arguments for persecution, but their central message was that Jews were alien, demonic creatures, subhuman and superhuman at the same time, who threatened "Aryans" with profound, almost inexpressible terror. Such fear and hatred have probably been a significant component of the antisemitic psyche for centuries, but they have not been given free rein. The persecution of political enemies, economic exploiters, and religious deviants must still be governed by a modicum of civilized restraint; though this restraint must have seemed invisible to the victims of the Crusades, it reappears, however dimly, when seen through the prism of the Holocaust. On the other hand, malevolent demons, terrifying aliens, and malignant vermin can only be extirpated with single-minded, ruthless ferocity.

The key question, therefore, is what role Christianity played in strengthening the image of Jew as demon, and the answer cannot be unequivocal. There is no doubt that the growth of such a perception of the Jew in the late Middle Ages was intimately connected with Christian ideas and served as an important explanation of the Jewish rejection of Christianity. Though this belief was manifested largely in popular Antisemitism, there was no shortage of clergy who endorsed and propagated it. At the same time, such a view is fundamentally alien to the central teachings of the medieval church, which protected Jewish life and looked forward to both the individual and the collective conversion of Jews. Demons, let alone vermin, are not candidates for conversion! Indeed, one could argue plausibly that it was precisely the weakening of religious grounds for Antisemitism in the modern period which opened the way for their replacement by the racial, demonic justification.

In sum, the Holocaust is not a Christian phenomenon, but it must weigh heavily on the Christian conscience. Many observers believe that it was this unparalleled catastrophe which led to the reexamination of Christian attitudes toward Jews and Judaism manifested in the last few decades. Several churches have even introduced ceremonies commemorating the Holocaust to coincide with the growing Jewish observance of *Yom Hashoah,* or Holocaust Day,[56] and the subject is a recurring theme in Jewish-Christian dialogues. It is a commonplace that the Holocaust has deprived Antisemitism of "respectability," at least temporarily, in what passes for civilized discourse, and it has served as an important reservoir of sympathy for the State of Israel. Many Jews, however, have begun to worry that this breathing space has passed, and Christian attitudes toward Israel, though often supportive and sometimes enthusiastic, have become a source of growing concern.

THE STATE OF ISRAEL

For nearly two millennia, Christians pointed to the destruction of the ancient Jewish state as proof that God had rejected the Jewish people and replaced them with "true Israel." In the context of such a theology, any manifestation of Jewish nationalism would inevitably be regarded as a defiance of the will of God, and the initial reaction of most Christians to the Zionist movement reflected precisely such an attitude. As Eugene Fisher has noted, however, the position of Vatican II on Jewish responsibility for the crucifixion would appear to render such a reaction obsolete and to leave no theological obstacle to Christian, or at least Catholic, support of the State of Israel.[57]

Fisher's logic is unassailable, and a 1973 statement by the bishops of

France declared that "the conscience of the world community cannot refuse the Jewish people . . . the right and means for a political existence among the nations."[58] Nevertheless, one wonders if the implications of Vatican II have been fully discerned in Rome; the official guidelines of 1975 are marked by a deafening silence concerning Israel, while the Vatican's failure to recognize the Jewish state remains a source of tension in Catholic-Jewish relations. This is an issue in which it is particularly difficult to disentangle politics and theology, but the official reasons, which speak of the ongoing state of war and the uncertainty of boundaries, do not carry much conviction.[59]

That Protestant churches would be divided about Israel is obvious and inevitable. In 1968, the World Council of Churches (W.C.C.) confessed its inability to reach a unanimous evaluation of the formation of the state, which, it said, brought Jews self-assurance and security only at the expense of injustice and suffering for Arabs.[60] This, of course, is a reservation not about borders but about the fundamental existence of the state. The W.C.C.'s most recent draft guidelines are a major step forward in this respect. They acknowledge an "indissoluble bond between the Jewish people and the Land of Israel, which has found expression . . . in the reality of the State of Israel. Failing to acknowledge the right of Jews to return to the land prevents any fruitful dialogue with them."[61]

Just as opposition to Israel can be based on either political or theological grounds, support for the state can also be formulated in secular or religious language. Jews have often spoken to Christians about the religious significance of the connection between Jews and the land, and such discussions can have two objectives. The moderate goal is to give Christians an appreciation of the depth and intensity of Jewish feeling on this matter; the more ambitious goal is to persuade them that Christian theology itself demands that Christians support this manifestation of the ongoing, unbroken covenant between God and the Jewish people. "The gifts of God are," after all, "without repentance" (Rom. 11:29).

For Christians who remain impervious to such persuasion, it can sometimes arouse resentment. One Christian, for example, was moved to make a grotesque comparison between Jewish efforts to convert Christians to friendship toward Israel and Christian efforts to convert Jews to Christianity, as if being asked to abandon your faith is analogous to being asked to revise your political opinions (even when those opinions have a theological dimension). He later modified the statement, but the initial reaction remains eloquent testimony to the potential for friction in this area.[62]

Even when Christians endorse the theological necessity of the State of Israel, some strange and unwelcome things can happen if the justification for its existence is made to shift almost entirely from the political to the theological sphere. A striking example of this phenomenon is a 1970 statement by the Synod of the Reformed Church in Holland. God's covenant with Israel, it says, is still in effect, and this includes the connection between Israel and the land. "Because of the special place of the Jewish people we endorse in the present situation the right of existence of the state of Israel." The founding of the state took place in an "all too human way, as is the case with practically every other state." But "the special place of Israel was never based on its moral qualities." God's "covenant-love" is not annulled by sin. "Therefore we ought not to dispute on moral grounds the right of the State of Israel to exist."

The document goes on to note that because of the Jews' special place, the State of Israel must behave in an exemplary way—to teach the world a new understanding of what a state is. The state's boundaries must offer the Jews a dwelling place, but the need to protect that dwelling place "should not induce the Jews to make it into a nationalistic state in which the only thing that counts is military power." In this respect, Israel must be better than other states. Finally, it is also called upon to exercise justice in an exemplary way by recognizing responsibility for the Palestinian refugees and giving Israeli Arabs *de facto* and not just *de jure* equality.[63]

Though Jews are inevitably pleased by a theologically oriented defense of Israel on the part of Christians, this document demonstrates the dangers of relying solely on theological grounds for such support; once the burden of Israel's existence is borne by theology alone, it becomes seductively easy to slip into the apparently unimportant concession that its survival is questionable on other, moral grounds. Such a concession is, of course, devastating to Israel's position in the eyes of anyone who does not share the particular theological perspective of this document. Moreover, the end of the statement is an exceptionally frank expression of the double standard often applied to Israel. To say that Israel is called upon to pass tests of prophetic stature is to make a demand that no state can readily meet; to imply, as this document does, that failure to pass these tests leaves Israel's right to exist untouched is not only of questionable value in the political sphere, but it is also—unfortunately—dubious theology. When the prophets made demands, failure to meet them had consequences. While Jewish title to the land remained in force *sub specie aeternitatis*, God reserved the right to suspend the lease. In short, this statement is destructive of Israel's moral and political position while providing very little theological consolation.

Christians hostile to Israel have a double standard in a far more egregious fashion. Daniel Berrigan, for example, made a famous speech after the Yom Kippur War in which he strongly implied that Jews must behave differently from others and denounced their failure to do so with the sort of scathing indignation appropriate only for acts of consummate evil.[64] Very recently, several hundred Christian clergy, including the head of the human-rights commission of the National Council of Churches, called for a reduction in U.S. aid to Israel because of alleged violations of human rights. Now, Israel depends on U.S. aid for its very survival. Its human-rights record is, by any standards, immensely superior to that of its adversaries; considering the circumstances, that record is so good as to be almost unbelievable. This Orwellian document is therefore urging that a state with an excellent human-rights record be placed in jeopardy in the face of a challenge from states with human-rights records ranging from poor to terrible—in the name of human rights![65] The signatories, of course, give the impression that Israel's sins *are* sufficiently severe to deserve comparison with those of notorious offenders, but this is a Big Lie of proportions that would have done Goebbels proud and merely underscores the application of a double standard.

Though the major Christian organizations have issued no statements as disgraceful as this one, a number of recent declarations have aroused considerable concern among Jews. The embrace of the Palestinian cause by third-world nations has not left liberal Christians unaffected, and the National Council of Churches has adopted a statement on the Middle East which pursues evenhandedness to the point where perfectly symmetrical demands are made of Israel and the P.L.O. Both must cease acts of violence, and each must recognize the other (apparently simultaneously); in Israel's case, this recognition must include the Palestinian right to establish a sovereign state. The National Council of Churches refused to single out P.L.O. terrorism or to make recognition of Israel a precondition for any change in Israel's policy. Even more recently, an

August, 1980, statement by the Central Committee of the World Council of Churches denounced Israel's annexation of East Jerusalem, equated the city's importance in Christianity and Islam to its importance in Judaism, and called on "member churches to exert through their respective governments all pressure on Israel to withhold all action on Jerusalem."[66]

These statements have virtually no theological content, and we have already seen that Jews have attempted to introduce a theological dimension into the Christian approach to this issue. The central point, however, is not a theological one. Positions of Christian religious groups which reflect indifference or worse toward the fate of Israel are interpreted by Jews as "indifference or even antagonism to the survival of the Jewish people";[67] such positions suggest that, despite protestations to the contrary, the history of Christian Antisemitism has not sufficiently sensitized even some sympathetic Christians to the specter of the mass destruction of Jews.

This is a strong assertion, and it is important at this point to consider briefly why active *Jewish* anti-Zionism is no longer admissible in the mainstream of Jewish life, despite its respectable antecedents in the first part of the century. There are various explanations, including the Holocaust and a growing pride in Israel's achievements, but the main reason is the new implications of anti-Zionism created almost overnight once the State was established. Before there was a state, the anti-Zionist position simply said that no such state should be established; after May, 1948, active anti-Zionism meant that the existing State should cease to exist. But the only reasonable scenario for its destruction would have to be drenched in torrents of Jewish blood. This dilemma is illustrated sharply in the almost pathetic hope expressed in the fiercely anti-Zionist work of the late Satmar rabbi; Jews, he wrote, should pray that Israel be destroyed—but not through the actions of the nations of the world.[68]

By this time, the critical importance of Israel to Jewish survival extends far beyond its boundaries. So many Jews have become psychologically dependent upon the existence of the State—so many perceptions of Jewish history, Jewish identity, indeed of Judaism itself, have been linked to its success—that the destruction of Israel would mean not only the mass extermination of its inhabitants but the spiritual death of a majority of diaspora Jewry. This is a statement of simple fact, and yet it gives the impression of heated, perhaps overblown rhetoric and consequently exemplifies a serious challenge facing Jews who wish to communicate their apprehension. Many well-intentioned listeners react by attributing such fears to an understandable "post-Holocaust" syndrome which must be respected but which hardly reflects objective reality. In this case, however, the paranoiac has real enemies; ironically, it is the detached observer who distorts the dangers by viewing them through the prism of a seductive psychological construct which appears to diminish them.

Ultimately, then, it is the identity of the consequences of anti-Zionism and Antisemitism which has created a nearly universal consensus among Jews, whatever their ideology, that protecting Israel must be one of the crucial priorities of the Jewish people, and it is this perception which leads to resentment and even anger at certain Christian statements on the Middle East. A feeling of moral outrage cannot justifiably result from a failure by Christians to develop their theology on Israel in a manner pleasing to Jews; it can and does result from the conviction that routine Christian denunciations of Antisemitism are virtually meaningless when combined with policies which, in Jewish eyes, jeopardize the security of the State and hence the survival of the Jewish people.

This combination of opposition to Antisemitism and espousal of positions dangerous to Israel does not necessarily demonstrate hypocrisy. We have already seen that non-Jews often fail to perceive the magnitude of the danger or to recognize the link between the threat to Israel and the threat to both Jewish lives and Jewish survival. There is also, of course, the existence of a conflicting moral claim made in the name of Palestinian Arab nationalism. The attractions of this claim are enhanced by its association with the aspirations of groups who have elicited considerable sympathy in the leadership of both the National Council of Churches and the World Council of Churches (the third world, victims of colonialist oppression, and the like), particularly in light of the categories of liberation theology.[69]

This is not the appropriate forum to argue the merits of this moral claim in detail. Nevertheless, the moral relevance of several well-known factors is worth noting. There is a Palestinian Arab state named Jordan, which is somehow not accepted as a legitimate locus for the realization of Palestinian national aspirations. Palestinian Arab nationalism was generated in part by the Jewish immigration and has tended to define itself, at least to the international community, only in relation to the territory that Jews happen to control (note the lack of interest in a separate Palestinian West Bank before 1967); that is, once Jews control an area, it becomes a focus of the Palestinian desire for self-determination. In a sense, then, a specific Palestinian nationalism (as distinct from a broader Arab nationalism) originated in resistance to Jewish national self-expression and was nurtured in the bitterness and frustration of a refugee status artificially prolonged by Arab states—precisely because of hostility toward Israel. The moral standing of a nationalism both generated and defined largely by relentless animosity toward the Jewish national presence (not to speak of the moral questions regarding the manner in which this nationalism is being pursued) cannot be accepted uncritically merely because it uses the terminology of self-determination. A positive Palestinian nationalism should be able to achieve fulfillment in Jordan (including, perhaps, much of the West Bank); the sort of Palestinian nationalism which is now dominant, given a mini-state in the West Bank and Gaza, will pose a mortal danger to Israel. Moral considerations surely require that the natural tendency of decent people to sympathize with the powerless be tempered by a reasonable assessment of what is likely to happen should they gain power.

Let me emphasize that this argument does not mean that Jews have the right to express righteous indignation whenever Christians or Christian organizations criticize Israel; Jews themselves are not always reticent in expressing disagreement with Israeli policies, and the self-censorship practiced by some Jews in these matters can hardly be demanded of Christians. I think, however, that a question can be formulated which might serve as a rough criterion for a fair Jewish reaction to Christian statements and for self-scrutiny by Christians professing concern for Jews: "Is this position rejected by at least ninety per cent of Israeli Jews on the grounds of national security?"

Israel is a democracy with a diverse and opinionated population; a positive answer to this question almost surely means that the position rejected is fraught with peril. Christians who find that they espouse such a position, particularly if this occurs with any frequency, are probably deceiving themselves about their concern for Jews; in reality, they are prepared to face the destruction of the Jewish people (not only the State of Israel) with relative equanimity.[70] For their part, Jews can hardly be faulted for reacting with deep disappointment when Christians maintain such views, and the National Council of Churches' statement falls into this category. The usefulness of dialogue is called into question when a major Christian body in the United States takes a stand which jeopardizes the survival of Israel. To make matters worse, this stand is less sympathetic than the position taken by both American public opinion and the policy of the United States government itself. It may be unrealistic to expect dialogue to have produced an attitude more favorable than that of the average citizen in a given country, but if the position of the churches is less favorable, many Jews cannot help but feel disillusioned about the entire process of interfaith discussion.

The picture, nevertheless, is not unrelievedly bleak. Veteran interfaith activists such as Franklin Littell, John Oesterreicher, and the Eckardts remain passionately devoted to the defense of Israel. For theological reasons, many Christian fundamentalists have spoken out on Israel's behalf, and, although we have already seen that many Jews feel ambivalent about this support, others have welcomed it with genuine enthusiasm. Given the discouraging atmosphere on the Israel issue as well as the Moral Majority's recent efforts to shed its antisemitic image, rejection of such support is becoming more difficult to justify, and it is especially noteworthy that Southern Baptists were conspicuous by their absence among the signatories of that document condemning Israel for violating human rights.[71] The irony that precisely those groups which participate least in dialogue are the strongest supporters of Israel should not go unnoticed, but this does not mean that dialogue has not helped produce Christian friends of the Jewish state—some of them quite influential. Israel is now inextricably linked to the spiritual and physical survival of world Jewry, and Jews must pursue every avenue to ensure its security. Interfaith dialogue is one such approach, and it must be cultivated with both deep sensitivity and uncompromising vigor.

ETHICS AND PUBLIC POLICY

Religion has something to say about social issues, but precisely what is not always clear. Wide differences on these questions exist not only among "religious" people in general but also among members of the same faith or even the same denomination. For interfaith dialogue, such a situation presents opportunities and pitfalls at the same time.

In some contexts, the existence of flexibility, divergent opinions within a single religious tradition, and overlapping views cutting across religious lines diminishes the adversarial relationship that can occasionally threaten the atmosphere of dialogue. In dealing with issues such as poverty and civil rights, all parties share the objective of maximizing social justice in an imperfect world, and discussions can constitute a combined effort to articulate the best means of attaining that end. It is not always clear, however, that such discussions are religious dialogue as much as they are a consideration of proper social policy by individuals who happen to be religious. The fundamental ethical principles are largely shared by all decent people, and choices must be made on the basis of calculations that are not radically different for the person of faith and the secular humanist. In other areas of Jewish-Christian dialogue, theological concerns can become too prominent; here, the specifically religious dimension can become little more than window dressing.

With some exceptions, Jewish and Christian participants in dialogue have tended to be theologically and politically liberal. Until fairly recently, this has made cooperation on social issues in the United States relatively straightforward. In the 1960s, for example, the civil rights movement was fighting for a cause whose justice was unassailable, and Jewish religious leaders were particularly prominent in a struggle which exemplified prophetic ideals and evoked no hesitation or ambivalence.

Things are no longer quite so simple. For reasons involving both ethical ideals and practical self-interest, many Jews have profound reservations about affirmative action quotas, and, even in less sensitive areas, the recent conservative trend has not left Jews unaffected. Since many Christian ecumenists have gone along with the sort of redefinition of liberalism which requires support for quotas, it has become somewhat more difficult to find common ground on a topic that once served as a fruitful, noncontroversial area for interfaith cooperation. There should surely be grounds for satisfaction that the civil rights issue has reached a point where ethical people can legitimately disagree about key policy questions, but from the more parochial perspective of Jewish-Christian dialogue (and Jewish-black relations in general), unanimity has been sacrificed on the altar of progress.

Other problems of public policy are marked by a more direct engagement of religious interests. With respect to public school prayer, which almost all Jews oppose, the liberal orientation of most Christian interfaith activists creates a commonality of opinion with Jews which does not mirror the views of the ordinary American Christian. On the matter of aid to parochial schools, where vigorous Catholic support means that there are deep divisions among Christians, the religiously liberal orientation of most Jewish ecumenists creates an illusion of greater Jewish consensus than really exists. The relative absence from dialogue of Orthodox Jews distorts the picture, and one Catholic leader has told me that awareness of significant Orthodox support for such aid is important in moderating Catholic resentment toward Jews because of this issue.[72]

Finally, there are the sensitive, occasionally explosive moral questions exemplified by the abortion controversy but also including such problems as euthanasia, homosexuality, and pornography. Here, too, the failure of Orthodox Jews to participate actively in dialogue can lead to skewed perceptions of what Judaism has to say about such matters. On abortion, for example, a number of Jewish organizations concerned with interfaith relations have declared that Jewish ethics are in essential conformity with the Supreme Court decision allowing abortion on demand before the last trimester. In fact, however, such a decision would have been rejected by every Jewish authority before the twentieth century, and, while Orthodox attitudes are neither monolithic nor entirely identical with Catholic views, they are far more restrictive than the public perception of the "Jewish" position.

On this and related matters, an appreciation of the Orthodox stance would contribute to a relaxation of tensions with both Catholics and fundamentalist Protestants. In any case, developments in biology and medicine have moved forward at such a dizzying pace that all religious traditions must take a fresh look at an almost bewildering variety of questions; in this context, abortion is only the proverbial "tip of the iceberg,"[73] and there is every reason to expect that such problems will receive continuing, urgent attention from theologians.[74] Though interfaith discussions will hardly play a decisive role in this process, they are likely to be stimulated and invigorated by confronting some of the most complex issues facing contemporary religious ethics.

CONCLUSION

No area of Jewish-Christian relations has been left untouched by the fundamental transformations of the last two decades. The revolution inevitably remains incomplete, and both opponents and supporters of the interfaith enterprise can cite abundant evidence for their respective positions. The most straightforward achievement of increased Jewish-Christian discussions is the least controversial; ordinary human relationships inevitably improve in the context of regular, sympathetic contacts. From this perspective, at least, even those with the deepest reservations about interfaith dialogue can only wish the participants well as they confront the theological, political, and moral dynamics of a relationship marked by danger, challenge, and genuine promise.

NOTES

1. The major statements, both Catholic and Protestant, have been compiled by Helga Croner in *Stepping Stones to Further Jewish-Christian Relations* (London and New York: Stimulus Books, 1977) (hereafter, Croner). For highlights of the developing Catholic position, see Leonard Swidler, "Catholic Statements on Jews—A Revolution in Progress," *Judaism* 27 (1978): 299–307; and Jorge Mejía, "Survey of Issues in Catholic-Jewish Relations," *Origins* 7.47 (May 11, 1978): 744–748. An excellent bibliographical survey has been provided by A. Roy Eckardt, "Recent Literature on Jewish-Christian Relations," *Journal of the American Academy of Religion* 49 (1981): 99–111.

2. On the current situation in Western Europe, see the summary articles in *Face to Face* 7 (Summer, 1980): 1–16. For obvious reasons, Israel provides a special, atypical environment for Jewish-Christian discussions; in addition to such ongoing groups as the Israel Interfaith Committee, the Ecumenical Theological Research Fraternity, and the Rainbow, the Director General of Israel's Ministry of Interreligious Affairs has recently established the Jerusalem Institute for Interreligious Relations and Research as a public, nongovernmental body (*Christian News from Israel*, vol. 27, no. 2 [1979], p. 62). In general, see *Face to Face* 2 (Winter/Spring, 1977).

3. "A Decade of Catholic-Jewish Relations—A Reassessment," *Journal of Ecumenical Studies* (henceforth cited as *J.E.S.*) 15 (1978): 243–260.

4. The phrase (which Siegman does not use) is from the first sentence of the Vatican II statement. On the impact of this asymmetry on early Jewish-Christian contacts, see my discussion in *The Jewish-Christian Debate in the High Middle Ages* (Philadelphia: Jewish Publication Society, 1979), pp. 4–8.

5. Paul J. Kirsch, *We Christians and Jews* (Philadelphia: Fortress Press, 1975), pp. 122–141.

6. Eugene Fisher, "A Roman Catholic Perspective: The Interfaith Agenda," *Ecumenical Bulletin* 44 (November–December, 1980): 11–12.

7. Edward Flannery, "Response to Henry Siegman," *J.E.S.* 15 (1978): 505. Cf.

also David-Maria Jaeger, "Catholic-Jewish Dialogue," *Christian Attitudes on Jews and Judaism* 69 (December, 1979): 1–3.

8. "Basic Issues of the Jewish-Christian Dialogue: A Working Paper of the Workshop on 'Jews and Christians' of the Central Committee of Roman Catholics in Germany," *Encounter Today* 14 (1979): 105–113, 125; and *Service International de Documentation Judeo-Chrétienne* (henceforth cited as *SIDIC*), vol. 13, no. 2 (1980), pp. 28–32.

9. *Zur Erneuerung des Verhältnisses von Christen und Juden* (1980), pp. 12–28. Partial English translation by Franklin H. Littell in *J.E.S.* 17 (1980): 211–212.

10. *A Christian Theology of Judaism* (New York: Paulist Press, 1980), p. 134; citation from Flusser's article in *Concilium*, new series, 5.10 (1974), p. 71.

11. Dom Louis Leloir, "One of the More Burning Issues in Jewish-Christian Dialogue: Unity and Trinity in God" (the title is noteworthy), *Encounter Today* 13 (1978): 101–110. Cf. also note 22, below.

12. "Has Interfaith a Future?" *Judaism* 27 (1978): 311.

13. This point was made by Richard Lowry in a paper presented to a Catholic-Lutheran-Jewish conference in the Fall of 1980.

14. Siegman, "A Decade," p. 257.

15. See, however, Gerald Blidstein's remarks about the need for Jews to reassess the image of Christianity (*Tradition* 11 [1970]: 103–113), cited approvingly by Siegman, "A Decade," p. 254.

16. "Confrontation," *Tradition* 6 (1964): 5–29.

17. "The Achievements and Trials of Interfaith," *Judaism* 27 (1978): 319.

18. *New York Times*, February 5, 1981. Several months after this was written, the individual involved was removed from his post.

19. *Face to Face* 8 (Winter, 1981) is devoted in its entirety to an important collection of reactions to this movement by both Christians and Jews.

20. Cf. William Harter's paper delivered to the Synagogue Council of America on December 7, 1972 (available at the library of the American Jewish Committee); William Sanford LaSor, "An Evangelical and the Interfaith Movement," *Judaism* 27 (1978): 335–339; M. Tanenbaum, M. Wilson, and A. J. Rudin, eds., *Evangelicals and Jews in Conversation* (Grand Rapids, Mich.: Baker Book House, 1978); and A. J. Rudin, "A Jewish Perspective on Baptist Ecumenism," *J.E.S.* 17 (1980): 161–171.

21. Eva Fleischner, ed. *Auschwitz: Beginning of a New Era?* (New York: KTAV, 1977), p. 106. The case for non-intervention in internal Christian theology was expressed eloquently by Siegman in "A Decade," p. 257.

22. See Pinchas Lapide and Jürgen Moltmann, *Jewish Monotheism and Christian Trinitarian Doctrine* (Philadelphia: Fortress Press, 1981); "Jews and Christians in Joint Worship: Some Planning Principles and Guidelines," *Ecumenical Bulletin* 44 (November–December, 1980): 36–39.

23. John Shelley Spong, "The Continuing Christian Need for Judaism," *The Christian Century*, September 26, 1979, p. 918.

24. The classification is borrowed from Harold Ditmanson's article in *Face to Face* 3–4 (Fall/Winter, 1977): 7–8.
25. Sheerin, "Has Interfaith a Future?" pp. 308–309.
26. Note, e.g., the statements of the World Council of Churches (1968) and the Lutheran Commission on World Missions (1969) in Croner, pp. 79, 91.
27. Daniel Polish, "A Jewish Perspective: This Moment in Jewish-Christian Relations," *Ecumenical Bulletin* 44 (November–December, 1980): 8–9.
28. Siegman, "A Decade," p. 256.
29. Paragraph 2.4 of the Guidelines (*Ecumenical Bulletin* 44 [November–December, 1980]: 30). See note 61, below.
30. "Study Outline on the Mission and Witness of the Church," *SIDIC*, vol. 11, no. 3 (1978), p. 32.
31. *The National Catholic Register*, July 10, 1977.
32. Sheerin, "Has Interfaith a Future?" p. 311.
33. Swidler, "Catholic Statements on Jews," pp. 305–306, citing Croner, pp. 7, 12, 18, 51, 64.
34. "Mission and Conversion in Roman Catholic History and Contemporary Debate: The Mission to the Jews," presented at the Kennedy Institute Trialogue, October 13, 1980.
35. Croner, pp. 81, 128–129, 148.
36. Rudin, "A Jewish Perspective," pp. 162–163.
37. Siegman, "A Decade," pp. 257–258.
38. "From the Viewpoint of Contemporary Judaism," *Face to Face* 3–4 (Fall/Winter, 1977): 13.
39. See *National Review*, June 23, 1978, p. 763.
40. See *Jews and "Jewish Christianity"* (New York: KTAV, 1978).
41. Annette Daum, *Missionary and Cult Movements: A Mini-Course for the Upper Grades in Religious Schools* (New York: Union of American Hebrew Congregations, 1979) is another example of a response that maintains a civil and respectful tone.
42. The status of this problem in the late 1970s was summarized by Mark Cohen in "Missionaries in Our Midst: The Appeal of Alternatives," *Analysis*, no. 64 (March 1978).
43. Swidler, "Catholic Statements on Jews," pp. 301–302.
44. Croner, pp. 70, 82–83; Draft Guidelines 2.1; Rudin, "A Jewish Perspective," p. 164.
45. Rosemary Ruether, "Anti-Judaism Is the Left Hand of Christology," in R. Heyer ed., *Jewish-Christian Relations* (New York: Paulist Press, 1974), pp. 1–9; Ruether, *Faith and Fraticide* (New York: Seabury Press, 1974); idem, "Anti Semitism and Christian Theology," in Fleischner's *Auschwitz*, pp. 79–92; and Alan Davies, *Anti-Semitism and the Foundations of Christianity* (New York: Paulist Press, 1979), p. xv.
46. The classic sociological study attempting to demonstrate the connection between certain Christian beliefs and anti-Jewish attitudes is Charles Glock

and Rodney Stark, *Christian Beliefs and Anti-Semitism* (New York: Harper and Row, 1966). Note also the later, much more limited survey by B. Cohen and A. Lacognata, *A Pilot Study on Christian Beliefs and Anti-Semitism*, 1976 (available in the library of the American Jewish Committee).

47. Cf. John Oesterreicher's reaction to Jewish support for Ruether, cited in Siegman, "A Decade," p. 257. For Christian denials of an inevitable link between Christology and Antisemitism, see Fleischner, *Auschwitz*, pp. 93–94, 195–197.

48. Robert Willis, "A Perennial Outrage: Anti-Semitism in the New Testament," *Christian Century*, August 19, 1970, pp. 990–992. See also note 17, above.

49. Cf. Eugene Fisher, *Faith without Prejudice* (New York: Paulist Press, 1977), pp. 54–58. For a general discussion of this issue, see also P. van Box and M. McGrath, "Perspectives: Anti-Jewish Elements in the Liturgy," *SIDIC*, vol. 10, no. 2 (1978), pp. 25–27.

50. *A Commentary on the Oberammergau Passionspiel in regard to Its Image of Jews and Judaism* (New York: Anti-Defamation League, 1977). See also Swidler's brief guidelines in *Face to Face* 7 (Summer, 1980): 19–20.

51. (Philadelphia: Fortress Press, 1978; German original 1975).

52. Croner, p. 14.

53. John Pawlikowski has presented an excellent summary of both proposals and problems, in Fleischner's *Auschwitz*, p. 172–178. See also *Face to Face* 2 (Summer/Fall, 1976): 3–8.

54. T.A. Idinopulos, "Old Form of Anti-Judaism in the New Book of Common Prayer," *Christian Century* 93 (August 4–11, 1976), pp. 680–684; John T. Townsend, " 'The Reproaches' in Christian Liturgy," *Face to Face* 2 (Summer/Fall, 1976): 8–11.

55. See Fisher, *Faith without Prejudice; Encounter Today* 13 (1978): 111; W.C.C. Draft Guidelines 3.3; J. Pawlikowski in Fleischner, *Auschwitz*, pp. 162, 171; and David Hyatt, "The Interfaith Movement," *Judaism* 27 (1978): 273. For a pessimistic comment on the situation in France, see *Encounter Today* 14 (1979): 152.

56. See *Face to Face* 7 (Winter, 1980): 11–14, 18–19, 27–29.

57. *Origins* 9.10 (August 16, 1979), 158–160.

58. Croner, p. 63.

59. See Marcel Jacques Dubois, "The Catholic Church and the State of Israel— After Thirty Years," *Christian News from Israel*, vol. 27, no. 2 (1979), p. 64. Some Catholics have argued that Vatican contacts with Israeli officials constitute *de facto* recognition. *De jure* would be an improvement.

60. Croner. p. 76.

61. Guidelines 5.1. The Protestant Church of the Rhineland (see note 9, above) has recently described the creation of the State of Israel as a "sign of God's faithfulness to his people." In subsequent drafts of the W.C.C. Guidelines adopted well after the completion of this article, this passage—and the one discussed at note 29, above—have been attenuated to a point where they

no longer retain the significance I have attributed to them. From a Jewish perspective, the discussion of Israel is no longer a step forward and is, in fact, quite disappointing.

62. See *Christianity and Crisis*, October 28 and December 23, 1974. Cf. also the remark by Willard Oxtoby in *The Christian Century*, October 13, 1971, p. 1193, cited in F. Talmage, *Disputation and Dialogue* (New York: KTAV, 1975), p. 185.

63. Croner, pp. 104–105.

64. *American Report*, October 29, 1973. For Arthur Hertzberg's response, see ibid., November 12, 1973. See also Robert Alter, "Berrigan's Diatribe," *Commentary*, February, 1974, pp. 69–73.

65. *New York Times*, January 8, 1981. For Christian comments criticizing the double standard, cf. Fleischner, *Auschwitz*, pp. 232–233; and Kirsch, *We Christians and Jews*, p. 119. On Christian criticism of Israel, see Judith H. Banki's excellent report, "Anti-Israel Influence in American Churches" (1979), prepared for the Interreligious Affairs Department of the American Jewish Committee.

66. *Current Dialogue* 1 (Winter 1980/81): 10.

67. Polish, "A Jewish Perspective," p. 9.

68. Joel Teitelbaum, *Sefer Va Yoel Mosheh* (Brooklyn: Jerusalem Book Store, 1981), p. 8.

69. See Rael Jean Isaac, "Liberal Protestants versus Israel," *Midstream* 27 (October, 1981): 6–14, especially pp. 12–13.

70. After this was written, Steven E. Plaut proposed a virtually identical criterion to define "What is 'Anti-Israel' " (*Midstream* 28 [May, 1982]: 3–6).

71. See the Eckardts' warning against relying on the theological arguments for Israel which provide the underpinning of the evangelical position (*Judaism* 27 [1978]: 320). On the other hand, support for Israel on other grounds than particularistic theology is not unheard of among evangelicals. Cf. Carl Henry in *Face to Face* 3–4 (Fall/Winter, 1977), p. 17. See especially A. Roy Eckardt, "Toward a Secular Theology of Israel," *Christian Jewish Relations*, no. 72 (September, 1980), pp. 8–20.

72. For a recent work dealing with a variety of social questions, see Eugene Fischer and Daniel Polish, eds., *The Formation of Social Policy in the Catholic and Jewish Traditions* (Notre Dame, Ind.: University of Notre Dame Press, 1980).

73. Hyatt, "Interfaith Movement," p. 275.

74. See "The Bio-Medical Revolution: Applying Jewish Values to Public Policy-Making," *Analysis*, no. 62 (April, 1977).

Index

About the Editor

NAOMI W. COHEN is a professor of history at Hunter College and the Graduate Center of City University of New York. She is the author of numerous books, her most recent being *The Year after the Riots: American Responses to the Palestine Crisis of 1929–30*.